An original Standard Pneumatic Action Company factory worker adjusts the valves in a standard stack.

A typical advertising piece from the 1920's, issued by one of the most prominent manufacturers of player mechanisms for installation by piano builders. The player piano was an important sociological influence in the first 2½ decades of the 20th Century.

P·L·A·Y·E·R P·I·A·N·O
SERVICING & REBUILDING

...A treatise on how player pianos
function, and how to get them back
into top playing condition if they
don't work

---

by Arthur A. Reblitz

Vestal Press

Lanham · New York · Oxford

VESTAL PRESS, Inc.

Published in the United States of America
by Vestal Press, Inc.

4501 Forbes Blvd, Suite 200
Lanham, Maryland 20706

Library of Congress Cataloging-in-Publication Data

Reblitz, Arthur A.
  Player piano servicing & rebuilding.
  Includes bibliographical references (p. 213) and index.
    1. Player-piano—Construction. I. Title. II. Title:
  Player piano servicing and rebuilding.
  ISBN 0-911572-41-40-6 (alk. paper)—ISBN 0-911572-41-4
  (cloth : alk. paper)
ML1070.R4   1985
789'.72   85-3140
                                    CIP

PLAYER PIANO SERVICING AND REBUILDING
TABLE OF CONTENTS

ABOUT THE AUTHOR

Arthur A. Reblitz began restoring automatic musical instruments and arranging rolls for them in 1964, and opened his shop as a full time business in 1972. Since then, his shop has restored instruments for many prominent collections across the United States. A 1968 high honors graduate of the University of Illinois, Art is a registered tuner/technician member of the Piano Technicians Guild. His work has appeared on nationwide educational television, the 1987 National Geographic television special "Treasures from the Past," "Ripley's Believe It or Not," in the Rose Bowl Parade and Radio City Music Hall, and his music rolls have been used for promotional work for McDonalds, Anheuser Busch and Coca-Cola, among others. He has made numerous contributions to *The Guidebook of Automatic Musical Instruments and The Encyclopedia of Automatic Musical Instruments* by Q. David Bowers, and the "Bulletin" of the Automatic Musicial Instrument Collectors' Association (AMICA), and he has written regular monthly columns for the "Technical Bulletin" of the Musicial Box Society International (MBS) and "The Coin Slot" magazine. He has also written for the Vestal Press Technical Series. In 1982 the author received the Q. David Bowers Literary Award from the Musicial Box Society International for outstanding literary contributions to the field of automatic music.

ACKNOWLEDGEMENTS

The author wishes to thank Bob Gilson, John Hovancak, Mike Kitner, Dave Ramey and Tom Sprague, for sharing their knowledge of automatic pianos and restoration techniques generously for many years, Harvey Roehl, for publishing all sorts of literature in the field of mechanical music, Durrell Armstrong, for making a wide variety of restoration supplies available over the years through his Player Piano Co. of Wichita, Kansas, and Fred H. Reblitz for proofreading the text.

Most of the disassembled player mechanisms pictured in this book were photographed during restoration. The author's full-time employees - Joseph Cossolini and Bob Grunow – deserve special thanks for their willingness over a five-year period to bring their work to a halt, time after time at a moment's notice, help set up photographic equipment, pose the pictures, and then resume working.

Thanks also to the following restorers and collectors who helped to make this book more complete by contributing illustrations and technical information: Terry Borne, Q. David Bowers, Jim Bratton, Larry Broadmoore, Craig Brougher, Ron Cappel, Jere DeBacker, Dave Gaudieri, Richard Groman, Randolph Herr, Rex Kennedy, Dick Kroeckel, Tom Marshall, Hayes McClaran, Jeffrey Morgan, Bill Pixley, Dave Saul, R.L. Schommer, Bob Taylor, Ross Waters, and Don Wick.

OTHER REFERENCE BOOKS BY ARTHUR A. REBLITZ:

Piano Servicing, Tuning and Rebuilding, A Catalogue of Music Rolls for the Mills Violano, Treasures of Mechanical Music (with Q. David Bowers), and *The Mills Violano-Virtuoso* (with Mike Kitner).

The author provides a technical consultation service for a fee through the mail only, and he may be contacted by writing to him c/o the Vestal Press. This service is not available by telephone.

AUTHOR'S PREFACE

Player piano design and manufacturing is an 80-year old industry, but the art of restoring old player pianos to factory-new condition is a relatively new one. Most of today's restoration techniques didn't need to be considered by those who manufactured and serviced player pianos from the 1920's through the 1950's; they have been developed since the early 1960's, when old instruments became valuable enough to be worth restoring.

The information contained here is based on more than fifteen years of actual hands-on, full-time experience. From 1965 through the time this is being written in 1984, my employees and I have spent over 50,000 hours rebuilding, servicing and tuning a large number of instruments for private individuals and many well-known collections and museums. These instruments have included all varieties of player pianos, reproducing pianos, coin pianos, orchestrions, table top organettes, player reed organs and band organs, ranging in size from simple Gem roller organs to several immense, extremely complex Hupfeld Pan Orchestras. Many of the instruments which we have restored have been played tens of thousands of times per year in heavy commercial use, demonstrating which materials are the most long-lasting and which ones wear out prematurely. During this time, I have constantly tried to find the most efficient ways to do the most durable, airtight repairs which will preserve the authenticity of the instrument, while always putting special emphasis on making each instrument *sound* good.

Over the years many individuals, as listed in the acknowledgements, have shared their knowledge and experience, but one person in particular - Dave Ramey - deserves a great deal of credit for developing and sharing his methods of making pneumatic components work right. His restoration of pneumatic mechanisms has, to me, always been the finest example of airtightness and efficient operation. This book reflects his enthusiasm, as well as my own, for the careful preservation and restoration of automatic musical instruments. I hope at least some of our enthusiasm will rub off onto whoever reads this book!

Art Reblitz
August 1984

DEDICATION

To Al and Flo Svoboda, who for over thirty years accumulated and displayed one of the largest, most interesting collections of nickelodeons and other mechanical antiques in their Nickelodeon Tavern and Museum in Chicago Heights, Illinois, and who gave the author his start there in the mid 1960's.

Left to Right: Dave Ramey, Flo and Al Svoboda and the author standing by the front door of Svoboda's Nickelodeon Tavern in April 1984.

FOREWORD

by Harvey Roehl

In 1963, The Vestal Press published the first book in recent years to deal with how to put derelict player pianos back into working order — Larry Givens' classic work, REBUILDING THE PLAYER PIANO. Since then close to 50,000 copies have been sold World-Wide, and this publisher takes a great deal of pride in knowing that thousands — perhaps tens of thousands — of instruments that otherwise would surely have ended up being scrapped are now giving musical pleasure to their owners, thanks to this information having been made available.

The time has now come for a more comprehensive book on the subject — to put in print much of the knowledge of restoration techniques both general, and specific to particular makes of player pianos, that has been developed in the intervening years. There is no one better qualified to do this than Art Reblitz, who not only is considered one of America's top authorities on the subject of the refurbishing of automatic pianos, orchestrions, and band organs, but who is the author of what has become the standard book in the World on piano technology in general — his outstanding work PIANO SERVICING, TUNING AND REBUILDING to which the book you are holding is now a companion volume.

While player pianos are back in production in small numbers, the great hey-day of the instrument was from 1900 to 1930, and the major interest in them was from 1910 to 1925 — just fifteen short years! Something on the order of 2.6 million players were produced in America alone during the period, and there are a lot of them left. The 'straight' piano used to be the pre-eminent musical instrument of the American home, and the addition of mechanical playing equipment made it all the more so until newer technologies by way of improved phonographs and the development of radio diverted the attention of the public to other entertainment devices.

Today the player piano is not considered a serious musical instrument; rather, its function is primarily to provide enjoyment for those who derive pleasure from hearing piano music created by mechanical means. It follows, then, that the object of this book is to help folks get more fun from player piano music (in addition to helping the author and the owners of the Vestal Press make a living!). If the book causes a few more happy faces to appear on the scene, the efforts in writing and producing it will have been well-spent.

HARVEY N. ROEHL
Vestal, New York 13850
October, 1984

September 16, 1911   **THE LITERARY DIGEST**

The Passing of the Silent Piano

A daily scene in all the world's large cities—the Pianola Piano displacing the piano of older type.

CHAPTER ONE
LOOK MA, NO HANDS

This book is a comprehensive, illustrated guide to the repair and restoration of paper roll operated, suction powered player pianos and piano playing mechanisms. It contains detailed step-by-step information on how player pianos work, why they malfunction, and the techniques, tools, supplies and materials which are needed to completely recondition the player mechanisms so they will look, work and sound like new.

Player Piano History in a Nutshell

The pneumatic player piano mechanism, played by perforated paper music rolls and powered by suction, made its big public debut in America in the late 1890's in the form of the Aeolian Pianola, a "push up" external piano playing

Illus 1-1. The Pianola pushup piano player, introduced shortly after the turn of the century. A rather cumbersome contraption, this early device was obsolete once the inner player, or self contained player piano, was perfected.

device. From that time until a few years after 1908 when 88-note music rolls were standardized, many early brands of mechanisms were developed and incorporated into push up piano players *and* player pianos. Although early player actions such as those by Wilcox & White (Angelus), Melville Clark (Apollo) and Farrand (Cecilian) were mass produced and mass marketed, they are regarded today as developmental because they are crude and cumbersome by comparison to the mechanisms which were manufactured after the early 'teens.

Early Pianolas used 65-note music rolls, later ones used 88-note rolls, and some deluxe instruments could play both types. Some other brands, including certain Cecilian and Angelus instruments, used different, non-standard rolls, and at least one model of Melville Clark Apollo player could play 58, 65, 70, 82 and 88 note rolls! (58-note rolls were used on many Aeolian player reed organs, 65- and 88-note rolls were the more common piano rolls, and 70- and 82- note rolls were very short-lived styles which are next to impossible to find today).

Illus 1-2. A typical player piano of the 1920's.

The heyday of the home player piano extended from about 1910 through about 1925; during this era, a high percentage of all pianos made in America - upright and grand - were player pianos. Some of the largest manufacturers of player actions were independent companies which specialized in supplying piano companies with player actions; these included the Standard Pneumatic Action Co., Simplex Player Action Co., Amphion Piano Player Co., Pratt-Read Player Action Co., and Auto Pneumatic Action Co. (Autopiano). Many of the larger piano manufacturers, however, produced their own player actions, including Aeolian, Baldwin, Cable, Gulbransen, Kimball, Story and Clark, and WurliTzer.

In the late 1920's when electronic amplification enabled the phonograph and radio to provide musical entertainment at a fraction of the cost of an automatic piano, the player piano met its demise, and the economic depression of the 1930's practically wiped out the whole piano industry. When the piano business was revived after World War II, new pianos were without player actions. Finally in the late 1950's, player pianos were mass produced once again. Since then, several modern brands - Aeolian, Kimball, Universal, WurliTzer and others - have been made, although in nowhere near the quantities of the 1920's.

Illus 1-3. One model of the Universal player piano made in the 1980's.

Throughout this book, the term "early" refers to those developmental player piano mechanisms manufactured prior to approximately 1910; the term "modern," refers to those made after the late 1950's. Unless one of these terms is used, information is generally directed toward the "average" player pianos made between the early 'teens and the late 'twenties.

Varieties of Player Pianos

Reproducing pianos, coin pianos and orchestrions operate on the same pneumatic principles as ordinary foot-pumped home player pianos, and they require similar rebuilding techniques.

Reproducing pianos have sophisticated expression mechanisms in addition to the regular player actions, enabling them to reproduce the playing of human pianists by means of special music rolls. Most were grand pianos, but uprights and a few spinets were also made. Leading American brands of reproducing actions were the Ampico, Duo-Art and Welte Licensee, while popular European brands were Hupfeld and the original Welte Mignon. Reproducing player actions were also built into external push-up cabinets and were known as *vorsetzers*. Most of these were manufactured by Welte, although some were also made by Hupfeld and others. A few reproducing pianos were also made without keyboards.

Coin pianos have motor-driven pumping bellows, large

Illus. 1-4. The reproducing piano is a sophisticated instrument which not only plays the notes, but also duplicates the expression of the human artist by means of specially coded music rolls. All of the great classical and popular pianists who lived during the player piano era recorded reproducing piano rolls, and their artistry may be enjoyed today by playing the rolls back on a beautifully restored reproducing piano.

multi-tune music rolls, and automatic mechanisms for starting when a coin is deposited, shutting off at the end of each tune, and rewinding after the last tune on the roll. Most coin pianos have a mandolin attachment controlled automatically by the roll, and many have an extra instrument like a xylophone or rank of organ pipes. *Orchestrions* incorporate several extra instruments - xylophones, orchestra bells, organ pipes, drums and traps, etc. - in addition to the piano. Coin pianos and orchestrions were made with and without keyboards. The most popular American brands of coin pianos and orchestrions were Seeburg, WurliTzer, Coinola, Link, Cremona, Nelson-Wiggen, Peerless and Western Electric (a subsidiary of Seeburg; no relation to the manufacturer of telephone and electronic apparatus), while their European counterparts included Hupfeld, Imhof & Mukle, Philipps, Popper, Gebr. Weber

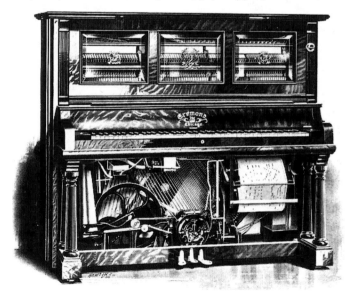

Illus. 1-5. A Cremona coin piano of the 1910 era with mandolin attachment. A coin piano has motor-driven pumping bellows, a coin mechanism for starting the motor, automatic rewind and shutoff, and a large multi-tune music roll, usually below the keyboard.

(no relation to the American Weber piano company), Welte and others. (The Mills Novelty Co. in America also produced the very popular Violano-Virtuoso, but this instrument is played by electromagnets, solenoids and motors rather than a suction system, so it is not included in this book. See *The Mills Violano-Virtuoso* by Mike Kitner and Art Reblitz, published by The Vestal Press.)

The word "nickelodeon" frequently is used as a nickname for coin pianos and orchestrions, but it correctly refers to early-day silent movie theatres, and was not used by the original manufacturers as a name for their automatic pianos.

Illus. 1-6. The Seeburg style KT was—and still is—a popular small keyboardless orchestrion. Made during the 1915-1925 era, it contains a 61-note piano, mandolin attachment, tambourine, triangle, castanets, and either xylophone or a rank of flute or violin pipes, playing style G or 4X 10-tune rolls. The cabinet front features a spread-wing stained glass eagle illuminated from the inside. All types of coin pianos and orchestrions are extremely rare and they deserve the finest quality restoration.

Home player pianos account for about 95% of all automatic pianos in existence today, reproducing pianos probably represent a little less than 5%, and coin pianos and orchestrions add up to less than 1%. For detailed information on the history of player pianos, reproducing pianos, coin pianos and orchestrions, refer to the books listed in the bibliography.

Operating Principles

Player piano actions, like any mechanisms, behave according to certain mechanical principles, and anyone possessing dexterity with tools, a good measure of mechanical aptitude and a lot of patience can learn how to repair them correctly. Although a few mechanical parts of a player piano mechanism such as the music roll drive transmission and various mechanical linkages are out in the open and are easy to understand, most of the parts are hidden away inside and are totally unlike anything found in *any other*

mechanical device (with the exception of certain pipe organ components). Player actions are powered by a limited amount of suction generated by the pumping bellows; ease of pumping and efficient operation depend upon the airtightness of sealer in hundreds of tiny channels running through various wooden parts, along with the airtightness and flexibility of hundreds of pieces of rubberized bellows cloth, rubber tubing, hoses, leather gaskets, valve facings, valve seats and pouches, all of which deteriorate over a period of time.

Illus. 1-7. This WurliTzer style CX tall keyboard-style orchestrion was restored by the author and his employee Joseph Cossolini in 1982; it is now in the Sanfilippo collection. It contains not only a piano, mandolin, flute and violin pipes, orchestra bells, bass drum, snare drum and triangle, but also a six-roll automatic music roll changer and a rotating jewelled wonder lamp surrounded by mirrors.

Because player actions are entirely different from anything else ordinarily encountered by the do-it-yourselfer, they require entirely different repair techniques. A typical restoration involves carefully disassembling all of the parts, breaking apart many wood-to-wood glue joints which incorporate air channels of various sizes, sealing these channels, making new wooden parts to replace any which splinter during disassembly, replacing all perishable leather and rubberized parts, cleaning and polishing everything, regluing loose and disassembled glue joints so they are airtight but not clogged with glue, adjusting moveable parts - sometimes within tolerances of several thousandths of an inch - and carefully reassembling, testing and troubleshooting everything. Fine quality player piano rebuilding involves repairing hundreds of old wooden parts and making new ones as necessary; an interest in sophisticated woodworking techniques and tools are prerequisites to successful restoration, either as a hobby or a vocation.

Illus. 1-8. Immense orchestrions were built in Europe by Hupfeld, Weber, Welte and others. This Hupfeld Pan orchestrion restored by the author for the Sanfilippo collection of Chicago in 1985 measures over twelve feet wide and eleven feet high. It contains a reproducing piano, six ranks of pipes, xylophone, orchestra bells, and a full complement of drums and traps, all controlled by a ten-roll automatic roll changer!

The design and operation of certain pipe organ components resemble player piano mechanisms, but pressure-operated organs have a much greater tolerance for air seepage than suction-operated player pianos do. It is desirable, of course, for organ components to be as airtight as possible, but a pipe organ will play reasonably well while enduring an amount of air leakage which would stop a player piano dead. The reserve capacity of a typical organ blower is far greater in proportion to the operating needs of the instrument than that of a typical player piano pump, permitting the traditional use in organs of soft valve leather which is noiseless in operation but which is not absolutely airtight. Also, the pouches ("primaries", in organ terminology) in an electropneumatic pipe organ are powered by electromagnets which are mounted nearby, while the pouches in a player piano are powered only by the tiny amounts of air which enter the tracker bar several feet away, through the holes punched in the music roll; these minute air signals in a player piano can be lost because of a leaky gasket which would have little effect on the performance of a pipe organ. Many good pipe organ technicians have had difficulty getting a player piano to work right for no other reason than their use of techniques, materials and standards which are considered acceptable for organ repair.

Quality and Standards of Repair

The net result of a good quality restoration is an automatic piano which *looks, works, and sounds* like it did when it was new. The extent of repairs which are economically justifiable for a given piano depend on its potential value, either monetary or sentimental. As old 88-note player pianos have become older, requiring more and more extensive repairs, inflation and constantly increasing demand have caused their value to rise, making the ever increasing cost of repairs economically practical. Many players needed new tracker bar tubing by the 1940's, - an inexpensive, simple repair - and with the replacement of this tubing they worked for another ten or more years. By the 1950's many instruments needed to have the bellows and pneumatics recovered, so during this time period a "completely rebuilt" player piano usually had new rubber cloth, tubing and hoses but still had its original pouches, valve leather and gaskets, along with original piano strings, tuning pins, hammers and other action parts. By the late 1960's most of the original materials had gone bad, requiring the replacement of all leather as well as rubberized parts in order for a player to work right. Since the introduction of modern players in the late 1950's, the value of an old home player piano in good working condition has approximately paralleled the price of a more expensive new one; by the early 1980's, the prices of new players - and thus the value of old ones - rose to a level at which it finally became economically practical to do beautiful cosmetic restoration as well as complete mechanical restoration, in-

Illus. 1-9. This fine Knabe art case Ampico reproducing grand piano was sold as being "completely restored." The "restorer" glued the pneumatics on in the wrong place, requiring 90° mending plates from the hardware store to connect each pushrod to the incorrect neighboring pneumatic. This picture was taken within a few months after the "restoration", and some of the mending plates had already broken off of the pneumatics. Poor repairs of this sort reduce the value of a piano and make a correct restoration much more difficult than if the piano had been left alone.

cluding extensive rebuilding of the piano itself - the soundboard, bridges, tuning pins, strings, hammers, action parts, cabinet and finish.

Each era of "restoration" had its technicians who stayed

4

in a rut, and through the 1970's many older piano tuners who were accustomed to an earlier era when player pianos were practically worthless still tried to rebuild them using cheap materials and without replacing any of the pneumatic and bellows hinges, leather gaskets and valve facings, or piano parts, leaving behind a trail of instruments which need to be completely restored today in the 1980's, and which are harder to restore than they would be if they had been left alone.

Fortunately today, many piano technicians are interested in the pursuit of excellence in their work, and they either specialize in player pianos or leave them alone. Of course, all through the years, some technicians who really liked player pianos performed fine quality work, but these careful people were the exception rather than the rule. Coin pianos and orchestrions, followed by reproducing pianos, have always been the most rare and valuable automatic pianos, and the finest rebuilders have traditionally specialized in restoring these instruments. Unfortunately, some player specialists have had no interest in piano servicing and have created a reputation for themselves among piano technicians as people who fool around with player pianos, but the finest, most dedicated player rebuilders pay equal attention to soundboards, pinblocks, bridges, actions, keyboards, and other piano parts as they do to the player mechanisms, knowing that a player or reproducing piano, coin piano or orchestrion is only as good as the piano itself.

All old player pianos - particularly reproducing pianos and coin operated instruments - are irreplaceable antiques, and repair shortcuts which alter a mechanism or make it difficult or impossible to recondition again in the future are the trademark of an unethical butcher. A conscientious rebuilder leaves every part in a condition which will be no more difficult to repair the next time the rubber and leather parts must be replaced.

In order for a restored instrument to work *and* look like new, cracked and split wooden parts should be reglued or replaced, not patched with silicone sealer or plastic wood. Wood containing stripped screwholes should be replaced, not filled with toothpicks or epoxy. There should be no tell-tale rebuilding tracks on any of the parts, inside or out. This means the careful rebuilder leaves no damaged screw heads, gouges in internal wooden parts, scratches in the finish, poorly-trimmed edges on bellows and pneumatics, clamp marks, sloppy hand-written numbers where there were none originally, etc. Over-restoration is also to be avoided; this includes such things as chrome plating to replace the original nickel plating, and high gloss paint on mechanisms which were originally finished with shellac or semi-gloss black enamel. It is always a pleasant surprise to find a thirty year old rebuilding date inside a player action which looks perfectly original, and it is always disgusting to find large blobs of white glue, silicone caulking compound, auto body filler, splinters and cracks, broken

screws, and other trademarks of a sloppy previous job. Eight out of ten player pianos restored in the author's shop during the 1980's were poorly repaired previously by someone else, requiring far more extensive (and *expensive*) repairs than would have been required otherwise.

If you view old automatic pianos as something to "monkey around with," monkey around with something else for the sake of the remaining instruments and people who care about them. On the other hand, if you are sincerely interested in trying to help preserve a fascinating, unique part of history, and you have the patience to do something over if necessary until it works right, then you will be rewarded with the wonderful feeling of bringing broken-down treasures back to life.

How This Book is Organized

Chapter 1, of which this section is a part, includes some background material on various types of automatic pianos, plus the author's restoration philosophy and various exhortations which usually are contained in prefaces and forewords. It is presented here in a real chapter of its own, in hopes that it actually will be read!

Chapter 2 contains an in-depth look at all the various parts of player pianos and how they work, along with instructions for playing a player piano.

Chapter 3 tells you how to intelligently choose an old player piano which is worth reconditioning.

Chapter 4 takes you through a typical restoration from beginning to end, component by component. It provides you with an overview of the whole job, showing you a logical plan of attack, and referring you to detailed instructions in Ch. 5 as necessary.

Chapter 5 includes detailed information on restoration techniques, supplies, materials and tools. In this chapter you will learn how to break apart and repair glued wooden parts, how to replace leather valve facings, pouches and gaskets, how to clean, rehinge and recover all sizes and shapes of pneumatics and bellows, how to make the parts look like new, and other tricks of the trade which are common to the repair of all player action components. You will also learn how to select the best materials for each job, along with what tools are necessary to get the job done right.

Chapter 6 provides useful tips for rebuilding specific brands of players.

Chapters 7 and 8 discuss the intricacies of reproducing pianos, coin pianos and orchestrions - how they work, and how to make them work like they should.

Chapter 9 summarizes useful servicing and maintenance techniques, for taking care of player pianos which are already in working condition, along with tips for the care and preservation of music rolls.

Before attempting to recondition a player piano, study Chapter 2 until you understand exactly how each part works. Then familiarize yourself with the restoration procedures in Chapters 4 and 5, along with any material in Chapter 6 which is appropriate to your specific piano. It is obvious that a person not experienced in rebuilding player actions should not tackle a valuable and rare reproducing piano, coin piano or orchestrion without having previously rebuilt, and rebuilt to high standards of craftsmanship, one or more ordinary player pianos.

UPRIGHT ACTION DRAWING

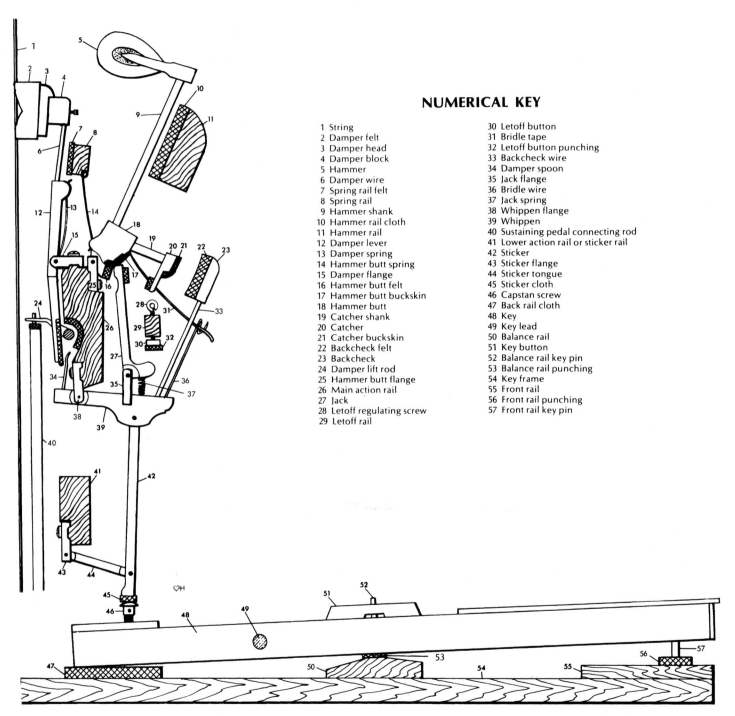

NUMERICAL KEY

1	String	30	Letoff button
2	Damper felt	31	Bridle tape
3	Damper head	32	Letoff button punching
4	Damper block	33	Backcheck wire
5	Hammer	34	Damper spoon
6	Damper wire	35	Jack flange
7	Spring rail felt	36	Bridle wire
8	Spring rail	37	Jack spring
9	Hammer shank	38	Whippen flange
10	Hammer rail cloth	39	Whippen
11	Hammer rail	40	Sustaining pedal connecting rod
12	Damper lever	41	Lower action rail or sticker rail
13	Damper spring	42	Sticker
14	Hammer butt spring	43	Sticker flange
15	Damper flange	44	Sticker tongue
16	Hammer butt felt	45	Sticker cloth
17	Hammer butt buckskin	46	Capstan screw
18	Hammer butt	47	Back rail cloth
19	Catcher shank	48	Key
20	Catcher	49	Key lead
21	Catcher buckskin	50	Balance rail
22	Backcheck felt	51	Key button
23	Backcheck	52	Balance rail key pin
24	Damper lift rod	53	Balance rail punching
25	Hammer butt flange	54	Key frame
26	Main action rail	55	Front rail
27	Jack	56	Front rail punching
28	Letoff regulating screw	57	Front rail key pin
29	Letoff rail		

Illus. 1-10. Upright piano action parts identified. For a complete explanation of upright and grand pianos, information which is prerequisite to learning about player pianos, study *Piano Servicing, Tuning and Rebuilding* by the same author and publisher as this book.

CHAPTER TWO
HOW PLAYER PIANOS WORK

Almost everyone who has ever sat down and pumped a player piano knows that the pumping pedals are connected to large bellows, and as the music roll turns, the holes in the paper somehow cause the piano keys to play. Few people, however, are aware of just how many parts a player piano mechanism actually has and how they work. The average hobbyist who thinks it will be possible to repair a player piano by patching the proverbial hole in the bellows and replacing a few pieces of broken tubing has a rude awakening upon disassembling a player piano for the first time and finding that there are nearly *one hundred* bellows and hundreds of other parts all glued and screwed together!

A knowledge of how pianos work and what their various parts are called is prerequisite to learning about player pianos. This book uses standard piano terminology and discusses piano problems which are relevent to the player mechanisms, on the assumption that the reader already understands ordinary non-player pianos. If pianos are new to you, learn the names of the parts shown in illus. 1-10, or better yet, obtain and study a copy of *Piano Servicing, Tuning and Rebuilding* by the present author, also published by the Vestal Press. A player piano is only as good as its piano!

Throughout this book, the term piano pedals refers to the soft pedal, sustaining pedal and other pedals of an ordinary non-player piano. The term pumping pedals refers to the pedals of the player action. In most player pianos, mechanisms or levers are provided for control of the piano pedals since they are inaccessible when the pumping pedals are in use.

PNEUMATIC PRINCIPLES

Suction, Atmospheric Pressure and Pneumatics

Player pianos work by means of *suction*, created by the pumping bellows in the bottom. Suction causes the keys to go down, the music roll to turn, and in some pianos, the sustaining and soft pedals to work. For each mechanical function in the piano requiring movement, there is a *pneumatic* (small bellows). When suction is connected to the inside of a pneumatic, it collapses and performs its mechanical function—playing its note, lifting the damp-

ers, pushing on the hammer rail, etc. Each pneumatic has a *valve* which turns it on and off by connecting it to suction or atmospheric pressure, respectively. (Technically, when the air pressure *inside* a pneumatic is reduced by the evacuation of some of the air, the atmospheric pressure *surrounding* the outside *pushes* it shut. Detailed explanations of the physics involved--the elasticity and molecular activity of air, how atmospheric pressure is measured, etc.--may be found in any encyclopedia, but this theory is unnecessary for the understanding of how player pianos work, providing that the reader knows what suction and atmospheric pressure are).

In the player piano repair field and in this book, the word *pneumatic* is used in two ways. When it is used as a noun, (i.e. "there are many *pneumatics* in a player piano), it refers to a small bellows. When it is used as an adjective (i.e. "*pneumatic* systems should be restored so they are as airtight as possible) it means "suction- or pressure-operated."

In this book, the terms "atmospheric pressure" and "atmosphere" are used interchangeably. Although the word "vacuum" is used by many technicians to describe the condition inside a player piano, its use is imprecise because it implies "total vacuum", something which is impossible to attain within the earth's atmosphere. Because of this inaccuracy, and the clumsiness of the term "partial vacuum," the word "suction" is used instead throughout this book.

How Suction Is Measured

The air under reduced pressure which moves around inside player piano mechanisms has two important properties: the *strength* of the suction, or the *suction level*, and the *volume* of air. To compare suction to electricity, the suction level is analogous to voltage, while the volume is analogous to amperage.

The suction *level* is measured in inches of water displaced in a water gauge, as shown in illus. 2-1. While an actual water gauge as illustrated is valuable for very precise measurements of the suction level in a reproducing piano, a good substitute for most other uses is a small vacuum gauge with a dial calibrated in inches of water. Be careful not to connect a water gauge to a suction source which is higher than the maximum level measured by the gauge, or the water in the gauge will be pulled into the player action.

VALVES

There are five main types of valves in a player piano: *inside* valves, *outside* valves, *pallet* valves, *flap* valves and *slide* valves. (The slide valve category also includes *knife* valves and *rotary* valves). How they work is presented here separately from the description of player ac-

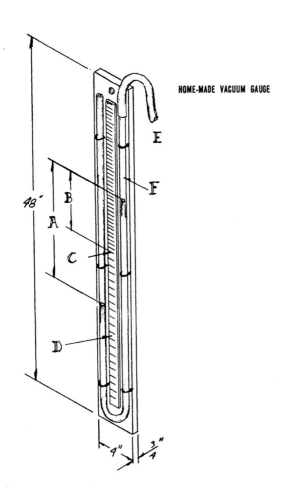

HOME-MADE VACUUM GAUGE

Illus. 2-1. A dial type vacuum gauge (above) and water gauge (left). The dial gauge is portable and is adequate for most uses, but for precise measurement of suction levels in reproducing pianos, use the water gauge.

F is either clear plastic or glass tubing, with an inside diameter of at least ¼". It is formed to a U-shape, and fastened to the board by any convenient means. If glass is used, a neoprene tube can be used to form the U at the bottom. D is a scale marked off in inches. One end of the tubing is left open to atmosphere, and the other at E is connected to a piece of neoprene tubing which is used to connect the gauge to the suction source being tested.

The tubing is filled to its midpoint C with water colored with ordinary food coloring to make it easier to read. Make sure that the 0 inch mark always coincides with the level of the water at rest, either by making the scale adjustable, or by adjusting the amount of water.

When suction is introduced at E, the water will rise in that side of the tube, and total amount of suction is indicated by the number of inches between the tops of the water columns, as at A. This will be the difference between the numbers of inches on the scale D.

A direct reading gauge can be made by marking a scale with half inches indicated as inches. This arrangement is easier to work with, as the readings can always be made directly such as at B.

tion mechanisms because the operation of valves is basic to everything else. If you don't understand the operation of valves and pouches, you won't understand how anything in a player piano works. If you learn this material well first, everything else should be easier.

Inside Valves

Illus. 2-2 is a simplified cross section showing a typical *inside valve*. (It is called an inside valve because it rests *inside* of the valve seats which it opens and closes). The suction chamber labelled vc is connected permanently to a supply of suction, represented in the illustration by arrows pointing in the direction of air flow. The chamber in which the valve is located is called the *valve well*, and the output of the valve well is connected directly to a pneumatic in this illustration by an airtight channel in the wood. When the valve is *down*, atmosphere enters the valve well and pneumatic through the top valve seat, and the pneumatic remains open. When the valve is *up*, it opens the bottom valve seat, admitting suction to the valve well and pneumatic, and simultaneously closes the top seat, closing off the atmosphere, so the pneumatic closes. When the valve goes *up*, its output is *suction*, so the pneumatic *closes*; when the valve goes *down*, its out-

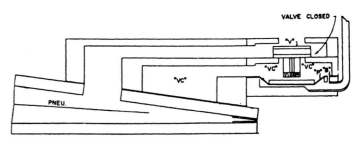

Illus. 2-2. An inside valve in the off position. The valve is down, and the pneumatic is connected to atmosphere.

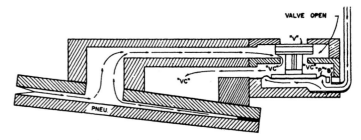

Illus. 2-3. Inside valve in the on position. Atmosphere inflates the pouch, the valve is up, and the pneumatic is connected to suction.

put is *atmosphere*, so the pneumatic *opens*. When the valve is up, it is *on*; when it is down, it is *off*.

Beneath the valve is the *pouch*, a flexible, airtight diaphragm which is larger than the valve. The pouch is glued over the *pouch well*, which has a small input channel leading to the music roll. There is also a tiny channel called a *bleed* connecting the suction chamber to the pouch well. The bleed is shown here as a small channel in the wood; theoretically, it is the same as a tiny hole in the pouch. In actual practice, the bleed is usually a tiny brass cup (or rarely, a celluloid or cardboard disc) with a hole in it; some player actions have adjustable bleeds with a pointed screw controlling the size of the tiny hole. The *valve stem* connects the valve to the pouch, and allows the pouch to push the valve up, or the valve to push the pouch down, depending on whether there is atmosphere or suction under the pouch.

When the pouch input channel is *open*, as shown in illus. 2-3, atmosphere enters the pouch well through the channel. Suction in the suction chamber simultaneously tries to pull the valve down and the pouch up, but since the pouch is larger than the valve and has more power, the pouch lifts the valve. Simply put, atmosphere inflates the pouch, lifting the valve.

When the pouch input channel is *closed*, as shown in illus.2-2, atmosphere to the pouch well is shut off. Suction from the suction chamber travels through the bleed, equalizing the suction below and above the pouch. With no atmosphere under the pouch, it no longer pushes upward on the valve stem. Suction pulls the valve down, and the valve pushes the pouch down.

The input channel to the pouch well is substantially larger than the bleed, so when the input is open to atmosphere, the pouch inflates immediately, even though a tiny amount of air continues to pass through the bleed. The bleed is large enough, however, to allow the suction to become equalized below and above the pouch immediately after the input channel is closed, allowing the valve to close almost instantly. In fact, a typical valve/pouch assembly in a player piano can turn on and off faster than 10 times a second!

A widely held but erroneous theory is that when the pouch input channel is closed, the pouch *pulls* the valve back down to its lower seat. The only way that this could possibly happen would be if the pouch, valve stem and valve were all glued together, and if suction below the pouch were *higher* than the suction above it, a condition which can not exist when the entire pneumatic system is operating on the same suction level. Actually, unless the pouch has a heavy disc attached to it which is pulled down by gravity, it floats directly under the valve stem. After a certain amount of use, the pouch *remembers* this position and never again assumes its original fully dished shape.

Outside Valves

Illus. 2-4 shows a typical *outside* valve, in the off position. (As its name implies, the body of the valve is *outside* of the valve seats). Everything works the same as in the above example of an inside valve, except when the valve is off (down), the valve well is connected to suction,

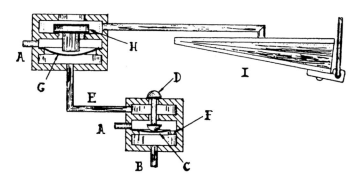

Illus. 2-4. This drawing depicts a double valve system, with the outside valve—the primary valve, in this case—toward the bottom, and the inside valve between the outside valve and pneumatic. D is the outside valve, A is connected to the suction supply, and B is the input to the pouch. As described in the text, an outside valve amplifies a small signal (atmosphere in = atmosphere out, or suction in = suction out) while an inside valve reverses the signal. The pouch for the primary valve has the usual bleed; the secondary pouch does not need one.

and when the valve is on (up), the valve well is connected to atmosphere. Therefore, when the valve is off, the output is suction, and when it is on, the output is atmosphere.

Summary—Inputs and Outputs

Every inside valve and outside valve assembly has an *input* and an *output*. The atmosphere signal which controls the pouch is always the input, and the suction or atmosphere produced by the valve is always the output. The input and output of an *inside* valve are always *opposite* (atmosphere in = suction out; suction in = atmosphere out). The input and output of an *outside valve are always the same* (atmosphere in = atmosphere out, suction in = suction out).

Primary and Secondary Valves

While the terms "inside" and "outside" valve denote a specific *type* of valve, the terms "primary" and "secondary" denote a specific *usage*. Since the input and output of an outside valve are the same (suction in = suction out, atmosphere in = atmosphere out), an outside valve can be used as a sort of amplifier to boost a small signal. Illus. 2-4 shows how a small outside valve can be connected to a larger inside valve, to improve the response of a weak signal. Valves which are connected like this are traditionally called "primary" and "secondary" valves, because in some player pianos, a set of small outside (primary) valves boosts the signals from the music roll to a larger set of inside (secondary) valves which control the pneumatics. There are many instances, however, particularly in orchestrions, where a small inside valve controls a large outside valve, so always be sure of the actual configuration to avoid confusion.

Pallet Valves

A *pallet* valve is simply a channel or an orifice covered by an airtight pad which can be opened by a button, lever or mechanical linkage, as shown in illus. 2-5.

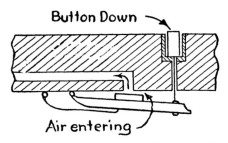

Illus. 2-5. A pallet valve simply opens and closes an orifice or tubing connection when a button is pushed or a lever is moved.

Flap Valves

A flap valve is a flexible piece of leather, often spring-loaded, and sometimes backed with metal, which covers one or more holes, allowing air to pass through in one direction but not the other. Large flap valves are used in pumping bellows to prevent air which is pumped out of a player action from being sucked back in; smaller ones are used as check valves in certain pneumatic control devices and expression mechanisms.

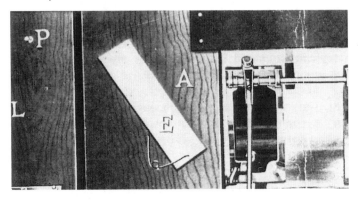

Illus. 2-6. A flap valve permits air to flow in one direction only

Slide, Rotary and Knife Valves

A slide valve, as its name implies, is a sliding block of wood or metal which covers and uncovers one or more channels. Some slide valves are solid and either open a channel to atmosphere or close it; others are hollow, and connect several channels to each other, or disconnect them. Some slide valves are quite complex, performing several functions at once.

A variation of the ordinary slide valve is the rotary valve, a metal disc which covers or uncovers, or connects and disconnects channels as it turns. See illus. 6-85 on p. 126.

A typical knife valve is shown in illus. 2-7. Located inside a pneumatic, with a spring trying to pull the pneumatic open, the knife valve regulates the suction flowing through it. When suction entering the pneumatic in-

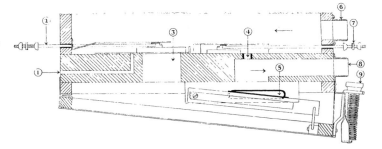

Illus. 2-7. This cross sectional drawing of a Duo-Art wind motor governor shows a knife valve (#5), and two slide valves controlling ports #3 and #4.

creases, the pneumatic pulls harder against the spring, closing the valve a little; when suction decreases, the spring pulls the pneumatic and valve open a little. The resulting suction which passes through the knife valve remains at a constant level despite changes in suction supply level. Some regulator pneumatics sometimes contain a pallet valve in place of the knife valve.

MAJOR COMPONENTS

Illus. 2-8 shows the major parts of a typical player action. ("Player action" = player mechanism). Most old player pianos have the parts located approximately as shown, although in some early players and most modern ones, the entire player action—except for the music roll mechanism—is below the keybed.

Above the keybed is the *stack* which plays the piano action by means of 88 pneumatics, valves and pouches. Most player pianos have a *single valve* action, with one

Illus. 2-8. Overall view of player action in skeleton piano cabinet.

valve and pouch for each pneumatic, all contained within the stack. Some players, however, contain a *double valve* action, which has a separate *primary valve* chest in addition to the stack. The primary valve chest contains 88 small outside valves which control the 88 larger inside valves in the stack. The primary valve chest, if present, is located on top of the stack.

Above the stack is the *head* which handles the music rolls. In the center of the head is the *spoolbox*, which holds the roll and carries it over the *tracker bar*, a brass bar with a row of holes which "read" the holes in the roll. To the right of the spoolbox is the *wind motor*, a suction-powered assembly of pneumatics and valves connected to a crankshaft, which turns the roll. To the left of the spoolbox in many player pianos is the *tracking device*, which keeps the roll aligned with the tracker bar.

Below the keybed are the *pump* which provides a constant supply of suction to the other components, and the suction control mechanisms, including the *wind motor governor* which keeps the music running at a constant speed, the *tempo control* or *speed control* which does just what its name implies, the *accelerator* which causes the roll to rewind at high speed, and the *action cutoff* which prevents the piano from playing backwards while the roll rewinds.

Pneumatic mechanisms for operating the piano pedals, if present, are usually attached to the sides of the cabinet, either above or below the keybed. In a few player pianos, there are additional mechanisms, usually located near the pump and controlled by levers or buttons mounted on the keybed, which provide expression by regulating the amount of suction available to the stack.

Mounted along the front of the keyboard and inside the music roll compartment are levers and buttons for controlling rewind/play, tempo, loud/soft, sustain, and sometimes additional features such as fast forward, expression, mandolin attachment, etc. Suction is fed from the pump to various pneumatic mechanisms by hoses, and various parts are mechanically linked by connecting rods.

THE STACK

Illus. 2-9, 10 and 11 show the front, back and cross section of a double valve stack made by the Standard Pneumatic Action Co. A large hose at the bass end connects the stack suction chamber to the pump. The 88 pneumatics are glued to three *decks*, and each pneumatic has a finger and pushrod which transfer its motion to the piano action. Inside the stack are the 88 valves and pouches; the front of the stack is the pouch board. Wherever wooden parts of the stack are screwed together, a leather gasket is installed to make the joint as airtight as possible. The entire stack may be removed from the piano in one piece for servicing, after several screws at each end are removed.

Illus. 2-9. Front view of a double valve Standard stack and head

Illus. 2-10. Rear view of the double valve Standard stack & head

The primary valve chest is mounted on top of the stack, under the head. Air signals from the tracker bar operate the primary pouches, which control the primary valves. The output signals of the primary valves pass through channels in the wood to the input channels of the secondary pouches, activating the secondary valves and the pneumatics.

The stack shown in illus. 2-9 etc. has the valves and pouches located inside, in the *valve board* and *pouch board*, forming the *valve chest*. The pneumatics are glued to deck boards, or *decks*, which are attached to the valve chest, usually with screws and gaskets. Illus. 6-7 shows another common type of stack, the *unit valve* stack, in which the pneumatics are glued to decks, but each valve/pouch assembly is contained in its own separate valve block attached to the front. Each unit valve is individually removable for servicing. Yet another type of stack is shown in illus. 6-123, the *unit pneumatic* stack. In this type, there are no deck boards, each pneumatic contains its own valve and pouch, and the whole pneumatic unit comes off separately for servicing.

There are a number of configurations for the fingers or pushrods which connect the stack to the piano action. The pneumatics always have wood or metal fingers which are built into or attached to the moveable boards. Many stacks, such as most of those built by Standard, Autopiano, Simplex, and Pratt-Read have a set of 88 flanged wooden fingers mounted above the top row of pneumatics, as shown in illus. 2-11, connected to the pneumatic fingers by metal or wooden pushrods. The flanged fingers push upward on the piano whippens to play the action.

11

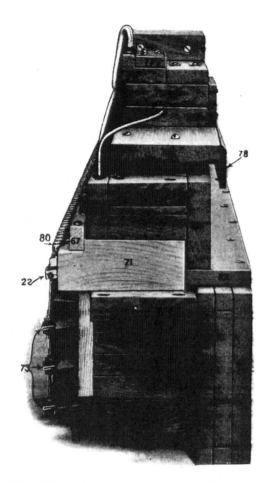

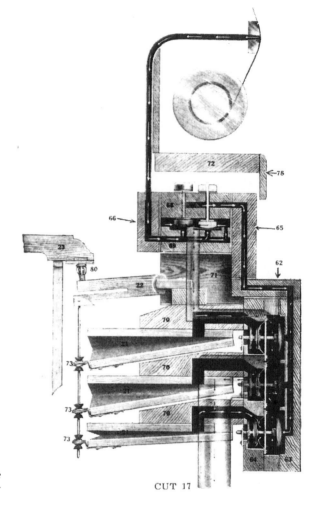

CUT 17

Illus. 2-11. End view and cross section of the Standard double valve stack. The end view shows the many individual boards which are attached to each other with leather gaskets in between.

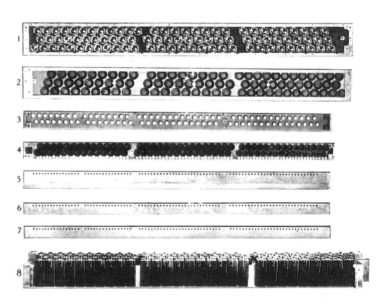

Illus. 2-12. From top to bottom: secondary valve board, secondary pouch board, primary valve board, primary pouch board, three channeled connecting boards, and the pneumatic decks of a Standard double valve stack.

Other stacks, including Beckwith, Story and Clark, and some made by Gulbransen, simply have wooden pushrods held in a guide rail which play the whippens, with no flanged fingers, as in illus. 6-43. Some stacks have no pushrods at all, but instead, the pneumatics push directly on regulating screws or bumpers which are attached to the stickers. The Gulbransen stack in illus. 6-56 has the pneumatics facing the piano action, with fingers which lift the stickers. The Baldwin stack in illus. 6-21 has upside-down pneumatics facing the front of the piano, with the fingers extending over the hinges to lift the stickers. A few stacks have upside-down pneumatics facing the front of the piano with complicated assemblies of levers on top of the stack (Cable Euphona) or underneath it (Jacob Doll) which convey the motion to the whippens. A few WurliTzer coin pianos and orchestrions have pneumatics mounted traditionally, facing the piano action, but with levers which push down on the fronts of the piano keys just behind the fallboard.

Most grand player and reproducing pianos, some early uprights, and nearly all modern players have the stack located *below* the keybed, with pneumatic pushrods pushing up on the bottom of the piano keys near the back end. Some of these pianos, including many Ampico "A" grands, simply have pushrods which pass through a guide rail mounted in the keybed. Other Ampico grands have flanged fingers attached to the stack, and Duo-Art grands have a pushrod guide rail attached to the stack, simplifying installation in the piano.

As the above examples illustrate, pouches, valves, pneumatics, fingers and other parts were put together in every conceivable way by player piano manufacturers, but they all work on the same principles of suction and atmospheric pressure.

In all player stacks, the fingers or pushrods touch the piano action but are not attached to it. When a piano key is depressed by hand, it pushes up on the piano action, lifting the action away from the stack, so the stack has no effect on the piano when it is played by hand. The idea that a player piano is necessarily sluggish because of interference from the player action is a myth perpetrated by jealous piano teachers in the 1920's who were afraid the player piano would cause them to lose business - which it undoubtedly did! Certain player pianos *do* have problems when it comes to hand playing, of course. It is impossible for a tall person to sit comfortably in front of an Ampico, Welte or other reproducing grand which is equipped with a drawer. The keys in Duo-Art grands are extra long, in order to accomodate the music roll mechanism, but in some Duo-Arts, the exposed portions of the keys (in front of the fallboard) are *shorter* than usual. The extra overall length makes the action stiffer than in a comparable non-player piano, and the shorter exposed portion of the keyboard makes the piano awkward to play by hand. In general, however, most player pianos play perfectly well by hand if they are regulated properly, and the difference in "feel" between a player and non-player of the same size is no greater than the difference between any two pianos of two different sizes.

THE HEAD

The head sits on top of the stack, with the spoolbox in the middle, the wind motor on the right, and the tracking device on the left, as shown in illus. 2-9.

THE SPOOLBOX

The *spoolbox* contains the *music roll spindles* (or *chucks*), *takeup spool*, *tracker bar*, *transmission*, and *spool brakes*. In some players it also contains the rewind/play lever, a switch for turning the automatic sustaining pedal on and off, a music transposing control, and the automatic tracking device. In players with no *automatic tracking device*, a manual roll alignment knob is sometimes located here.

The music roll spindles support the music roll during play, and turn it backwards during rewind. If an automatic tracking device is used, it usually aligns the roll by moving the spindles slightly to the left or right. The left spindle is spring-loaded, and the right one—the rewind drive spindle—is keyed to fit into the right hand music roll flange to drive the roll during rewind. In standardized 88-note players, the right spindle has a flat blade which fits into the socket in the roll flange; in 65-note players, the right spindle has a slotted socket which holds the eared pin end of the roll. (See next page).

Running across the middle of the spoolbox is the *tracker bar*, a brass bar with 88 holes for the 88 playing notes of the stack, plus an extra large hole on the left side for the automatic sustaining pedal mechanism, if present. (Most 88-note piano rolls are perforated for automatic sustaining pedal; its perforation is always to the left of the 88 note playing holes). In some cases, there are also one or more holes surrounding the edges of the paper for controlling an automatic tracking device. The back of the tracker bar is fitted with brass nipples, which are connected to the pouch input nipples of the stack with small tubing appropriately called *tracker bar tubing*. Some 88-note players have 80 or fewer pneumatics, with four or more pneumatics and valves omitted from each end of the stack; their tracker bar holes are either unconnected or they are teed to holes one octave away.

Many players have a *transposing* tracker bar which can be moved to the left or right a few holes to play the music in a higher or lower key, to suit a vocalist's singing range. Two types of transposing device are shown in illus. 2-13 and 2-19.

Below the tracker bar is the takeup spool, which winds the roll around it during play.

On the right side of the spoolbox is the *transmission*, a framework supporting shafts, gears, sprockets, chains, and a shift lever which is connected to the manual rewind/play control lever. One shaft of the transmission is connected to the wind motor, either directly or with sprockets and a chain, and the wind motor always turns this shaft in the same direction. With the lever in the "play" position, power is transmitted from the wind motor through a pair of gears to the takeup spool. With the lever in the "rewind" position, the takeup spool gears are disconnected, and power is transmitted through a clutch, sprockets and chain to the right hand music roll spindle, which rapidly rewinds the roll.

The transmission also usually contains the *takeup spool brake* (or *lower brake*) and the *music roll brake*, (or *upper brake*). These brakes apply controlled drag on the takeup spool shaft during rewind and the music roll spindle during play, causing the paper to wind up snugly. In most

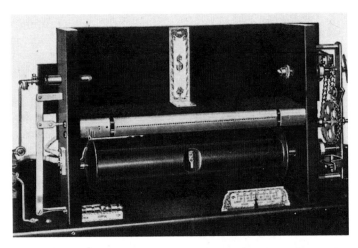

Illus. 2-13. Closeup of a Standard spoolbox with a transposing tracker bar. The lever in the lower left hand corner of the spoolbox latches into one of five slots, locking the bar into five different positions.

players, the brakes are turned on and off mechanically by the rewind/play lever, but in some instruments they are controlled by pneumatics.

88-Note vs. 65-Note Music Rolls

Prior to 1908, various types of piano rolls were made with various hole spacing across the width of the paper, with the 65-note format being the most common. At a conference of manufacturers held in Buffalo NY in 1908, common agreement was reached that everyone should produce rolls compatible with the full 88-note scale of the piano—and this standard has prevailed to the present day, all over the world. One very compelling reason for abandoning the 65-note scale was the recognition that the player piano could never be taken seriously for reproduction of classical compositions with such a limited capability; only with the full piano scale being used would the player piano be competitive in the world of serious music.

Both 65-note and 88-note rolls have a paper width of 11¼"; 65-note rolls have the 65 holes spread across the paper width at a spacing of 6 holes per inch, while 88-note rolls have all 88 holes in the same paper width, spaced at 9 holes per inch. 65-note rolls are also known as "pin end" rolls, because each flange has a small metal pin at its axis. The left pin is round, and the right pin is shaped to fit into a slotted drive socket in the spoolbox. The flanges of 88-note rolls have round sockets for the spoolbox roll support spindles. The left flange socket is round, and the right one is slotted. 65-note rolls are quite rare today, but they do pop up in an antique store or piano roll auction now and then. Prior to 1905, other non-standard rolls were also used on home player pianos, but these are extremely rare today. During the transitional era, a few players were made which accepted both types of rolls; these are known today as 65/88 note players. They

are equipped with a tracker bar with two rows of holes and a switching device to turn one row on and the other off, (or more rarely, interchangeable tracker bars) and interchangeable roll drive spindles for the two types of spool ends.

Unless a 65-note player action is mentioned specifically in this book, all text is directed toward standardized 88-note players, although most information is also applicable to 65-note instruments with a little translation.

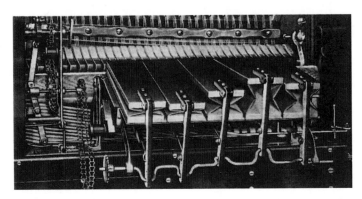

Illus. 2-14. A Standard wind motor tilted forward to provide room for tuning the piano, showing the pneumatics, connecting arms and crankshaft. By April 1917, Standard had produced over 120,000 of these wind motors!

THE WIND MOTOR

The *wind motor*, which turns the music roll, is an assembly of pneumatics and slide valves connected to a crankshaft. Each pneumatic turns the crankshaft part of one rotation, the crankshaft moves the slide valves, and the slide valves feed suction to the pneumatics in sequence, causing the crankshaft to turn. Most wind motors have either four, five or six pneumatics. In a five point (five pneumatic) wind motor, for example, each pneumatic turns the crankshaft a little more than one fifth of one rotation, with enough overlap between the pneumatics for perfectly smooth operation. Early pushup piano players have three point wind motors; these have a belt running to a cast iron flywheel which smooths out the steps between the three pneumatics. Four point wind motors work fairly smoothly without a flywheel, but the standard adopted by the late 'teens was the five or six point motor. Most six point wind motors are arranged with three pairs of double pneumatics, each pair of pneumatics sharing a double-acting slide valve; Gulbransen wind motors use two triple-acting rotary valves. All wind motors turn in one direction only; the direction of the music roll is reversed for rewind by the transmission.

THE TRACKING DEVICE

Every 88-note home player piano has some means of adjusting the alignment of the roll with the tracker bar, either manually or automatically.

Illus. 2-15. The simplest form of roll tracking adjustment, the manual tracking knob. In this piano, it serves the purpose of adjusting for rolls which are out of line, as well as shifting the bar several steps to the left or right for transposing.

Manual Tracking Devices

The simplest form of tracking device is the manual *roll adjuster*. This is either a thumb wheel or lever which moves the tracker bar or music roll to the left or right. The thumb wheel shown in illus. 2-15 moves the tracker bar, the Kimball keyslip lever moves the *top* roll spool, and the early Aeolian push-up piano player spoolbox lever moves *both* spools. If a music roll is in perfect condition, with both edges trimmed straight, perfectly straight flanges, the holes punched correctly and the end tab centered at the beginning of the leader, the manual roll adjuster may be set once at the beginning, and the roll will play through in perfect alignment with the tracker bar from beginning to end.

Automatic Tracking Devices

Unfortunately, many rolls—both old and new—are less than perfect, requiring adjustment now and then while they play, so most player pianos contain an auto-

matic tracking device (or *automatic tracker*) instead of a manual roll adjuster. Usually mounted directly on the left side of the spoolbox, or on the shelf to its left, the automatic tracker aligns the roll with the tracker bar by sensing continuously where the edges of the paper are, and by moving either the top spool or the tracker bar as necessary. Most automatic trackers move the top spool by means of a cam which adjusts the right hand roll spindle; very few move the tracker bar, by means of large pneumatics. The latter method was seldom used because it involves moving the whole bundle of tubing as well, making the tracking device sluggish.

Automatic trackers are either *mechanical* or *pneumatic*. All mechanical trackers sense the position of the roll with one or two sensing fingers; some pneumatic trackers use sensing fingers and others use sensing holes in the tracker bar.

Mechanical Automatic Trackers

In a mechanical tracking device, the spring in the left hand music roll spindle constantly tries to push the roll to the right, pressing the right hand spindle shaft against the adjusting cam. As the cam moves up and down (or left and right, or whatever), the roll moves to the left or right. In most examples, (Simplex, Story and Clark, and Gulbransen), the cam is rotated by a "fishing pole" and string wound around a shaft. This shaft is turned by a friction wheel clutch which is propelled by the transmission. The sensing finger or fingers are mechanically linked to the clutch and cause the two friction wheels to engage or disengage. If the roll wanders to the *left*, the sensing finger(s) disengage the clutch, allowing the spring in the left hand music roll support spindle to push the roll to the *right*; if the roll wanders to the *right*, the sensing fingers engage the clutch, winding up the string, pulling the fishing pole down, and moving the roll to the *left*. The roll does not lurch abruptly to the left or right; rather, the clutch floats in the ideal position, making minor adjustments constantly.

Another form of mechanical tracking device, used in some Fayette Cable players and possibly other brands, incorporates a gear train in place of the fishing pole. As in the fishing pole tracking device, sensing fingers manipulate a friction wheel clutch.

Many mechanical automatic tracking devices were made for player piano manufacturers by the Brand Player Accessories Co. of New York, N.Y.

An unusual mechanical automatic tracker is the one used in many modern WurliTzer player pianos. A sensing finger is connected to a microswitch, and a small reversible electric motor drives the roll adjusting mechanism. The motor pushes the roll to the right until the sensing finger trips the switch. This reverses the motor, pushing the roll to the left, until the finger trips the switch in the

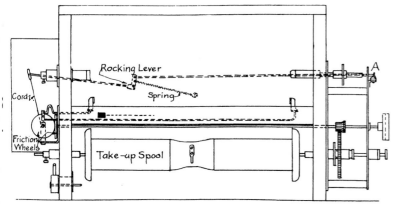

Illus. 2-16. The "fishing pole" type of mechanical automatic tracking device of a Story & Clark player. This senses mistracking by feeling the paper edges with two fingers, and adjusts the music roll spindles to the left or right as necessary by means of the fish pole and friction wheels. Its adjustment is covered in the Gulbransen section on p. 125.

other direction, reversing the motor again. The top spool constantly moves left and right, wearing the edges of music rolls faster than most other tracking devices.

Illus. 2-17. Another type of mechanical automatic tracker. In this version made by the Brand Player Accessories Co.and found in a Fayette Cable piano, the fish pole is replaced by a pulley and tracking cam. Numerous other varieties also exist.

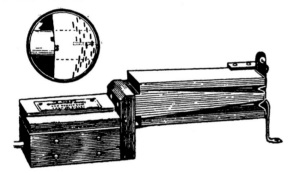

Illus. 2-18. The common Standard pneumatic tracking device, which takes care of paper alignment with four tracking holes which control a pair of pneumatics. Its sophisticated operation is described in detail on pp. 143–145.

Pneumatic Automatic Trackers

Pneumatic tracking devices have one or two pneumatics which push the roll to the left or right in response to sensing fingers or holes in the tracker bar.

The simplest form of pneumatic device was used in early Aeolian, some Hardman and some Price and Teeple players, with one hole or sensing finger on the left side of the tracker bar connected to a single pneumatic. During play, the pneumatic is connected to suction through a bleed. When the sensing hole or finger is completely closed, the pneumatic collapses slowly; when the hole or finger is completely open, the pneumatic opens because the sensing hole is larger than the suction supply bleed. During play, the pneumatic pushes the roll sideways until the edge of the paper nearly covers the sensing hole or almost closes the finger. At that point, atmosphere entering the pneumatic balances the suction supply, and the pneu-

matic floats in that position, holding the roll in alignment. To accomodate rolls of slightly different sizes, the sensing finger or the portion of the tracker bar containing the sensing hole is adjustable in relation to the note holes. This system works satisfactorily in play but tends to damage rolls during rewind (see below).

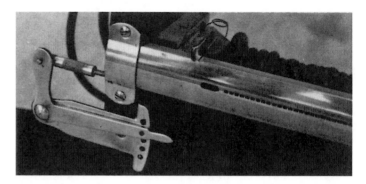

Illus. 2-19. This Fayette Cable transposing mechanism has a lever which shifts the entire tracker bar left or right; the tracker bar has an extra wide hole for the sustaining pedal, and the paper edge sensing fingers for the automatic tracking device remain stationary.

A much better type of sensing finger arrangement, used in most old Aeolian and Amphion players, has a double pneumatic connected to a constant source of suction, with each finger opening a tube connected to one of the pneumatics. When the edge of the paper pushes on one finger, air bleeds into that pneumatic, pushing the roll in the opposite direction. Usually there are constrictions (bleeds) between the pneumatics and suction supply, slowing the movement of the pneumatics to make the tracking device work smoothly. This type of tracker works well with rolls of one specific width. Wider rolls hold both finger valves open, and narrower rolls open neither one; both conditions render the tracker less sensitive, as the roll must wander over a wider range before correction can take place.

Somewhat more complex is the device used in players manufactured by Baldwin, using floating sensing fingers which are linked to little pallet valves with a balanced T lever. This device works regardless of paper width. (See the Baldwin information later in this book for further information).

Another slightly more elaborate system is found in some Jacob Doll and Pratt Read players, in which a double pneumatic responds to a pair of edge sensing holes, with one hole on each side of the roll. The sensing holes are drilled in little brass blocks which can be adjusted sideways in slots in the tracker bar to accomodate rolls of different widths. In some pianos, a manual control is provided for adjusting the sensing holes at the beginning of each roll; in others, a complicated mechanism automatically floats the holes in to the edges of the paper and then keeps the roll centered on the note holes while it plays.

The most common form of pneumatic automatic tracking device is found in Standard, Autopiano and modern Aeolian players. This device has two staggered sensing holes on each side of the roll, as shown in illus. 2-18, connected to a mechanism containing six pouches and four valves which control a large double pneumatic and tracking cam. When slightly wider rolls are played, the tracking device responds to the outer tracking holes, and when slightly narrower rolls are used, it ignores the outer pair of holes and responds to the inner ones. Details of its operation are included in the section on Standard player pianos in Ch. 6.

Combination Manual & Automatic Trackers

An automatic tracking device keeps the roll aligned properly as long as both edges of the roll are in good condition, or are worn equally. When one edge of a roll is torn and folded over, the automatic tracker doesn't know what to do, so it pushes the roll grossly out of alignment. Some rolls play better without an automatic tracker; others play better with one. An interesting tracking mechanism was used in early Balwin players. This gadget incorporates the usual Baldwin automatic tracking device plus a manual roll adjusting knob, with provision for turning the automatic mechanism off and locking the roll in a centered position. Details are included in the Baldwin section of this book.

Automatic Tracking Devices and Rewind

Note that most automatic tracking devices work *during play only*, and not during rewind. During play, when the roll is too far to the left, the tracker responds by pushing the upper spool a little to the right. Because the paper is unwinding slowly off the spool, the tracker moves the spool *and* the paper, correcting misalignment with the tracker bar. If the automatic tracker worked during rewind, however, it would tear the edges of the paper. For example, if fingers or edge holes sensed that the paper was too far to the left, the tracker would push the spool to the right, tearing the left edge of the paper on the upper left flange as it rewound rapidly. For this reason, all automatic tracking devices are disengaged during rewind. In a mechanical device, the friction wheel clutch is disengaged; in a pneumatic device, the suction is cut off. Simultaneously, the upper spool is locked into a centered position.

Unfortunately, some automatic trackers with one pneumatic and one edge sensing finger (early Aeolian, Price and Teeple, Hardman) shred music rolls during rewind if suction is disconnected. Instead, suction is connected all the time, and the tracker works backward during rewind, which also damages rolls. There is no simple remedy for this problem short of changing the tracking device to a more reliable style.

Transposing Tracker Bars

In players with a transposing tracker bar, the center section of the bar which contains the note-playing holes is mounted so it can be moved to the left or right in steps, allowing the music to be transposed to suit the vocal range of someone who wishes to sing along. This is done in a way which does not interfere with the automatic tracking device. If the device uses edge sensing fingers, the whole bar moves to the left and right for transposition, while the fingers remain stationary. If the tracker uses edge sensing holes in the tracker bar, the bar is cut into three segments as in illus. 2-13; the outer segments containing the sensing holes (and sometimes the sustaining pedal hole) remain stationary, and the center segment containing the note playing holes is adjustable. In rare examples, the edge sensing holes are mounted in separate brass blocks which fit in horizontal slots cut into the tracker bar; the whole bar moves from side to side around the stationary sensing holes.

THE PUMP

The pump includes the two *pumping bellows* connected to the pumping pedals, and one or more *reservoirs* which serve to smooth the suction output between pumping strokes. The pumping bellows and reservoirs are usually all fastened to a common suction chamber called the *trunk*. Each pumping bellows has one or more external springs which hold it *closed* and hold the pumping pedal *up*. Each reservoir has one or more internal springs which hold it *open*.

The pumping bellows have internal and external *flap valves* which control the flow of air as the bellows are

Illus. 2-20. The complete pump of a Standard player action, including the two pumping bellows connected to the pedals, two large reservoirs, action cutoff and wind motor controls.

17

pumped. Each flap valve allows air to pass through only in one direction. When a pumping pedal pushes the bellows *open,* suction inside the bellows pulls the external flap valve shut, causing air to be pulled out of the trunk. When the pedal is released, the spring pushes the bellows closed again, creating air *pressure* inside the bellows. This higher pressure pushes the internal flap valve shut, trapping the lower pressure inside the trunk, and exhausting the contents of the pumping bellows through the external flap valve. Thus, each time the bellows is pushed open, it pulls air out of the player action through the internal flap valve, and each time it is released, it dumps this air into the atmosphere through the external flap valve.

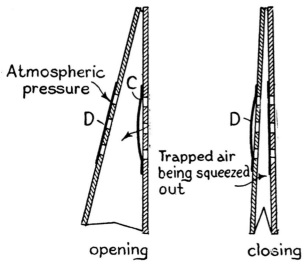

Illus. 2-21. When the pumping pedal is pushed down, the inside flap valve C opens and the outside valve D closes, causing air to be drawn out of the player action into the pumping bellows. When the pedal is released and the spring pushes the bellows shut again, the inside valve closes and the outside one opens, exhausting the air into the bottom of the piano. The author has seen many players in which the owner erroneously sealed the outside flaps shut to "keep them from leaking."

To keep the suction output of the pump at a constant level, one or more reservoirs are included. When each pumping pedal is pushed down, the suction level inside the trunk increases, and the reservoirs pull shut, absorbing some of the increase. Between pumping strokes, the suction level decreases, and the internal reservoir springs push the reservoirs partially open, compensating for the decrease. The result is that as the pumping pedals are pumped alternately, the reservoirs pulsate in and out, and the suction output of the pump remains fairly constant.

SUCTION CONTROLS

The suction control mechanisms below the keybed include the *action cutoff,* and the *wind motor governor, speed control* and *accelerator.* In some players, all of these parts are built into the pump; in others, they are mounted separately.

The Action Cutoff

The action cutoff is simply a large valve which blocks or passes suction from the pump to the stack. During rewind, the action cutoff closes, preventing the stack from playing the music backwards. In some players, (Standard, Autopiano), it is in the form of a large slide valve which is opened and closed by the manual rewind control lever, as shown in illus. 2-20. In others, (Gulbransen, H.C. Bay, Schulz) a pneumatic mounted on the pump does the work of opening and closing a valve inside the trunk; the pneumatic has its own valve and pouch, controlled by a pallet valve connected to the rewind linkage. Another variety is simply a large pouch with a cutoff valve attached directly to it, controlled by a small valve which is actuated by the rewind linkage pallet, as in Amphion players.

In pianos with sustain and soft pedal pneumatics, a mandolin pneumatic or other accessories, the action cutoff usually cuts off suction to these during rewind also.

The Wind Motor Governor

The wind motor has three suction controls: the governor, the tempo control, and the accelerator. The governor regulates the flow of suction to the wind motor, keeping the speed constant regardless of pulsations in the suction supply or soft or loud playing. It consists of a medium size pneumatic with a knife valve inside and a spring which tries to pull it open. When the suction level increases during loud playing, the pneumatic pulls harder against the

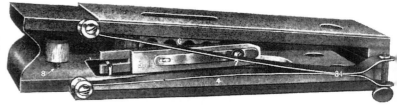

Illus. 2-22. Cutaway view of the Standard governor, showing the internal knife valve and external adjustable spring.

spring, closing the knife valve a little, and when the suction level decreases during soft playing or between pumping strokes, the spring pulls the pneumatic and valve open a little. This keeps the level of suction fed to the wind motor constant, regardless of the level inside the pump, allowing the player pianist to vary the volume level without varying the speed of the music.

The Tempo Control

The tempo control is a slide valve (in Gulbransens, a rotary valve) which admits more or less suction to the wind motor as adjusted by the tempo lever. The orifice controlled by the slide valve is usually shaped as shown in illus. 2-23. The tempo lever also moves a small pointer in the spoolbox, which indicates the speed of the roll on a numbered scale. Each increment of 10 on the tempo scale indicates one foot of paper travel over the tracker bar per minute; 70 = seven feet per minute, 80 = 8 feet per minute, etc. There is no correlation between this standardized tempo scale and the number of beats of music per minute; the scale is simply a guide for setting the speed of a music roll to the suggested tempo printed on the roll leader. The printed tempo is merely the opinion of the musician who arranged the roll, and it is not necessary to adhere to this tempo if a slower or faster speed is desired.

In most Angelus, some Autopiano and a few other players, two tempo controls are provided: an ordinary one with the usual tempo scale, and a spring loaded ritard/accelerate lever which returns to normal when released. This permits the player pianist to pause, or to reduce or increase the tempo for artistic effects, without changing the basic tempo setting; after the temporary speed change, the wind motor reverts to the previous tempo.

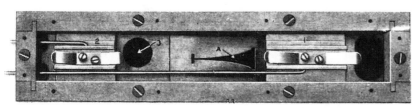

Illus. 2-23. The Standard wind motor control box with its cover removed. The accelerator slide valve to the left is shown in the rewind position with port 3 open, and the tempo control slide valve is shown at the fastest setting with port A all the way open.

The Wind Motor Accelerator

The accelerator is a valve located between the suction supply and wind motor, which bypasses the governor and tempo control valve. It remains closed during play, and opens during rewind, causing the wind motor to rewind the roll at a high speed. Like the action cutoff, the accelerator is controlled directly by the rewind lever in some player pianos, and is controlled by a pneumatic or pouch in others. The action cutoff and wind motor accelerator operate together, and are usually controlled by the same lever or pallet valve.

The Silencer

In some players, a control button called the *silencer* operates the action cutoff and wind motor accelerator at the same time, *without shifting the transmission into rewind,* causing the wind motor to wind the roll forward quickly. This is useful for skipping over unwanted songs in a multi-song roll.

Expression Regulators

A few player pianos have the stack divided into treble and bass, with a separate suction regulator for each half. Each expression regulator works on the same principle as a wind motor governor, causing the stack to play at a constant volume level regardless of pumping speed. Levers are provided for manual control of the regulator spring tension, giving independent expression control of the bass and treble. Sometimes, accent buttons are also provided; these control large valves which bypass the regulators, admitting full pump suction to the stack for quick bass or treble accents. Refer also to Themodist expression pianos in Ch. 7.

ACCESSORIES

Hammer Rail Controls

The hammer rail in most player pianos is made in three pieces, with two small hammer rails—one for bass and the other for treble—attached to the full length rail. The two inset rails are connected to levers or pneumatics, and

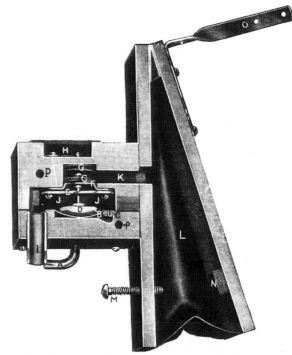

Illus. 2-24. Most player pianos have some means of softening the bass and treble separately, either by manual control levers, or by buttons which actuate large control pneumatics like the one shown here.

they allow the player pianist to soften the bass and treble independently. The main rail is connected to the piano soft pedal, and it works like the hammer rail in any upright piano. When hammer rail pneumatics are used, they are located on the sides of the cabinet, sometimes above the keybed and sometimes below it; in some pianos, each pneumatic contains its own valve and pouch, and in others, the valves are contained in the piano stack or in a separate valve box under the keybed. The soft hammer rail pneumatics are controlled by button-operated pallet valves in the piano keyslip.

Sustaining Pedal Controls

As mentioned in the description of tracker bars earlier in the text, many players have an automatic sustain pneumatic which works from a large hole to the left of the note playing holes in the tracker bar. The sustain pneumatic is usually quite large and has one or more large valves in order to have enough power and speed to do its job. It lifts the sustaining pedal dowel by a linkage which gives it further mechanical advantage. The tube from the tracker bar hole is invariably interrupted with a *sustain on/off* switch in the spoolbox. This blocks or passes the signal to the pouch input of the sustain valve, giving the player pianist the option of using this accessory or not, depending upon the effectiveness of the sustain perforations in each music roll. The sustain pneumatic and hammer rail pneumatics usually are supplied suction from a section of the pump supply trunk which is shut off during rewind.

In pianos with no automatic sustain pneumatic, there is a lever in the keyslip for manual control of this function.

Illus. 2-25. The Standard automatic sustaining pneumatic, which works in response to a finger button or the hole to the left of the note playing holes in the tracker bar.

The Mandolin Attachment

Some player pianos contain a *mandolin attachment,* a wood or metal bar with a leather or bellows cloth curtain slit into as many segments as there are treble notes in the piano, with a metal or wood tab attached to each segment. The mandolin swings up and down on supports which are screwed to the sides of the piano; it is turned on by lowering it between the hammers and strings with a lever in the spoolbox or with a pneumatic actuated by a keyslip button. When the mandolin is lowered into the "on" position, the piano hammers bounce the tabs against the strings, producing a tinny sound. There are no tabs for the wound bass strings because the tabs are harder than the copper windings and cut through them if used in this range. The mandolin is also known as the "harp," "zither," " banjo," "Rinky-Tink" (TM Schaff Piano Supply Co.) and "Ukelano" (TM Aeolian Corp.).

A different type of mandolin attachment was used in Schiller player pianos, and in Coinola and Cremona coin pianos and orchestrions. In this type, a long narrow wooden tray holding little wood-tipped rods or flat wooden blades rests between the hammers and dampers. When turned off, the rods or blades lie between the hammer shanks. To turn the mandolin on, the tray is moved sideways so the rods or blades are aligned with the shanks, and when a note plays, the shank hits the rod, bumping it into the strings. The hammer hits the strings at the same time, and the resulting tone is a combination of the mandolin device and the hammers. This type of mandolin does not wear the hammers.

Illus. 2-26. The mandolin attachment produces a tinny sound when the metal- or wood-studded tabs are lowered between hammers and strings.

Electric Suction Pumps

Most modern player pianos and a few old ones have an electric pump or suction box in addition to the foot pump. Modern instruments (and very few old ones) have a high speed turbine powered by a universal motor (with commutator and brushes) of the type used in most household vacuum cleaners. If an old player has an original motor driven pump, it is usually similar to the type used in reproducing pianos, with four bellows connected to a crankshaft turned by a large pulley, driven by a 1200 rpm induction motor with a small pulley. In pianos having both electric and foot pumps, there is a check valve which automatically closes the hose from the electric pump when the foot pump is used.

Automatic Rewind

This accessory is found in modern player pianos which have an electric pump, to prevent the roll from being torn off the spool in case the piano is left playing unattended, although a few modern players without an electric pump also have this feature. Most 88-note rolls made since about 1930 never use the last few playing notes in the bass and treble, but these holes are all punched simultaneously at the end of every roll. The automatic rewind pneumatic contains its own valve and pouch, with the input tube connected to one of the highest or lowest tracker bar note holes. If the piano is not manually switched into rewind after the music stops at the end of a roll, the rewind unit automatically pulls the transmission into rewind. Electric reproducing pianos have automatic rewind devices, described in detail in Ch. 7.

Automatic Shutoff

The automatic shutoff is provided in electric player pianos to turn the motor off when the roll is rewound completely. In some pianos, a microswitch falls into a groove in the takeup spool when the roll comes off, turning off the motor, and in others, the paper uncovers a small hole in the takeup spool or a non-note-playing hole in the tracker bar, actuating the valve for a pneumatic which throws the switch. Automatic shutoff mechanisms are described in detail in the sections on modern Aeolian players and reproducing pianos in Ch. 6 and 7.

DIFFERENCES BETWEEN ORDINARY PIANOS AND PLAYER PIANOS

Uprights

An upright player piano is basically the same as any other upright piano, with a few structural and mechanical differences. The player piano cabinet is about four inches deeper from front to back, to accomodate the player action, and it contains doors for access to the spoolbox and pumping pedals. The pedal door either slides left and right, slides up and down, or folds up and down in two pieces, and there is usually some sort of lever or handle to open and close it. In some pianos, the two spoolbox doors are connected with a mechanical linkage so when one is opened, the other opens at the same time. A few players (Cable Euphona, Kimball, some Pratt Read) have one large lever mounted under the keybed, which opens the pedal door and then lowers the pedals. Nearly all players have two keyslips: a large hollow one which folds down, exposing the control levers, and a thin one which remains in place in front of the keys. Exceptions are early Baldwins, in which the keyslip is like an ordinary one, old Kimballs, in which a small center portion of the keyslip folds under when the pedal door lever is operated, and Cable Euphonas, in which the center part of the keyslip pulls out on metal slides to expose the levers.

In most players, the hammer rail has split inset rails, as described above in the section entitled Hammer Rail Controls, for individual control of treble and bass.

Old players usually have a *key lock*, a hinged rail under the fronts of the piano keys which may be swung into po-

sition with a small lever under the keybed to prevent the keys from moving when the player is used. This allows the player action to play quickly repeated notes a *little* better at *extremely* soft playing levels, particularly in upright reproducing pianos. Its effect is so negligible that few people ever use it.

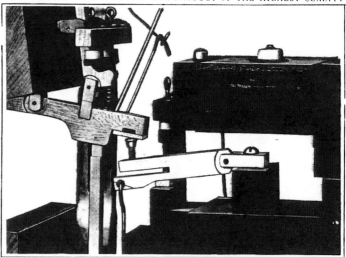

THE FLEXIBLE FINGERS

Illus. 2-27. In this action model of one note in a Standard double valve system, the stop rail is mounted on the stack, with a regulating screw and button positioned above each "flexible finger." Other players have a similar stop rail mounted on the piano action, with the regulating buttons positioned over the ends of the whippens. The stop rail prevents the pneumatic from pushing the whippen up too far.

Most players have a *stop rail* to limit the travel of the whippens. When a piano is played by the *keyboard,* the keys go down until they stop on the front rail punchings; the thickness of these punchings regulates the amount of key travel. If there were no front rail punchings, the keys would push the whippens up too far, causing the hammers to block against the strings. To prevent the *player action* from pushing the whippens up too far, the stop rail is mounted either on the stack, limiting the motion of the flanged fingers, or on the piano action, limiting the motion of the whippens. In old players, there is usually a regulating screw and button for each note, providing individual adjustment; in many modern Aeolian players, the stop rail is simply a wood strip with a piece of action cloth suspended over the backs of the keys.

In most upright players, the piano pedals are connected to the damper and hammer rail dowels with metal rods running across the bottom, which take up less space than the large wooden trap levers found in most non-players.

Grands

Ordinary grand pianos, and grand player and reproducing pianos also have a few differences. Pianos housing the music roll mechanism in a drawer under the keybed (Ampico, most Welte Licensee and Recordo grands) have a regular size cabinet, but in pianos with the roll mechanism above the keyboard (most Duo-Art and European grands), the cabinet is elongated between the fallboard and pinblock to accomodate the spoolbox, wind motor and other parts. In pianos with a drawer, the controls are all inside the drawer; in pianos with the spoolbox above the keyboard, the controls are usually behind a hinged keyslip, but are in the spoolbox compartment in a few instruments. The stack is nearly always mounted under the keybed, and a large slot is cut into the back of the keybed to allow the pushrods to push up on the back ends of the keys, which are cushioned with felt or action cloth. (A few grands have the stack located in the drawer, with linkages connecting the stack to the pushrods whether the drawer is open or closed). In many player grands, one or more of the beams under the piano are altered or missing, to accomodate the pump and other mechanisms. The cabinet usually has side skirts to hide the player action, and most grands have a *belly cloth* covering the bottom to help quiet mechanical noises. In most player and reproducing grands, the piano pedal trap levers are completely different than in ordinary grands, to get around parts of the player action.

Spinets and Consoles

Nearly all modern players have the stack mounted under the keyboard, with the pushrods pushing up on the back ends of the keys. Exceptions are the first Hardman Duo players made by Aeolian in the late 1950's, in which the stack is above the keyboard as in old uprights. Ampico spinets have the stack, pump, motor, and expression mechanisms all squeezed under the keyboard.

SUMMARY OF MANUAL CONTROLS

Now that you are familiar with all commonly encountered mechanisms, a review of the manual buttons and levers will summarize the operation of a typical player piano:

Bass/treble soft levers or buttons: operate the bass and treble split hammer rails, softening half of the piano to bring out melodies in the other half.

Door opening lever: opens the pedal doors; sometimes simultaneously pulls the pedals down and rarely also opens the keyslip.

Key lock: prevents the keys from moving while the player action plays the piano.

Mandolin lever or button: causes mandolin rail to drop between hammers and strings, producing tinny sound.

Rewind/play lever: shifts the transmission and operates the action cutoff and wind motor accelerator.

Ritard/Accelerate lever: temporarily modifies the speed of the wind motor for artistic interpretation of the music.

Roll adjuster: adjusts the tracker bar from side to side for correct alignment with the roll.

Illus. 2-28. Because modern pianos are smaller than old ones, the stack is located under the keybed, with the pushrods pushing up on the back ends of the keys.

Silencer button: operates the action cutoff and wind motor accelerator but leaves the transmission in "play."

Sustain lever or button: lifts the dampers off the strings, like the piano sustaining pedal.

Sustain on/off switch: turns sustain hole in tracker bar which is tubed to automatic sustain pneumatic mechanism on and off.

Tempo lever: adjusts the speed indicator and the speed of the wind motor.

Transposing lever: adjusts the tracker bar in steps to play the music in a lower or higher key.

MECHANICAL VARIETY

In the early days of the player piano, manufacturers didn't stay with a particular design for long, so early players have all sorts of unusual mechanisms and features. Melville Clark, for one example, was a great experimenter and innovator, and it is unusual to find any two Melville Clark Apollo player pianos which have the same exact features. All varieties of unusual expression mechanisms, pumps, stacks, tracker bars and spoolboxes which play odd music rolls, spring-wound roll motors, and other curiosities are the norm rather than the exception in these early players. In fact, even the player pianos which were mass produced in huge quantities during the 1920's underwent a continuous evolution of design, resulting in every conceivable combination of valves, pneumatics, pushrods, fingers, transmissions, tracking devices, wind motors and other components. To the mechanically inclined technician, this variety is one factor which makes player piano restoration fascinating. Each new job represents the possibility of something unknown, and if the technician views this as a challenge rather than an obstacle, restoration is always interesting.

HOW TO PLAY A PLAYER PIANO

A well-restored player piano is *easy to pump*. What does easy to pump mean? It means the player action is as airtight as possible, so the pumping pedals meet resistance on the way down. A player piano which is truly hard to play offers no pumping resistance, requiring fast, full pedal strokes to make any music at all. Inexperienced player pianists sometimes sit down at an airtight instrument and complain that it is hard to pump, because the pedals are hard to push down. While they struggle, fortissimo music comes out of the piano, the stack threatens to break piano action parts, and the hammers are on the verge of breaking strings! Other novices use a quick succession of very short pumping strokes, wasting most of each pedal stroke. Still others attempt to push each pedal all the way down in time with the music. Needless to say, these approaches are all wrong. Here's the correct way to play a player piano.

Remove the music roll from the box, and before inserting it in the piano, drop the right end (with the drive flange) into the right hand several times. This straightens the paper, reducing the amount of correcting which will be necessary by the automatic tracking device or roll adjusting knob. Insert the left end of the roll into the spoolbox and push it to the left, align the right end with the drive spindle, and make sure the spindle seats in the socket in the right flange. Put the rewind/play lever in the rewind position to allow the takeup spool to be rotated by hand. Pull the roll leader down over the tracker bar and attach it to the hook on the takeup spool, and turn the takeup spool by hand until you see the tempo printed on the leader and all the tracker bar holes are covered with smooth, unwrinkled paper. Set the tempo. In players with automatic shutoff, be sure to wind at least one full turn of paper around the takeup spool to prevent the player from turning itself off the moment you turn it on.

Switch the rewind lever to the play position, and begin pumping with full, gentle strokes. In the words of one attraction owner who displays a foot pumped instrument for the enjoyment of tourists who have never pumped a player piano before, pump it like a bicycle, one pedal after the other. Just before one pedal hits bottom, start pushing the other one slowly, and release the first one quickly so it will be ready for its next turn. When the music starts, keep pumping with full strokes, and observe that by pressing harder the music gets louder. Pump no harder than necessary to play the music at a medium volume, and learn to use expression, constantly varying the volume with the phrases of music. Accent the melody by giving the pedal a little extra push; when a soft filler passage occurs in the music, let the piano coast for a brief moment. If the wind motor governor is regulated properly, pedal-induced expression will not cause annoying speed changes in the music.

Player pianos with large pump reservoirs and large stack pneumatics and valves are less sensitive to minute pumping changes, because the reservoirs even out the suction flow. Players with small reservoirs, valves and pneumatics, (such as old Aeolians and Gulbransens) feel tighter; in fact, as each note or chord plays, it can be felt in the pedals. To provide more pumping expression capability, Standard pumps, which have two large reservoirs, have a small reservoir cutoff pneumatic inside one reservoir, allowing the player pianist to make quick accents while still providing reserve suction for coasting.

If the piano is equipped with an automatic sustain pneumatic, try playing various rolls with it turned on and off. Note that each time the sustain pneumatic works, its momentary suction drain on the pump can be felt in the pedals. Because of this, many player pianists prefer to leave the sustain pneumatic turned off, and use the manual sustain lever instead (in instruments which have both). Do your own sustaining with the lever or button when there are arpeggios (broken chords running up and down the keyboard) in the music, or when the accompaniment "sits" on the same chord for several beats. *NEVER sustain over chord changes, blurring dissonant notes together.* Although the sustaining lever is called the loud pedal in some players, its purpose is *not* to make the music louder by holding the dampers off the strings over chord changes.

When an interesting melody occurs in the treble (right hand), subdue the bass with the bass soft lever or button; when something interesting plays in the bass, subdue the treble. Use both soft controls together for playing pianissimo (extra soft) once in a while, and release them both for loud finale passages.

Once in a while it is nice to increase or decrease the speed of the music with the tempo lever during the music. While this is not usually the case in ordinary popular rolls, it is very desirable in classical music, and necessary in most modern medley rolls, which frequently have musically questionable tempo changes between one piece and the next.

At the end of the roll, rewind it gently, and remove it from the spoolbox. Before putting it in its box, tap the paper to the right again by dropping the roll into the right hand. Leave the piano in rewind, ready to accept the next roll.

With lots of practice, it is possible to become quite adept at using the tempo, sustain and soft controls, and pumping with expression, all at the same time, creating music which is interesting to listen to. People who just sit and pump one loud boring piece after another soon lose interest in a player piano, but those who creatively try to make real music continue to find the instrument fascinating over a long period of time.

CHAPTER THREE
HOW TO BUY AN OLD PLAYER PIANO

(You spent all that money on *WHAT?*)

Where to Look for an Unrestored Player Piano

Finding a good *unrestored* player piano isn't the easy job that it was in the 1950's, when a prospective buyer could find a nice selection for under $100 each just by "asking around." A high percentage of all old players have had at least some of the tubing, hoses, and pneumatic cloth replaced, with the result that they play, but they don't play well. In the eyes of many owners these instruments have been "restored" and are worth restored prices, even though the previous repairs usually must be redone.

Unrestored instruments *do* turn up now and then, however, so with diligence you can still find one. How? Study the local want ads, and let all of your friends and acquaintances know that you are looking for one. You might try searching antique stores and piano dealers in your area, but it is unusual for a good player piano to turn up here, because most dealers have been "stung" by at least one old player which needed a lot more work than they thought it would, and they would rather stock merchandise which can be turned over without a large additional investment in repairs.

Use caution if you decide to purchase an instrument which is advertised something like this: "major repairs have already been done, but this piano doesn't work quite right so we are selling it for an *unrestored* price." (Once during the 1970's, a well known American dealer actually had the nerve to advertise an old Seeburg electric piano nation-wide as being "completely restored, except we didn't have time to attach the electric power cord, so we're not sure how well it works." Whoever bought it deserved what he got!) Once in a while, the previous repairs will save you a little work, but it is far more common to have to spend a substantial amount of extra time *undoing* what was done, so it is wise to consider a non-working previously repaired instrument as worth *less* than one which is actually unrestored! *Either buy an instrument as completely restored—if it works perfectly — or consider it to be completely unrestored. Never buy one which is "in between" hoping to complete the restoration with a little extra work, unless you are technically competent to disassemble the entire instrument and examine every single piece prior to your purchase!*

Picking a Good One

If you decide to find a player piano on your own without the appraisal of an expert, you will have to check each part of the piano and player action to verify its condition. Take the owner's description of the piano with a grain of salt. As mentioned above, most owners think their player pianos are restored, even if the only repair ever made was the replacement of one main hose. Actually, the typical owner knows far less about the inside of a player piano than about most household appliances, but this lack of knowledge does not prevent the owner from repeating vague statements like "my tuner said the only thing wrong is a small hole in the bellows which *anybody* could fix, but he doesn't work on player pianos."

Before taking anything apart, ask the owner if the player mechanism still works. If the answer is "yes," have *the owner* sit down and demonstrate the piano. If you so much as sit down at the piano and try to play it, and it doesn't work, there is the chance that you will be accused of breaking something.

After the owner's demonstration, open the lid and remove the upper and lower front panels from the piano. Some player pianos still work even though the tubing and hoses are as brittle as uncooked macaroni. If this is the case, be extremely careful not to loosen or break any of them; you will have to evaluate the condition of the piano without taking anything apart. However, if you find that the tubing and hoses have been replaced, or if the owner tells you that the player mechanism hasn't worked for years, you can safely remove the stack and pump to check out the piano action, bridges and other parts, because you won't risk "breaking" the player action by breaking a piece of brittle tubing. *NEVER* adjust a transposing tracker bar in an unrestored player piano which still plays, unless you want the opportunity of replacing all of the tracker bar tubing for the owner at no charge!

The Piano

Pianos do not last forever, as many people think they do. Unfortunately, pianos continue to put out some kind of sound long after major repairs are necessary, leading the uninformed to believe that they are indestructible. As stated elsewhere in this book, the music produced by a player piano is only as good as the piano itself, and the condition of the piano depends on the condition of thousands of parts! Begin your evaluation of the player piano by checking the piano; in many instances, you can rule out the purchase of an instrument without even looking at the player mechanism.

Pull the piano away from the wall (or look under the bottom of a grand) to see if any glue joints of the frame and cabinet are coming apart. In extreme examples, the back of an upright piano will remain leaning against the wall when the keybed and sides are pulled out for an inspection. If the frame is falling apart, decide whether the piano is really worth complete disassembly, major woodworking and re-gluing.

Is the cabinet in good condition? Loose veneer and other loose cabinet parts indicate a piano which has been too humid and then too dry. Is the bottom of a vertical piano glued together, or does it bow down when the piano pedals or pumping pedals are used? Are the legs of a grand wobbly? How much woodworking will it take to put the cabinet in good looking, structurally sound condition?

Is the cabinet finish acceptable as is, or would you want to refinish it? Refinishing a piano with a smooth piano finish is much more work than refinishing other furniture.

Check the plate, soundboard, ribs and bridges. Is the plate cracked? If so, don't buy the piano. Is the soundboard still glued to the frame and pinblock all the way around? Are sections of the soundboard warped away from the ribs? Small soundboard cracks aren't important, but large ones are usually accompanied by loose sections of soundboard which make the piano sound like a bad loudspeaker.

Illus. 3-1. When a piano soundboard is cracked and loose from its ribs like the one shown here, an annoying buzzing sound is produced, and major repairs are necessary.

If the piano has a bass bridge shelf, is it in one piece? Are the bridge and shelf glued together, or will they have to be repaired? Are the bridges in good condition, or are they cracked or split around the bridge pins? Recapping or replacing the bridges is usually only worthwhile in a valuable piano.

If the above parts are in good condition, turn your attention to the strings and tuning pins. Are the bass strings reasonably clean, or are they rusty and caked with dirt and corrosion? Are the treble strings, pressure bar and tuning pins so rusty that the strings will break during tuning? A certain amount of tarnish isn't serious, but actual rust means the piano should be restrung.

In what condition is the pinblock? In a grand piano, the bottom layer can be inspected after the piano action is re-

Illus. 3-2. The bass bridge in this Seeburg style F coin piano is being recapped and the soundboard is being reglued. Always check a player piano thoroughly prior to buying it to find out if it needs extensive piano repairs.

moved. The bottom lamination doesn't tell you how tight the tuning pins are, but it does tell you if the whole pinblock is falling apart. In some vertical pianos, the face and upper edge of the pinblock show, giving you some idea of its condition, but in others the whole pinblock is hidden, and the only way to tell its condition is to measure the tightness of the tuning pins with a torque wrench (unless you are an experienced piano tuner). Have the pins been "doped" with pin tightener, indicated by stains on the pins or plate? Or have they been driven in until the music wire coils touch the pinblock or plate? These are signs that the piano will have to be restrung in order to stay in tune reasonably well. If the pins are the original ones and are extremely loose, it is usually possible to restring the piano with larger pins, but if the piano has already been restrung once and the pins are loose or squeaky, the piano probably needs a new pinblock, a major job, particularly in a vertical piano.

Next, check the condition of the keyboard and piano ac-

Illus. 3-3. Before purchasing a player piano, be sure you know whether it is tunable or not. In some old pianos, oversize tuning pins and new strings will do the trick, but in others a new pinblock is necessary. Replacing a pinblock is a costly job worth doing only in exceptionally valuable pianos like this Seeburg style G orchestrion.

tion. Are the keytops in good condition or should they be replaced? How are the fronts of the keys? Are the keys warped, with the front leaning to one side and the back to the other? How are the hammers? Look down on the striking points from above to see how much felt is really left in the deep grooves. Original hammers are usually uniformly dirty, but if they have been reshaped, they will be much cleaner where they have been filed, and they will usually be unevenly shaped. How are the center pin bushings? The key bushings? Do hammer butts and other action parts wobble and click? Some clicks are caused by loose flange screws, but other clicks indicate the need for new felt action parts. How are the bridle tapes? These are usually the first parts of a vertical piano to go bad, and they are the easiest to replace.

In summary, if a piano has an unglued frame, unglued or cracked cabinet parts or veneer, a broken plate, rusty metal parts, large cracks in the soundboard and bridges, loose tuning pins, worn-out or moth-eaten hammers and action felts, severely warped keys, clicking action parts or keys which play more than one note at a time, look for another piano, or plan to do major piano repair work before even thinking about repairing the player action.

The Player Action

If you are purchasing an unrestored player piano with the intention of rebuilding it yourself, the brand of the player action and how well preserved or how badly abused it is determine the ease or difficulty of the rebuilding job. Guidelines regarding player action and piano brands are included later in this chapter, and specific restoration information for various brands is included in Ch. 6.

In general, the condition of the piano is some indication of the condition of the player action, providing that the latter is actually unrestored. If the metal parts in the piano are bright and shiny, and if the wooden parts have not suffered moisture damage, the player action will also reflect this. If the piano has been stored in a swamp-like environment, the player action will show just as much deterioration as the piano does. If the piano passed your thorough examination, go on to inspect the player action just as carefully.

Make sure that there are no missing wooden or metal parts, but don't worry about the condition of the tubing, hoses, rubber cloth and leather parts, because you will replace these during the restoration anyway. Are the pumping pedals and linkages intact, or were they discarded to make room for an added suction box? Is the wind motor all there? If the piano originally had a tracking device, is it still in place? These parts are rarely missing, but now and then you will run across a piano in which the wind motor was replaced with an electric gearmotor, or a makeshift automatic tracking device was added.

If you can remove the stack from the piano without causing it to quit working by breaking brittle old tubing and

hoses, do so. Since it is impractical to disassemble the stack in a piano which you are considering purchasing, you will have to tell by looking at the outside whether or not any internal damage is likely. If everything in the piano is covered with the same 50 year accumulation of dust, and none of the screw heads are damaged, chances are good that all of the internal parts are intact.

Finding a Good Restored Player Piano

To find a good *restored* instrument, locate an expert technician who specializes in player piano restoration either as a hobby or full-time profession. One word of mouth recommendation from a satisfied customer is worth more than any amount of advertising, and if you keep getting referred to the same technician by several happy player piano owners, this might mean that the technician is a good one. Such an individual will either have a good instrument for sale, or will try to find you one, or will appraise one which you have located, for a reasonable fee. The sales personnel in many music stores and antique shops which sell low-priced, poorly restored player pianos, and the owners of most low-budget antique museums are likely to describe a fine technician as being "good, but he charges *way* too much." Conversely, they are saying their own low-priced technician "isn't very good, but at least he's *cheap*." By all means, check out several technicians, compare their workshops and tools, and scrutinize instruments which they have restored. Find out how long a backlog of work the technician has; most excellent rebuilders have a waiting list for major restoration jobs. If you are searching for someone to restore an instrument for you, be suspicious if a rebuilder jumps at the opportunity to begin restoring your piano tomorrow; if no one else wants his repair work, do you? A fine technician doesn't have time to answer a lot of dumb questions, but if you learn the material in this book first so you understand how player pianos work and know what to look for, any reputable rebuilder will be proud to show you examples of his or her work.

Here are some general guidelines for evaluating a restored player piano. As in appraising an unrestored instrument, check the piano first. The word "restored" is used carelessly and it means different things to different technicians; in many instances, a "restored" player piano has had no major work done to the piano at all! If the piano is truly restored, it should have new strings, tuning pins, hammers, damper felts, perfect bridges and soundboard, attractive keytops, shiny action springs and perfect action felts; if any of these parts are still original, they should be clean and shiny with no signs of wear or deterioration. In other words, the piano should look, work and sound like a new piano of comparable size. Is the player action easy to pump? A well restored player piano should play soft and loud when you vary the pumping speed, and should coast a little after you stop pumping. You should be able to play through any number of rolls without getting tired, and it shouldn't be too much work to play a roll with one pumping pedal. The music should play at a constant speed regardless of how soft or loud you play, and the tempo control lever should adjust the speed of the roll from a complete stop (or very, very slow) to a speed faster than you would ever want to use. All control levers should work without binding or squeaking. With the owner's permission, disconnect the hose attached to the wind motor, cover the nipple or elbow with the palm of your hand, and try to turn the motor backwards with your other hand. If it is airtight, it will be almost impossible to turn. Reconnect the hose. With no roll covering the tracker bar, pump fast to see if all 88 notes will play at once. If the system is airtight, they should. Remove the large hoses from the pump, tape off the connections with masking tape, and pump one pedal until the reservoir(s) are pulled shut. It should take at least sixty seconds for the reservoirs to open completely. Put everything back together, put a test roll on the piano, and check the repetition of each note. Do all the valves and pneumatics work right? If a note doesn't repeat right, check the holes in the test roll— many test rolls are perforated poorly here and there, causing poor repetition on certain notes, but this cause is obvious if you look closely at the roll.

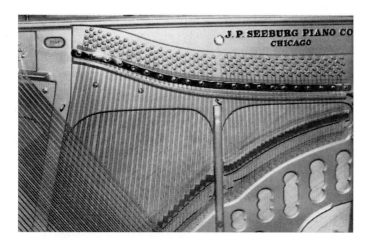

Illus. 3-4. The back of this piano has been restored, including a new shiny gold finish on the plate, a reglued, shimmed and refinished soundboard, repinned bridges, new strings and tuning pins, and the hardware replated with nickel plating. With new hammers, hammer butts, action springs and felts, damper felts and other parts, the piano looks, works and sounds like a new piano. Anything short of this is not actually restored.

Before paying for your new treasure, get a signed statement itemizing all repairs which have been done, with the terms of any warranty spelled out in writing. Failure of major components should be covered by a warranty, but tuning, regulation and minor adjustments which become necessary due to use will be excluded. In other words, a reputable rebuilder should be willing to guarantee that the pouches, pneumatics, valves, etc. will continue to work for

the life expectancy of the materials involved, but don't expect a free service call if the chain comes off the wind motor, a seasonal humidity change throws the piano out of tune, or a hyperactive child yanks something loose.

If you are contemplating the purchase of an instrument which was previously repaired but not completely restored, check carefully to see if any of the prior repairs are still good, or if they will just make the player action harder to restore. Pick at the edges of exposed gaskets and try to examine the exposed leather top valve facings—are they rotten, or have they been replaced with the correct material? Try to tighten accessible screws. Are they tight, or do they keep turning, indicating that the threads in the wood are stripped? Are the pneumatics stiff? Check the condition of the bellows cloth— is it flexible, or does it crunch when folded? Is the wind motor pneumatic cloth cracked along the folds, or has it been patched at the corners? Does the wind motor turn smoothly, or does it lurch? If bellows and pneumatic cloth was replaced, are the edges trimmed neatly, or is the wood scarred with scissors marks? Are there blobs of glue which oozed out around the edges, or around glue joints? If the stack has pneumatics glued to the decks, check for white glue which indicates that previous repairs have been done. It is much harder to remove from old wooden parts than the original hot glue is; consider this when purchasing a previously repaired piano. Do the hoses fit properly, or are undersize or oversize hoses forced over the nipples or held on with automobile radiator hose clamps? Familiarize yourself with problems and their symptoms discussed in Ch. 9; this information will help you to assess the repair work which might be necessary after you get the piano home.

Readers are encouraged to use the checklist reproduced in the appendix for appraising player pianos, estimating repair jobs, and describing repair work which has been completed.

Brand Names

Many of the finest American pianos of the player piano era, including Chickering, Knabe, Mason & Hamlin, Steinway and Weber, were marketed in substantial quantities with reproducing player actions, but only in very limited quantities with ordinary player actions. Fortunately, many other companies also made excellent upright pianos during this era, so finding one with good potential isn't too difficult. Now that old players are over 60 years old, the state of preservation is just as important as the maker. An ordinary good quality old upright player with excellent soundboard and bridges, and new strings and hammers, sounds far better than a fine quality brand name piano of the same size with deeply grooved, packed hammers, corroded bass strings, loose bridge pins and no sound board crown. Nevertheless, given two old pianos in identical states of preservation, the one which was better when new has greater potential, given equal restoration. Fine brands which are more commonly encountered than the ones listed above include Apollo (Melville Clark), larger Baldwin pianos (with various brand names, listed in the Baldwin section of Ch. 6), A. B. Chase, Jacob Doll, Heintzman, Ivers & Pond, Marshall & Wendell, Packard, Stroud, Vose, and Wing. In fact, any fully restored player piano has a rich full sound, providing that careful attention is paid to every detail of the piano as well as the player action during restoration. Even "ordinary" brand name pianos such as Gulbransen, Kimball, WurliTzer and hundreds of others, are so much larger than modern consoles and studio uprights that their sound is far superior, again providing that high quality restoration is performed or that all components are preserved exceptionally well.

Since the author resides in America and the large majority of instruments which he has repaired have been of American manufacture, he does not have extensive experience repairing the many fine makes of players and pianos sold in overseas markets, particularly England, New Zealand, Australia and Continental Europe. But the principles of player piano operation and construction, and the characteristics of the work that must be done to put them in shape, know no national boundaries!

When purchasing an unrestored player piano which you plan to restore yourself, consider the difficulty of restoring certain player actions. Aeolian, Amphion (unit valve type), Autopiano, Pratt-Read (screwed together, not glued type), Standard, and Story & Clark player actions are easier for the beginner to restore correctly than Angelus (glued together pouch-pneumatic type), early Apollo (Melville Clark), H. C. Bay, early Cecilian, Gulbransen, Schulz, Simplex and WurliTzer actions, with Baldwin and Kimball somewhere in between.

Empty Player Pianos

Many old uprights had the player actions removed after they quit working in the 1940's, and few of the orphan player actions were saved, so empty player pianos far outnumber sets of extra parts in existance. If you run across an empty player piano, don't buy it in hopes of finding the correct action for it someday. On the other hand, if you run across a good restorable set of parts, hang on to them; you just might find a piano in which they can be installed, among all the other empty players in which they *won't* fit. Exceptions are players made by Gulbransen, which were standardized to a greater extent than most other brands. Of course, empty reproducing pianos, coin pianos and orchestrions, and orphan parts for them, are worth preserving for collectors who specialize in restoring these rare and valuable instruments.

Dating Player Pianos

Along with other misconceptions (like "solid oak" cabinets, "upright grands," and "solid brass frames,") many people think their player pianos *must* have been made in the 1800's. Actually, nearly all 88-note players in existence today were made after about 1912, with the large majority made in the early and middle 1920's. The only way to date a piano— unless an accurate piece of paperwork such as an original sales invoice exists—is to look up the serial number in the Pierce (formerly Michael's) *Piano Atlas*. This standard reference includes serial number dating lists for thousands of piano brands. Some listings are inaccurate or incomplete (such as those for Aeolian Co. reproducing pianos of various brands) and other listings are correct for ordinary pianos but not for players made by the same company. Also, many pianos carry names of department or music stores rather than their actual maker, and thus may not appear in the Piano Atlas. Nevertheless, the book is a valuable reference for dating many better known pianos.

Summary

When searching for an old player piano, the more you know about what you're buying, the happier you will be when you finally purchase one. Learn as much as you can about pianos and player actions by reading and by visiting with others who share your interest. Don't buy on impulse, don't underestimate the amount of time it takes to perform good quality major repairs, and don't kid yourself about minor repairs which have already been done. Filed hammers, new keytops and new bridle tapes don't constitute a rebuilt piano, just as recovered pneumatics and new tubing don't make a restored player action, and they don't mean the piano will necessarily last for years of additional use. Whether you buy a restored instrument or restore one yourself, you will have a large investment of money or time in it; a mechanical musical instrument with thousands of parts which are over sixty years old is not the place to be "cheap." A corner cut here and a dollar saved there will result in a disappointing instrument, but time and money taken to get the job done right will give you a piano which will provide many years of enjoyment.

CHAPTER FOUR
OVERVIEW OF
A COMPLETE
RESTORATION,
COMPONENT BY
COMPONENT

This chapter presents an overview of the complete restoration of a player action, showing you a logical procedure, component by component, without going into great detail. The subsequent chapter describes and illustrates specific restoration techniques, tools and materials in detail. While at first glance it might seem more logical to present all of this information in the order of an actual restoration, a single chapter attempting to cover the overall plan as well as detailed restoration techniques would be extremely long and confusing because there is no "typical" restoration. For example, instructions for replacing gaskets might occur in the section on restoring the stack, even though gaskets are also found in other components, and some stacks contain no gaskets at all! To avoid this confusion, the general plan and detailed techniques are presented separately. This way, you can get an idea of the scope of a restoration here first, and then learn all of the details in Ch. 5, using the cross references between chapters as necessary once you actually begin the job.

The sequence described here is a typical routine used by many rebuilders, but there is no reason that you can't change the order in which you restore major components, for variety from one job to the next, or if you are waiting for supplies to come in the mail. In whatever order you tackle a set of parts, however, solve problems as they occur, rather than hopping from one part to another every time you come to something difficult, only to wind up with a huge mountain of problems after all of the easy work is done!

The more observant you are about small details during a restoration, the easier your job will be. Throughout this section you will be admonished to observe, measure, notice, sketch, keep track of, check, and observe some more. It is easy to think you have made note of every important detail when you have totally forgotten an important measurement, so pay attention to what you are doing from the

time you first take the front of the cabinet off until you proudly demonstrate your finished piano to a friend.

DISASSEMBLING THE PIANO FOR CLEANING

Remove the front cabinet parts of the piano. Open the lid and look down inside the upper front panel to see how it is attached. All pianos have latches at the upper corners, and a few also have folding braces at the lower corners (which hold the front at an angle to support sheet music) which must be slipped off their pins. Loosen these latches and remove the front. If the side columns don't come out with the front in one piece, they are attached to the sides with two large screws each; remove them. In many American pianos made before 1910 and most European pianos, the music shelf and fallboard slip out of the piano without removing any screws, once the front panel and pillars are removed, but in most post-1910 American player pianos, these parts are secured by screws. Remove the large screw at each end of the music shelf, remove the shelf and fold the fallboard (keyboard cover) shut, and you will find the screws which hold the fallboard in the piano: either one large screw at each end, or one hinge at each end with three small screws (some Standard/Autopiano and H. C. Bay pianos). Remove the cheek blocks and both key slips—the thick one which folds down to expose the control levers (if present) and the thin stationary one which covers the front of the key frame. Remove the bottom front panel by pushing up on the trap spring and swinging the top of the panel forward, lifting it off of its pins. (Some European pianos have one or two large wooden turn latches instead of the trap spring).

If this is your first restoration and if all of the original hoses and tubing are still in place, now is the time to make a sketch showing where the tubes and hoses connect, and how they are attached to the sides of the case and bottom of the keybed, before disassembly causes any of them to break. If you actually understand how a player piano works, you should be able to figure out where each tube should go, but in some pianos, small tubes connect to junction blocks or connectors whose function will remain unknown until you can see the inside of various components, so making a sketch might help during reassembly. Also, in some pianos the original routing is the best way to fit the tubing and hoses into the smallest possible space, and if you ignore the original placement of tubing within bundles, or the route of the wind motor hose, you may have to retube the piano more than once before you figure out how to make everything fit! Note, however, that there is probably a 50% chance that one or more of the tubes have been placed incorrectly during a previous repair attempt, so your notes will be subject to correction when you figure out how everything works.

With the front panels, pillars, music shelf and fallboard removed from the piano, and a sketch made of tubing, hoses and any other details which might be confusing later, you are ready to remove the player action. In nearly all cases, the entire upper action—stack and head—comes out in one piece. If the piano has a mandolin, disconnect the control lever mounted on the spoolbox. Remove the spoolbox brace from the piano plate, pull the large hose off the left end of the stack from below the keybed, pull the smaller hose off the wind motor without breaking the end of the motor or crushing the nipple, disconnect any small tubes running from the ends of the stack downward, and disconnect any spoolbox linkages from their control rods mounted on the sides of the case. Some players have two large hoses for the stack, one at each end. If the piano still has its original tubing and hoses, they might be rock hard and stuck to the nipples, discouraging easy removal. Grasp the hose and turn it until it comes off or breaks more or less flush with the nipple, then break the remaining pieces off with pliers or cut them away with a knife, preserving the nipple or elbow if possible. If lead or cast zinc pot metal nipples and elbows are corroded so badly that they crumble in your hands, they will have to be replaced. Remove the screws or bolts at the left and right ends of the upper action which hold it in the piano. In some cases the screws run horizontally through the action into blocks behind it; in others, they run vertically, usually through the spoolbox shelf which overhangs the stack at either end. Some players have only two large screws, while others have six or more.

After you are convinced that the stack is completely disconnected, slide it forward until it bumps into the cabinet or cheek blocks, and lift it out of the piano. As you lift, *watch the stack fingers,* being careful not to push them against any part of the piano action. Although the stack is very heavy, you will run less chance of breaking something if you remove it by yourself, rather than risking having a helper push while you pull. If the stack will stand up by itself, stand it upright on the floor; if it will tip over, lay it on its face on a blanket, cushioning tracker ears or any other delicate mechanical parts which protrude from the front. Mark and retain any loose cardboard or wood shims found between the stack and its mounting points.

The stack in Standard/Autopiano players is secured to a suction supply manifold at the left end with four large oval head screws, and the right end is held in the piano with one large screw, usually accessible through a hole in the spoolbox shelf. By removing these five screws, the wind motor hose, spoolbox brace and two control linkages at the right side, the stack may be removed, leaving the suction supply manifold in place on the keybed.

Next, remove the pump. Disconnect all hoses, control tubing, and mechanical linkages, making note of how the linkages were connected. If there is a bewildering forest of control wires above the pump, figure out how to disconnect only those wires which are *directly attached to the pump itself,* leaving in place everything else which is suspended from the keybed. Some pumps are fastened only at the top, with one or more large screws or nuts and bolts; others are also fastened with screws at the bottom. In some pianos, the pump may be removed by lifting it off of the elaborate mounting brackets which are fastened to the piano bottom; in others, the pump is fastened to the brackets and some of the screws must be removed. Analyze the situation carefully to avoid breaking anything, and if you find that you actually removed a lot more parts than necessary, reinstall or number and sketch them before you forget how to put them back. In some pianos, there is very little clearance between the keybed and the top of the pump, and it is necessary to remove some of the rods which are connected to the control levers in order to swing the pump forward. In others, it is necessary to lift the pump and swing the bottom out first. Some WurliTzer pumps are impossible to remove without loosening the vertical support rod attached to the keybed and pushing it down into the pump. Lay the pump aside.

Remove the sustaining and soft pedal pneumatics and their finger buttons, if present, and remove any other miscellaneous pneumatic control mechanisms.

Remove the piano action: disconnect linkages for the bass and treble soft pneumatics or levers, unscrew the four action nuts, pull the action forward, unhook the pedal dowels, and lift the action out of the piano. Vacuum the keys, number them toward the back end or draw diagonal lines across each section behind the key buttons to assist putting them back in the right order, and remove them from the piano. In most pianos, the original numbers which are stamped on the keys just behind the keytops are hard to decipher if the keys get mixed up, and any numbers toward the front end of the keys will be removed if new keytops are installed.

REMOVING DECADES OF DIRT AND DEBRIS

Now that all major parts are out of the piano, move it and the parts out onto your patio or into your garage, and get a vacuum cleaner, an air compressor, a face mask good for filtering dust out of the air, a bucket of warm water with a tablespoon of white vinegar, and a damp rag. First vacuum the large quantities of accumulated dirt off of the parts and out of the inside of the piano, being careful not to scratch the old finish or to vacuum up any of the cloth or paper punchings from the key guide pins. Then blast the piano with compressed air, (again being careful not to damage keyboard punchings), creating a large, satisfying cloud of dust, some of which will settle on everything in sight, including you and the piano. Blow the dirt out from the windings of the bass strings, behind the plate, behind the keybed, along the bridges, under the piano pedals, and everywhere else it has accumulated. Alternately use the vacuum and compressed air until all removeable dirt is gone. Don't forget about the gravel, bits of drywall, dead leaves

Illus. 4-1. The player action, piano action and keys have been removed from this Cable Nelson player in preparation for a thorough cleaning and final evaluation of any major repairs which might be necessary.

and other organic matter, arms from old dolls, buttons, piano teachers' gold stars that fell off of a piece of sheet music in 1928, streetcar tokens and vermin which have collected in the crevices behind the soundboard, particularly at the bottom ends of the ribs among the back posts. When the compressed air no longer produces any more dirt, wipe the parts clean with the rag dampened with warm dilute vinegar water. Apply the same treatment to the player action parts, removing as much accumulated dirt as possible from between pneumatics, under deck boards, etc. Don't worry about removing every bit of old grease from metal player action parts yet, which you will do thoroughly later when they are disassembled. Blow out the piano action with compressed air, but don't wash it with the damp rag, which will just make any remaining surface dirt soak into the unfinished wood and felt parts. Obviously this is not a job to be done when a gentle breeze is blowing in the direction of your neighbor's wash hanging on the line, if anyone still follows such an old fashioned procedure in this age of talking clothes driers!

In the absence of a source of compressed air, remove as much dirt as possible with the vacuum cleaner and a variety of stiff nylon brushes, a toothbrush, etc. Once you clean a piano with compressed air, however, you will agree that borrowing or renting an air compressor for the "once every fifty year cleaning" is well worth the trouble.

The old finish on many player action parts, including the gloss black paint on many spoolboxes and other visible stack parts is shellac based. Cleaners containing alcohol (including many household cleaners) and strong detergents will ruin this finish. The safest cleaner is warm water with a little vinegar.

After you have cleaned everything, scrutinize the condition of the back, soundboard, bridges, strings & tuning pins, action, keyboard, pedal actions and other parts, or have a professional piano technician check everything for you. Although you should have done this before you bought the piano, it is a good idea to check everything again now, to find any major problems like a bad pinblock before wasting a lot of time and money restoring the player action and refinishing the cabinet only to find out that the piano is unusable.

ORDERING PARTS AND MATERIALS

Before you get involved in restoring and refinishing the piano itself, order materials which you will need for restoring the player action. By the time you are done with the piano, your pneumatic and bellows hinge material and cloth, tubing and hoses, valve, pouch and gasket leather and other parts will be on hand; otherwise your repair job will come to a standstill while you wait for everything to be delivered.

If you plan to restore only one player piano, order just enough materials to get the job done. If you plan to restore a number of player pianos, you might as well order larger quantities of materials to begin with. This way, you won't have to spend a lot of time taking careful measurements just to avoid ordering a little too much material, and you will also be able to take advantage of quantity discounts.

For your first restoration, use ordinary cotton rubber cloth with hot glue for the stack pneumatics and for the wind motor if it has small pneumatics, motor cloth with hot glue for the wind motor if it has large pneumatics and for small pedal control pneumatics, the wind motor governor, mandolin control pneumatic and automatic tracker pneumatics, and medium weight (fuzz back) bellows cloth with hot glue for the pumping bellows and reservoirs. After gaining experience with these materials, you might want to try others; see pp. 75–79 for detailed descriptions of pneumatic and bellows covering materials, and pp. 47–49 for descriptions of various types of glue.

Examine the player action to determine approximately how much gasket and valve leather you will need; partially disassemble the stack if necessary to measure the thickness of the original leather. Decide whether to order pouch leather or rubber cloth for new pouches (see pp. 82–85), and make a list of other materials such as fibre discs, new valve stem guides, valve seats, blotter paper rings, bleeds and other parts which might be necessary. List how many feet of each size of tubing and hose will be needed. As mentioned elsewhere in this book, don't skimp on the quality of materials; their cost represents only a small fraction of the value of the total restoration, and trying to save a few dollars by buying cheap or incorrect materials is foolish economy!

REPAIRING AND REFINISHING THE PIANO

If the original finish on the piano is satisfactory, decide what repairs should be made to the piano. Every unrestored old piano needs at least a major regulating job, and most old player pianos need quite a bit more work than this. If you wish to do this work yourself, obtain a copy of *Piano Servicing, Tuning and Rebuilding,* a companion volume to the present book by the same author and publisher. This book shows you how to do everything from simple regulating to major restoration of the soundboard, action and other parts. If you want to leave the piano work to a professional, you should still have a copy of this book on hand so you will be able to communicate with your piano technician about the work that will be done. Whether or not you do the work yourself, put the piano into excellent condition, or the nicest player action restoration will be disappointing.

If you are not going to refinish the piano, proceed with all necessary repairs and regulating.

If you are going to refinish the piano or have it refinished, tip it on its back and remove the bottom. Leave the piano pedals and trap levers attached to the bottom, but be careful to press the pedals down to keep them from scratching the toe board as you pull the bottom away from the piano. Remove the toe board, the front legs or pillars, and the key bed. Completely remove and disassemble all hardware—hinges, brackets, control levers, pedals, etc.—from all of the cabinet parts, carefully marking where everything came from. This will allow you or your refinisher to strip, stain, fill, seal and finish everything without having to worry about the finishing materials running into hinges, locks, and other parts.

If the back of the piano needs to be restored, remove the strings, tuning pins and plate, repair the soundboard, bridges and pinblock, and mask the new finish on the soundboard *before* the piano is refinished. Wait to install the plate and restring the piano until *after* the cabinet is refinished.

Refinishing a piano is *a lot of work!* Many player piano owners who have refinished a whole house full of antique furniture are astounded at the amount of work that it takes to strip a piano and apply a beautiful piano finish. Complete refinishing information would fill another whole book, but an acceptable piano finish can be produced by the following method. First reglue loose veneer and repair cabinet damage. If the old finish scratches easily with your fingernail, scrape it off with a narrow paint scraper, being extremely careful not to scratch the veneer with the corners of the scraper. (In fact, it is a good idea to round the corners of the scraper just a little). Be careful not to round any edges on corners of the veneer! Keep the scraper sharp, and you will have the old finish off faster and with less mess than with using chemical stripper. Or, if the old finish is too tough to scrape, use chemical stripper. Observe all precautions on the can regarding ventilation, skin protection and other safety measures; it is now known that benzene, which was previously used in paint stripper, can be carcinogenic, and methylene chloride, a constituent of many products manufactured at the time this is written, might cause heart trouble and other problems.

When all parts are stripped, you will find that most of the cabinet is veneered but possibly a few parts like the pillars, the front of the keybed, the keyslip and other shaped pieces are solid maple, which will absorb less new stain than the veneered pieces. Sand everything with the grain, with 320 open coat paper, and apply oil stain of your choice. Allow the stain to dry completely, and keep applying additional coats to the lighter pieces until everything is the same color when viewed from various angles.

Obtain the darkest available paste wood filler (not plastic wood, but paste wood filler which is available only from specialty refinishing suppliers or full-line paint stores), thin it per the directions on the can, and brush it into the pores of the veneered pieces. Let it dry for the recommended time, and rub the excess off of the surface with burlap. This important step is omitted from most modern furniture, but if you don't fill the pores, your completed piano will resemble the boring veneer of a modern Philippine mahogany interior door, and everyone who sees it will remark "Oh, you refinished that, didn't you!" instead of saying "That's *beautiful*—is that the *original* finish?"

After the filler dries, apply one or two coats of sanding sealer followed by several thin coats of lacquer with a spray gun, allowing each coat to dry and scuffing with 320 paper before applying the next coat. If you don't have access to spraying equipment, one or two coats of "Deft" brushing lacquer or equivalent will produce an acceptable amateur finish. After the finish is completely dry, polish it out with appropriate polishing compound on a rag, and apply a coat of paste wax as a finishing touch. Of course, you may use varnish if you want to duplicate the lustre of the original finish, but be prepared to spend *weeks* of spare time rubbing out the dust specks, brush marks and other imperfections with pumice and rottenstone!

After the cabinet is refinished, install the plate and restring the piano if you removed these parts previously. Then refinish and repair the piano bottom: remove everything from the bottom while it is out of the piano, repair any cracks or unglued spots, replace the white shellac or black paint, clean and polish the parts, have the pedals replated if necessary, replace broken springs, and reassemble everything, installing appropriate felt or action cloth cushions above and below the pedals. Install the key bed, toe board, front legs and bottom, and stand the piano up. As you assemble the cabinet parts, polish and lacquer the hinges, locks, control levers and other hardware as you go. Repair the keyboard and action as necessary and install them, and completely regulate the piano.

MAKING A NEW MANDOLIN CURTAIN

If the piano contains a mandolin attachment, check the curtain to see if it is brittle or if any of the clips are missing. If it needs to be replaced, measure the old one and remove it from the support rail. Select a piece of chrome tanned calf skin which doesn't stretch but which is fairly flexible

Illus. 4-2. The first step in making a new mandolin curtain is to glue a piece of appropriate chrome tanned leather to the mandolin rail, cut out the notches for the piano action support posts, apply chalk to the strings and install the rail in the piano. Lower it into position and press the leather against the chalk to make plain impressions of the strings.

and cut it to the outside dimensions of the old mandolin curtain. Sand the shiny finish off the front of the leather where it will be attached to the rail, and glue it to the rail with hot glue, securing the leather every 6" with a #2 carpet tack as shown. Cut out the large notches for the action posts, and install the rail in the piano. Apply chalk to the strings directly behind where the rail is located in the "on" position, and press the leather against the chalk to make plain impressions of the strings. Remove the mandolin from the piano, lay it with the leather face down on the bench, and with a small square, draw lines on the leather representing the cuts which will be made to separate the curtain into individual tabs. Draw a line from one end of the leather to the other showing the top of the cuts,

Illus. 4-3. Remove the mandolin from the piano and lay it flat on the bench. In this closeup, lines have been drawn between notes with a ball point pen.

and punch a small hole at the intersection of this line with each pair of cross lines. Then cut out the individual tabs as uniformly as possible with a sharp knife. Find paper fasteners the same size as the original ones at a large office supply store, center one on the end of each tab with the sharp point facing the strings, and secure it to the tab by squeezing it together firmly with pliers. Install the mandolin rail in the piano; if you marked and cut everything carefully, the new tabs will line up perfectly with the strings with a little adjustment of the rail.

Never install mandolin tabs for wound tenor and bass strings; the mandolin clips are harder than the string windings, and they will cut through the windings, ruining the wound strings.

Regulate the piano action to the same dimensions as any other upright piano, but adjust the letoff to $1/8''$ *with the mandolin turned on.* This will result in approximately $3/16''$ total letoff, permitting the hammers to bump the clips into the strings without blocking.

Use the mandolin sparingly when playing rolls. It provides a nice effect once in a while, but if you use it all the time, the hammers will wear out quickly from rubbing on the curtain.

Illus. 4-4. To complete the mandolin attachment, punch a series of small holes as described in the text, and then make two cuts to separate each tab from the next. After attaching paper fasteners to the ends of the tabs, the new mandolin is ready to be installed in the piano

ADDITIONAL PIANO ADJUSTMENTS

Many player pianos contain a stop rail mounted on the piano action, manual control levers for sustain, bass hammer rail soft, treble hammer rail soft, and a key lock rail under the keys, all of which must be regulated.

When a piano is played by hand, the travel of each whippen is limited by the cloth and paper punchings under the front of the key. Since the player action in most player pianos pushes up on the whippen, there must be an additional provision for stopping the whippen when the player action is used. Most player pianos have a stop rail for this purpose, mounted either on the stack (as in most Standard/ Autopiano players) or on the piano action itself. If the rail is on the stack, regulate it later as described toward the end of this chapter. If it is mounted on the piano action, remove it prior to regulating the piano. When the piano action is completely regulated, including the key dip and backchecks, every hammer should check at the same distance from the strings when the keys are played with uniform touch. Then install the stop rail, turn all of the regulating buttons up so they have no effect on the action, and gradually turn each one down until the hammer checks at the same point whether you play the key or push up on the whippen with the same amount of force.

If the piano has manual control levers, adjust the sustain lever so it has a little play—usually about ³⁄₁₆″ at the tip — before it lifts any of the dampers, and so it raises all of the dampers before it hits the stop. In order for this lever or an automatic sustaining pneumatic to work properly, the piano must be regulated perfectly, with all of the dampers adjusted to lift off the strings at precisely the same moment with the damper lift rod; see *Piano Servicing, Tuning & Rebuilding* for this and all other necessary regulating procedures. A human can manipulate the sustaining pedal of a piano far enough and fast enough to compensate for the sloppy damper regulation of many old pianos, but the sustain lever or pneumatic of a player action has nowhere near as much travel. Adjust the soft bass and soft treble hammer rail control levers, if present, so they stop when the split halves of the hammer rail push the hammers half way to the strings. Replace the lever stop cushions with new thicker or thinner pieces cut from backcheck felt, if adjusting the linkages doesn't do the trick. If moving the hammers half way to the strings by pushing on the hammer rail causes any of the dampers to lift, either the dampers, the damper spoons or the bridle tapes are regulated wrong.

If you think you or anyone else will ever use the key lock, the hinged rail below the front end of the keys, regulate this by adjusting the rockers or other means of adjustment so the rail prevents the keys from going down without pushing any of them above their normal rest position. For precise adjustment of individual keys, glue little strips of paper on the bottoms of the keys as necessary. Preventing the keys from moving has very little effect on the operation of a properly working player action, but you might encounter a few rolls with extremely short repeated holes which will work slightly better on very soft playing with the keys locked.

THE UPPER PLAYER ACTION

As noted earlier in the book, player stacks are made in many configurations—with deck boards, unit valves, unit pneumatics, flanged fingers, dowel pushrod, etc. This section presents generalized information to steer you through the restoration of any screwed-together stack; for specific restoration information, see Ch. 5 and 6.

The upper player action consists of two or three major components: the head, the pneumatic stack, and if the player has a double valve action, the primary valve chest. The first step of a restoration is to separate these major parts from each other.

During disassembly of all player mechanisms, try to tighten all screws before removing them, and place a bit of masking tape next to any screw holes which are stripped or overdrawn. Every screw must be absolutely tight, and the only way you will know which screwholes need repair is to mark them prior to disassembly. This goes for the hundreds of screws which hold some stacks together as well as all the other screws in the pump, regulators, control and accessory pneumatics, and all other parts.

How the head separates from the rest of the stack depends on whether the lower end of the tracker bar tubing attaches to a junction board which is part of the head, or directly to the pouch board. If the head has a junction board (Standard, Autopiano), remove the row of screws which hold it down and any other screws holding the bottom board of the head to mounting blocks attached to the top deck of the stack. The head will now lift off. The tracker bar tubing junction board attaches directly to the pouch board in a single valve action, or to the primary valve chest in a double valve action. If the stack has a primary valve chest, remove the screws holding it down, and lift it off the rest of the stack.

In a stack with the tracker bar tubing connected directly to the pouch board, cut the old tubing with scissors (or break it out if it is brittle). Leave the old tubing stumps on the tracker bar for now, but remove all remaining tubing from the pouch board nipples.

Most heads with lead tracker bar tubing have a junction board, permitting removal of the head without disconnecting any tubing. If you encounter one with lead tubing connected directly from the tracker bar to the pouch board with no means of disconnecting or separating it, cut it apart, and replace it later with neoprene tubing as described on p. 38. Be sure to install the new brass nipples before installing the pouches!

Disassembling the Stack

Lay the head and primary valve chest aside, and turn your attention to the pneumatic stack. The order in which you will disassemble it depends on the type of fingers and pushrods it has. If the pneumatic fingers push directly on the piano action (Baldwin, some Gulbransens) skip the following paragraph and disassemble the decks.

If the stack has a row of flanged wooden fingers mounted on a rail on top, these fingers and the pushrods which connect them to the pneumatic fingers must be removed first. In some stacks with a flanged finger rail, the whole row of fingers may be removed at once after disconnecting their wire pushrods from the pneumatic fingers and removing the stop rail, if present. In a Standard, Autopiano or similar stack, disconnect the wires from the pneumatic fingers by removing the lower leather nuts. Rotten leather nuts may be removed quickly by crushing them with pliers. The flanged finger rail is held to the top deck with flat head screws *under* certain flanges, which must be unscrewed and broken loose to expose them. In a Simplex, simply loosen the leather nuts and slip the pushrods out of the slots in the metal fingers of the pneumatics. In an Amphion, either unscrew the pneumatic fingers and break them off the pneumatics, leaving them attached to the pushrods, or unscrew the upper wood finger flanges individually and unhook the wires from the pneumatic fingers. In a Gulbransen with flat wooden pushrods glued to buckskin rectangles on both ends, slice through the buckskin on the pneumatic fingers and remove the upper finger rail with all the fingers attached to it. In a Gulbransen with dowel pushrods, remove the upper guide rail and lift the dowels out of the holes in the pneumatic fingers. Whatever the configuration, the simplest method for removing the fingers and pushrods will be obvious with a little study.

Always number parts before removing them, starting with 1 in the bass. If there are several rows of parts, such as pneumatic fingers or pneumatics, number the top row starting with T1 in the bass, the middle row starting with "1" or "M1", and the bottom row with "B1." By numbering everything including the mounting boards according to this simple rule, you will always be able to figure out where everything goes. Locate your numbers where they won't be sanded off during restoration, and where they won't be seen after reassembly.

As you take things apart, put the screws for each component in a separate small container like a plastic cottage cheese dish or baby food jar, labelling them so you will be able to figure out where they came from during reassembly. You will be amazed at the number of screws and other small parts in some player actions.

After the stop rail, flanged fingers and pushrods are removed from the stack, disassemble the rest of the stack into its various deck boards, pouch board(s), valve board(s), or unit pneumatics, unit valve blocks, etc.

Restoring a Deck Type Stack

With the pneumatic decks removed from the valve board(s), or with the unit valve blocks removed from the pneumatic decks (as in an Amphion), measure the overhang of the pneumatics on each deck, and measure the pneumatic span, recording this information in your notes. In many stacks, the overhang is different on each deck. If the pneumatics still have wood fingers glued to them, number the fingers, remove the screws, break the fingers off (see p. 54) and lay them aside in order. Then number the pneumatics, mark their positions on the decks, and remove them from the decks as described on pp. 52–53. If possible, number the moveable boards so the numbers will show through the holes in the stationary boards, permitting you to glue them back in the correct order without having the numbers show after the stack is reassembled. Repair or replace pneumatic boards as necessary, sand, hinge and

cover the pneumatics (pp. 60–72). After the glue dries, test each pneumatic for airtightness.

Some player pianos contain no stop rail for the stack or piano action, but instead rely on the pneumatic span and internal stop bumpers to control the travel of the whippens. In such pianos, pay careful attention to the span. If you have too much, the hammers will block against the strings, and if there is too little, they will bounce. In either case, there will not be anything you can do to correct the problem short of covering the pneumatics again. If in doubt about the correct span, measure the travel of the whippen at the point at which the stack pushes on it, and make sure the pneumatic fingers move exactly this distance with the stop bumpers installed.

As you proceed with sanding and scraping off old glue, you will remove original black paint or shellac from some surfaces. Note where this original finish was, and replace it immediately after sanding, with all glued areas masked off.

Sand the deck boards, repair any cracks or other damage, plug and redrill screw holes if necessary (pp. 56–60), test the channels for airtightness and add new sealer if necessary. Reglue the pneumatics to the decks (p. 73), *precisely where they were originally glued*, and test each pneumatic again for airtightness by collapsing the pneumatic, holding your finger or thumb over the suction supply hole in the deck, and trying to pull the pneumatic open. It should not open, or open very slowly. If the pneumatic finger screw holes leak, hold your thumb over them while trying to pull the pneumatic open.

Replace any gaskets on the deck boards. Reattach the fingers to the pneumatics, using thin hot glue for wooden fingers and thick burnt shellac for metal ones.

If the stack has the valves and pouches mounted in large boards, remove the old leather and glue from the pouch board(s), test the channels for airtightness and seal them if necessary, and replace the pouches (pp. 82–85), sealing them if they were originally sealed. Remove the bleeds, clean them, and replace any with damaged holes. Press them back into the wood, applying a tiny collar of burnt shellac to seal any which are not tight (p. 85). Block each bleed with your finger and blow and suck on each pouch again; apply another coat of sealer to any which exhibit more leakage than the average.

Regasket the pouch board(s) if they originally had gaskets (pp. 79–81). After the glue for the pouches is dry, test each pouch by blowing and sucking (with your mouth, not your lungs) on a tube connected to the input nipple. Each pouch should have the same amount of bleed, determined by the porosity of the leather and the size of the bleed cup.

Number, mark the orientation of and disassemble the upper valve seats (Gulbransen, Amphion, etc.) or the lower seats (Standard, Autopiano, etc.) and remove the valves. Clean, polish and seal the seats, seal the valve wells if necessary, releather the valves or seats, replace any gaskets, reassemble the valve board(s) and calibrate the valve travel (pp. 86–89). As you install the valves, test each one for airtightness if possible, both on the top and bottom seats.

Attach each pouch board to the valve board, calibrate the pouch to valve stem clearance (pp. 89-90), and reassemble the stack. In Standard and similar stacks, it is a good idea to assemble the pouch and valve boards and test the valves before attaching the pneumatic decks. Refer to Ch. 6 for specific instructions.

In a unit valve stack, sand and disassemble the valve blocks (pp. 54–56), check the parts for airtightness and replace the sealer if necessary, replace the pouches and valve leather, reglue the pouch blocks to the valve chambers, install the valves, regulate the pouch to valve stem clearance, calibrate the valve travel and attach the upper valve seats.

Leave the flanged finger rail and pushrods off until after you test the stack, in case you find a problem which requires further disassembly.

Testing a Single Valve Stack

To test the stack, set up a regulated suction supply—a test pump and reservoir with adjustable spill valve, or a suction box with an electronic speed control—and adjust the suction level to 7" with a suction gauge. A rotary pump and reservoir with adjustable spill valve makes the best test pump, but in the absence of an old electric piano pump, a suction box with electronic speed control will do. If a stack conforms on the bench to the tests given here with a rotary pump, it will work well in the piano. A suction box moves a larger volume of air than a rotary pump does, so test results made with one of these are less valid. You will learn with experience how the performance of a stack or other component tested with your own test pump relates to its performance in the piano.

Attach appropriate supports to your workbench and clamp the stack to the supports. Plug off each pouch input nipple with a short knotted piece of tracker bar tubing if the nipples are installed, or with a piece of masking tape if they aren't, and connect the suction supply to the stack. In a single valve stack, all of the valves should immediately seat, and the reservoir should quickly pull down. Measure the suction at one of the pouch nipples; the gauge should read the same as it does when connected directly to the test pump without the stack. If you made all of the separate tests recommended above during the restoration, you know that each pneumatic, channel, pouch, valve, seat, etc. is airtight. A significantly lower gauge reading— 1" less than the output of the test pump—indicates that the gaskets, lower valve facings or lower seats are leaking and that the stack will not perform well.

Open each nipple and listen to the valve on the top seat, either holding your ear or a stethoscope or ear tube close to the top seat. You should be able to hear absolutely no leakage on the top seat. If you hear a faint hissing noise not at-

Illus. 4-5. A rotary test pump If you don't have one, test each component with a suction box as described in the text.

tributable to the top valve facing or seat, it might be air moving through the bleed or an internal bleed channel. Connect a 3' long tracker bar tube to the input nipple, and hold the open end under the bench so it will muffle the sound emanating from the nipple. In some stacks—particularly old Aeolian stacks and valve boxes with bleeds inside—a confusing hissing noise occurs inside the seal cloth, so be careful to differentiate between this bleed noise and top valve seat leakage.

Test each note individually by removing its knotted tube or tape and "playing" the nipple rapidly with your finger. By causing your hand to flutter you should be able to cover and uncover the nipple about eight times per second, and the pneumatic should snap up and down just as fast, on 7" or less. If the pneumatic closes quickly and opens slowly, there is an atmosphere leak under the pouch, or too little bleed. If it closes slowly and opens quickly, there is too much bleed or suction leaking under the pouch. If the pneumatic is sluggish in both directions and if you know that the valve is airtight on the lower and upper seats, you have too little valve travel. Pneumatics often appear to be sluggish in opening simply because there is no force to open them except gravity and the stiffness of the cloth; simulate the weight of the piano action by resting your index finger on the pneumatic while testing it. If the valve makes a spitting noise, you have too much travel. Disassemble the stack and make adjustments as necessary.

If there is any question about the promptness of a valve turning on, connect the pouch input nipple to a note playing hole in the tracker bar with a piece of tracker bar tubing, and test the valve again by opening and closing the tracker bar hole with your finger. If a valve barely lifts when its pouch input nipple is open, it might not lift at all when the tracker bar is connected because the latter is smaller.

If you have a few notes which leak on one seat or the other, make sure you haven't caused problems by inserting screws that are too long, entering a valve chamber or channel. Many Standard/Autopiano and other stacks leak over from one note to the next during testing due to the absence of the screws which hold the head to the pouch board. Once these holes have screws in them, the leakovers disappear. Other causes for problems (after each individual component checked out airtight during assembly) are tiny chips of wood lodged between a valve and a seat, cracks which were spread open when screws were inserted, and leaky gaskets, particularly gaskets with pouch input channels running through them. Be persistent in solving dead notes and ciphers (notes which play all the time). A player piano with one dead note or cipher is no fun to play.

For one final test, turn on the test suction supply and remove the knotted tubes or pieces of tape one by one. A tight stack should have no trouble playing all 88 notes at once on low suction (6" or so), although it will become very weak by the time the last tubes are removed due to atmosphere entering all 88 bleeds.

Testing the stack with the test pump should remove all dust, talcum powder and other loose matter from the stack. After all lacquer and rubber cement vapors are gone, block off all of the input nipples and suck on the main suction supply by mouth. If the stack is tight, it should be like sucking on a blocked-off hose. This is the real test for the tightness of the inner valve seats; all 88 inner seats seal off suction at once, and a minute leak at each one will add up to a gross overall leakage.

When you have solved all problems and the stack passes all of the above tests, replace the upper leather nut and any punchings on each pushrod, regulating them to approximately the position of the old nuts. Install the flanged finger rail, reconnect the pushrods to the pneumatics, and install the lower punchings and leather nuts.

Illus. 4-6. To install new leather nuts, make a nut holding tool by cutting slots into the end of an appropriate nipple and bending the resulting prongs slightly outward. Chuck the tool in a variable speed electric drill, and slowly turn the nuts onto the threaded pushrods.

Testing a Double Valve Stack

A double valve stack is harder to check for lower valve seat leakage because without the primary valves, the only suction below the pouches is whatever leaks through the pouch leather and wood. Orient the stack with the pouches down so gravity can pull the valves to their lower seats before you close off the input nipples or holes. On low suction, the valves will usually seat after a few seconds. Test for tightness with all of the valves turned off. Then open one input at a time and listen for top seat leakage. A valve with no bleed will not repeat quickly, but it will return to the lower seat a moment after you close the input channel.

Restoring and Testing a Unit Pneumatic Stack

After removing the head, and the flanged fingers and pushrods if the stack is so equipped, remove the front cover board, exposing the screws which hold the pneumatics to the trunk board. Completely remove any tubing located inside the cover board. Number the pneumatics, unscrew and remove them from the trunk, turning any of the elbows which get in the way of the screws.

Number and mark the orientation of the top valve seats, and remove them from the pneumatics. If the seats are metal and are pressed into countersunk holes in the wood, as in a Simplex, be careful to remove every bit of sealer before attempting to pry them loose, or you will bend them and wind up with a leaky stack. Keep each valve and seat in order, in case the thickness of the valves or shape of the seats varies.

Measure the span, remove the cloth and moveable boards, sand the pneumatics (pp. 55, 60), crack the pouch boards off the valve chambers (p. 55); and replace the pouches (p. 82–85). Clean and seal the lower valve seats if necessary, and glue the pouch boards back onto the valve chambers. Sand lightly once again to remove the bead of glue at the pouch board glue joint.

Hinge and cover the pneumatics (pp. 71–72), and gasket the hinge ends. Test each pneumatic individually on a jig like the one shown in illus. 6–125, making sure that the valve is airtight on the lower and upper seats, and that the pneumatic will repeat positively at 7" or less. A problem isn't going to solve itself by your ignoring it until after the stack is assembled. Make any necessary adjustments or repairs now; if you put them off until later you will just waste a lot of time disassembling and reassembling parts.

Clean and regasket the front cover board (pp. 79–81), and repaint the front side if necessary. Reattach the pneumatics in their original locations, install the internal tubing, seal around the elbows if necessary, and attach the front cover board. Now test the stack again as described above for testing a deck type stack. Ciphers or general leakage in a unit valve stack can occur if the gaskets do not perfectly seal the pouch input holes, so if every unit tested perfectly airtight on the jig but the assembled stack is leaky, make sure all of the pneumatics are screwed down square and flat, and that the gaskets are tight. When everything works right, install the flanged fingers and pushrods if the stack is so equipped, replacing all leather nuts.

REGULATING THE STACK TO THE PIANO

After restoring and testing the stack and regulating the piano, install the stack in the piano with its original shims, without the head, in order to regulate lost motion and the stop rail. These adjustments are very important, and they are impossible in most player pianos once the head has been mounted on the stack.

If the stop rail is in the way of lost motion regulating capstans, remove it. Adjust the stack shims (or Amphion support bolts) to eliminate as much lost motion as possible; this will often take care of about 80% of the lost motion regulation. Then tighten the stack down and adjust each regulating screw or capstan so there is just a tiny amount of movement of the flanged finger before the whippen begins to move. Check this by lifting each finger with a small hook, as illustrated on p. 143.

Install the stop rail, block off the pouch input nipples with knotted pieces of tracker bar tubing, and connect your test pump to the stack to regulate the stop rail. Play each note by removing the knotted tube and opening and closing the input nipple with your finger; adjust the stop regulating screw so the backcheck catches the hammer butt at the same place when the pneumatic plays it as when you play the key by hand. If the stop is too high, the hammer might block; if it is too low, it might bounce.

To regulate a double valve stack without the primary valves, tape over the pouch input channels with masking tape and apply suction. Although there are no bleeds, the small amount of bleed through the pouch leather will permit the valves to seat after a few moments. To test each note, open the input channel and alternately apply suction and atmosphere by mouth with a small piece of tubing.

RESTORING THE PRIMARY VALVE CHEST

A primary valve chest is simple, compared to the rest of a stack, but every part must be repaired just as carefully. Disassemble the chest, remove the pouch board, and remove the valves (p. 90). Resurface and releather the valves, install them and calibrate their travel. Check the bleeds for damaged or plugged holes (p. 85). Sand the pouch board, seal the channels if necessary (pp. 49–50), replace the pouches (pp. 83–85) and pouch discs, if originally used. Regasket everything (pp. 79–81). Prior to reassembly, recheck the valve travel in case any of the buttons slipped on the stems before the glue dried.

Reassemble the primary chest, tape over the output holes, plug off the input nipples with knotted tubing, connect the chest to your test pump, and test each valve for repetition as described on p. 36. Listen closely for leaks on the outside or inside seats, and when you are satisfied that everything works properly, attach the chest to the main part of the pneumatic stack. Connect the stack to your test pump and test each note once again, checking for airtightness and repetition. If the stack and primary valve chest passed all tests individually, the combined assemblies should pass with flying colors, but it is still a good idea to check everything before attaching the head and installing the stack in the piano.

RESTORING THE HEAD

Remove the wind motor, and pneumatic tracking device if present, from the shelf, and disassemble the spoolbox far enough to remove the metal parts which need cleaning. If you want the spoolbox to look like brand new, you will need to completely disassemble everything in order to polish and lacquer the takeup spool flanges and other hard-to-get-at parts. Whether or not you go that far, remove the tracker bar if it had rubber tubing, to remove the remains of the old tubing and to polish and lacquer it as described on p. 94.

If the tracker bar was tubed with lead tubing, check the condition of the lead inside and out. Cut several tubes apart - one toward the upper end, one toward the middle and one toward the lower end—with a new single edged razor blade, to see if there is any corrosion on the inside. If the inside is shiny with no hint of corrosion, splice your cuts back together with neoprene tubing. Often lead tubing which looks perfectly shiny and smooth on the outside is badly corroded inside; if you find white powder inside, replace the tubing. Cut most of the tubing away with a scissors, remove the tracker bar and chip off the hard shellac or cement where the lead joins to the tracker bar nipples, being careful not to damage the delicate brass. Chip away the shellac where the lead is attached to the junction board. If you can't remove the lead stumps by pulling them out of the wood, cut them off flush, select a drill bit just a little larger than the inside diameter of the lead, and screw it into each stump to pull the lead out of the wood. Now you have a junction board with oversize holes where the 5/32" tracker bar tubing is supposed to connect. Either plug the holes and drill the plugs for 5/32" nipples or elbows, or obtain a set of appropriate reducing nipples or elbows with one end large enough to fit snugly into the junction board and the other end having 5/32" outside diameter.

If the transmission and music roll spindles are shiny underneath a coating of old grease, soak them in odorless paint thinner and brush away all of the old dirt and grease with a toothbrush. If shafts, sprockets and other parts are tarnished heavily, make a careful sketch of the transmission, completely disassemble it, polish each part individu-

Illus. 4-7. Reducing nipples or elbows may be used to connect neoprene tracker bar tubing to a pouch board which originally had lead tubing.

ally, and rinse everything to remove all traces of polish. Lubricate all friction points during reassembly (p. 95).

If the spoolbox has a manual roll adjuster or a mechanical automatic tracking device, clean, polish, and lubricate it. Use a drop of sewing machine oil on each of the tiny bearings of a mechanical automatic tracking device. Do not put any oil on the friction drive contact surfaces.

Nearly all spoolboxes in old player pianos have two spool brakes which apply drag on the music roll, the upper brake during play and the lower brake during rewind. These brakes take many forms, including flat spring loaded fingers which rub on brake hubs, devices which pinch the spool shafts, pads which rub against drive gears, etc. Be sure to clean all of the old grease from the friction pads, brake hubs, etc., so you will be able to adjust the amount of drag. The takeup spool (rewind) brake is controversial, but most music roll collectors and modern day roll manufacturers favor its removal. With the brake installed, the spoolbox will rewind rolls snugly but will sometimes fray the edges of fragile old rolls no matter how well the spoolbox is aligned; with the brake removed, the rolls will rewind loosely, requiring gentle hand tightening before putting them away. To be safe, remove the brake or a connecting link and store it in the bottom of the piano.

Reassemble the spoolbox and transmission but do not install the wooden tracker bar cover, or the back and top spoolbox panels yet. If the bottom board of the head is a junction board equipped with tubing nipples, tube the tracker bar now. (If the tracker bar tubing attaches to nipples mounted in the pouch board, install the tubing after mounting the head on the stack - see p. 42). If the tracker bar has an adjusting knob or transposing lever, slide the bar all the way to the treble, and starting with playing note #1, attach a tube from the junction board to the tracker bar. Leave just enough slack in the tubing so it isn't pulled tight; even a little too much tubing will get in the way of the backchecks in many players. Proceed to tube the tracker bar to the junction board from bass to treble, and when you are half way done, slide the bar all the way toward the bass, and finish tubing all the way to playing note #88. It is frequently necessary to push each tubed tracker bar nipple tightly against the ones which are already tubed to create enough room to install the next tube; when doing this, be careful not to deform or break the tracker bar nipples. If a nipple breaks off the tracker bar, you will have to remove the bar from the spoolbox and expertly solder a new nipple in place without loosening the adjacent nip-

Illus. 4-8. Neat new tracker bar tubing.

ples. Unless you are skilled at difficult soldering jobs, take the tracker bar to a good band instrument technician, who should be able to make the repair without damaging anything. In some cases it is possible to reattach a broken tracker bar nipple by holding it in place while building up quick drying epoxy around it.

If the piano still has lead tubing in good condition and has a transposing tracker bar, connect the short links from the tracker bar to the lead now.

Restoring a Pneumatic Tracking Device

Pneumatic automatic tracking devices come in various shapes and configurations, as described on p. 16. Sketch and disassemble the mechanism, and clean, rehinge and recover the pneumatics. It is extremely important that the pneumatics are airtight and perfectly flexible for prompt response. For your first few restorations, cover the tracking pneumatics with the thinnest available motor cloth and hot glue; after you feel comfortable covering double pneumatics (p. 73), switch to nylon pneumatic cloth (polylon) or bilon, which is just as durable and much more flexible. If the tracking device contains valves, pouches and gaskets, make sure all of the channels in the wood are airtight and that the screw holes are tight, and replace all of the leather carefully and accurately.

Refer to Ch. 6 for specific instructions on a variety of automatic tracking devices. Reassemble the tracking device, mount it on the head, and attach the mechanical links which connect it to the spoolbox.

Setting Up and Aligning the Spoolbox

The spoolbox and tracking device must be aligned perfectly in order for a variety of music rolls to play correctly. Although the method of adjusting the mechanism varies with the design of the head from one brand to the next, all spoolboxes require the same basic adjustments, performed in the following order.

First, center the takeup spool on the tracker bar. If the tracker bar is moveable from side to side, adjust it to approximately the centered position. In some pianos, set screws in the takeup spool flanges or collars control the sideways position of the spool; in others, a large adjustable machine screw, sometimes with a lock nut, pushes one end of the takeup spool shaft against a flat spring bearing against the other end. Adjust the spool as necessary so if a new roll with a good leader is wound around it, the roll is centered on the tracker bar holes. In some pianos (notably Baldwin) the takeup spool is not meant to be moved on the shaft, and large set screw indentations are provided in the shaft showing the correct location for the spool. Pianos with a non-adjustable takeup spool usually have an adjustable tracker bar. After adjusting the spool, make sure it will coast five or six full turns if you give it a good spin; if it slows down immediately, it is too tight and it will tear rolls during rewind.

After centering and aligning the tracker bar and takeup spool, turn your attention to the music roll support spindles and manual roll adjuster or tracking device. All moving parts should be clean, lubricated, and as free of friction as possible. If the spoolbox has a manual roll adjuster which acts on the upper roll spindles, regulate it so the roll is centered on the tracker bar when the manual control knob or lever is in its center position, allowing some travel to either side.

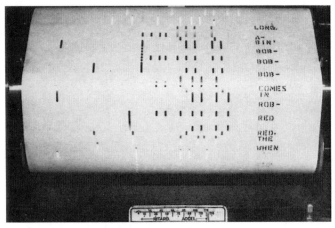

Illus. 4-9. A well aligned spool box with music roll in place, equidistant between the flanges of the takeup spool. The holes in the roll are aligned with the tracker bar holes, and the automatic tracking device - not shown in the picture - is centered within its range of travel

If the spoolbox has an automatic tracking device, adjust the linkages so when the pneumatics, fishing pole or other power source is at its midpoint, the music roll is centered on the tracker bar and takeup spool, and the edge sensing fingers (if present) begin to do their job if the roll is moved $\frac{1}{32}$" to either side of its well-centered position. Install any tubing for the tracking device. For final regulation, apply suction to the tracking device (if suction operated), put a roll on the spoolbox and turn the drive sprocket by hand, checking to see that the tracking device keeps the roll perfectly centered on the tracker bar holes and that the roll winds up centered on the takeup spool. It is easier to make any final adjustments now with the spoolbox on the bench than after it is installed in the piano. Illustrated instructions for various brands are included in Ch. 6.

Insert a roll in the spoolbox, shift the transmission to "play," turn the sprocket by hand, and adjust the top spool brake just tight enough to keep the paper between the supply spool and tracker bar from fluttering.

Restoring the Wind Motor

Wind motors have either one or two pneumatics per slide valve. The most common type, with one pneumatic per valve, either has the pneumatics glued on a common trunk or has them connected to each other with short pieces of fibre tubing. Whichever the type, begin by sketching and removing the crankshaft and its supports, the slide valves, pneumatic fingers and connecting linkages. Keep the parts in order. Measure the position of each slide valve on its connecting wire. If the slides still happen to be adjusted to their original factory setting, reassembling them in their original positions will make the job of timing the motor easier. Remove cover boards, brackets, and other strips of wood or metal which are attached to the pneumatics. Clean and polish all of the hardware, being careful not to bend the crankshaft. Once bent, a crankshaft is very difficult to straighten again. After cleaning all of the bushings with alcohol, see if any of them are loose enough to cause a knocking noise in the wind motor. This noise is particularly offensive in a reproducing piano, so replace any bushings which have obvious play (p. 93).

Illus. 4-10. Most wind motors have the pneumatics glued to a common trunk

If the motor has a row of pneumatics glued to a common trunk, measure the span and overhang, and mark the positions of the pneumatics on the trunk board. Cut the pneumatics open, number and remove the moveable boards, scrape off the old glue surrounding each pneumatic and score a line in the trunk indicating where each board is glued. Carefully remove the pneumatics from the board, using heat if necessary. If you must damage some of the wood, damage the pneumatic boards and replace them rather than damaging the trunk. If the face of the trunk— often $\frac{1}{8}$" thick mahogany—splits, either repair it or sand it all the way off and replace it with a similar piece of wood.

Clean, hinge and cover the pneumatics; for your first few jobs, use motor cloth on large pneumatics (Standard, etc.) or cotton rubber pneumatic cloth on small ones (Schulz, Story & Clark, etc.). Check the trunk channels for airtightness, seal them if necessary, lap the slide valve seating area and impregnate it with graphite (p. 95). Reglue the pneumatics to the trunk *exactly where they were glued originally*, padding your clamps so they will not leave marks on the slide valve seats. After the glue dries, check each pneumatic for airtightness, taping the finger screw holes if necessary. Correct any leaks before proceeding.

Lap the sliding surface of each slide valve on 320 sandpaper on glass. If the valves are covered with motor cloth, replace it with new motor cloth and hot glue. Replace any slide bushings if necessary, and graphite the sliding surface of each valve (p. 95).

Reassemble the crankshaft, slide valves, pneumatic fingers and connecting linkages; usually all of these parts form one assembly which is all installed at once. Assemble the mounting brackets, cover boards, etc. Replace any leather nuts on the slide valve connecting wires.

Illus. 4-11. A wind motor with unit pneumatics connected to each other with short fibre or brass tubes. The timing of this motor is set by turning the dowels which are between the crankshaft and slide valves.

Restoring a motor made of individual pneumatic blocks assembled with short pieces of fibre tubing is easier because the pneumatics don't have to be broken off of a common trunk board. After removing the crankshaft, slide valves and pneumatic fingers, pull the pneumatics apart from each other and follow the same restoration procedure as for a trunk board wind motor.

If the motor has each pair of pneumatics ganged together with a thin connecting board as in illus. 6-144, there is a strong possibility that the screws for the connecting board will pull the moveable boards of the pneumatics out of line during reassembly. Either cover and reglue the pneumatics *precisely* as they were originally, or replace the moveable

boards and drill new screw holes in the pneumatics for the connecting boards *after* the pneumatics are glued to the trunk.

If the motor has double pneumatics, cover them as described in the Aeolian and Gulbransen sections of Ch. 6.

Setting the Timing of the Wind Motor

One of the most important adjustments in a player action is the timing of the wind motor. A well-adjusted motor turns the music roll perfectly smoothly; a maladjusted one causes the music to "lope" or "lurch," spoiling the fun of playing the piano.

Setting the timing of a motor which has one slide valve for each two pneumatics is easy: adjust each valve so it moves exactly the same distance from the center hole in both directions. Setting the timing of a motor which has one valve per pneumatic is a little more difficult, but if you measured the original locations of the valves carefully, they will usually be very close to their correct positions. Measure the maximum distance from the edge of each slide valve to the edge of its hole, and set all of the valves to this distance. Apply a little suction to the motor, hold the crankshaft back by hand, and allow it to rotate slowly. Watch the cloth on the first pneumatic; as you allow the crank to turn, see if suction pulls the cloth in just as the crank arm moves beyond the imaginary line extending from the center of the crank to the center of the pneumatic finger flange pin. If suction is applied too early, causing a "knee lock", ritard the adjustment of the slide valve a little. Then turn the crank 180°, and make sure that atmosphere is admitted to the pneumatic a little *before* the crank approaches the imaginary line. If the pneumatic still has suction when the crank is parallel with this line, advance the slide valve a little. When you think this pneumatic is adjusted right, with suction admitted to it only during the correct arc of crankshaft rotation, measure the maximum distance from the slide valve to the hole, and adjust the other five slide valves to this distance.

If necessary, check each pneumatic as you did the first one. If the entire motor—pneumatic, slide valves, channels, etc.—is airtight, if the pneumatics are flexible, if the bushings and slide valves are free of excess friction, and if the timing is set correctly, the motor should now turn perfectly smoothly even at a very slow speed—20 rpm or less. If you hold your hand over the suction supply nipple and attempt to turn the motor backwards, it should not move or just barely move, showing that all pneumatics and slide valves are airtight. Any leakage will manifest itself as a hissing noise or as uneven resistance to being turned against its will. For a final test, hold a hose connected to your test pump about ¼"-½" away from the nipple; the motor should turn smoothly.

Attach the wind motor to the head, and connect the chain. Always install a ladder chain so the ends of the wire which forms each link are toward the outside and point in the direction in which the chain moves, as in illus. 4-12. This way, the largest and smoothest part of each link approaches the sprocket first, helping to keep the chain from derailing. If a transmission has a second chain connecting the drive shaft to the top shaft, this chain does its work during rewind but merely idles during play. Orient it with the ends of the links pointing in the direction it moves during rewind, when it is moving at a higher speed.

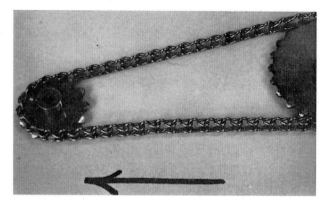

Illus. 4-12. Connect the chain so the ends of the wire forming each link point in the direction of rotation, on the outside of the chain

If a player piano has two different size sprockets for the wind motor and transmission, and if the shafts are the same diameter, place the larger sprocket on the wind motor and the smaller one on the transmission. This will enable the wind motor to run at a slower speed, consuming less suction.

ASSEMBLING AND INSTALLING THE UPPER ACTION

Remove the stack from the piano, and attach the head (and primary valve chest). If you haven't already installed the tracker bar tubing, do so as explained on p. 39. After installing the 88 playing note tubes, connect a tube from the sustaining hole in the tracker bar to the pedal on/off switch, and any other control tubes which might be present.

With the complete stack on the bench, apply suction, insert a test roll, and wind through the roll by hand, checking each note for good repetition. Recheck the adjustments for the automatic tracking device (if present). If you tested everything carefully as you went along, you will have no problems, but if you find a note which doesn't repeat right, fix it now, even if that means completely disassembling everything again! After everything works like new, install the tracker bar cover and the spoolbox back and top panels, and reinstall the upper action in the piano.

RESTORING THE LOWER ACTION

The lower action includes the pump and all of the associated parts which are mounted on it including the action cutoff, wind motor governor, speed control and accelerator. Sketch the linkages and other parts which might get mixed up, measure the span of *all* bellows (note that the two reservoirs often have different span, and that the pumping bellows are usually different from the reservoirs), and check for stripped screw holes. Remove the pumping pedals and connecting rods and lay them aside. Remove all cover plates, pneumatics, valve blocks, external springs and other parts which are screwed to the trunk or reservoirs.

When all of the control mechanisms, linkages and other attached parts are removed, you will be left with the pumping bellows and reservoirs attached to the main trunk. In some players these large bellows come off by removing a number of large screws; in others, they are glued on. If they are screwed and gasketed in place, remove them now. If the bellows are glued solidly to the trunk and are widely separated from each other, permitting cleaning, glue removal, flap valve replacement, rehinging and recovering without removing them from the trunk, leave the stationary boards in place. If the bellows are glued close to each other, remove all screws, remove the moveable boards, and attempt to break the stationary boards off of the trunk. If the boards or the trunk split beyond repair, they will have to be replaced. Heat sometimes helps to soften the old animal glue holding the bellows in place, but it usually also softens the glue holding the laminations of plywood bellows boards, causing them to come apart just as effectively! If you use heat to remove the boards, separate and reglue all delaminated spots in the plywood.

Remove the springs from the inside of the reservoirs. Handling these springs can be very dangerous, so proceed with caution. Cut a hole in the old cloth in one side of the reservoir, large enough to reach in and compress the spring by hand, remove it from the reservoir, grasp it with both hands and release the tension. If there are two springs, cut another hole in the cloth on the other side. Some bellows have access covers which permit removal of the springs through a large hole in one of the boards; if this is the case, be extra careful not to let the spring fly apart when you try to pull it out through the hole.

Pull or cut as much of the old cloth as possible off of the bellows, separate the two boards at the hinge, remove the old flap valves, and sand or scrape the boards clean of all old glue and cloth (pp. 61–62). Replace the inside flap valves (pp. 90–92), and test *each hole* by mouth (not with your lungs!) for absolute airtightness. Leaky flap valves are the most common reason for an otherwise well restored pump to lose suction. Prepare the outside flap valves so you can test them, but don't install them yet, or they may become damaged when you slide the bellows around on your bench during hinging and covering. Rehinge the bellows (p. 66) and recover them. Use the original cardboard stiffeners if they are in sufficiently good condition, or make new ones if necessary (p. 74). After recovering the bellows, replace the outside flap valves.

Cover reservoirs which have internal springs as described on p. 75.

If the trunk contains cutoff valves, pouches, gaskets, etc., releather them before attaching the bellows to the trunk. Lap and regraphite any slide valves. If the trunk contains a speed control, clean accumulated dirt from the orifice carefully. If the orifice is a separate piece of wood, brass or celluloid, make sure it is flat and sealed to the wood, and make sure the slide valve seats properly. If the wind motor governor or a small expression regulator bellows is hinged directly to the face of a reservoir (Gulbransen, Price & Teeple and others), rehinge and recover it prior to assembling the pump.

Reattach the bellows to the trunk. Some rebuilders install very thin leather gaskets between each bellows and the trunk in pumps which were originally glued together, gluing *both sides* of each gasket, to make future disassembly possibly a little easier. Without gluing the gaskets on both sides, the pumping bellows will work their way loose after several humidity changes and a certain amount of pumping. Have the screws handy, preheat the wood, coat the surface with hot glue and quickly assemble and screw the parts together.

Rehinge, recover and regasket any detachable bellows, valve blocks or other parts (like the wind motor governor in a Standard, or the action cutoff pneumatic of a Gulbransen), test them for airtightness and install them on the trunk. When restoring the wind motor governor, attempt to reassemble it with all parts adjusted as they were. In case some of the settings were never tampered with, this will make it easier to regulate later, when you are putting the finishing touches on the piano. If the motor governor contains a knife valve, lap the mating surfaces and regraphite them, checking for airtightness and smooth operation. Always install new inside and outside hinges in spring loaded regulator pneumatics.

Regasket all flanged hose connectors, and seal around all unflanged nipples and elbows with burnt shellac.

Many pumps (Standard, Autopiano, Amphion and others) contain an accent pneumatic inside one reservoir, which collapses quickly when the suction in the trunk increases suddenly, blocking the suction flow through the reservoir. This permits the player pianist to produce a quick accent with a sharp push on one of the pumping pedals, feeding the accent to the stack and preventing the reservoir from absorbing the momentary burst of higher suction. If present, rehinge, recover and regasket this pneumatic, releather its valve (if it has one), and install it in the reservoir. Never discard an accent pneumatic just because it looks like too much extra work to fix it; player pianos which have this device need it because of the large size of their reservoirs.

If the old rubber pedal mats on the pumping pedals still have most of an original logo -- the Standard backwards S or the Gulbransen baby, for example -- keep them, but if they have holes worn all the way through, obtain replacements from a supply company, or get some rubber stair tread material with fine parallel lines from a large hardware or building supply store. Remove the old pedals from the frames, remove the old material and sand off the old glue, and glue the new mats in place with contact cement. Clean and polish the pedal linkages, repair or replace any worn bushings or connecting pins as necessary, reassemble the pedals and install them on the pump. Install any external springs. Apply a drop of oil to each connection in the pumping linkage, and clean off the excess so it won't drip on the floor.

Testing the Pump

Stand the pump up on your bench, seal off all of the nipples with duct tape or airtight masking tape (some masking tape is surprisingly leaky, spoiling your test), and depress one of the pumping pedals a few times until the reservoirs are pulled tightly shut. A well restored pump will hold suction for a minute or more before the reservoirs become completely relaxed. If the reservoirs open after ten or fifteen seconds, your player piano will be hard to pump. Check carefully to eliminate every possible source of leakage: under screw heads, under the bellows cloth at the corners, through gaskets, cracks in the wood, etc. After you pump the reservoirs shut, if you see the cloth on a pumping bellows gradually pull in as if it has suction inside, the inside flap valve leaks. If you gently pull the outside flaps away from their seats and the reservoirs open noticably faster, this is an indication of significant inside flap valve leakage. With leaky inside flaps, the pumping bellows will pump a certain amount of air back and forth between each other during play, wasting that amount of suction, which should be available for playing the piano. If the pumping bellows have removable plates for access to the inside flap valves (a rare feature), disassemble them and repair the flaps as necessary so you can't detect any seepage into the pumping bellows. If not, you will have to decide whether tearing the pump apart again to repair the flap valves properly will be worth the additional effort.

Test the operation of the action cutoff and wind motor controls. Remove the tape from the stack supply nipple (leave it on the wind motor supply nipple for now), and manipulate the action cutoff lever (or actuate the cutoff pouch or pneumatic) to see if it completely blocks the flow of suction from the stack supply. If not, adjust the cutoff valve so it seats properly. Seal the stack supply nipple again, and open the wind motor supply nipple. With the accelerator valve off, turn the speed control all the way off and check for leakage. With the speed control still turned off, operate the accelerator to see if it connects full unregulated suction to the nipple. Adjust as necessary. Ignore the wind motor governor for now. You will adjust it later after everything is installed in the piano.

MISCELLANEOUS ACCESSORIES AND PNEUMATIC CONTROLS

Now that the main upper and lower actions are completely restored and tested, the only remaining parts are the sustaining and soft pedal pneumatics, mandolin pneumatic and any expression regulators which are not physically attached to the pump. Restore each one of these with the same careful attention that you paid to the stack, tracking device and other intricate parts, and test each completed part for airtightness and quick, efficient operation. Many large sustaining pneumatics have two or more valves and pouches, but usually have only one bleed sufficiently large to feed both pouches.

One of the most neglected, most easily repaired parts in the whole player piano is the control button pallet valve assembly. If you haven't done so already, *take it out of the piano*, releather the pallets or their seats, and test for airtightness.

INSTALLING AND REGULATING THE PLAYER ACTION

Assuming that you have diligently tested every component, repaired and installed the mandolin, repaired, regulated and tuned the piano, and regulated any manual control levers, you are now ready to install the player action in the piano. After all of the time that you have in the project, now is no time to become impatient! Continue doing each step in the right order, and don't skip over something which will cause you to have to disassemble something else later. The first and most time consuming step in installing the player action - installing and regulating the stack - is already done, as described on pp. 38 and 42.

Installing the Control Mechanisms and Small Tubing

Install the control buttons and their pallet valves. Make sure the buttons are free to move down and up without binding. Replace the cloth bushings surrounding the buttons in the keybed if necessary; you don't want something as simple as a leaky or binding button pallet to make you think there is something wrong with the mechanism which it controls.

Install the sustaining pedal pneumatic, and connect and adjust its linkages now. The open end of the pneumatic should be able to move approximately ³⁄₁₆" before engaging the pedal dowel; this will insure that it won't hold the dampers off the strings when it is off. The sustaining pedal pneumatic should have a spring or some other means of holding it in the fully open position, in addition to the

springs of the dampers. If it is missing or if the pneumatic never had one, install one, and adjust it so the pneumatic does not move when the sustaining pedal is operated manually. Adjust the stop screw in the pneumatic, if present, to limit the travel just to the point where all of the dampers lift free of the strings. When making this adjustment, you will find out whether or not you or your piano technician did a good job of regulating the dampers to the damper lift rod. When everything is adjusted right, the sustaining pneumatic should be able to lift all of the dampers with a minimum of motion.

Install the soft hammer rail pneumatics, connect their linkages, and regulate them so they move the bass and treble hammers half way to the strings.

If the pedal pneumatics or manual control levers cause squeaks when they move, locate and eliminate the squeaks now. They are usually in connecting linkages toward the back of the keybed, which are impossible to fix once everything is installed in the piano.

Connect the small diameter tubing from the finger buttons to the pedal pneumatics, following the original route through any staples in the keybed and on the sides of the piano. Install any other small tubes which run from the top to the bottom, through staples or wooden retainers, for the action cutoff or other parts, leaving enough extra length at each end so they will reach their destination on the stack and pump.

Installing the Pump and Hoses

Install the pump and connect the control linkages. Connect the upper control linkages to the tempo pointer and transmission on the head. Install the wind motor hose, routing it so it doesn't interfere with any of the control linkages or piano action parts, and connect it to the pump and the wind motor. If it kinks, install elbows as necessary. Install the main stack hose(s) and the suction supply hoses to the pedal and other control pneumatics. Finally, install and connect any remaining small tubing for the action cutoff and other mechanisms.

Regulating the Control Levers and Mechanisms

Put a test roll on the spoolbox and wind it onto the takeup spool. Move the rewind/play lever to the play position, and regulate the linkage so the takeup spool gears are

Illus. 4-13. Many player actions have adjustable linkages connecting the controls levers to the pump and other parts, making the levers easy to regulate.

44

engaged but not binding, and so the action cutoff admits suction to the stack. Move the rewind lever to the rewind position to see that the rewind gears are engaged and the action cutoff shuts off the suction supply to the stack.

Regulate the tempo indicator in the spoolbox so it is at 0 when the tempo lever in the keyslip is all the way to the left. When the pointer and lever are regulated correctly, they will move simultaneously all the way from the extreme left to the extreme right, with the arrow moving from 0 to the highest number on the scale.

Move the rewind lever to the play position, and move the wind motor accelerator and speed control slides on the pump to their off positions so the wind motor stops turning. Opening either of these controls will cause the motor to turn, so each one must be turned off in order to regulate the other. Regulate the accelerator to work only when the rewind lever is in the rewind position, and regulate the tempo control mechanism so the motor just barely begins to turn when the tempo pointer is set at the first tempo graduation on the scale - usually 10. Remember that opening either the speed control valve *or* the accelerator on the pump will cause the motor to go faster, so don't let their interaction confuse you.

Regulating the Wind Motor Governor

Now everything is ready to use, with all control levers connected and adjusted, but the wind motor governor still needs to be regulated. Lay your test roll out on a long table, and measure the tempo regulating markings, which are supposed to be spaced at one foot intervals. Many test rolls have these marks printed completely wrong; if yours is wrong, make your own marks, one every foot for seven feet. Put the test roll on the piano, and recheck the adjustment of the top spool brake so it just barely prevents the paper from fluttering. Make sure the tempo lever and valve are set so the motor does not turn with the lever set at 0 and just begins to turn with the lever set at 10. Have a digital watch or stopwatch handy, and set the lever at 70. Lift one

slide valve slightly off its seat to keep the wind motor from turning, pedal to provide a normal playing level of suction, and release the slide valve at the moment that you begin timing. This is more accurate than starting the test by jerking the tempo lever from 0 to 70. A speed of 70 means seven feet of paper should pass the tracker bar in one minute, so the marks on your test roll will tell you whether the roll is running too slow or too fast. If the tempo test shows that the motor is running too fast, weaken the spring on the wind motor governor. If the motor runs too slow, strengthen the spring. If the motor stalls on extremely hard pumping, turn the stop screw on the governor pneumatic in ¼ turn at a time until this is cured. If the motor races on hard pumping, back the stop screw out ¼ turn at a time. If you carefully readjusted the governor spring during rebuilding to the setting that you found when you took it apart, it might be too tight because at some time in the past, a technician tightened it to compensate for general leakage in the player action. Take your time regulating the wind motor; this finishing touch will make the difference between a player which is fun to play and one which seems to have its own ideas about tempo.

If the player has expression regulating governors, adjust them so the piano plays at a medium or medium soft level when they are in operation. This will provide pleasant contrast to ordinary loud pumping.

THE MOMENT YOU HAVE BEEN WAITING FOR

After you are happy with all of the adjustments, give the piano a final tuning if necessary, and put the cabinet together. If you can breeze through most music rolls by pumping with one foot without getting tired, if you can uncover the tracker bar and play all 88 notes at once by pumping vigorously, if all of the controls and accessories do what they should, and if you can play any passage of music very soft or very loud without having the music change speed, pat yourself on the back. You did a good job.

CHAPTER FIVE
REBUILDING
TECHNIQUES,
TOOLS, AND
MATERIALS

Now that you are familiar with the general routine of restoring a player action as described in Ch. 4, you are ready to learn all about specific rebuilding procedures and the tools and materials used.

Illus. 5-1. Part of the author's workshop, where components and instruments are disassembled and reassembled. Another room is equipped with woodworking tools for doing the dirty work. In this picture, Bob Grunow reassembles an Ampico expression mechanism.

The number of instruments which you intend to restore will have a bearing on how heavily you should invest in tools and supplies. If you plan to restore just one player piano for yourself, you will be able to get the job done with a certain minimum number of hand tools and with access to a few power tools, perhaps in a friend's wood shop, and with a small quantity of materials and supplies. Purchase wood screws, paint, metal polish, pneumatic and bellows cloth, leather, tubing, hoses, rubber pedal mats, glue, etc., only as needed for the job at hand.

If you intend to pursue restoration as a hobby and you feel that you will remain involved over a long enough period of time to justify spending more money on tools and supplies, a few essential power tools of your own and a small inventory will make life much easier. This should include the more commonly used types of cloth, leather, tracker bar tubing, hoses, glue, solvent and hardware; this stock may be acquired gradually without a huge lump expense by purchasing a little more of each material than needed for the job at hand. The stock of useful supplies will grow gradually, and you won't end up buying a large quantity of something which you will hardly ever use.

If you decide to restore instruments professionally for others, you will want to order larger quantities of supplies and materials in order to take advantage of discounts offered by suppliers, and you will need to stock a good supply of maple, poplar, tubing, hoses, tubing connectors, cloth, leather, solvents, at least one box of 100 of each useful size of wood screw,—in short, everything recommended in this chapter. You will want to keep all materials in stock, which means reordering them before running out. You will also need a fully equipped wood shop in order to make new pneumatics, pumping bellows, and more complex items on a routine basis. Most of the work of today's full time restorer includes sophisticated woodworking comparable in skill to the finest cabinet making, and if owning and caring for a whole shop full of tools doesn't interest you, don't plan on making a career of player piano restoration!

In this chapter, several repair methods are included for certain jobs: one method for getting the job done with a minumum of tools, and another faster method for those who possess a complete woodworking shop. Individual tools and their uses are described in detail; at the end of the chapter are checklists of tools recommended for the beginner, the more advanced hobbyist and the professional rebuilder.

Player piano restoration involves the use of many types of pneumatic and bellows cloth, leather, glue, lubricants, solvents, etc., which must be obtained from a number of sources. Some materials, such as various weights of pneumatic and bellows cloth, are available in a wide variety from different supply companies, with every supply company claiming that its materials are superior, making it confusing for the beginner to choose the right material for each specific task. To make matters worse, if the novice asks ten restorers for their opinions, ten different recommendations are likely to be made. In this chapter, many materials are described in detail, including those which are preferred by the author, others which are considered acceptable but are not the preferred choice, and still others which should never be used. The materials which are given the highest recommendation have a proven durability record; they will not make a future restoration more difficult, and they are used by the finest rebuilders*. Don't cut corners by buying inferior materials! Even though quite a few different materials and supplies must be on hand for a restoration, their cost is insignificant compared to the amount of labor involved.

*Unfortunately, all types of supplies are subject to change at the whim of the manufacturer, making it difficult to rely on the same exact material being available year after year. To learn what the best currently available materials are, discuss this with a reputable restorer.

Piano Supplies and Tools

Do you intend to perform your own piano repairing and regulating, or will you hire a piano technician to do this important part of your restoration? Piano supplies and specialized tools and procedures which are necessary for piano repair and regulating are only mentioned here and there in the present book as they apply to player piano work, but they are described in detail in the companion volume to this one, *Piano Servicing, Tuning and Rebuilding*, by the same author. Remember, a player piano is only as good as the piano itself!

GLUE

This section gives a preview of various types of glue used in player action repair, together with basic instructions for using hot glue. Further details for specific uses are given throughout the book.

Hot Glue

Hot Glue (hide glue, animal glue), the old standby for many gluing jobs in a player action, is composed of hydrolyzed collagen, a protein constituent of animal skins, connective tissue and bones. It is sold by the pound in granular form —small crystals or flakes —by piano, organ and woodworking supply companies. It possesses the advantages of sticking quickly, staying stuck, and being easy to sand off of wood. If applied correctly, it is very strong; for example, if a piece of thick, rugged chrome tanned cowhide is glued to a piece of wood with hot glue, an attempt to pull it loose will either tear the leather or pull a layer of wood loose. Hot glue may be mixed thin for gluing pouches and valve leather, or thick for covering large bellows with thick fleecy cloth. Its stickiness and fast drying

Illus. 5-2. The glue pot, an essential tool for player action restoration. In lieu of a commercially made thermostatically controlled electric glue pot, hot glue may be mixed in a double boiler on a hot plate or stove.

time make it the ideal glue for felt, action cloth, pneumatic and bellows hinges, and bellows covering leather. Use hot glue to glue all pneumatics on decks, fingers on pneumatics, and all other wood glue joints which will have to be broken apart again in the future, for gluing pneumatic and bellows hinges, for valve leather and gaskets, and for covering all pneumatics and bellows with rubber cloth or leather.

Although any wood to wood glue joint, including one assembled with hot glue—such as a pneumatic glued to a deck board—can be stubborn to disassemble, the advantage of using hot glue is that when the parts are separated in the future, the old glue may be removed easily by sanding; this is not the case with other common woodworking glues such as white and aliphatic resin glue. The only real disadvantages of using hot glue are the experience which is necessary in order to judge how thin or thick to make it, and the dexterity required to apply it neatly in the short time before it begins to gel.

Hot glue does not stick to finished wood nor to metal, so it can not be used for sealing around hose connectors, sticking metal fingers to pneumatics, sealing valve plates or other similar applications. See "sealer" on pp. 49–50.

How to Use Hot Glue

Hot glue crystals are mixed with water and heated in a glue pot. If you plan to restore more than one player piano, obtain a thermostatically-controlled glue pot from a piano or organ supply company. If you intend to restore only one piano and want to avoid the expense of a "real" glue pot, construct a simple double boiler by placing a glass jar in a kettle of water on a stove or thermostatically controlled hot plate.

Whether you make your glue in a genuine glue pot or in a double boiler on the stove, use a candy thermometer to check the temperature, which should be kept between 135-145° Fahrenheit. The thermostat in some commercially available glue pots is sometimes set a little too high; if a check with a thermometer proves this to be the case, remove the little hex head screws which hold the glue pot together, gently remove the outer liner without disturbing the power cord connections, and adjust the thermostat as necessary. It is normal for the temperature to swing approximately ten degrees F., but the thermostat should be adjusted so the highest temperature does not exceed 145°. If glue is heated beyond this temperature, it can harden in the pot after being heated for just a few hours.

Many commercial glue pots come with a wire crosspiece inserted for wiping the excess glue off the brush. This wire will accumulate large clumps of partially dried glue, and will gradually rust away, depositing flakes of rust in the glue. Discard the wire and replace it with a wood dowel wedged in place. The wood rod will neither deteriorate nor accumulate stalactites of glue.

To make a batch of glue, fill the container of your glue pot about ⅓-½ full of dry glue crystals. This will produce plenty of glue for an average work session. If you plan to use a lot of glue, as when covering or assembling a large pump, make a larger batch, but if the pot is more than ½ full you will waste a lot of time wiping extra glue off the handle of the brush! If you make much less than ⅓ of a pot, the glue will dry out quickly, making it necessary to add water frequently.

Slowly add cold water until there is about ¼″ of water on top of the glue. Don't stir yet; the water will mix in by itself, and if you stir the water into the glue crystals, you might be tempted to add too much water. Cover the pot and let the glue dissolve overnight. Turn on the heat the next day about an hour in advance, and when you are ready to start working you will have a batch of glue of approximately the right consistency for gluing pneumatics to deck boards. Each time you withdraw a brush full of glue, stir the glue well; this will insure that the consistency will remain uniform. The consistency should be something like thick pancake syrup, thicker than water but thinner than molasses. This can be judged only when the glue is hot; as soon as it is applied to a piece of wood, or even when a brush full is held in mid air, it begins to cool and thicken.

Prior to applying the glue, preheat the surface of the wooden parts with an iron or heat lamps to a temperature no hotter than that of the glue pot. Apply and spread the glue with a stiff brush as quickly as possible—within a few seconds after removing it from the pot. When two pieces of wood are preheated, the hot glue is stirred and applied to the wood, and the two parts are assembled and clamped within five seconds or so, the consistency of the glue is correct if just a little glue squeezes out of the joint, and if it is difficult or impossible to slide one piece against the other a few moments after assembly. If the two pieces of wood feel like they have a spongy cushion between them, either the glue was too thick in the pot, the glue was not stirred well enough immediately before use, too much was applied to the wood, the parts were not preheated adequately, or too much time was taken to assemble the parts. (Beginners often find all of the above to be true)! On the other hand, if no glue squeezes out, it is mixed too thin. In either case, quickly separate the parts, remove the glue and start over.

When gluing gaskets, pouches, and other thin pieces of leather, add a little extra water to make the consistency thinner. When gluing thick leather or bellows cloth, allow the glue to become a little thicker. In all cases, warm the wood to which the leather will be applied with an iron to give yourself a little more working time, and keep the heat in your work room turned up to at least 70 or 75°.

Make a cover for your glue pot and use it! A rubber disc sold as a polishing and sanding accessory for an electric drill makes a nice heavy glue pot cover which won't slide around, but the plastic lid from a coffee can or margarine dish will also work. It is important to keep the glue covered

at all times while the batch is initially dissolving and cooking, and as much as possible during actual use. If the glue is left uncovered while it is mixing the night before, the top ½″ or more will be composed of froth which will remain after the glue is cooked for several hours. When this mixture is stirred, the froth will permeate the glue with thousands of air bubbles which will gradually return to the surface as another layer of froth. A good batch of glue should not be full of air bubbles. The more the cover is left off of the glue pot during actual work, the sooner the glue will have a hard crust on top, particularly in dry climates, requiring additional water, thorough stirring and more waiting for it to mix again. Keep your glue pot covered as much as possible, and add water as necessary to keep the consistency right for the job.

Hot glue may be reheated many times for jobs where great strength is unnecessary, but clean your glue pot and make a new batch when gluing a set of pneumatics to their deck boards, covering pressure operated pneumatics or bellows, or gluing other parts where strength is important.

Other Types of Glue

Liquid hide glue is hide glue with thiourea added as a drying retardant. Like hot glue, it can be sanded off wood easily, but it dries very slowly and does not possess the strength of hot glue. It is not strong enough to hold pneumatics on deck boards reliably, and professional rebuilders view its slow drying time as a nuisance; once you are used to the speed of hot glue you will not use something which takes a long time to set.

White glue such as Elmer's Glue-All (TM Borden, Inc.) was the most popular glue for player piano repair during the 1950's when few rebuilders cared about how hard it would be to restore the player piano again twenty or thirty years later. Now that thirty years have elapsed, white glue's disadvantages have become painfully obvious. The main disadvantage of white glue is the difficulty of removing it from wood, because it is too hard to remove by scraping, and sanding only turns it gummy and sticky, ruining the sandpaper. Because of the difficulty of removing it from pneumatics and bellows, decks, gasketed areas, pouch boards and other large surfaces, it should never be used for any of these jobs.

Aliphatic resin glue such as Titebond (TM Franklin Chemical Industries) and Elmer's Carpenter's Wood Glue (TM Borden, Inc.) is excellent wood glue, but it is as difficult to remove from large areas as white glue is, so its use should be confined to articles which will never have to be disassembled, such as gluing broken pieces of wood, assembling parts of valve boxes and other permanent glue joints. Do not use it for covering pneumatics and bellows, or for gluing valves, gaskets, pouches, etc. When using it for regluing veneer or broken cabinet parts in a piano which will be refinished, make your repairs prior to removing the old finish. This will help to keep the glue from soaking into bare wood and causing stains which will show through the new finish. If this type of glue is used in a wood joint which was originally hot glued, all traces of the old hot glue must be removed, or the two will mix together, forming a soup that has little strength; the same thing applies to white glue mixed with hot glue.

Contact cement is used only for gluing new rubber mats to pumping pedals. Because of the difficulty of removing it from wood during subsequent restorations, never use it for gluing gaskets, pouches, pneumatic or bellows cloth, etc.

Epoxy is handy for filling voids in wood which are difficult or impossible to fill with wood, and for helping to secure small wires to wooden parts, such as wire valve stems to wood pouch buttons, where great strength is not necessary. It is also useful for gluing clean breaks in metal castings like transmission frames, providing that the glue joint is also reinforced with a pin, machine screw and nut or some other mechanical connection.

PVC-E (plastic glue) is used for recovering pneumatics with nylon cloth. It is also handy for gluing leather to metal, such as the leather valve facings on metal pallet springs (for keyslip pedal control buttons), and leather gaskets on flanged hose connectors. Although some rebuilders use it for everything from gluing pouches to sealing around hose connectors, anyone who has had to remove it from wood will never use it on wood again except for covering small pneumatics with nylon cloth, where no other glue will stick. Don't confuse this with the thin, volatile, toxic PVC cement which is used for plastic plumbing; PVC-E looks like white glue and smells completely different from PVC plastic pipe cement. It is available only from piano and organ supply companies, not hardware stores. In case PVC-E is found to be toxic, use it with adequate ventilation and skin protection.

When nylon cloth (polylon, bilon etc. - see p. 76) and PVC-E glue are used for covering pneumatics, the cloth slips around on the wood more than it does when ordinary rubber cloth and hot or white glue are used. Because of the greater dexterity required to do a neat job, the beginner should cover several sets of player piano stack pneumatics with rubber cloth and "conventional" glue (hot or white) before attempting to use nylon cloth and PVC-E.

Super glue is rarely used in player piano repair. Use wood glue, not super glue, to repair wood.

Hot melt glue, used in a glue gun, has no use in player piano repair. Although it is very sticky when melted, after it cools it has almost no strength at all. If you attempt to cover a bellows with this glue, you will find yourself recovering it again when the cloth or leather falls off within a short time!

SEALER

Sealer is used for making internal channels in wooden parts airtight, for making leather pouches and leather bellows coverings airtight, for sticking things together where great mechanical strength is unnecessary, and wherever an airtight joint is desired where glue will not work, or where parts must be disassembled in the future. For example, where unflanged tubing and hose connectors fit tightly into holes in wooden parts, a bead of sealer around the outside of the connector is necessary to prevent leakage; the only glue which will stick to metal *and* wood will cause damage to the wood during future disassembly (like epoxy) or is difficult to remove from the wood (like PVC-E). Various applications require different types of sealer.

Shellac was the most common wood sealer used in the "old days"; most internal channels, pouch wells and other chambers were given a liberal coating of shellac to make the wood reasonably airtight. The shellac which is available today is often too thin to make wood absolutely airtight, particularly when it is used to seal new wood. The thickness of shellac is measured by "pound cut;" four pound cut has four pounds of dry shellac mixed with one gallon of alcohol. If you can find a source for shellac crystals, mix your own six pound cut. This will seal the wood somewhat better than the canned shellac sold by most hardware stores.

Thick shellac was used originally for sealing around hose connectors, sealing leather nuts to threaded wires, sticking metal pushrod fingers to stack pneumatics, and reinforcing wooden pieces, such as mounting blocks, which are screwed together but need to be disassembled in the future. It is still the best material to use for these purposes today. Old-timers in the field made it by burning some of the alcohol out of

Illus. 5-3. A neat bead of thick shellac around a hose connector, valve plate or other wood-to-metal joint forms a permanent airtight seal but permits disassembly in the future. Hot glue, white glue, and other types do not stick to the metal, while epoxy causes wood to break during future disassembly.

pre-mixed orange shellac, so it used to be called "burnt shellac." A better and safer method is to mix a small amount of alcohol with dry shellac flakes available from woodworking supply companies. Make the mixture thick enough so it won't run when applied to a vertical surface. Although thick shellac takes a week or longer to dry, it sticks to wood, metal, and other parts for years, and it can be removed by chipping it off or heating it without damaging the parts. Metal parts coated with thick shellac (i.e. Simplex and right-side-up Amphion top valve plates) are easily cleaned by soaking them in alcohol. Since shellac is a basic player-piano-restoration supply, it is always on hand, and it is the only readily available, easily removable substance which sticks to shellac, paint, and other finishes which are already on the wooden parts. Once you get used to having a supply of thick shellac on hand in a small squeeze bottle, you will wonder how you ever lived without it.

Lacquer—the liquid variety, not aerosol —is probably the best material for sealing pouch wells, channels, etc. in new wooden parts because it soaks in, builds up and dries faster than shellac does. It is also used for resealing old parts, but it is more brittle than shellac, so there is a possibility that it may crack and flake loose after a long time, particularly if a thick layer of lacquer is applied over old, flaky material. When using it for new parts, beware of lacquer soaking all the way through porous wood like poplar, making it difficult or impossible to glue anything to the other side.

Liquid *rubber cement* (such as Carter's), available in various size cans from office supply stores and thinned down 50/50 with rubber cement thinner (naphtha), is used for sealing leather pouches, and for coating the inside of the leather covering on pumping bellows to make them airtight. After applying several thin coats to a pouch, or several thick coats to the inside of a bellows, coat the rubber cement with talcum power to eliminate stickiness. (Some brands turn hard and shouldn't be used on pouches).

PVC-E glue can be used as a sealer in places where its perpetual stickiness won't have a detrimental effect on surrounding parts. For example, it can be used as a substitute for shellac for sealing around unflanged tubing nipples, but it obviously can't be used for sealing channels in wood, where it will become clogged with dirt, or in pouch wells, where the pouches will stick to it. PVC-E is also useful for sealing the inside of bellows leather to make it airtight; it gets the job done with one medium coat, followed by a coat of talcum powder, instead of the two or three coats of rubber cement which are necessary.

Beeswax is used in some player actions (including Cable Euphona and Kimball) for sealing around the heads of countersunk flat head screws which hold valve chests together. It remains soft for many years, is easily scraped off for disassembly, and is easily remelted into place during reassembly. Do not use it for any other sealing applications.

What Not To Use for Sealer

Beginners who learn the joys of using hot glue often decide that it should be used everywhere, including for sealing metal hose connectors to wooden parts. Unfortunately, hot glue doesn't stick to metal *or* finished wood, and since most deck boards and other wooden parts are shellacked or painted, hot glue applied as sealer not only comes loose from the nipples and elbows within a few days after it is applied, but it also comes loose from the surrounding wood! White and aliphatic resin glues stick to metal and finished wood somewhat better, but if used as a sealer around tubing elbows, these glues break loose if an elbow is turned even the slightest bit for alignment.

As mentioned in the section on gaskets, never use any type of caulking compound or rubber paint for sealer.

CLEANERS AND SOLVENTS

Solvents and chemical cleaners are used for removing dirt, grease and tarnish from old metal and wood parts. Some jobs may be done with relatively safe ordinary household cleaners, but others can be done much more efficiently with more toxic solvents. Go to whatever lengths necessary to protect yourself from the harmful effects of these solvents. They not only damage lung tissue by inhalation, but can also cause kidney damage and other problems by direct absorption through the skin. If you are a smoker, be aware of the fact that smoking inhibits the cleaning action of the cilia in lung tissue which ordinarily remove foreign substances, compounding the danger. Some products which were in widespread use through the 1960's are now considered to be so unsafe that they are no longer available for consumer use. These include benzene, a known carcinogen, carbon tetrachloride, whose vapors are lethal even in tiny doses, and others. Gasoline, of course, never was considered to be a safe solvent because of the explosive nature of its fumes, as well the health hazard connected with breathing them. Assume that some substances which are in use today will probably prove to be unsafe in the future, and use them accordingly, with rubber or neoprene gloves or other skin protection, and adequate ventilation. This means having some way of breathing a continuous ample supply of fresh air, not just having a nearby window open a little. Heed the same precautions when using paint, lacquer, shellac and other finishing materials, and when working with tools which generate fine powdered wood. If your only alternative is to wait until the weather is good enough to work outdoors, so be it.

Odorless paint thinner appears at this time to be the safest solvent for cleaning transmissions and other greasy metal parts.

Lacquer thinner works faster than odorless paint thinner, but is potentially harmful to your health; use it only with appropriate skin and lung protection.

Denatured ethyl alcohol is used to remove old shellac from metal parts. It takes a while for it to dissolve old shellac, so pour some into a bottle, add the parts and let them soak. *Methyl alcohol* is considered to be less safe because among other problems, it can cause damage to the optic nerve and lead to blindness.

Naphtha is the thinner for rubber cement which is used for sealing pouches and bellows leather. It is less volatile than lacquer thinner but may pose some of the same health hazards; never apply suction to pouches by mouth while rubberizing them.

Paint and varnish remover contains toxic solvents. Use it only as directed on the container. If you find an old can of paint and varnish remover which contains benzene, do not use it!

WOODWORKING TECHNIQUES

Player piano actions, with very few exceptions, are made primarily of wood, and a large part of their restoration involves careful woodworking. In addition to more ordinary skills such as cutting, sanding and drilling, player action restoration involves unique procedures such as breaking apart tightly glued components (in which tiny channels conduct suction or air across glue joints), replacing internal leather and rubber cloth parts, and then regluing the wood so the channels are perfectly aligned, airtight and not clogged with glue. While some wooden parts are fastened together with screws and can be taken apart and put back together easily, others are glued, and their correct disassembly and reassembly requires a high level of patience, skill and dexterity. This section describes basic skills which are necessary for disassembling wooden player action parts, removing decomposed rubber cloth and leather from them, repairing the wood and reassembling the parts.

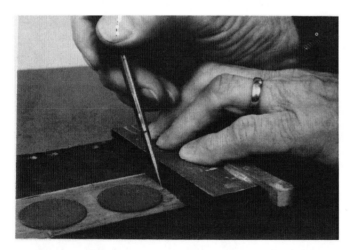

Illus. 5-4. After chipping the glue away, mark the original location of a pneumatic carefully prior to removing it. If the pneumatics are all perpendicular to the edge of the deck, a dot made with an awl will suffice. Otherwise, score a line on the deck with a knife.

Preparation for Disassembly

Wooden parts are fastened together with glue, screws or both, and certain preparatory work—checking the tightness of screws, and measuring and sketching the orientation and fit of glued parts—must be performed prior to taking anything apart. Many beginners jump right into the disassembly of components without performing this preparatory work, at best causing needless backtracking during reassembly, or at worst causing problems which prevent the player mechanism from ever working right again. The preparatory work is simple; get in the habit of doing it now and you will save yourself many headaches later.

Illus. 5-5. If there is any danger of sanding the marks away during cleanup, neatly mark the edges of the deck board

Check the tightness of every screw before removing it! In order for a player action to be airtight, the screws holding gasketed parts together must be very tight. How tight? As tight as possible without crushing the wood beneath the screw heads, and without having the screws break. Whenever you encounter a screw which keeps turning without beginning to compress the wood as you try to tighten it, mark the wooden part which holds the threaded part of the screw, with chalk or a small bit of masking tape. Later, during repairs and cleanup, your marks will remind you which screws were overdrawn, and you will decide which holes have to be plugged and redrilled, and which ones will be tight with the substitution of longer screws. To your dismay you might find entire rows of screw holes which are stripped, and you might be tempted to ignore them, or insert toothpicks into the holes, but if you do, you will end up with a leaky, hard to pump player action.

If you find during disassembly that long slender screws — longer than 1" x #6, or 1-½" x #8 —are rusty, particularly where they were surrounded by old leather gasket material, obtain new screws, and check for tightness by removing each old screw and temporarily inserting and tightening a new one, to avoid breaking any of the old screws off in the wood.

After checking the tightness of all of the screws, decide whether it will be necessary to mark the parts or to make a quick sketch of them to help during reassembly. Many small valve boxes and cover plates are square or rectangular with nearly symmetrically located screw holes, and the orientation of these parts in relation to each other should be marked to prevent confusion or error during reassembly. Always mark the parts in a way that the marks won't show after the parts are put back together. There are several professional ways of doing this, including stamping the matching wood surfaces with ⅛" steel number stamps, or marking with one or more small dots made with a sharp scratch awl, or stamping with one or more small lines made with the end of a small screwdriver. Don't stamp the wood in a place where it will be covered with a gasket or seal cloth, or where the mark might disappear during sanding or scraping. Don't scratch numbers into the wood, write numbers on wood with a ball point pen or magic marker, or stamp marks in obvious places where the marks will show. If you number parts with chalk, or with pencil or ballpoint pen over old shellac or other finish, the numbers are likely to disappear before you are ready to reassemble the parts. If there might be any possibility of a question about how the parts should be reassembled, make a quick sketch, or take a closeup picture, showing as many details as necessary to reassemble them correctly. Remember, despite your best intentions, you might not reassemble the parts until weeks after you disassemble them, and the best memory for small mechanical details is aided by good written records.

Prior to disassembling glued parts such as pneumatics and decks, pneumatics and fingers, and other components where one smaller part is glued to a larger surface of another, measure and mark as necessary so the parts can be reglued in the same precise location. If a pneumatic overhangs a deck board or other mounting surface, measure the amount of overhang, or if one end is flush, make note of this. Mark the locations of the sides of the smaller part by scribing lines into the surface of the larger part with an awl, or by punching with a sharp chisel. Most glue joints have a certain amount of glue surrounding the smaller part; chip this glue away prior to scribing the location, or your marks will be inaccurate. If you observe that every single pneumatic on a deck board is glued down perfectly square in relation to the front edge of the board, you may mark the location of each side of each pneumatic by punching the deck with an awl, as shown in illus. 5-4. This method does not provide accurate enough information when the pneumatics were glued down crooked, however, and it is sometimes desirable to duplicate the original positions of crooked pneumatics in order for the fingers to line up with the piano action, providing that the crookedness originated in the factory and not during a previous repair job. When pneumatics are glued to the deck with pouch leather or paper gaskets in between, mark the locations of the pneumatics on the edge of the deck; marks made on the gasket will disappear during sanding and cleanup. If the pneumatics were glued on crooked in a previous job, make a scale stick showing the alignment of the whippens, and transfer the alignment marks to the deck boards to align the pneumatics and fingers properly. See p. 35 for further information on disassembling a stack.

After marking and measuring a component so its correct reassembly will be obvious, you are ready to disassemble it.

Disassembly of Glued Parts

Most wooden parts which must be broken apart during restoration fit into one of two categories: a thin, somewhat flexible piece of wood glued to a thicker rigid piece, or two rigid pieces glued together. The first category includes small wooden pushrod fingers glued to pneumatics, and most stack pneumatics glued to their decks, while the second includes unit valve blocks, unit pneumatics, and most larger pneumatics and bellows. Both involve the use of sharp chisels of various widths, a mallet or small hammer, and a putty knife which has been sharpened to a thin edge. Putty knives are made of softer steel than the tool steel which is used for chisels and other cutting tools, so you will not be able to create a true knife edge on one, but try to make it as sharp as possible. Contrary to the rules of sharpening chisels, if you sharpen a bevel on both sides of the putty knife blade it will have less tendency to dig into either wooden part. You will drive the putty knife into glue joints with a hammer, so obtain a knife with a solid steel blade extending all the way to the top of the handle, and remove the handle so the blade can be driven deeper into the wood. Use a putty knife approximately the same width as the pneumatics which you are removing —usually 1", 1¼ "or 1½."

Removing Small Pneumatics

To remove a thin pneumatic from a thicker, more rigid deck board, begin by removing as much of the old glue on the deck surrounding the pneumatic as possible, by cutting or scraping it away with a chisel or other sharp tool. Measure the span of the pneumatic (see p. 68) and its location on the deck, slit the old pneumatic cloth, mark both boards of the pneumatic with matching numbers, cut the hinge apart and lay the moveable board aside. Now you are ready to begin separating the glue joint with your sharpened putty knife. It is always desirable, of course, to try to preserve both pieces of wood, but in many instances where the old glue is exceptionally strong, one piece of wood will probably be damaged. This is usually the piece with the grain running in the direction in which you pry. Since is is normally easier to make a new pneumatic —or a whole new set of pneumatics, if necessary —than to make new deck boards, pry with the grain of the pneumatic, not with the grain of the deck board.

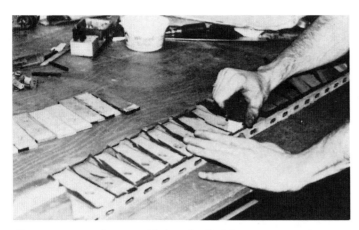

Illus. 5-6. Cutting the moveable boards off of the pneumatics after numbering them.

Clamp the deck board on edge on a solid surface to prevent it from flipping over as you work on it. Under good light, position the sharp end of the putty knife precisely along the glue joint at one end of the pneumatic and hit it gently with a hammer. If nothing happens, check to make sure the blade is aligned perfectly with the glue joint, and hit it again a little harder. As soon as the end of the glue joint pops open, turn the deck around and repeat the process on the other end of the pneumatic. When that end begins to come apart, move back to the first end, alternating from one end to the other until the pneumatic either pops loose from the deck in one piece or breaks. In most stacks, a few pneumatics come off easily, others are very stubborn and the rest fall somewhere in between. In some stacks, however, all of the pneumatics pop loose undamaged with little force, and in others, nearly every pneumatic board cracks before coming loose. The first time you attempt to remove a set of pneumatics, work on each pneumatic until it comes loose, alternating from the hinge end to the open end, until you learn just how hard to drive the knife with the hammer. With experience, you can go all the way down the row of pneumatics from one end of a deck to the other, loosening the hinge end of every pneumatic, then turning the deck around and loosening the open end of

Illus. 5-7. The deck board with the moveable pneumatic boards removed, ready for removal of the stationary boards.

every one, rather than continually flipping the deck as you go from one pneumatic to the next.

Although the sharpened putty knife is the standard tool for removing pneumatics, some rebuilders favor using a sharp wood chisel. Since you should have a good selection of wood chisels on hand anyway, try one to see which tool works better for you.

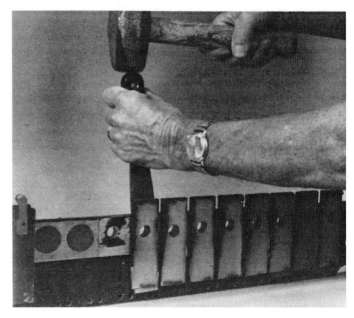

Illus. 5-8. Separating a pneumatic with a sharpened putty knife. In some instances, a sharp chisel does less damage; try each to see which works the best.

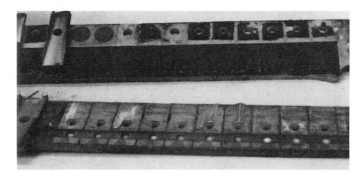

Illus. 5-9. Two deck boards with the pneumatics removed, ready for cleanup. The early Amphion (above) has gaskets, the remains of which show as black squares. The Schulz deck (below) had the pneumatics glued to it without gaskets.

Some rebuilders find that heating the glued down stationary pneumatic boards with an old iron helps to soften the old glue, helping the glue joint to pop apart with the putty knife or chisel. This works only if the old glue still contains a certain amount of moisture; if so much heat is applied that the old glue becomes baked, the pneumatic will be harder to remove than if no heat had been used. It is also very common for the heat to warp the thin pneumatic board, ruining it.

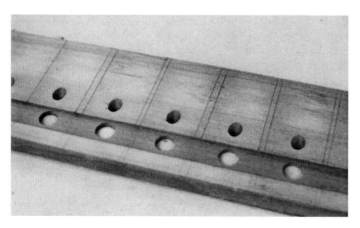

Illus. 5-10. Properly scribed marks still show plainly after glue removal and sanding of the deck.

Removing Glued Wood Fingers from Pneumatics

Most wooden pushrod fingers are attached to the pneumatic with glue and one or two screws. After removing the screws, chipping away the surrounding glue and numbering both parts, try popping the finger off the pneumatic by applying downward pressure to the glued end with your thumb, and upward pressure to the free end with your index finger, as shown in illus. 5-11. In many instances, 90% of the fingers in a stack can be removed this way

Illus. 5-11. Some fingers will pop off by prying as shown.

undamaged. If the first two or three fingers break, however, try removing them with a sharpened putty knife or chisel, or with parallel jaw pliers. Keep the fingers in order; unlike pneumatics and decks which must be sanded prior to regluing, most fingers can be reglued (with hot glue) where they came from without sanding, by perfectly aligning the small mating fragments of wood, providing that they were not previously reglued with white glue.

Disassembling Unit Valve Blocks and Unit Pneumatics

Unit valve blocks (Amphion) and unit pneumatics (Simplex, late style Gulbransen, Coinola, etc.) must be broken apart in order to replace the pouches. These parts represent

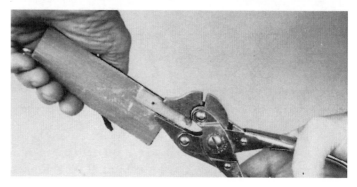

Illus. 5-12. Two other methods of removing stubborn fingers: a parallel jaw pliers, and a chisel.

a different disassembly problem because they are rigid, unlike ordinary pneumatic boards which are thin and somewhat flexible, and both parts have the grain oriented the same way. With the right technique, however, they separate more easily than ordinary pneumatics usually do.

Illus. 5-13. An "upside down" Amphion unit valve removed from a stack.

Illus. 5-13 shows an unrestored Amphion upside down unit valve block, with its original coating of thick orange shellac intact. After numbering and removing each valve block from the trunk board, cut or scrape off as much of the old cork gasket as possible with a knife. The top valve seat is glued down to a blotter paper gasket; cut it apart with a sharp knife, number the valve seat and lay it aside. Then carefully sand the back of the block (where the gasket was), the front and both sides, as shown in illus. 5-15. If you use a stationary belt sander, use a fine sanding belt, and sand gently until you remove most of the old orange shellac finish. By leaving just a trace of the shellac (or glue, on the

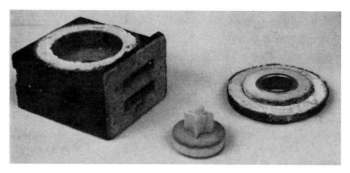

Illus. 5-14. Remove the top valve seat by cutting through the blotter paper gasket.

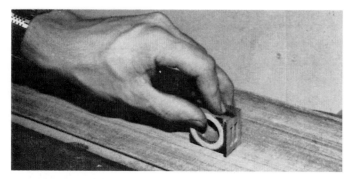

Illus. 5-15. Gently sand the shellac off the four sides of the block to expose the glue joint.

Illus. 5-16. Separate the pouch board by placing a very sharp chisel or felt and leather knife precisely on the old glue line and tapping gently with a mallet.

Illus. 5-17. If each step is performed with care, the pouch board will separate from the valve block almost perfectly. These instructions are applicable to any glued together block; for further information on Amphion valves, see the Amphion section of chapter VI.

gasketed side) on the wood, you will know that you didn't sand away too much wood. If you do not have access to a stationary belt sander, sand the blocks by hand on a piece of fine sandpaper on a ¼″ thick piece of glass. When the block is clean, with only a trace of old finish or glue remaining, you will be able to see the glue joint clearly all the way around. Sharpen your best chisel (or felt and leather knife sold by piano and organ supply companies), place the blade precisely on the glue line on one side of the block, and tap gently with a hammer, creating an indentation along the glue line. Repeat this process on all four sides of the block, and then go around the block again, tapping a little harder. Most blocks will pop apart with little splitting if you use a sharp chisel and are careful to stay on the original glue line. Since the glued surface of an Amphion or similar unit block will be sanded prior to reassembly, tiny slivers of wood which break loose don't matter, but slivers which are large enough to leave a void should be cut off with a single edged razor blade and reglued to the piece where they came from.

Any unit valve block which resembles the one illustrated here can be broken apart in the same way. For further details of other styles of Amphion blocks, refer to the section on Amphion and Ampico player actions on pp. 104 and 169.

To replace the pouch in a unit pneumatic, clean and sand the pneumatic as described on pp. 60–61, number and remove the moveable board, top valve seat and valve, and then separate the pouch block and valve chamber just like a unit valve block.

Illus. 5-18. Simplex unit pneumatics. From left to right: complete unit; one with moveable board removed; another with pouch board separated from valve board.

A possible alternative for separating certain unit valve blocks and unit pneumatics is to heat them in a microwave oven, which will ruin the old glue before it damages any of the wood, permitting easy disassembly without splintering. At the time this is being written, this is still considered to be an experimental technique. *Never place metal objects in a microwave oven;* this goes for bleeds, metal valve seats, internal threaded metal plates, or other small pieces of metal hidden inside wooden valve units! A microwave oven heats objects from the inside out, so by the time you see a tiny wisp of smoke coming from a valve block, damage has already been done to wood inside the block. Also, if you heat a block for disassembly, count on having to replace every bit of old sealer inside, as this will be ruined along with the old glue. Like heating glued parts with an iron, heating in a microwave works like magic in some cases, and only seems to make the glue stronger in others.

For additional information on unit pneumatics, refer to the sections on Simplex, Gulbransen, and other specific brands later in this book.

Removing Medium Size Pneumatics

Most medium size control pneumatics for governors, sustaining pedals, soft pedals and other accessories are gasketed and screwed to their mounting surfaces, providing easy disassembly. Others which are glued to a pouch block or entire valve assembly are the same size or are larger than the part on which they are mounted, permitting rehinging and recovering the pneumatic without breaking it loose. It is sometimes necessary, however, to break a medium size pneumatic loose. To do this, follow the procedure used for separating unit valve blocks and unit pneumatics described above. Measure the span and mounting location, sketch the unit as necessary, remove any surrounding glue and old pneumatic cloth to expose the glue joint all the way around. If any portion of the glue joint is covered with thick shellac or other finish, sand this off to expose the glue line for accurate alignment of the chisel.

Removing Large Pumping Bellows

Large pumping bellows and reservoirs are sometimes gasketed and screwed to the trunk board, providing easy removal, but when they are glued they are usually difficult to remove because of the large area of the glue joint. Additionally, plywood bellows often split apart because the glue holding the laminations together is no better than the glue holding the bellows to the trunk board. If enough space exists around the perimeter of a large bellows to clean and recover it without removing it from the trunk, don't remove it, providing that the old glue joint is indeed good and is still airtight. When less than 2″ or so exists between two bellows, at least one of them will have to be removed. Remove all hardware, measure the span and carefully remove the reservoir springs, marking their positions and orientation for correct reassembly later. They are dangerous-handle them with care! Remove the old cloth and the moveable board, and then remove any screws which hold the bellows to the trunk board. In some cases there are screws entering the bellows from the outside of the trunk and more screws inside the bellows (which are usually accessible through a detachable cover plate or holes in the moveable board). Check and double check to make sure every screw holding the bellows to the trunk has been removed, to avoid irreparable damage. Remove all old glue and rubber cloth so a sharpened putty knife may

be placed precisely along the glue joint, and work your way all the way around, gently tapping the knife with a hammer at first, and then gradually driving it deeper and deeper into the glue joint until the bellows comes off. If you are tempted to use an iron to heat the old glue prior to removing a plywood bellows, remember that you will loosen the laminations of the wood just as much as the glue joint which you are trying to disassemble. No matter how careful you are, you will inevitably crack or break a bellows board now and then, so be prepared to make a new duplicate board if necessary.

Separating Chunks of Maple

Where one piece of maple is glued to another larger piece, such as a large maple "finger" on a soft pedal pneumatic, it is sometimes possible to separate them with little or no damage by supporting the larger piece on an absolutely solid surface (like a concrete floor) and shearing the glue joint by hitting the smaller piece of wood on the end with a small sledge hammer and intermediate piece of maple, as shown in the Gulbransen section of Ch. 6. Drive the glued piece and intermediate piece *only on the end grain!* This works only on pieces of maple at least ¼″ thick; smaller pieces, and other types of wood—including poplar —usually break before the glue does.

Repairing Damaged Wood

During the course of a typical restoration, some of the wooden parts crack, split or break as the old glue joints are broken apart. At best, one or two small pneumatic fingers might break, require regluing, or at worst, a whole set of stationary pneumatic boards and pumping bellows are broken beyond repair. Whether you will reglue a broken part or replace it will depend upon just how bad the damage is, how hard it will be to make a duplicate part, and how many tools you have. Whenever a piece of wood cracks or breaks, decide right then whether you will repair or replace it. If you decide to repair it, do so right away! By doing this promptly, the glue will be drying while you proceed with

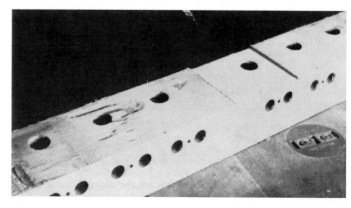

Illus. 5-19. A WurliTzer pneumatic deck board which was badly splintered from a previous repair. This picture shows the area under one pneumatic which has been cut away with a dado blade on a table saw.

56

Illus. 5-20. The same deck with new poplar glued in place, sanded to the correct size, and ready to have the new pneumatics glued on.

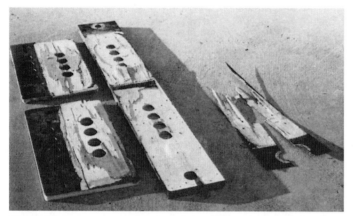

Illus. 5-21. In many cases, damage is inevitable when separating large glued parts, as in this Amphion pump.

Illus. 5-22. The Amphion trunk board with the entire layer of splintered wood removed.

Illus. 5-23. Clamping a new face board on the trunk. When repairing large pieces of wood, the more clamps the better.

Illus. 5-24. The newly refaced trunk with the screw holes and suction channels drilled; one pumping bellows having its splinters glued back where they came from. The object is always to end up with two perfectly smooth, flat pieces of wood to glue back together, to form an airtight glue joint.

Illus. 5-25. The repaired and sanded bellows ready for repainting, new flap valves, rehinging and recovering prior to regluing to the trunk.

disassembly of the rest of the parts, and when you are ready to clean and sand the set of parts, the broken part will be ready. Also, it is better to glue a broken part before sanding it, because the old finish will prevent the glue from soaking into surrounding areas and leaving a stain on the wood after the part is refinished. Furthermore, if a lot of broken parts accumulate, they may exceed the number of clamps which you have, causing a slowdown if you make all wood repairs at once. And finally, it is a good habit to solve problems as they occur rather than to let them accumulate until all of the easy work is done, at which time you will have to face a whole mountain of problems.

To reglue a broken or cracked part which will not have to be disassembled in the future, use aliphatic resin glue (Franklin Titebond, Elmer's Carpenter's Wood Glue or equivalent) and always use clamps with wood clamping blocks to prevent the clamps from leaving marks on the part. Assemble the parts dry first, prepare the clamps and clamping blocks, coat each part with a thin layer of glue (or inject glue into the crack with a hypodermic needle, or insert it with a thin narrow knife blade), reassemble the parts in perfect alignment, place a piece of wax paper over any area where glue will squeeze out onto a clamping block, and put on the clamps. In most cases, C clamps are better than spring clamps for repairing broken wood, because the amount of pressure can be controlled. Be careful to align the parts perfectly so the repair job will be strong and invisible.

Broken and Splintered Pneumatics

Although some other texts recommend regluing splintered pneumatics to the old splinters on deck boards, professional rebuilders always sand the mating surfaces of pneumatics and decks to insure that the new glue joints will be perfectly airtight. Regluing two splintered parts is a good way to insure a leaky player action, particularly if the parts were already broken and reglued once before, so always sand the mating surfaces, and replace all pneumatic boards which have voids left by missing splinters.

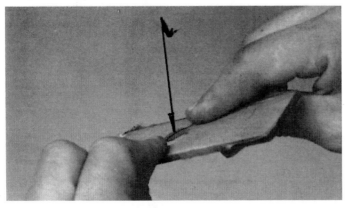

Illus. 5-26. Some cracks in pneumatics are more obvious than others. Always test each pneumatic to find any internal cracks.

Many pneumatics crack when removed from the deck boards; some of these cracks are obvious, but many others are subtle and are visible only when pressure is applied to the board as shown in illus. 5-26. Check every pneumatic board for hidden internal cracks, and reglue or replace the boards as necessary. In some cases, so many pneumatics will break that you will decide to replace all of the stationary boards even though you have already repaired some of them. In some stacks, most of the pneumatics come loose from one deck with no damage, half of them on another deck break into unusable splinters, and none of them survive on the third deck. After removing the pneumatics as carefully as possible, decide whether it will be easier to repair the damage or to make a whole new set. Since a substantial percentage of the time invested in making new pneumatic boards is setup time, it doesn't take much longer to make a whole new set than to make fifteen or twenty. Repair an old stationary board only if the repaired part will have enough wood left to be sanded flat for airtight regluing; if the pneumatic is splintered so badly that there will be voids in the glue joint, replace it. Forget about filling voids with plastic wood, automotive body filler or other patching materials; these have no place in the shop of a skilled player piano restorer.

Separating Other Parts

When separating other glued parts, use the same precautions and techniques as used for pneumatics and deck boards. Analyze the situation before proceeding, and if there is any chance of damage to one of the parts, always try to preserve the part which will be harder to duplicate.

Channels

Many pneumatic components contain channels which are separated from each other only by a tiny remaining piece of end grain wood, heavily sealed with thick shellac. Seal one end of each channel with airtight masking tape (some tape is surprisingly porous) or duct tape, and suck on each channel by mouth to check for airtightness. Generate suction with your mouth only, as when using a straw; *never apply suction by drawing air in with your lungs!* If you detect internal leakage, determine whether it is due to a crack in the wood or faulty sealer, and repair as necessary.

Removing Broken Screws

In player actions which have been subjected to a humid environment, it is common for screws to break off flush with a glue joint or gasket, where moisture penetrates easily. It is a wise practice to replace all of the screws in a player action if any of them are rusty, because many perfectly good looking screws with internal corrosion will break when tightened adequately during reassembly. It is far easier to replace $15 worth of screws than it is to remove a broken stump from a restored action component without contaminating new pouches and internal channels with sawdust! (See the section on hardware on pp. 94–95).

To remove the stump of a screw embedded in a piece of wood, first attempt to grasp any remaining portion of the screw with good pliers, and try to unscrew the stump. This occasionally works, but in most cases if the screw is rusted into the wood solidly enough to break in half, a tiny stub will break off too. If you can't unscrew the stump, drill a hole immediately adjacent to it, using a drill bit equal in diameter to the threaded portion of the old screw. With an awl, push the top of the stump into the new hole and back into the old one several times until it is loose enough to be unscrewed with needle nose pliers. Then repair the screwhole as described below.

Repairing Stripped Screw Holes

In many places where screw holes are stripped, the wood is thick enough that new screws of the same diameter as the old ones but ¼" longer will solve the problem. If longer screws will come out the other side or break out of the wood into internal channels, or if the hole is damaged by removal of a broken screw stump, repair the hole by replacing the wood surrounding the threads of the screw.

Illus. 5-27. In some cases, an ordinary dowel rod may be cut into plugs, but in others, it is necessary to use a plug cutter to make new plugs of the correct type of wood with the grain oriented the right way.

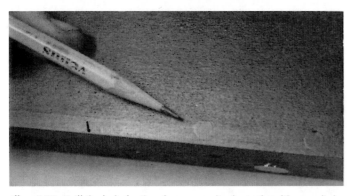

Illus. 5-28. Drill the hole for the plug perpendicular to the old screw hole; knurl the plug and glue it in with Titebond or equivalent.

Drill a hole perpendicular to the screw hole with a sharp drill bit, and using a plug cutter, make a new plug out of poplar, maple, or whatever the surrounding wood is. Knurl the plug, or file small gooves in it, to relieve the hydraulic pressure of the glue, and draw a pencil line on the end of the plug indicating the orientation of the grain. Glue the plug in place with Franklin's Titebond or equivalent, with the grain of the plug parallel with that of the surrounding wood; the pencil line will help you to orient the plug if the glue obscures the grain pattern.

If a hole for a plug enters a suction chamber, glue seal cloth over the plug to prevent leakage.

In the middle of a large surface of wood where it is impossible to drill a hole for a plug perpendicular to the screwhole, you will either have to move the screw to a new location, plugging the old hole for airtightness, or make a new wooden part. The top cover plate of an Ampico A pump is particularly prone to having most of the screw holes for the action cutoff box stripped, requiring replace-

ment of the cover. See the section on Ampico pumps in Ch. 7.

How Not to Repair Screw Holes

Never replace a screw with one of larger diameter in hopes of making it tighter. While it will *seem* tighter because the unthreaded shank will bind in the outer piece of wood, the threaded portion will be no tighter and will probably crack the inner piece of wood. Never use toothpicks or matchsticks; the sharp threads of the screw will cut them to bits, rendering them useless. Never drill out a screw hole to insert a dowel; this is no better than toothpicks because the grain is oriented the wrong way and the screw threads will shred the end grain. Never drill out a screw hole to insert a plug, even with the grain oriented properly; even with the plug epoxied in place, the screw will eventually pull the plug up into the gasket, losing all of its holding power.

Replacing Wooden Parts

It is a fact of life that many player action parts must be replaced due to disassembly damage or the butchery of a prior repair job. Most American player action parts were made of maple or poplar, with some bellows made of maple or poplar plywood; many European action components were made of European beech. When a maple or poplar part must be replaced, *use the same type of wood that was used for the original part!* Manufacturers usually understood wood and knew which type was correct for a given purpose. Of the more common lumberyard woods, pine cracks and does not hold screws well enough to keep things airtight, and oak, mahogany and walnut are too porous; so stay with poplar and maple, which are available from wood specialty shops and larger "home building centers." Although birch is a reasonable substitute for maple for some structural cabinet parts, it is more porous and requires much more sealer than maple does when used for valve blocks and other pneumatic components. When it is necessary to replace old delaminated plywood for bellows, use new high quality plywood with no internal voids, faced with birch veneer. For maximum strength, use plywood known as "Baltic plywood," "Russian plywood," or "multi-laminate European beech." Specialty plywood is available from large lumber wholesalers, although it may be necessary to find a retailer through whom to place your order. Never replace a large, spring loaded plywood bellows board with solid wood; this will invariably crack under the spring tension.

Early player actions—generally, those made prior to 1910, including many player reed organ mechanisms—had some parts such as gasketed valve box cover boards made of sugar pine. Many of these parts must be replaced because they are cracked and split. Replace them with poplar, which will last longer.

When making a new set of stack pneumatic boards, obtain a poplar board at least at thick as the pneumatics are wide, and have it surface planed *immediately prior to cutting it*, to avoid having it warp while in storage in your shop; cutting a large warped board on a table saw is dangerous because of the tendency to bind and kick back. Saw the pneumatic boards off the edge of the large board, and resaw them to the correct width if necessary. This saves having to plane a large amount of wood down to the thickness of the pneumatics. When cutting out new wind motor pneumatics, obtain a poplar board already planed down to the correct thickness (unless you own or have access to a surface planer), and cut them to size on the table saw.

After cutting out new parts, seal them with lacquer or a thick coating of shellac in the areas that were sealed on the original parts. The sealer will soak into the wood, making it difficult or impossible to glue anything to it, so avoid getting sealer on areas which will be glued down, hinged, covered, gasketed, etc.

Removing Old Rubber Cloth, Leather and Glue

Removing the decayed old materials from wooden parts is the dirtiest part of player action restoration, but it is a process which must be done with as much precision as any other step. In some player actions, the old leather and rubber cloth separates from the wood with ease, particularly if it is still relatively strong and was not glued well to begin with, but in others, the old materials tear into fragments, leaving a mess of animal glue, leather and powdered rubber stuck tenaciously to the wood. These rotten remains must be scraped and sanded from the wood without damaging or altering the size or shape of the wood itself. To make matters worse, many player actions have already been "restored" in the past, with new materials glued in place with white glue or contact cement, which is much harder to remove without damaging the wood.

Sanding Pneumatics

After measuring the span, numbering, marking the location, removing a set of pneumatics from their deck boards, and repairing the broken pneumatic boards, pull off as much of the old cloth as possible and remove the remains of the cloth hinges.

Sanding small stack pneumatics includes sanding all edges, the glued surface of the stationary board, and the area where the hinge is attached inside both boards. Most restorers use a combination belt and disc sander, sanding the long sides of pneumatics on a fine grit sanding belt, and sanding the narrow ends on a fine sanding disc, as shown

in illus. 5-29, 30. Stop often to check for possible crookedness or excess removal of wood. It is particularly easy for a beginner to remove too much wood when holding a pneumatic directly on the table of a disc sander, because in this position it is harder to feel exactly how fast material is being removed from the pneumatic. If the pneumatics have not been sanded crooked previously, try to sand off 90% of the old glue, leaving a trace of glue all over the edge of each board; this will insure that you are not sanding anything crooked. Check *every* pneumatic in *every* plane for squareness. Crooked pneumatics which have been sanded down to various sizes look terrible and are a mark of a careless, sloppy mechanic. If you are re-restoring a set of crooked pneumatics, do your best to straighten crooked edges and keep all of the pneumatics the same size, or replace them.

Illus. 5-29. Sanding the sides of a stack pneumatic. Have all of the pneumatic boards numbered prior to sanding to keep from mixing them up.

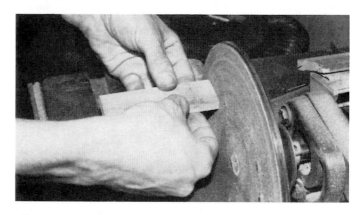

Illus. 5-30. Be very careful to sand the ends of the pneumatic straight and square.

Some rebuilders advocate gang sanding whole bunches of pneumatics, but it is difficult or impossible to hold them tightly enough to keep some boards from slipping, causing uneven sanding. For the nicest looking results, sand one pneumatic at a time.

After sanding the edges of each pneumatic, sand the glued surface of the stationary board as shown in illus. 5-31. Then sand off the remaining hinge materials and glue as shown in illus. 5-32. Hold the pneumatic very carefully to keep your fingers away from the sandpaper, and to keep from sanding a slope onto the inside surface of the pneumatic!

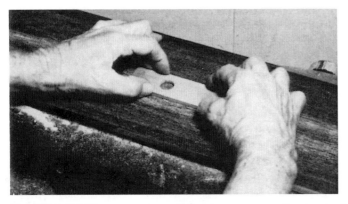

Illus. 5-31. Hold the pneumatic carefully when power sanding the glued surface to avoid sanding your fingertips!

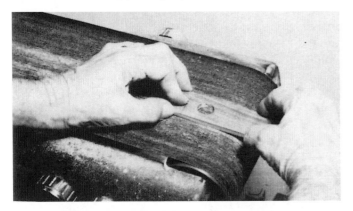

Illus. 5-32. Sanding the remains of the old hinge.

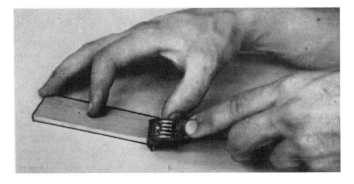

Illus. 5-33. Carefully clean the glue off of the bevelled surface.

If the sides of the pneumatic boards were originally bevelled toward the hinge end to enhance flexibility of the pneumatic, gently clean this area as shown in illus. 5-33. Be careful not to exaggerate the bevel, making the area where the cloth will be glued too small.

Run a narrow paint scraper over all four inside edges of each pneumatic board, and around the glued side of the hole, removing all traces of sharp glue, as shown in illus. 5-34.

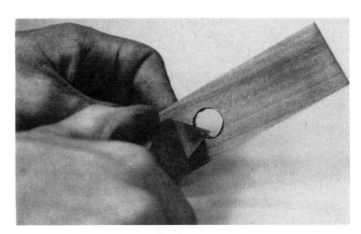

Illus. 5-34. Cut the bead of hardened old glue away from the inside of the pneumatic and the hole with a small paint scraper or knife blade.

It is a good idea for the beginner to practice sanding a set of pneumatics *without* built in fingers before advancing to those with fingers.

If you have replaced any of the stationary boards with new ones, pair them with orphaned moveable boards, number both parts and sand them just like old pneumatics. This will insure that both boards for each pneumatic are the exact same size.

Sanding Large Bellows

Cleaning larger control pneumatics and bellows is similar to cleaning small stack pneumatics, but on a larger scale. Unfortunately, the rubber in some old bellows cloth turns to fine powder, and the weakness of the rotten cloth causes it to delaminate in small pieces instead of coming off the wood neatly. Fortunately, old cloth and animal glue chars at a much lower temperature than wood does, so the judicious use of heat can be very helpful in its removal. If a lot of old shredded bellows material remains on a large piece of wood, try scorching it and the old glue with a pencil flame burner on a propane torch turned down to the lowest possible setting. With extreme care, you will be able to turn the remaining glue and other material to a crunchy black crust, which you can then remove by relatively gentle scraping with a small paint scraper, with absolutely no damage to the wood. *Don't try this for the first time on a small delicate part!* Gain your initial experience on a large bellows with an area covered with old glue which is much larger than the area heated by the flame. When you can do this reliably *without darkening the color of the wood*, graduate to somewhat smaller parts. Scorching the glue is also helpful if you don't want to use a belt sander or can't use one for a certain application; with the old glue turned into a charred crust, you can scrape it off easily with a small paint scraper. Because of all the fine, highly flammable particles of wood, glue and cloth which will surround your work, keep a damp towel and container of water handy just in case a spark lands in the wrong place. It is also advisable to use a respirator with filters suitable for smoke, to keep from inhaling irritating or toxic fumes.

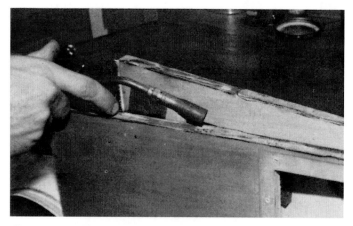

Illus. 5-35. Scorching the old hot glue without scorching the wood takes a little practice, but it makes the job of glue removal easier.

Some rebuilders prefer an old iron, set at the maximum heat, for broiling old glue, leather and cloth. If you try using one, be careful not to spread sticky old glue and other materials around on clean wood with the charcoal-covered sole plate of the iron!

Scraping the edges of large bellows is probably the safest way for a beginner to clean them, and it is the best way to remove most of the old material after using a torch, but experienced rebuilders finish the job by sanding all four edges on a fine sanding belt, just like sanding the long edges of a small pneumatic. Learn to "float" the board in the air immediately above the sanding belt, and then carefully lower it so the entire surface touches the belt at once, being careful not to let the moving sanding belt drag the wood. It is good practice to move large parts around on the surface of the sanding belt; this provides tactile feedback regarding where the most material is being removed, and it also prevents the belt from gouging the work piece. Since it is usually too cumbersome to sand both boards of a large pumping bellows at the same time, be very careful to sand each board identically so they are both the same exact size when you are done.

After sanding the edges of each board, scrape or sand the old glue from the hinge spacer block, being careful not to

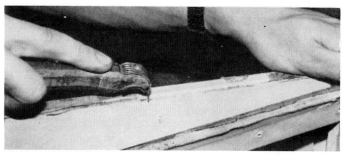

Illus. 5-36. With careful use of the torch, clean white wood will appear after the glue is removed with a narrow paint scraper.

alter its shape, and remove the old glue from the gasketed or glued surface where the bellows is fastened to the trunk. Then remove all sharp edges of glue with a scraper. This is a good time to double check for delamination of plywood bellows boards; insert Franklin's Titebond glue or equivalent and clamp as necessary. Be sure to remove all glue which oozes out, or it will prevent the hot glue from holding the new bellows cloth on the edge of the wood.

Removing Old Gaskets and Their Glue

After disassembling a component and exposing its gasketed surfaces, make note of the location, width and thickness of each gasket. The thickness is particularly important in valve boxes in which there is a gasket between the pouch board and valve chamber. Changing the thickness of gasket also changes the distance between the valve stem and pouch, and installing a new gasket which is too thick or too thin will make the pouch/valve stem clearance excessive or insufficient. Disassemble any other removable parts such as top valve seat plates, valves, mechanical linkages, etc., and lay them aside.

Pull as much of the old gasket as possible off the wood by hand, then try to scrape more of it loose with a sharpened putty knife or chisel, being careful not to cut into the wood. If the remains are negligible, sand the wood carefully on a stationary belt sander until 90% of the old glue is gone. By leaving a trace of old hot glue in place, you will know that you haven't removed any wood. Then *gently* finish sanding the piece, with *very little pressure on the component*, until the last trace of glue is gone. As when sanding bellows, move the work piece around on the sanding belt to keep from sanding too much wood in one spot. After you gain experience with the sander, you will be able to sand all of the old glue off more quickly, but until you feel comfortable with the power and speed of a belt sander, take it easy! More damage has been done to player action components and the ends of fingers by careless power sanding than any other single repair procedure.

If large pieces of old gasket stubbornly resist removal by pulling or scraping, broil the old leather and glue with a pencil flame propane torch or iron, using the same precautions as when heating old bellows material as described above.

Illus. 5-37. Be gentle when scraping around holes; it is very easy to dig into the wood, ruining the flat surface.

When scraping the wood surrounding a hole, be careful not to dig in to the narrower portion, removing too much wood, as shown in illus. 5-37. If you keep your scraper sharp, you will be able to control the amount of material removed without using as much pressure.

Removing Glue from Other Parts

When it it necessary to sand glue or old finish off of the side of a valve block or other component which is made of several layers held together with screws, sand the entire component prior to disassembly to insure even sanding of the entire surface.

Illus. 5-38. When scraping old glue or sealer out of pouch and valve wells, scrape in the direction of the four arrows to keep from digging into the wood.

Illus. 5-39. If the right size drill bit is available, drill the old glue out of the pouch well without removing any wood. A Forstner or multispur bit is preferred, but it is possible to do this job with a new flat high speed wood bit with the point removed.

Many pouch boards are flat and may be sanded all at once on a stationary belt sander, but other pouch boards and many unit pneumatics and unit valves have countersunk pouch wells. Remove glue from these wells with a narrow paint scraper or chisel. A better alternative for a rebuilder who owns a drill press is to obtain the correct size Forstner bit, multispur bit or even high speed flat wood boring bit with the point broken off, and drill out the old pouch material and glue without removing any wood, as shown in illus. 5-39.

Removing old White and Aliphatic Resin Glue

White and aliphatic resin glue is much harder to remove from wood than old hot glue is, because the heat generated by sanding it with a power sander causes it to melt just to the point at which it turns into a soft sticky mess. The best

way to remove either type of glue is to heat it a little bit at a time with a torch, and scrape most of it off *while it is still hot* with a *very sharp* paint scraper! Perform this smelly job with excellent ventilation, preferably with a suitable respirator. Anyone with any common sense who ever has to endure removing large amounts of old white or aliphatic resin glue from old deck boards or pumping bellows will never contemplate using this glue for anything that ever has to be taken apart and sanded!

Dissolving Old Glue

Some technicians who are not equipped or experienced to do careful woodworking enjoy removing old glue with water, acetic acid, white glue (*white glue??*) or other liquids. Needless to say, wooden parts warp when exposed to water and the wood fibers soften and deteriorate when soaked with acid. For the best, quickest results, stay with scraping and sanding.

PNEUMATICS AND BELLOWS

Pneumatics and bellows come in all possible sizes and shapes, from tiny Schulz pouch pneumatics to large pumping bellows. Every pneumatic and bellows must be hinged and covered with materials which are flexible enough to permit freedom of movement but strong enough to provide great endurance. The following section begins with a description of hinge materials and techniques, continues with pneumatic and bellows covering techniques, and ends with detailed descriptions of the many types of cloth and leather which are used for covering pneumatics and bellows.

Hinges

The ideal hinge for a pneumatic or bellows is strong, doesn't stretch, stays glued to the wood, holds the boards together to prevent wobble, and is flexible enough to permit completely free movement. The idea that a thinner hinge is necessarily better than a thicker one is a fallacy. In any suction-operated pneumatic or bellows, the hinge material should be thicker than the covering material, to provide adequate clearance between the two boards at the hinge end. Without this clearance, the pneumatic will pinch the covering material every time it collapses, making it hingebound and wearing the covering material prematurely.

Hinging Small Pneumatics

The best material for stack pneumatic hinges is "pillow ticking" available from well-stocked fabric stores. A thin glue-absorbent canvas, this material resembles heavy *cotton* blue jean denim, but has alternate blue and white

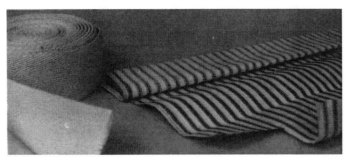

Illus. 5-40. The best hinge materials are white reed organ pedal webbing and cotton pillow ticking, for large and small bellows and pneumatics, respectively. Never use rubberized material for hinges, which makes them stiff

stripes. Make sure the material you purchase is really cotton, which absorbs hot glue and stays stuck; thin polyester material is available with the same striped pattern, but this is totally useless for hinges.

Illus. 5-41. First cut the hinge material into strips, then cut and fold it into individual hinges. (Shown right to left.)

To make hinges for small pneumatics, decide on the dimensions so you can cut the material into strips, fold the strips from end to end and then cut the folded strips to the width of the individual hinges. An advantage of using striped pillow ticking is that the stripes can be used as a cutting guide, eliminating most of the measuring.

Illus. 5-42. The width of a hinge should equal the width of the pneumatic board between the two bevels

First, decide how wide to cut the long strips; their width will determine the *length* of the folded hinges, as shown in illus. 5-41. The *length* of an unfolded hinge is usually about the same as the *width* of the pneumatic, but is rarely less than ¼″ nor more than 1½″. Cut a long strip of ticking, fold it in half lengthwise and iron the fold to

crease it. Then cut it into pieces a little narrower than the width of each pneumatic; if the inside surfaces of the pneumatic boards are bevelled toward the hinge end to provide folding room for the cloth, make the hinges the same width as the remaining unbeveled portion of wood, as shown in illus. 5-42. Cut pieces of waxed paper *wider than the pneumatics*, and insert one in each folded piece of hinge material; this will prevent the two halves of the hinge from sticking together during gluing.

Illus. 5-43. Apply glue to both pneumatic boards.

Illus. 5-44. Quickly lay the hinge in place

Pick up both halves of a pneumatic as shown in illus. 5-44, quickly but accurately lay a thin coating of hot glue across the hinged area of each board, press a hinge on one board in the precise location shown in illus. 5-42, and grasp the waxed paper as shown in illus. 5-45. Quickly place the other board on the hinge, press the two boards together and wipe excess glue out with your fingernail. Then place a spring clamp on the pneumatic, and double check all the way around the pneumatic boards to make sure the clamp does not cause them to slide out of alignment. Inset the hinge from the tail end of a small pneumatic by about 1/32″ to insure that it won't stick out after the glue is dry, but do not inset a hinge any more than this, or the pneumatics will be hingebound.

As with any hot gluing operation, keep a dish of warm water, a damp rag and a dry rag on hand to clean your fingers *every time you get glue on them*, to keep from spreading glue all over everything!

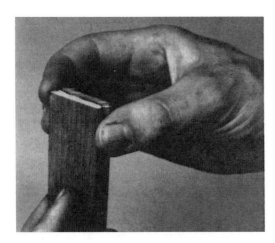

Illus. 5-45. Pull the waxed paper down to hold the hinge in position, and press the other board on the hinge.

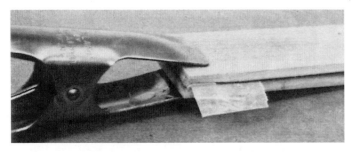

Illus. 5-46. After positioning the spring clamp on the pneumatic, recheck to make absolutely certain that the boards are still aligned

Keep the pneumatics in order as you install the hinges; when you run out of clamps, you can go back and unclamp the first three or four pneumatics, putting them all in one clamp, and freeing several clamps for reuse. Again check each pneumatic to make sure the clamp does not push the boards out of alignment.

Some rebuilders lay the pneumatic boards flat on a table with the hinge ends touching each other, brush glue onto the boards, lay the hinge material on the glue, and wait until it dries before folding the pneumatics shut. This expedient saves time but causes loose wobbly hinges because a certain amount of hinge material is torn loose from the glue when the pneumatics are folded shut for the first time.

Some stack pneumatics, such as Simplex, did not have internal hinges, but relied on the strength of the cotton rubber pneumatic cloth and hot glue to hold the boards together. While this system worked for Simplex, the author has seen many pneumatics recovered with no internal hinges which have pulled apart. Until you are experienced in covering pneumatics, always install internal hinges whether the pneumatics had them or not.

Double Hinges

Small pneumatics which are subjected to unusual stress - such as hinge springs—originally had the advantage of added strength provided by the cotton rubber cloth covering the outside of the hinge. When these pneumatics are recovered with nylon cloth (polylon or bilon) and PVC-E glue, the new cloth does not reinforce the hinge, because the plastic glue does not soak into the fabric, allowing the hinges to pull apart and wobble. If you use nylon cloth and PVC-E glue to recover small pneumatics which have hinge springs, such as Duo-Art stack pneumatics and orchestrion snare drum pneumatics, always install inside *and* outside hinges made of pillow ticking and glued with hot glue prior to covering the pneumatics. A double hinge is shown in illus. 5-47.

Illus. 5-47. Always install a double hinge - an outer hinge and an inner one—in pneumatics with hinge springs or which are otherwise subjected to unusual stress

Hinging Medium Size Bellows

Many wind motor pneumatics and small control pneumatics were originally double hinged. Replace both the inside and outside hinges of small and medium size pneumatics with pillow ticking. Always replace outside hinges in pneumatics which originally had them, and always double hinge wind motor pneumatics which will be covered with nylon cloth and PVC-E glue. Whenever you plan to install an outside hinge, glue the inside hinge in place first, and orient the clamps along the sides of the bellows if possible so the outside hinge may be installed while the clamps are in place. This will help to keep the outside hinge flat, and the glue for both hinges will be dry at the same time.

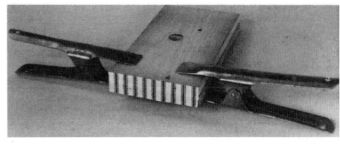

Illus. 5-48. If you clamp the inside hinge of a medium size double-hinged pneumatic as shown here, you can apply the outside hinge immediately so the glue for both hinges can dry at the same time

Old Aeolian wind motors have double "see-saw" pneumatics, with the two boards of each pneumatic hinged with a narrow strip of leather. In many wind motors these old hinges are still strong and airtight, but if they are bad, replace them with suitable firm leather with a suede surface on both sides. Measure the size of the hinge carefully before removing it, to preserve the correct separation between the two boards. Carefully remove the old leather from the slot in the wood with a hacksaw blade, without altering the shape of the slot, and install the new piece of leather with hot glue.

Gulbransen wind motor pneumatics have similar hinges made of a piece of leather wrapped with thin rubber cloth, but the moveable board swings between two stationary boards. As in old Aeolian wind motors, some Gulbransen hinges are still good, but if you find a bad one, replace it as described above.

Many Amphion and Ampico bellows are hinged with narrow strips of ticking alternating from the outside of one board to the inside of the other, as shown in illus. 5-49. If installed carefully, this type of hinge is strong and flexible, with no tendency to wobble. The author replaces crisscross hinges in pneumatics which originally had them, but uses ordinary hinges otherwise.

Illus. 5-49. Medium and large Amphion pneumatics and bellows typically have criss crossed hinges as shown. Glue the new hinge pieces to the inside surface of each pneumatic board and let the glue dry; then clamp the boards together and glue the hinges around the edges of the boards.

Rehinge medium size bellows such as pedal pneumatics, wind motor governors and expression regulators with white "reed organ pedal webbing," a tightly woven material used for connecting pump organ pedals to the pumping bellows, sold by piano supply companies. The process for making and installing the hinge is the same as for small pneumatics, except that C clamps are necessary when a bellows is too big for available spring clamps. Pedal webbing is much thicker than the pillow ticking used for small pneumatics, so apply an extra thick layer of hot glue to the wood prior to laying the hinge in place.

Hinging Large Bellows

Just like the hinges in control pneumatics, the hinges in large pumping bellows and reservoirs were made in several different ways, with mattress ticking (a thicker version of pillow ticking) or pedal webbing, inside only, inside and outside, criss-cross, or in various combinations. Installing these hinges is similar to installing hinges in medium size control bellows, but due to the large size, hot glue must be spread with extra speed to keep it from setting up before the boards are assembled. Pedal webbing is usually the ideal material for inside hinges, and if a large bellows originally

had both inside and outside hinges made of pedal webbing, replace them with the same material. When hinging large bellows, extra care must be taken to keep the boards from slipping out of alignment when the large C clamps are tightened. It is usually helpful to insert a block of wood between the boards at the open end, equal in thickness to the hinge wedge, and to use a C clamp at the open end to keep the boards aligned.

Illus. 5-50. Standard pumps are reinforced with ropes in addition to the usual tough hinge material.

Many Standard and Autopiano pumps had the hinges reinforced with pieces of rope which were glued and dowelled into holes in the boards, in addition to the usual inside and outside hinges, as shown in illus. 5-50. While it is possible to omit the ropes, it is a nice added touch to replace them for extra strength. Carefully drill out the old dowels and pieces of rope, clean the slots which accomodate the rope in the wood, sand new dowels to a blunt wedge shape on one end, and pound them in with hot glue to secure the new ropes into one board. Use cotton rope, which will absorb the hot glue. Clamp the wood to keep it from splitting. After the glue dries, clamp the two boards together, and secure the ropes with more dowel wedges in the second board. Finish by cutting off the excess dowels with a sharp chisel, being careful not to cut into the new ropes.

Some reed organ pumps and reservoirs are hinged with strips of leather; if you wish to use this instead of pedal webbing, use split cowhide with suede finish on both sides similar to the leather used for large gaskets.

What *Not* To Use for Hinge Material

Since the three important attributes of a good pneumatic hinge are flexibility, strength, and the ability to remain glued down, any material which does not posess all three characteristics should not be used. Any material containing rubber, such as motor cloth or bellows cloth, has the same effect on a hinge as adding an unwanted spring, and should *never* be used. Avoid materials which stretch a lot; they will continue to stretch after being glued inside a pneumatic, allowing the boards to separate or wobble. Likewise, fabrics which do not absorb glue are unsuitable. While self-adhesive hinge material is available, the author has never seen any self-adhesive material which didn't lose its adhesion or turn into a gummy mess within a short time.

Covering Pneumatics and Bellows

The many different types of pneumatic and bellows used in automatic pianos require a wide variety of covering materials, depending on size and shape, whether absolute airtightness is necessary, whether the covering should be rigid or perfectly flexible, how well the covering must stick to the wood, if springs are used or not, whether durability is the most important attribute, and other factors. For example, in some instances, bellows cloth wears out prematurely, requiring the use of leather; in others, leather is not airtight enough, requiring the use of bellows cloth. In general, larger bellows are covered with thicker materials; material which is too thick causes a pneumatic to be stiff, while material which is too thin is not strong enough. Obviously, no single material is best suited for all applications, so the size and other characteristics of each pneumatic or bellows must be taken into consideration when the covering material is chosen. The following discussion begins with instructions for covering pneumatics and bellows, continues with detailed descriptions of many commonly available materials with their recommended uses and adhesives, and ends with a summary of types and sizes of pneumatics with their recommended materials.

How to Cover Small Pneumatics

After finishing all of the preliminary work on a set of pneumatics—measuring the span, removing the fingers, marking, numbering and removing the pneumatics from the decks, repairing/replacing, cleaning and rehinging them—they are ready to be covered. Properly covered pneumatics must meet certain criteria. The two boards should be perfectly aligned, and the cloth should have no wrinkles. The pneumatic should be completely flexible. When the pneumatic is pulled open forcefully by hand, the cloth should be *evenly* taut all the way around. Any areas which become stretched will prevent the pneumatic from opening properly and have the potential of wearing out prematurely. The pneumatic should not be *hinge bound* due to excess glue or incorrect hinging. In fact, a pneumatic which is covered correctly with cotton cloth should be flexible enough to fall open and shut *under its own weight.*

Every pneumatic and bellows should have an internal stop cushion, to prevent it from clamping a hard crease in the cloth; the original pneumatic cloth which lasted the longest seems to be that which never received a sharp crease. (Of course, other factors such as the quality of the material and environmental pollution also enter into the longevity of rubber cloth).

After reading this section, including the detailed infor-

Illus. 5-51. Any pneumatic which closes completely when it operates needs an internal stop cushion to prevent the cloth from wearing out quickly. Exceptions are stack pneumatics which are prevented from closing completely by a stop rail on the stack or piano action.

mation describing all of the types of cloth which are available, decide what type of pneumatic cloth to use. For your first player restoration, you will probably choose ordinary thin cotton rubber cloth and hot glue. Pneumatics which are covered correctly with hot glue and rubber cloth are significantly more flexible than with any other type of glue. With experience you might switch to nylon cloth and PVC-E glue for a possibly more durable job, but for now, learn to cover pneumatics using the easier materials.

During the covering process, you will get glue on your fingers, the scissors and the jig. To keep from getting glue all over the pneumatics as well, keep a dish of warm water, a damp rag and a dry rag handy, and keep your fingers and tools meticulously clean.

The first step in covering pneumatics is to tear or cut the covering material into slightly oversize pieces. Most rubber cloth can be torn to size more quickly and accurately than it can be cut; some material tears equally well in both directions, while other material tears down its length but not across its width. In many cases, the end of a piece of rubber cloth as it arrives in the mail is not parallel to the "grain" or weave of the fabric, resulting in a crooked line the first time you tear it crosswise. Rather than wasting a large piece of cloth, begin by measuring about an inch in from the end, cutting a small incision with scissors and tearing this strip off. Grasp the material firmly and rip it forcefully, as when tearing a plastic bag off the roll at the produce counter in your grocery store. (If you try to tear the cloth gently, it probably won't tear straight.) This will either straighten the end so all subsequent tears will be parallel to the first one, or it will demonstrate that the material should be cut—at least crosswise—instead of torn. Next, unroll the cloth and make an incision at a point equal to the length of one pneumatic strip, which is equal to the perimeter of one pneumatic plus ½" for overlap at the hinge end. Tear this piece off, lay a ruler against the end, and mark the width of the strips, which will equal the original span of the pneumatic plus ¼" extra. (The span is the dimension shown in illus. 5-52). If you have a large enough cutting board, mark the strips with a knife; if you don't, use a ball point pen and scissors. Then tear all the strips apart.

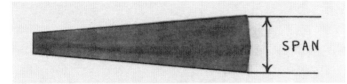

Illus. 5-52. The span of a pneumatic.

To insure that all pneumatics have the same span, use a "pneumatic covering jig," which is nothing more than a spacer which is inserted between the two boards. The handy jig shown here is an adjustable version marketed by certain piano supply companies, although if you plan to restore only one or two player pianos, you can make a simple non-adjustable jig for each job out of a piece of plastic or other non-absorbent material. Whatever sort of jig you use, adjust its width so when it is inserted snugly between the boards of a pneumatic, the outside span will be correct.

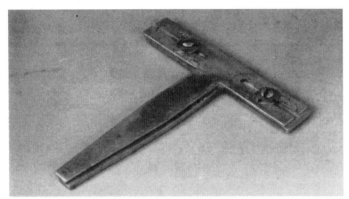

Illus. 5-53. One type of pneumatic covering jig, sold by supply companies. Other more complicated gadgets are also available, but the simple jig shown here is the most efficient.

After adjusting the jig, fold one strip of pneumatic cloth in half lengthwise and gently crease it, to mark the middle. Lay the strip on your workbench, with the long dimension running sideways, and stick a piece of masking tape to the bench at each end of the cloth. Center a pneumatic on the

Illus. 5-54. By placing masking tape markers on your bench, you will be able to center the jig perfectly over each piece of pneumatic cloth without measuring or guessing each time.

cloth, insert the jig, and stick another piece of tape on the bench to mark the position of the jig (illus. 5.-54). Now you are ready to cover a set of pneumatics.

Lay a strip of cloth between your marks on the bench, lay the jig in place, and pick up a pneumatic, holding it as shown in illus. 5-55. Apply a thin smooth layer of hot glue across the end of each board with a short, stiff brush, and press the pneumatic onto the cloth, making sure that the boards are touching the jig. Don't spread the glue with your finger; the cloth will spread it for you. With a little practice you will learn just how much glue to apply; if you use too little, you will be able to peel the edge of the cloth loose after it is trimmed, or if you use too much, an abundance of glue will squeeze outside and inside the pneumatic. Glue which oozes toward the inside of a pneumatic will form a sharp edge which will wear through the cloth. Carefully withdraw the jig, hold the pneumatic gently by one board and rock that board perpendicular to the bench, to press it flat against the cloth. Then gently hold the other board and rock the pneumatic the other way. Always rock the pneumatic toward the outside, to squeeze excess glue away from the inside. From now on the pneumatic must be manipulated without placing any stress on the boards which might cause the cloth to slip or become wrinkled. Gently lift one free end of the cloth with one hand while inverting the pneumatic with the other, and *lightly* press on the cloth to spread the glue and stick the cloth to the wood. Lay the pneumatic aside on its open end until the glue dries for a few minutes. When you become proficient at covering pneumatics you may omit this drying time.

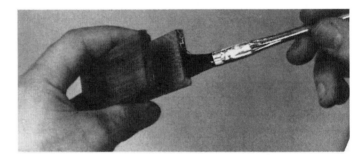

Illus. 5-55. Apply a smooth layer of glue to the end of each board.

Illus. 5-56. Press the pneumatic onto the cloth.

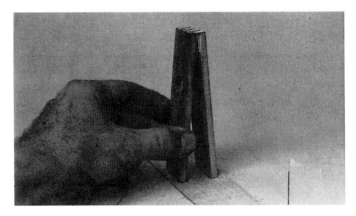

Illus. 5-57. Withdraw the jig, and rock the pneumatic first onto one board and then the other to press the cloth onto the wood.

Lay the pneumatic on one side, gently pulling the cloth flat underneath the pneumatic. Apply hot glue to each edge, pull the cloth straight to eliminate buckling, and with a wiping motion straight down the length of the pneumatic, secure the cloth to the wood. Gently rub to spread the glue, turn the pneumatic over and repeat the process on the other side. As you rub, first wipe along the inside edge, and then wipe again with more pressure toward the outside, forcing excess glue away from the inside edge of each board. After the glue sets a little but before it gets hard, nick the corners with a sharp scissors as shown in illus. 5-60, *being careful not to cut into where the cloth covers the wood.*

Illus. 5-58. With the cloth under the pneumatic pulled flat so it doesn't disturb the already glued open end, apply glue to the edges of the side facing up, and press the cloth into place.

Before the glue hardens, trim the excess cloth from the open end and both sides with *sharp* scissors, again being careful not to pull or stretch the cloth. By trimming *before* the glue turns hard, you will be able to do a neat job without gouging the wood. Note that there is a right way and a wrong way to hold the blades of the scissors against the wood, as shown in illus. 5-61 and 5-62. Held correctly, the

Illus. 5-59. Repeat the process for the other side.

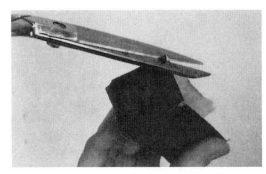

Illus. 5-60. Cut the cloth at the four corners to permit it to lay flat while the glue is drying. Be careful not to nick the corner of the pneumatic.

cutting edge of the stationary blade presses the cloth against the wood, and the moving blade snips the cloth off like a paper cutter. Held incorrectly, the rounded edge of one blade is between the cutting edge and the material, causing sloppy trimming. A bandage scissors with the bulb ground off the end makes a good pneumatic trimming scis-

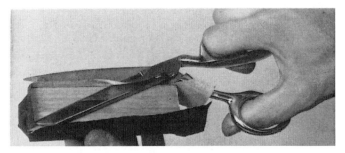

Illus. 5-61. The right way to hold the scissors against the wood when trimming a pneumatic.

Illus. 5-62. The wrong way to hold the scissors against the wood.

69

sors, as the angle of the blades makes them easy to hold against the edge of the wood.

Cover and trim the open end and sides of each pneumatic, laying the pneumatics in a row as you finish this step, and let them dry for a few hours.

When the glue is completely dry, you are ready to cover the hinge ends. If a pneumatic is in the open position while the cloth is glued on the hinge end, the cloth will have to stretch each time the pneumatic closes, causing it to be hingebound. To prevent this, tie each pneumatic shut with a rubber band while gluing the cloth on the hinge end. The rubber band won't leave an impression on the cloth if the glue is completely dry.

Illus. 5-64. With a rubber band holding the pneumatic shut, glue the first half of the hinge.

Illus. 5-63. Left: correctly folded pneumatic cloth. Right: incorrectly folded cloth.

Illus. 5-65. Trim the first half of the hinge, and glue the second half.

Close each pneumatic, coaxing the cloth into the proper shape as it folds. The internal stop cushion will prevent the cloth from receiving a hard crease, possibly prolonging the life of the material. If you cut the strips of cloth and positioned the jig on the pneumatic accurately, the two tails of cloth will be the same length, just long enough to overlap ½". Fold one over to see how much wood it covers, apply glue to that much wood, and press the cloth in place. Repeat this procedure for several pneumatics, until the glue on the first one begins to set but before it turns hard. Then go back to the first one, trim the first half of the hinge and glue the second half. Depending on your trimming skill, either put the pneumatic back in your assembly line long enough for the glue to set, or trim the second half immediately. You will learn just how long to let the glue dry for your own individual working speed, and you will have a row of pneumatics in various stages of completion as you work. When you finish a pneumatic, lay it aside, leaving the rubber band on it until the hinge glue dries. Remove the rubber bands promptly after the glue dries, and store the pneumatics in the open position until you are ready to glue them on their decks.

The various steps of covering your first pneumatic might take a total of fifteen or twenty minutes excluding the glue drying time between steps, but after your tenth pneumatic you should gain a little speed, and after you do several sets you should begin to feel comfortable. Most experienced restorers can cover a set of ordinary stack pneumatics with cotton rubber cloth and hot glue *neatly* in approximately

six hours, after cleaning and hinging them. Speed without loss of accuracy will come as you become proficient with several skills: learning to be gentle with the cloth to keep from pulling it out of line after it touches the glue on the wood, learning to apply precisely the right amount of glue on the wood, and learning to trim one whole side of a pneumatic with one snip of a sharp scissors without pulling the cloth out of line. Don't forsake accuracy for speed; covering a set of pneumatics correctly is just as important as any other step of a restoration, and it only represents a small fraction of the total time involved.

Illus. 5-66. A completed pneumatic. The cloth is perfectly smooth and unwrinkled all the way around, the edges are trimmed neatly without any gouges in the wood or rough edges of glue, and the pneumatic easily falls open and shut under its own weight.

To cover pneumatics with built in fingers, cut a square hole — a little larger than the width of a finger — in a piece of plywood and attach runners to the bottom to hold it up off the bench, as shown in illus. 5-67. After ripping strips of new cloth about ¼" wider than the pneumatic span and ½" longer than the pneumatic perimeter, hold each pneumatic over its strip and cut a small slit on each side of the finger, as shown in illus. 5-68. Make each slit the same length, just a little longer than the pneumatic board is *thick*, and make sure the distance between the two slits *precisely* matches the width of the finger. Since the fingers might be slightly different widths after cleaning off the old glue and cloth, use each pneumatic to slit the finger tab for its own strip of cloth. Cover the pneumatics just like ordinary ones, but place the strip of cloth with the slit tab over the square hole in the board, and apply a bead of glue to the open end of the pneumatic *including the finger where the cloth tab will cover it*. Carefully press the pneumatic onto the cloth, aligning the finger precisely between the two slits, pick the pneumatic up and rub the cloth, including the little tab which is now laying against the finger, being careful to keep the cloth flat and unwrinkled without pulling the cloth or the moveable board of the pneumatic off to one side. Like any other tricky procedure, you will get better with practice. If a pneumatic ends up having wrinkles in the cloth, remove the cloth and glue before the glue dries, and start over.

Covering unit pneumatics is just like covering any other pneumatics, except that a lot more preparatory work is

Illus. 5-69. Press the pneumatic onto the cloth with the finger extending down into the hole in the jig.

Illus. 5-70. The tab of cloth on the finger should lay flat. If necessary, apply a tiny drop of glue to each corner of the tab to make it airtight.

Illus. 5-67. A board with a square hole in it forms a simple jig for covering pneumatics with built in fingers.

Illus. 5-68. Slit the cloth for each pneumatic individually to account for fingers of slightly different sizes.

necessary: remove the finger, top valve seat and valve for cleanup, sand the whole pneumatic with the old hinge intact (if possible), separate and sand off the old hinge, split the pouch block off the valve chamber, renew any sealer on inside surfaces, replace the pouch, reglue the pouch block, gently sand off the small bead of new glue, blow the sanding dust out of the valve well without damaging the pouch, and hinge the pneumatic. (Whew!) Perform one step on all of the pneumatics, then procede to the next step. This saves a lot of time and helps to insure that you won't forget a step here and there on one pneumatic. The geometry of many unit pneumatics is such that the span of the cloth is much wider than it looks at first glance. Lay one pneumatic on its side and measure as shown in illus. 5-71; add ¼" and tear one strip of new material. Hold the pneumatic open to the correct span, lay the open end on the cloth, and wrap the cloth around the pneumatic to make sure you have made the cloth big enough. Then tear the whole set of strips.

If the unit pneumatics which you are covering have gaskets on the hinge end (Simplex, Coinola, late style Gulbransen, etc.), overlap the cloth ¼" on one *side* of the pneumatic toward the hinge end, instead of the usual ½" on the *hinge end,* as shown in illus. 5-72. This will permit the gasket to lay flat. Mark your working surface for the ends of the strip of cloth and pneumatic covering jig so the overlap occurs at the correct point on the side of the pneumatic. Glue the overlapping cloth with just enough glue to get the job done; an excess amount will be pinched between the boards when the pneumatic closes, causing it to be hingebound.

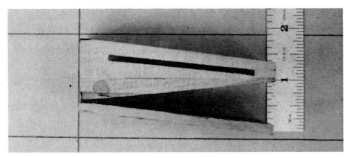

Illus. 5-71. Although the span of the open end of this Simplex unit pneumatic is only 1⅛", the cloth must be torn to a little over 2" due to the geometry of the pneumatic.

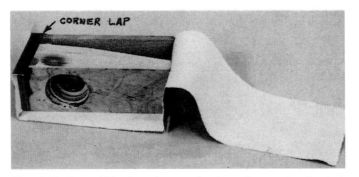

Illus. 5-72. To avoid having a lump under the gasket, overlap the cloth ¼" on the side as Simplex did originally.

To cover pneumatics with nylon cloth and PVC-E glue, increase the amount of time that you wait for the glue to set between steps. This doesn't have to slow your pneumatic covering job, because you can set up an assembly line with a few pneumatics waiting for the glue to set for each successive step, instead of gluing and trimming the open end and both sides of a pneumatic all at once as a professional does with cotton rubber cloth. PVC-E glue always remains somewhat rubbery, and nylon cloth is more difficult to trim neatly than cotton rubber cloth, but with practice and a sharp scissors it is possible to do an equally neat job. As you proceed with each step of covering, warm the cloth and glue with an iron to help the glue to set.

The above procedures may be used on stack, wind motor, automatic tracker, regulator, control and all other pneumatics up to six or eight inches long. (Refer to pp. 75–78 for recommended materials for various sizes of pneumatics). When using double weight motor cloth, try tearing a small strip to see if it tears neatly. If not, cut it with a scissors or knife. The larger the pneumatic, the wider the

Illus. 5-73. The cloth on this Hupfeld Phonoliszt Violina wind motor pneumatic was glued poorly and is falling off.

excess cloth should be; tear or cut the cloth for a large sustaining pedal pneumatic ½" wider than the span instead of the ¼" extra allowed for small pneumatics.

Hinge Springs

Many small pneumatics, including some Duo-Art stack pneumatics, have hinge springs as shown in illus. 5-74. If you reuse the original pneumatics, keep the springs in order and mark the location of each spring hole prior to recovering to facilitate correct reassembly. If original steel springs are rusty, make new ones of the same diameter music wire. If the originals are in bad condition and are made of phosphor bronze, brass or some other material, either obtain identical wire, or replace it with smaller gauge steel piano wire. To determine the right diameter replacement wire, press an original pneumatic with its spring in place on a postal scale, and measure the ounces or grams of force necessary to collapse the pneumatic. Check several pneumatics and take an average. If a stack has several sizes of pneumatics with hinge springs, take an average reading of several pneumatics of each size, in case the strength varies from one size to the next. Experiment with various sizes of new wire until you find the size which duplicates the strength of the original.

Illus. 5-74. A hinge spring of the type used in some Duo-Art grand stack pneumatics, most orchestrion xylophone pneumatics and others.

Illus. 5-75. Adjust each hinge spring so it doesn't pull the pneumatic off to one side like this.

Gluing Stack Pneumatics to Deck Boards

Before gluing a set of pneumatics onto the decks, test each pneumatic and each channel in the deck boards for airtightness. Prepare a new batch of hot glue, and make sure you can see all of the alignment marks on the deck boards plainly. Find the amount of pneumatic overhang in your notes, and set a combination square so the ruler sticks out this amount from the square. Lay the pneumatics for one deck in order, upside down, and heat the deck board with an iron. When the deck is warm, place the iron on the first pneumatic and apply glue to the deck. Press the warm pneumatic onto the deck, hold the end of the combination square ruler squarely against the deck and use the square to determine the correct overhang and to make the open end of the pneumatic square with the deck. Apply a spring clamp. By warming the wood, you will increase your working time. Make sure the clamp does not push the pneumatic out of alignment. If your hot glue is the correct thickness and if you work fast enough, the pneumatic will quickly stick to the deck. If it slips around as if on a soft rubber cushion, remove it, remove the glue and start over. Leave the clamp on each pneumatic for an hour or so.

If your hot glue is too thick, the pneumatic will feel spongy when you press it to the deck, and an abundance of thick glue will squeeze out. If the glue is too thin, none will squeeze out, the pneumatic might leak and might fall off. If you use too much glue, it might run down into the deck, or if you turn the deck over before the glue is dry it will run into the pneumatics.

After the glue dries overnight, test each pneumatic for airtightness once more. By taping off the feed hole in the deck or plugging it with your thumb, it should be impossible to pull the pneumatic open with your other hand.

If pneumatics or decks are too large for spring clamps, either use C clamps or press each pneumatic down for a minute by hand, returning to press the previous two or three pneumatics down after gluing each subsequent one. Hand clamping will work only if the pneumatics and decks are absolutely flat.

For illustrations of gluing pneumatics to decks, refer to the Gulbransen section in Ch. 6.

Covering Double Pneumatics

Some double pneumatics were originally covered with two pieces of cloth, and others with just one. Some pneumatics covered with a single piece of cloth are shaped so the cloth does not have to be slit down the middle of the sides of the center board; others require a slit. To be safe, if a pneumatic looked neat before you removed the old cloth, duplicate the method which was used originally. Refer to the Gulbransen section of Ch. 6 for step-by-step photos of the recovering of a wind motor double pneumatic. In any double pneumatic with an internal hinge, (as opposed to Ampico grand tracker pneumatics which have *external* hinges) cover the ends of the hinge with pouch leather, stopping the cloth short by ⅛", as shown.

See p. 101 for information on Aeolian see-saw wind motor pneumatics.

Covering Large Bellows

Always use hot glue for covering large bellows, to spare the next rebuilder (who might be you!) the horrible job of removing white glue from the edges of large boards. Make your hot glue thicker than for any other use, because the cloth or leather used for covering large bellows absorbs quite a bit more glue than thinner cloth does.

Illus. 5-76. This bellows is ready to have the cloth glued to the open end. The boards are held to the correct span with the narrow strip of wood temporarily tacked to one side with small brads.

Because of the difficulty in positioning the open end of a large bellows on a piece of cloth accurately, it is easier to invert the bellows and place the cloth on it. Tack a small strip of wood on one side of the bellows to hold the correct span while you cover the open end, and spread the glue with a stiff brush approximately equal in width to the edge of the board you are covering. Be careful not to drip glue inside the bellows. Some restorers favor gluing the cloth with one thinner coat of glue, peeling it back a few inches at a time and applying another coat of glue, although one layer of thick enough glue accomplishes the same thing in half the amount of time. Whether you apply one or two

Illus. 5-77. To melt the hot glue into the cloth and wood, iron the cloth with the iron set no hotter than the glue pot, to keep from scorching the glue. After the glue dries, bellows cloth or leather which is glued to wood correctly with hot glue will tear before pulling loose.

coats of glue, iron the cloth after securing it to the wood, with the iron set no hotter than the temperature of the glue pot. After covering the open end, wait for the glue to set, and trim the edges before it turns hard. If the bellows originally had the corners secured with small tacks, install a new #2 carpet tack at each corner, but never use rows of tacks or staples from one end of a bellows to the other.

The fastest and neatest way to trim thick cloth or leather is with a new single edge razor blade. Pull on the loose end of the cloth with one hand opposite to the direction you are cutting with the other, and guide the blade carefully to keep from cutting into the wood. Trimming leather will dull the sharpest blade quickly, so have a good supply of single edge razor blades on hand; professional rebuilders who use them purchase them by the hundreds. Some manufacturers apparently trimmed large bellows by waiting until the glue was dry and then running a coarse sanding block or file over the edge, leaving a rough edge on the wood and a frazzled edge of cloth. While some restorers use this method, it is slower and sloppier than using a razor blade to trim the cloth before the glue turns hard. After each bellows is covered, wash off any hot glue with a damp rag, and touch up the edges with a black marking pen if necessary.

Illus. 5-78. Trim heavy cloth or leather on a large bellows with a new single edge razor blade, pulling on the loose end of cloth in the opposite direction with your other hand as shown.

Illus. 5-79. Stiffeners are necessary in most large pumping bellows to prevent the cloth from buckling in and out during playing.

Large pumping bellows contain internal and external flap valves and usually have cardboard stiffeners glued to the inside of the cloth or leather. (These stiffeners are sometimes incorrectly referred to as "gussets"; a gusset is actually the flexible leather corner of a large wooden-ribbed pipe organ reservoir). To prepare for covering bellows with stiffeners, disassemble and clean them, replace the internal flap valves, and rehinge the boards. Moving the bellows around on the workbench might damage the outside flap valves, so install them after the bellows are covered. Many old cardboard stiffeners may be separated from the old cloth by peeling the cloth back, removing only a thin layer of cardboard. If you can preserve the original stiffeners, re-use them, noting their original positions on the cloth. Draw a center line down the length of the new strip of bellows cloth, (or an appropriately off-center line if one bellows board is thicker than the other) and glue the stiffeners to it with hot glue, carefully turning the material over to iron the stiffeners in place. Let the glue dry, and then glue the cloth to the bellows one edge at a time. Glue the material to the edge of the wood so the edge of the stiffener is snug against the wood *when the bellows is folded shut*. If the stiffener is too close to the wood, the bellows will be stiff; if it is too far from the wood (if there is too much cloth between the edge of the stiffener and the wood), the stiffener will pop in and out during pumping. Draw the lines and glue the stiffeners carefully and symmetrically to avoid making the bellows stiff; a pumping bellows which is covered with ordinary bellows cloth should be just as limber whether it contains stiffeners or not.

Illus. 5-80. Gluing a strap of pedal webbing across the open end of a reservoir with internal springs makes it easier to install the springs. The strap also relieves stress on the bellows cloth, possibly helping it to last longer.

To cover reservoirs which have strong internal springs, clean and rehinge the boards, and glue and tack a piece of pedal webbing across the open end to limit the opening to the correct span. Let the glue dry overnight, and then install each spring in the original location. The strap of webbing not only will facilitate the installation of the springs; it will also take most of the spring tension off of the rubber cloth, possibly increasing its life span.

To cover bellows which share one large stationary board, as in some player pianos and most reed organs, the only difference from regular covering is that the cloth glues onto the surface of one board instead of its edge. The first time you tackle such a pump it might look intimidating, but with careful measuring and gluing, it is possible to turn out a neat job. If there is room enough to tack a narrow slat of wood over the cloth between the two bellows, do so as insurance against its coming loose, but be sure the slat won't interfere with mounting the pump in the piano or organ.

It is customary for professional restorers to cover player piano and reed organ pumps with bellows cloth, and to cover motor driven reproducing piano, coin piano and orchestrion pumps with leather. (For further information, refer to the following section on various kinds of cloth and leather). When covering a large bellows with leather, seal the inside of the leather with several thin coats of rubber cement or one coat of PVC-E glue, followed by a thorough dusting with talcum powder. To apply the glue in the right place, glue the leather onto the open end of the bellows, lay the bellows over onto each side, and draw the outline of the inside of the boards on the leather with a ball point pen. Apply masking tape along the outside of the lines, brush the sealer onto the leather, let it dry, remove the tape, and cover as usual, being careful not to glue coated leather onto the wood (which won't stick).

Pneumatic and Bellows Covering Materials

Each piano and organ supply company has its own name for various weights of pneumatic and bellows cloth; material called "medium bellows cloth" in one catalogue might be called "heavy bellows cloth" in another. Refer to the *Vestal Press Resource Catalogue* for names and addresses of supply companies, and obtain a current catalogue and packet of pneumatic cloth and leather samples from each supplier (available for a small fee) when deciding what materials to order. Many supply companies sell wholesale only; their products must be ordered through a technician who already has an account with them.

Don't get too excited about every new material that comes along just because it's new and different, but don't refuse to use something just because it's new either. The most innovative newcomers to the rebuilding field switch from one material to the next each time any supplier promises a new discovery; the most traditional, conservative rebuilders won't try anything new. The best course to pursue

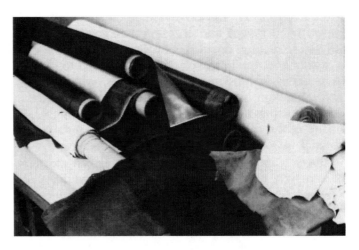

Illus. 5-81. The novice faces a bewildering array of materials for covering pneumatics and bellows. The following text will help to sort out the right material for each job.

is a middle one of intelligent, cautious experimentation. If a material is durable, airtight and sticks well, stay with it, but be open minded about possible improvements. Suppliers of rubberized cloth, tubing, etc., receive a lot of criticism from experienced rebuilders because of price, quality and lack of consistency. While some piano supply companies seem to purchase whatever their manufacturers sell them, regardless of quality, others really do try to provide durable materials. Remember, the supply companies have to rely on *their* suppliers, and many player piano restoration materials are so specialized that it is hard for supply companies to get the same identical product twice in a row. An old saying in the field is "if you like a particular type of pneumatic cloth, order enough to last for a *long* time, because next time you try to get some it won't be available."

Imported Materials

A note to readers who are convinced that the "finest imported materials" advertised at a slightly higher price by some supply companies are necessarily special: some European suppliers sell "the finest imported American materials," while some American suppliers sell "the finest imported European materials." Shipping bellows cloth across the Atlantic Ocean does not necessarily make it superior!

Cloth

Single weight rubber cloth ("pneumatic cloth"). Finely woven cotton cloth coated with a thin layer of rubber on one side, approx. .006"-.009" thick. Known everywhere simply as "pneumatic cloth," this is the old standby for ordinary stack pneumatics and other pneumatics up to about 2" wide and from about 2" to 6" long. It is also used for pouches in a few player pianos, including many Gulbransens and early Amphions, where absolute airtightness is desired, and where extremely low suction levels are not used. It is too thin to be durable enough for use on wind motors and accessory pneumatics, and too stiff for use on tiny "pouch pneumatics" such as those used in Schulz and Apollo players. It is also too stiff to be used for pouches in most reproducing pianos, which require rapid repetition of notes played at extremely low suction levels. The finer the weave of the cloth, and the higher the quality of the rubber, the more flexible and durable this material is. Good quality rubber coating feels somewhat "rubbery," and when applied to finely-woven cloth can be very thin, providing excellent flexibility and durability. Beware of rubber which may be pulled loose from the cloth or which cracks within a few weeks after being folded. Use hot glue; this cloth is traditionally glued down with rubber facing out.

Single weight nylon rubber cloth. Finely woven nylon cloth coated with a thin layer of *rubber* on one side. Marketed for a number of years as an alternative to ordinary single weight rubber cloth; not in production at the time this is being written, but mentioned to familiarize the reader with it in case it is encountered in a previously restored piano or in case it becomes available again. Most rebuilders glue the nylon side down, with the rubber facing out as in ordinary cotton rubber cloth; use PVC-E for gluing the nylon side, or hot glue for gluing the rubber side.

Schulz pouch cloth. Specially woven synthetic cloth covered with a very thin layer of rubber; approx. .005" thick. Made specially for covering Schulz pouch pneumatics (see the section on Schulz in Ch. 6), and other tiny pneumatics which are too stiff if covered with any other single weight cloth. PVC-E glue recommended.

Single coated nylon cloth ("polylon"). Thin, finely woven nylon, coated with thin layer of polyurethane on one side; approx. .004"-.005" thick. Resembles the material used for light weight raincoats but is completely airtight. Various colors are available from various suppliers. Used on stack pneumatics as an alternative to single weight rubber cloth, it has proven to be more durable than some brands of rubber cloth since it was introduced around 1970. The best quality material is quite flexible, but does not stretch when tugged diagonally. Use PVC-E glue only.

Double coated nylon cloth ("bilon"). Thin, finely woven nylon with a thin coating of polyurethane on both sides; approx. .005" thick. Used as a very durable pneumatic cloth where extreme flexibility is not necessary. Difficult to glue down around corners of small pneumatics, this is at its best when used on pneumatics at least 1" wide by 4 ½" long. The most durable, flexible cloth for wind motors. Use PVC-E glue only.

Double weight rubber cloth ("motor cloth"). Two layers of finely woven cotton cloth with a thin layer of rubber sandwiched in between; total thickness approx. .012"-.014". The traditional cloth for covering wind motors; particularly well suited to motors with large pneumatics such as old Aeolian, Duo-Art and 4 point Bald-

win and Kimball. Stiffer than bilon for smaller motors. The finer the weave and the harder it is to pull the two layers of cloth apart, the better the quality. If you want to use this on wind motors with small pneumatics—narrower than 2½"—try to find the thinnest available material. Also used for hammer rail pneumatics, small sustaining pneumatics, wind motor governors and other pneumatics between approx. 2½" x 6" and 4" x 8". Use hot glue.

Double weight nylon cloth ("nylon motor cloth"). One layer of finely woven nylon, and one layer of cotton or other absorbent material with a thin layer of rubber sandwiched in between; total thickness approx. .009". Marketed as a more durable alternative to ordinary motor cloth. The quality of this material has varied from mediocre to fine, with the poorer variety unwilling to stick to wood regardless of what glue is used, and the best variety really excellent for covering medium size bellows which receive constant hard use, such as Duo-Art expression regulators. If you decide to use this, experiment with various glues to see which sticks the best for you. Do not use this cloth on wind motors; it tends to remember the position where the motor last stopped, causing the motor to turn unevenly.

Light bellows cloth. Two layers of cotton cloth with thin layer of rubber between; total thickness approx. .020"-.030". Thickness and stiffness is between that of motor cloth and medium bellows cloth. Good for small reservoirs, large governors, sustaining pneumatics and other bellows between approx. 4" x 8" and 6" x 10". Use hot glue only.

Medium bellows cloth ("fuzz-back", "flannel back"). Two layers of medium weight cloth with thin layer of rubber in between; total thickness approx. .040". The inside layer of cloth is usually fleecy, hence the name. The old standby for covering pumping bellows and reservoirs in pedal-operated player piano pumps. Wears out quickly if used on motor driven reproducing piano and nickelodeon rotary pumps, which should be covered with leather. Use hot glue.

Heavy bellows cloth. Two thick layers of cloth with thick layer of rubber in between; total thickness approx. .045"-.050". Intended for use only on large organ bellows; some of this material encountered by the author is so stiff that if it is used on most player piano pumping bellows, the pedal return springs will not push the bellows all the way shut, decreasing the pedal stroke in some instances to half of what it should be. Really large bellows such as orchestrion pressure reservoirs, large band organ pumps, etc. should be covered with leather, not heavy bellows cloth.

Reed organ bellows cloth. One thick layer of cloth with rubber coating on one side, like the cloth originally used in reed organs; available in several thicknesses. Some restorers use this for the large pumping bellows and reservoirs in reed organs, while others use fuzz back bellows cloth. Not for use in player pianos. Use hot glue only.

Polyurethane Sheeting ("Perflex")

For several years during the early 1970's the latest "advancement" in the field of player piano and pipe organ restoration was "perflex," a thin transparent layer of polyurethane promoted by several suppliers as the perfect material for replacing pouches and covering small pneumatics. Unfortunately, within a few years of its introduction most of it had come unglued, stretched out of shape, and developed holes all across its working surface. It is no longer sold by major suppliers; if you find any in a stock of old supplies, discard it!

Leather

Pouch leather ("pneumatic leather," "tan pneumatic leather"). Thin tan or white leather available only from piano and organ supply companies, not leather shops. The old standby for most pouches; thickness varies from .010" for small primary pouches in reproducing pianos to .035" for covering pipe organ pneumatics. Very flexible, not as airtight as rubber cloth. Read information on pouches and bleeds on pp. 82–85 prior to changing from zephyr skin or rubber cloth to pouch leather, or vice versa. Use hot glue.

Cabretta. Available from piano and organ supply companies, and some well-stocked leather shops. Used by organ technicians for covering medium size pneumatics. Not recommended for player piano use because it stretches and splits, allowing the outer surface to move around after the inner face is glued down, making it messy, hard to work with, and not airtight enough.

Chrome tanned calf skin and cow hide ("garment leather"). Pre-stretched, relatively airtight, sticks well, extremely durable. The old standby for covering reproducing piano, coin piano, orchestrion and band organ pumps. Available from some organ and piano supply companies and large leather specialty shops; ranges from small skins approx .020" thick for covering medium size control and percussion pneumatics in orchestrions, to medium size skins approx .045" thick for covering small motor-driven rotary pumps, to skins which are half the size of a cow, approx .060" thick, for covering large band organ and orchestrion pumps. When shopping for this leather, make sure it doesn't stretch, and can't be peeled into two layers. Fold it over twice to see how thick and stiff it will be at the corners of a bellows. If it is too hard and stiff, it will be hard to glue, won't fold well and will wear out prematurely at the folds; if it is too soft and fuzzy it will stretch too much. Hold it up to sunlight to make sure it isn't full of pinholes. Watch for cattle brands and scars which will wear out or leak. The unfinished side should be moderately fuzzy, not extremely hairy (indicating that the leather will stretch and split) nor extremely smooth (indicating that it won't stick well to hot glue). Often available

in many colors; traditional rebuilders favor black or dark brown, although if the correct thickness is available only in a bright color, it may be used where it can't be seen, as inside a boxed-in Duo-Art or Ampico rotary pump. Use hot glue.

Alum tanned sheepskin. Available in various thicknesses from piano and organ supply companies. Not airtight enough for vacuum actions in player pianos, reproducing pianos or orchestrions, but widely used in pipe organs and for covering small and medium-size *pressure operated* bellows, such as band organ bass drum control and beater pneumatics. Also used for pallet valves in reed organs and orchestrion pipe chests. Use hot glue.

Zephyr skin. Extremely thin animal intestine sometimes used for covering pouch pneumatics in Schulz player pianos. Very sensitive, airtight and responsive, but it shrinks and swells with humidity changes like a skin drum head. Modern zephyr skin splits easily into several layers, and is hard to glue, so it is not the preferred choice of most rebuilders. If you try it, use hot glue, and after the glue is dry, add a thin layer of hot glue *on top of* the glued down portion of zephyr skin to help prevent it from splitting or coming loose.

Summary by Size of Pneumatic or Bellows

Tiny Pneumatics
(up to approx. ¾" wide x 2" long)

Cover Schulz and other pouch pneumatics which were originally covered with extremely thin rubber cloth with "Schulz pouch cloth" glued with PVC-E. Zephyr skin may be used instead, providing that it is glued down well with hot glue. Cover Apollo pouch pneumatics and others which were originally covered with leather with the thinnest available pouch leather, glued with hot glue. Cover Seeburg and Operators (Coinola, Reproduco) tiny spring-loaded setoff pneumatics with ordinary rubber pneumatic cloth, with hot glue. (These are the tiny pneumatics which convert vacuum output signals from the piano stack to atmosphere input signals to the pipe chest or xylophone).

Small Pneumatics
(approx. ¾"—2" wide by 2"—6" long)

Cover piano stack pneumatics with single weight rubber pneumatic cloth glued with hot glue (for traditional appearance and reasonably good durability, depending on the brand of the cloth), or with polylon glued with PVC-E (for better durability). For maximum durability, cover stack pneumatics which are at least 1" x 4½" with bilon, using PVC-E glue; bilon is too stiff for pneumatics which are smaller than this. In pianos with several sizes of stack pneumatics, (such as some Duo-Art grands), use the same type of cloth on all of them.

Cover small pneumatics located on the outside of expression mechanisms, pipe chests, percussion actions, etc. with pneumatic cloth or polylon; use pouch leather to cover pneumatics originally covered with leather, which are located inside organ pipe chests.

Medium Pneumatics (approx. 2"—4" wide by 4"—8" long)

Cover wind motor and automatic tracking pneumatics with motor cloth and hot glue (for traditional appearance), or with bilon and PVC-E (for maximum durability and smoothness of operation). Cover small wind motor governor, expression, hammer rail, rewind/replay, shutoff and other control pneumatics in home player pianos and reproducing pianos with motor cloth and hot glue (for flexibility and traditional appearance) or with nylon motor cloth and PVC-E (for greater durability). Cover Duo-Art accordion pneumatics with pouch leather and hot glue (for traditional appearance) or with polylon or bilon and PVC-E (for durability, and to reduce stretching). Cover medium size bass drum beater pneumatics, automatic rewind pneumatics, hammer rail pneumatics, expression regulators, etc., in coin pianos and orchestrions with thin chrome tanned calf skin and hot glue for maximum durability.

Medium Bellows (approx. 4"—6" wide x 6"—10" long)

Cover large governor and sustaining pedal pneumatics and other medium size bellows in player and reproducing pianos—such as Duo-Art expression regulators—with light bellows cloth and hot glue for traditional appearance, or with nylon motor cloth and whatever glue works the best for possible greater durability. Cover bellows of this size in coin pianos and orchestrions—including small vacuum reservoirs, pump bellows, large bass drum beater pneumatics, etc. with medium thickness chrome tanned cow hide and hot glue.

Large Bellows (over 6" wide and 10" long)

Cover player piano pumping bellows and reservoirs with medium weight bellows cloth, and cover the bellows in motor driven pumps with chrome tanned cow hide. The author has never encountered any modern bellows cloth which will last for more than a few months of heavy commercial use on a motor driven pump. If a home player piano will receive heavy use, apply sheepskin patches over the corners.

Illus. 5-82. To reinforce the corners of the pumping bellows - usually the first thing to wear out in a player piano—cover them with 1¼" diameter sheepskin punchings.

What Causes Pneumatics and Bellows to Wear Out?

The life span of pneumatic and bellows cloth depends on two equally important factors: how well it *ages*, and how well it *wears*. A material might wear well—showing no breakdown after a million cycles in a testing device, for example—but if it doesn't last for more than a few years because of changes in its internal chemistry due to aging, it shouldn't be used in a player piano. Conversely, a material might last on the shelf for 50 years, but if it breaks down after a bellows operates 100,000 times, it shouldn't be used either. (100,000 repetitions might sound like a lot, but considering that one note toward the middle of the keyboard can play over 100 times during the playing of one roll, playing 1000 rolls shouldn't cause the pneumatic cloth to show signs of wear).

While the only practical way to judge how well a material will *age* is to compare it to how other similar looking materials have aged in the past, certain controllable mechanical factors enter into how well a material will *wear*. If rubber or other materials are under constant stress, they wear out sooner; if a pneumatic is covered incorrectly with the cloth stretched tight in some places and loose in others, the stretched portions of the cloth will deteriorate prematurely. If pneumatics are allowed to collapse all the way, pinching the folds of the cloth together, the cloth will wear out rapidly along the folds, but this will not happen if internal stop cushions or external stop rails prevent the pneumatics from closing all the way. Similarly, the cloth used in pianos in which the pneumatics hang all the way open sometimes deteriorates faster than the cloth on pneumatics which rest on a support rail, preventing them from opening all the way. While it is acknowledged that the Aeolian Company used finer quality rubber cloth in their old player and reproducing pianos than many other companies did, the fact that Aeolian stack pneumatics neither hang all the way open (when not playing) nor collapse all the way (when playing) probably also contributed to the unusual longevity of the cloth. Before you condemn a material which failed prematurely, be sure it wasn't subjected to unusual stress due to improper installation, abuse or environment.

What *NOT* to Use for Covering Pneumatics and Bellows

Experienced rebuilders are constantly amazed at the variety of strange pneumatic and bellows covering materials encountered in previously repaired player pianos. These materials range from from pieces of flourescent orange hunter's jackets to vinyl upholstery material; they are usually not airtight and are almost always too stiff. Suffice it to say that if a material is not sold specifically by piano and organ supply companies for pneumatics and bellows, don't use it! Naugahyde and other materials which are available from fabric shops might last for years wrapped around the padded armrest of a reclining chair, but they will crack and fall apart within a few weeks of use on a pumping bellows!

GASKETS

Many suction operated mechanisms have two or more pieces of wood screwed together with gaskets in between, permitting disassembly for servicing. Ideally, a gasket keeps a component airtight as long as the parts are screwed together, but permits disassembly without damage to itself or to the wooden parts. In climates where the humidity is high in the summer and low in the winter, wooden parts shrink slightly during the dry season, causing enough air leakage through gaskets to affect performance of the player action. To combat this, many player action manufacturers glued each gasket to one piece of wood, and coated the mating piece of wood with a layer of thin shellac prior to assembly. With the gasket glued to one piece of wood and stuck to the other with shellac, it effectively prevented leakage even when the screws became slightly loose in the winter.

Leather Gaskets

When the correct non-splitting suede calf skin is glued to one piece of wood, with the other piece of wood coated with shellac prior to assembly, it is possible to disassemble the gasketed joint months or years after initial assembly by prying the shellacked board off of the gasket, without damaging the board or the gasket. The advantages of suede calf skin are its long life, authentic appearance, and airtightness through moderate seasonal humidity changes while allowing disassembly and reassembly without any damage to the gasket or surrounding parts. It also has just the right amount of softness; when parts are screwed together, the leather compresses a little, forming an airtight seal, but when the parts are disassembled, before the shellacked board pops loose, it pulls the nap of the leather up, providing softness and compression for reassembly. There are only two "disadvantages" of using suede calf skin. It takes a certain amount of experience to find a good leather shop and to select suitable skins of leather which are uniformly thin, will not split, will not stretch too much, and stick well. Also, it takes a certain amount of practice to make neat leather gaskets, because leather is somewhat more difficult to cut than cork and other materials. Careful practice, however, will result in consistently neat, long-lasting and airtight gaskets. Suede calf skin gaskets are the choice of experienced professional restorers.

Other Types of Leather

Sheepskin and cabretta are used widely for gaskets in pipe organs, where a certain amount of seepage is considered acceptable. These types of leather are not suitable for suction operated mechanisms because even when sealed to the opposing surface with shellac, they leak during dry seasons. If sealed, they also tend to split during disassembly, necessitating their replacement whenever a component is serviced. The author has encountered any number of otherwise well restored orchestrions which get weak or die completely during dry seasons for no other reason than seepage through their sheepskin or cabretta gaskets.

Making and Installing Leather Gaskets

Obtain the thinnest available split suede calfskin in an appropriate shade of tan, rust or white from a large leather supply shop or piano or organ supply company. Do not use leather which has a shiny finish on one side; the finished side will not stick if glued down, nor will it seal if it faces out.

Always cut leather on a cutting board with a sharp knife; never use scissors, because it is impossible to cut a perfectly straight line in leather with even the sharpest scissors. A long basswood board obtained from a lumber specialty store makes the best cutting board, because the grain is parallel to the length of the wood, and the wood is hard enough to support the leather but soft enough that it doesn't dull the knife. If you always cut with the grain, a piece of basswood will last for a long, long time. A sheet of masonite does not make a good cutting board because with each cut, more material flakes off the surface, resulting in a

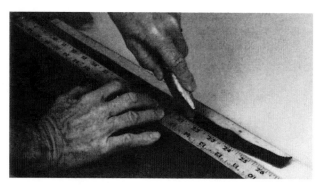

Illus. 5-83. A basswood cutting board has straight, parallel grain which makes it easy to cut straight lines. It is impossible to make neat gaskets with a scissors.

Illus. 5-84. To locate holes in a gasket, chalk the holes in the wood and press the leather against the chalk. Then cut the holes out with an appropriate punch.

crumbling, rough surface. The hardness of the glue in masonite also causes the knife blade to dull faster. Never use plywood or any other wood which has a pronounced grain pattern; this will deflect the knife, making it impossible to cut straight lines.

Gaskets which cover an entire surface of a piece of wood are usually made of one piece of leather. There are several ways of making new one-piece gaskets, depending on the size of the wood and whether or not the leather has holes in it. To gasket a small block of wood which has no holes in it, simply cut an oversize piece of leather, glue it to the wood, iron it with the iron set at the same temperature as the glue pot, let the glue set, and trim the edges before the glue becomes brittle. Orient the piece of wood on the cutting board so you cut with the grain, hold the knife steady, and pull it smoothly along to keep from slicing into the edge of the wood.

If a gasket has holes in it, measure and cut the leather to size before gluing it to the wood. To make a small gasket, press the piece of wood on the leather firmly enough to make an impression of the perimeter, lay a straightedge along the impression and cut the leather with a knife. If the gasket is larger than 6″ in either dimension, measure the size of the wood and transfer the measurements onto the leather with a ruler, and then cut the leather out. Lay the wooden part on your bench face up, rub chalk on the holes, and lay the precut gasket exactly where it will be on the wood. Press the leather against the chalked holes, carefully lift it off, and cut the holes out with appropriate squeeze, tube or arch punches. Then apply hot glue to the wood, lay the gasket in place, and press it with a warm iron. You have used the right amount of glue if a tiny, barely visible amount squeezes out around the edges. After the glue sets but before it hardens, check every hole and remove any collars of glue with a small knife or awl. If you don't, the screw will bind when installed, possibly cracking the wood. Careful chalking, marking, punching and gluing will produce factory-perfect gaskets.

Large pieces of wood are rarely completely covered with leather, but instead have a gasket running around the pe-

rimeter. To replace perimeter gaskets, measure the width of the old leather all the way around; in some cases, one strip is wider than another because of the size of the mating piece of wood. Cut a straight edge on one side of your skin of gasket leather, and then mark the width of the strips with ball point pen marks, one mark every four or five inches down the strip. Hold a 12″ steel ruler tightly on the leather and cut from one mark to the next, moving the ruler along as you go. If you measure carefully, press down hard enough as you cut, and hold the knife at the same angle from one end of the strip to the other, you will produce perfectly uniform strips. A new knife blade cuts leather easily with little downward pressure; excess pressure required by a dull blade causes sloppy results. Glue the strips with the ink marks toward the wood so they won't show. If it is necessary to splice long strips of leather in the middle, make a 45° cut for artightness, and match the ends of the leather for thickness to avoid a lump.

After cutting the strips, decide how you will join them at the corners to avoid having to glue the last piece *between* two previously glued pieces. Since the strips will stretch a little as you glue them down, it is impossible to fit one piece perfectly between two others. Instead, glue the first

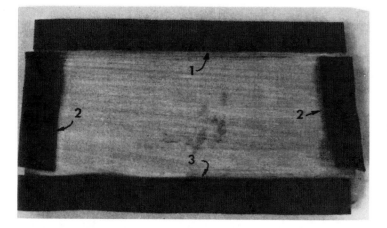

Illus. 5-85. Plan your perimeter gaskets so the last piece will cap off both corners. This produces a neater gasket than if you try to fit the last piece between two other pieces.

piece so it runs all the way across the wood; butt the next two pieces against it, trim them and cap them off at the other end. Illus. 5-85 shows the correct sequence for applying perimeter strip gaskets. When butting one piece of leather against another, be sure that the edges make good contact for an airtight seam. Apply the hot glue thin enough so it doesn't ooze up into the seam, spoiling the leather when you iron it. After the glue dries completely, try to pull the leather up. If you used the hot glue correctly, either the leather will tear or the wood will split.

If a perimeter strip has screw holes, which is usually the case, chalk the holes in the wood and carefully lay the strip in place. Press down on one end, smooth the leather out toward the other end and press on each successive screw hole as you go. Don't worry about the starting end of the leather pulling away from the end of the wood a little; as you smooth and press the leather from one screw hole to the next, the gentle stretching will closely duplicate the actual stretching which will occur when you glue the leather. Punch the chalk marked holes, and glue the leather a few inches at a time, ironing it as you go. Look ahead, and stretch or squeeze the leather a little if necessary to make each screw hole perfectly centered.

Illus. 5-86. Neat new gaskets. The corner joints are invisible and perfectly flat, the screw holes are all in the right places, and the edges are straight and flush with the edges of the wood.

Pouch Leather Gaskets

Some small components have thin pouch leather gaskets. When replacing these, mix your hot glue very thin to prevent it from oozing onto the face of the gasket when ironed.

Cork Gaskets

Cork was used as a gasket material by many player piano manufacturers. The best cork gasket material is reasonably airtight, if the components are screwed together very tightly, but cork leaks badly during dry seasons if it is not stuck to both surfaces. If it *is* stuck to both surfaces with the glue/shellac technique described above, as in Ampico A actions, it breaks into several (or hundreds of) irregular

pieces when disassembled, preventing reassembly without replacing the gasket. To solve this problem, some manufacturers such as WurliTzer used no shellac but instead installed strong compression springs with washers on the screws in an attempt to keep the wood squeezed together during seasonal humidity changes. Unfortunately, the springs were so strong that today many valve chests incorporating them have all of the screwholes stripped, requiring major wood replacement to make them airtight again.

The advantages of cork gasket material, which make it popular among inexperienced rebuilders, include its uniform thickness, easy availability and relative ease of cutting and punching, as compared with leather. Its disadvantages include its general leakiness between the particles of cork, its tendency to leak even more during dry seasons unless it is stuck to both surfaces (requiring replacement of the gasket after disassembly) or assembled with compression springs (which cause wood to crack and screwholes to become stripped), and the difficulty of removing old cork residue from wood in preparation for installing new gaskets. It is not the choice of experienced rebuilders.

In the Ampico B, well-designed springs hold the cork-gasketed parts together, helping them to remain airtight through humidity changes without shellac sealer. Also, some of the gaskets are faced with rubber cloth to make them even tighter and to keep them from sticking to the mating surface. This is one player action in which cork gaskets are acceptable, if an airtight variety of cork is used.

Blotter Paper and Cardboard Gaskets

Blotter paper valve chest gaskets leak badly during dry seasons because they have almost none of the resilience that good leather gaskets have; even if they are stuck to both surfaces, they tend to split and leak between laminations. Non-splitting cardboard gaskets were typically glued to both pieces of wood, with the edges of the cardboard sealed with a coat of shellac; these are airtight, but it is necessary to destroy them in order to disassemble the parts. Old paper and cardboard gaskets are the hardest of all to remove from wood when it is necessary to replace them, so these materials are not recommended for valve chests.

Many wooden ring type upper valve seats (i.e. Amphion) are gasketed with blotter paper rings. For this use, blotter paper is excellent; replace these as necessary with new blotter rings available from certain suppliers, or make your own from blotter paper obtained from an office supply or art supply store.

Other Materials

Sponge materials such as foam weatherstripping and closed cell neoprene lose all resilience within a short time of being installed as gaskets, and once they are compressed they not only stay compressed and leak, but they are also very difficult to remove from the wood, particularly if they have a self-adhesive backing, which combines with the gasket and wood to form a sticky, gooey mess. Other materials which should never be used for gaskets include "artificial leather," automotive gasket material, cardboard tablet backs, and silicone or any other type of caulking compound. Some varieties of cork/neoprene composite gasket material are somewhat more airtight than cork, but they still possess the drawbacks of cork. Learn to use the best quality leather for gaskets, and you will have the best results.

Pneumatic Deck Gaskets

In some player actions, the pneumatics are glued to the deck boards with a layer of thin pouch leather (old Aeolian), newspaper (Cable Co.) or cheesecloth (Amphion) in between, so the pneumatics can be removed without damage to either the pneumatics or the decks. Most player actions do not have these deck gaskets, and without them, it is still possible to remove the pneumatics as described on pp. 52–53 without damaging the deck boards. If you decide to install new deck gaskets, be sure the leather or paper which you use is thin and cohesive enough that it is perfectly airtight and will not split, allowing the pneumatics to come loose from the decks during fortissimo playing.

Sealing Gaskets

Never coat gaskets with oil or grease in hopes of making them more airtight. Never saturate them with liquid silicone in hopes of extending the life of leather which should be replaced; this will cause future gluing problems. Never run caulking compound, hot melt glue, rubber paint or other sticky materials around the edges of gaskets. Gaskets are either airtight or they are not, and running something sticky or gooey around the outside edges as a remedial action is a sign that the technician lacks the interest and patience to do the job right. The correct way to seal gaskets, as described above, consists of shellacking the mating wooden surface (*not the leather!*) prior to assembly.

Cheating

Although a conscientious restorer carefully repairs every stripped screw hole in a player action as described on p. 59, there are occasions where an otherwise perfectly good, intricate, hard-to-make piece of wood has a flanged connector attached to it in a location where it is impossible to repair the stripped holes without replacing the entire piece of wood. On such occasions it is permissible to apply a bead of PVC-E glue or other sealer around the perimeter of the gasket to make it airtight, if stress applied to the connector by the weight or stiffness of a hose won't pull it loose

from the wood. If absolutely necessary, apply a *tiny* bead of PVC-E directly on the gasket, recognizing that you will have to replace the gasket any time you have to disassemble the connection. Resort to cheating only in places where it is impossible to repair the screw holes, and where it would be ridiculous to make an entire new wooden assembly.

EDGE SEALS

Some player actions, such as old Aeolians, are assembled without gaskets. Instead, the seams which occur where wooden parts are joined have seal cloth glued over them. In other actions, including some by Hupfeld and Welte, the edge seams have paper glued over them. This method of assembly produced a long-lived airtight component, but the seal cloth or paper must be cut and replaced in order for the component to be serviced. When restoring an action which had seal cloth or paper, replace it with the same kind of material, with hot glue, so the replacement material and glue may be removed again in the future.

POUCHES AND BLEEDS

Pouches

Player piano manufacturers have used three materials for pouches: pouch leather (pneumatic leather), pneumatic cloth, and zephyr skin. Polyurethane sheeting (perflex) has also been used, but as discussed earlier, this material should never be used for *anything*.

The correct operation of a pouch and valve depend on the amount of bleed. (The word "bleed" is commonly used both as a noun identifying the brass bleed cup and also as a noun indicating the suction passing through it). Too much bleed causes a valve to be sluggish in turning *on*, while too little bleed makes the valve sluggish in turning *off*. The amount of bleed required for optimum valve repetition is dictated by the size of the tracker bar hole and the size of the pouch; given these two non-variable factors which are built into a player action, the correct amount of bleed is determined by the size of the bleed orifice and the porosity of the pouch material. Zephyr skin and rubber cloth pouches are completely airtight, but leather pouches are somewhat porous; airtight and non-airtight pouches require different size bleeds. Conversely, the size of the bleeds in a valve chest dictate the type of replacement pouch material.

In many old players including Ampico reproducing pianos, the leather pouches were sealed with one or more coats of very thin liquid rubber cement, rendering them airtight for a number of years. This treatment is not permanent, and when notes become noticibly sluggish the rubber must be renewed. See "sealing leather pouches" below.

Many pouches still look good, and appear to have enough dish, but are packed full of dirt. To be on the safe side, replace all pouches.

Choosing Pouch Material

In pianos which originally had leather pouches with no rubber sealer (indicated by the presence of very small bleeds) use thin pouch leather. Save the thinnest available pouch leather for reproducing pianos. In pianos which originally had sealed leather pouches, such as Ampicos, use leather pouches coated with rubber cement as described below. In a piano which had airtight rubber cloth or zephyr skin pouches, use sealed pouch leather if the pouch boards are removable for future resealing. If the pouches were originally rubber cloth and are located inside unit pneumatics or in valve chests which are glued shut, requiring recovering the pneumatics or major woodworking in order to gain access to the pouches, use the most flexible available rubber cloth.

Zephyr skin is very light weight, sensitive, airtight and responsive, but it shrinks and swells with humidity changes, making it impossible to keep the correct clearance between pouch and valve stem. Also, with repeated humidity changes, zephyr skin pouches shrink more and more until they hold the valves up off their seats during dry weather, causing gross leakage in a stack. Another drawback to zephyr skin is its appeal as food for certain insects. The author remembers a WurliTzer 105 band organ which was used in parades by a well known Chicago area nickelodeon collector during the 1960's, which was playing well one fall but wouldn't play a note when fired up the following spring. With the valve chest disassembled, it was found that the pouches were *gone*, entirely eaten by insects!

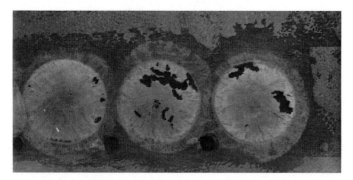

Illus. 5-87. Zephyr skin is extremely flexible, light weight and airtight, but unfortunately it changes size when the humidity goes up and down, and insects love to munch on it.

When deciding what material to use for replacing the pouches in a piano which was repaired previously with the wrong pouches or bleeds—a common occurrence—attempt to find another similar instrument for comparison, or try various size bleeds with one pouch until you find the right size.

What *Not* to Use for Pouches

Never use polyurethane sheeting (perflex) or any other type of unbacked rubber or plastic material for pouches. Use zephyr skin only if the humidity surrounding a piano will always remain constant in the future and adequate insect damage prevention will always be provided. Never use nylon or other non-absorbent pneumatic cloth with PVC-E; sooner or later, the suction will pull the pouches loose. Use hot glue; although PVC-E will work with absorbent materials, it is the most stubborn glue to remove from wood, making future pouch replacement much more difficult.

Installing Leather Pouches

Since most old pouches have shrunk, making it difficult to tell the original outside diameter, the best way for a beginner to determine the correct size is to make several samples. Most pouch wells are no deeper than $3/16''$, and the pouches should have enough dish to touch bottom at the center without stretching, ignoring any hole in the well. With the correct amount of dish, the diameter of the leather should be large enough to cover about $3/16''$ of wood around the edge, providing that this does not cause one pouch to hang over into the next well. In a primary chest with two closely-spaced rows of small pouches, cut the leather so it covers $1/8''$ of wood around the edge. When you have found the size which has adequate dish and gluing surface, cut out a whole set of pouches, with a few extras in case you spoil a few with too much glue. If you plan to restore only one or two player pianos, draw a slightly undersize circle with a compass on a thin cardboard disc, trace around it with a ball point pen on the bottom (rough) side of the pouch leather, and cut the pouches out with a scissors. If you would rather not cut out the pouches by hand, order a set of precut pouches from a supply company. If you plan to restore many pianos, buy an arch punch each time you need a different size set of pouches, and eventually you will have a complete set of punches. If you are trying to earn a living by restoring player pianos, the cost of a large arch punch will be returned in the time saved in just one or two jobs. Buy or make an end-grain maple punching block.

Pouches may be installed by hand, providing that you

Illus. 5-88. When installing a pouch without a suction operated pouch setter, apply the glue, wrap the edges of the pouch up around a suitable small disc, lay the pouch into the well, and then press the edges down onto the glue, to keep from dragging glue onto the working area of the pouch.

Illus. 5-89. A much more efficient way to install pouches is with a suction operated pouch setter. This tool forms the pouch with the correct amount of dish and presses it into place all at once.

are very careful not to drag glue down onto the working area of the pouch as you form the right amount of dish. Lay a small disc which is about ⅔ the diameter of the pouch well on the center of a pouch—a dime or nickel is handy for many pouches, apply hot glue around the edge of the well, bring the edge of the pouch up around the disc, place it in the center of the well and carefully lay the perimeter of the leather on the glue, pushing the leather around until the wrinkles all disappear. Any glue which is dragged onto the moving portion of the pouch will either cut through it or stiffen it, so be sure to create enough dish *before* you allow the leather to contact the glue. Wipe off any glue which squeezes out, and press the glued area of the pouch with a large washer or other round object. If the pouches are on the surface of a flat board—not in countersunk wells—press them with a warm iron. Wipe any glue off the iron with a damp rag after each pouch.

A much more efficient way to install pouches is to use a suction-operated *pouch setter*, as shown in illus. 5-89, available in a few sizes from certain supply companies. Used with a test pump or other suction source, a pouch setter helps to install pouches more neatly with more uniform dish in a fraction of the time required to install them by hand. The face of a pouch setter is milled with small slots which are connected to an internal channel running through the shank, the shank is connected by a rubber tube to the suction source, and the rubber tube has a large hole near where it attaches to the setter.

Apply glue to the rim of the pouch well, hold one finger over the hole in the connecting hose, lay a pouch on the setter, and the suction will form the leather to the correct shape. Press the pouch in place, open the hole in the suction tube, and remove the setter.

Non-suction-operated pouch setters are also made, but these are not recommended as they cause the pouch to drag glue onto its working surface as it is installed.

Continuous Pouches

Some pouch boards are faced with one continuous strip of leather instead of individual pieces. Repouch this type of board with one piece of leather like the original, being extra careful not to drag glue onto the working area of the pouch. Use hot glue, spread it over a few square inches of wood at a time, and press the leather with an iron after each portion of leather is glued, to melt the glue into the wood and leather.

Valve Stem Lifter Discs

In many player actions, each pouch has a fibre disc attached, to lift the valve stem without pushing an indentation into the pouch. A pouch disc should be glued only at its center, which allows the pouch its full travel; gluing the

Illus. 5-90. Gluing the pouch disc only at the center permits the pouch to have maximum travel.

disc all the way across severely limits the pouch travel. In some examples, a small leather punching is glued between the pouch and disc, offering even more flexibility.

Sealing Leather Pouches

In pianos in which the leather pouches were originally sealed, including Ampico reproducing pianos, seal the new leather with two thin coats of Carter's Rubber Cement or equivalent, thinned 50/50 with rubber cement thinner. Mix a solution of cement and thinner in a baby food bottle, smear a thin coat on the pouch with a circular motion of a pliable brush, and rub the cement into the leather with your finger. If the rubber cement pulls loose or rolls into little balls, it is too thick. Do all of the pouches once, allowing the first coat to disappear indicating that it is dry. Then apply the second coat. Some restorers apply suction to the bottom of the pouch by mouth, to draw the cement into the leather, but this is unnecessary and is undoubtedly harmful to the health. It does little good anyway, because with the proper dish, the pouch touches the bottom of the well, blocking off the suction except for a small area surrounding the input hole. After the rubber cement is dry, rub talcum power into it to eliminate all traces of stickiness.

To seal pouches which have fibre discs, place a round masking tape punching on the center of each pouch, apply the sealer, and then remove the punchings.

Keep the rubber cement very thin, to avoid making the pouches too stiff. Some rebuilders use mink oil to seal pouches because many brands of rubber cement turn hard after a short time. Beware of this problem when choosing pouch sealer!

Installing Rubber Cloth Pouches

Using cotton rubber pneumatic cloth for pouches is somewhat more difficult than using soft, pliable pouch leather. It is impossible to impart quite as much dish to rubber cloth, and it takes longer to press the wrinkles down until the glue holds. On the other hand, it is unnecessary to have as much dish with a rubber cloth pouch, because there is no shrinkage as there is with leather. Once the rubber cloth sticks to the wood all the way around, clamp it with an appropriate washer, spacer block if necessary, and a spring clamp. It is particularly important when gluing fibre discs to rubber cloth pouches to glue the center only, to maximize pouch flexibility and travel.

Unusual Pouches

Late style Schulz, late Otto Higel and probably a few other player actions incorporate removable pouch blocks suspended below the valve stems as shown in Ch. 6. Covering these is a relatively simple procedure, but be careful not to draw the leather too tightly around the sides, which will decrease the travel of the center of the pouch or cause it to push the valve stem off to one side.

Many European instruments, and a few American ones, use "envelope" or "pillow" pouches, as shown in illus. 5-91. Making new pouches of this type without getting glue all over the leather requires quite a bit of dexterity. There are several methods of folding and gluing the leather. In one method, a rectangular piece of leather with a hole punched in the center is glued to itself around a non-absorbent insert, the insert is removed, and the end pieces are glued on. A leather washer is then glued to the hole, reinforcing the point at which the pouch is glued to the pouch board. If you encounter pillow pouches, careful observation and a few measurements will tell you how to copy them. Never use cardboard washers even if the original ones were cardboard; suction surrounding the outside of the pouch will seep through the edges of the cardboard, increasing the bleed and making the note reluctant to play at soft levels.

Brass Bleed Cups

Make it a habit to remove all brass bleeds; even if they look clean from the top, they often have an accumulation of fuzz or verdigris on the bottom. Carefully pry each bleed out with a thin blade, soak them in lacquer thinner if necessary, and blow them out with compressed air. While the bleeds are removed, blow out the channels and test for airtightness. If the bleeds are very snug in the wood, press them back in; if they are the least bit loose, seal each one under the rim with a miniscule amount of burnt shellac.

In some Duo-Art pianos, two sizes of bleeds were used to compensate for pouch leather of different porosity. When replacing the pouches, seal them with rubber cement, and open the smaller bleeds to the larger size. The stack will not work properly if uniformly sealed pouches have various size bleeds.

Replacing Paper or Celluloid Bleeds

If paper or celluloid bleeds are damaged, or if the bleed holes are all different sizes, replace the entire set with brass bleed cups. If the bleeds were all in one row and if the holes in the wood are too large to hold the brass bleed cups tightly, rout a slot in the wood and glue in a piece of wood of the same type with Titebond or equivalent. Drill the holes for the new bleed cups, blow out the sawdust and wood particles, seal the new wood, and insert the new bleeds. Replacing old paper or celluloid bleeds with brass bleeds sometimes poses quite a challenge, but with ingenuity there is always some way to do it. Make sure that the brass bleeds are airtight around their perimeter and will stay tight with humidity-induced changes in the wood.

Bleed Covers

Some player actions have access holes for cleaning dirty bleeds. The holes are sometimes covered with rubber cloth

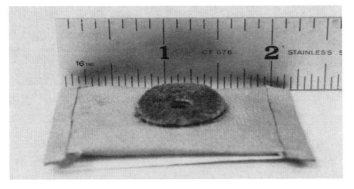

Illus. 5-91. Making new "envelope" or "pillow" pouches requires meticulous work to avoid getting glue on the material.

85

patches, sometimes with large machine screws, and sometimes with rubber plugs. The latter are usually too hard to form an airtight seal; remove them and cover the holes with rubber cloth patches.

Adjustable Bleeds

Some player pianos have pointed adjustable bleed screws which may be adjusted individually. These have a habit of collecting a lot of dirt; remove and clean the screws, and blow out the channels. When testing the valve chest, regulate each bleed by connecting its pouch input nipple to a tracker bar hole, playing the tracker bar with your finger, and turning the bleed screw until the valve repeats correctly. If the valve is slow to come up, turn the screw in; if it is slow to go down, turn the screw out. For fine regulation after the screw is close to the correct position, turn it no more than 1/8 turn at a time.

VALVES AND SEATS

Types of valves include *inside* valves (ordinary stack valves and all others which are inside of their seats), *outside* valves (the primary valves of most double valve actions, with the valve buttons outside of the seats), *pallet* valves, *slide, rotary* and *knife* valves, and *flap* valves. The airtight functioning of *all* valves in a player action is essential to efficient operation, so if the following material seems too long and detailed, that's just an indication of the amount of attention which valves deserve. This section includes general information on a variety of valves; further details are included in the specific brand section in Ch. 6.

Inside Valves and Seats

Inside valves and their stems are made of various combinations of materials and take many forms, including leather-faced wood buttons with wood stems (Amphion, old Aeolian, Gulbransen, some Hupfeld, Simplex, late style Seeburg), wood buttons on wire stems (old Aeolian, some Hupfeld, Pratt Read, Welte), formed bakelite buttons (H. C. Bay), metal discs on wire stems (Baldwin), fibre

Illus. 5-92. Valves come in all sizes and shapes, but all can be categorized as either rigid or wobbly. From left to right, the old Aeolian valve is rigid on its stem, while the Amphion, Baldwin, Gulbransen and Standard valves are all wobbly.

discs with fluted wood stems (Coinola), fibre discs on wire stems (Autopiano, Standard, early style Seeburg, Cremona), celluloid discs with fluted wood stems (Cable Co.), formed neoprene buttons with fluted plastic stems (modern Aeolian) and other materials and configurations. All inside valves can be broken down into two important categories: those which *wobble* and those which are *rigid*, as shown in illus. 5-92.

Seats for inside valves are usually smooth wood, metal plates, grommets, brass tubing or molded bakelite inserts. Usually either the valve or the seat, but not both, are faced with leather. A leather-faced valve on a smooth wood or metal seat, or a wood button on a leather seat, provides a nearly airtight seal, but leather seating on leather does not. A few early player actions including early Melville Clark Apollos had leather valve facings *and* leather-faced seats, but these were not as airtight as ordinary actions and did not hold suction quite as well. (Melville Clark got around the problem in early Apollos by using a spring motor to operate the music roll, so all of the suction from the pump could go to the stack instead of 25% or more going to the wind motor as in other brands. Some later Apollo pianos with conventional valves and seats also have conventional wind motors).

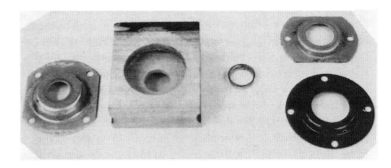

Illus. 5-93. A variety of valve seats: Old Aeolian, Amphion, Gulbransen Standard (above) and Autopiano (below)

What to Use for Valve Facings

To reface valves or leather-faced seats, use only leather, as close to the original type and thickness as possible. Two types of leather were used originally: suede leather, with suede finish on both sides for wood seats (i.e. Standard outside facings), and leather with suede finish on one side and shiny finish on the other for metal seats (i.e. Standard inside facings). Choose new leather as close to the original as possible. The nap should be perfectly smooth, not hairy or fuzzy, or air will leak through the facing edgewise. Usually the thinnest available calfskin, or an appropriate thickness of pouch leather is suitable, glued with hot glue. The lower valve facings of inside valves are prone to being pulled loose by the suction inside the valve chest, so the leather used for these must be absorbent enough for the hot glue to stick the leather tightly to the valve. When pouch leather is used for lower valve facings, the fuzzy side is glued to the valve disc with the shiny side facing out. (Never attempt to glue the shiny side of finished leather to anything; sooner or later, it *will* come loose).

Pigskin, available from large retail/wholesale leather shops, makes fine valve leather, particularly for small primary valves, if you can find some which isn't so porous that it allows glue to squeeze through. Punch your own valve facings with an arch punch and end-grain punching block, or purchase them already punched from a supply company.

Releathering Valves

Refer again to illus. 5-92 and 5-93, which show various wobbly and rigid valves and their seats. Wobbly valves have no trouble seating easily, if they have enough wobble. When you releather wobbly valves, be careful to maintain or exceed the original amount of wobble—old stiff leather sometimes doesn't wobble as much as it did when it was new. When deciding what size to make the valve stem hole in the leather, analyze how the valve originally wobbled without leaking around the stem. In many cases, a leather facing is glued to the valve disc only around the perimeter, to allow the center of the leather to flex while hugging the stem.

Valves with fluted stems often have a tiny punching between each button and stem. Replace this punching when replacing the valve leather. Amphion valves have a small round head nail countersunk into an indentation in the lower face of the valve button, as shown in illus. 5-94. The nail head is somewhat larger than the countersunk hole, providing stem wobble. When releathering these valves, push each nail through a leather punching, glue the punching to the valve, and then press the stem onto the nail.

Releathering rigid valves poses more problems, because their airtight seating depends on the precise placement of each stem guide and seat. Prior to disassembling any valves, rigid valves in particular, number and mark the orientation of every seat and guide, so you will be able to install them in their original locations. A serious mistake made by novices is to assume that mass produced parts are

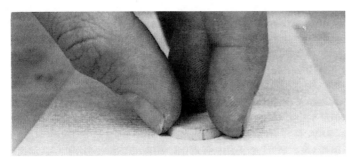

Illus. 5-94. When sanding the old glue off of a valve button on fine sandpaper taped to a piece of thick glass, be extremely careful to press evenly to avoid ruining the valve.

identical, but it is common for small variations to occur in the locations of screw holes and stem guide holes, causing serious leakage if valve parts are mixed up or if guides or seats are put back in the wrong orientation. A good rule to follow when working on valves is: IDENTICAL-LOOKING PARTS USUALLY AREN'T.

Clean all traces of old leather and glue off of the old valve discs or buttons. First pull off as much of the leather as possible by hand, and then sand on 180 grit sandpaper taped to a ¼″ thick piece of glass, pressing evenly and moving the valve in a circular motion. Polishing a valve perfectly smooth and shiny with finer sandpaper reduces the adhesion of hot glue, so the small sanding scratches left by 180 paper are desirable. Check the valve for flatness as you sand it; if you sand through the glue on one part of the valve face before the rest, you are either pressing and sanding unevenly or the valve is warped. Either sand the valve until it is perfectly flat, or replace it. Check new replacement fibre valve discs for flatness before using any of them; sometimes they are warped worse than the old ones are! To detect a small warp, lay the disc on a perfectly flat surface and see if it rocks, or hold it up to a light to see if any light shows through.

Hot glue usually sticks leather to wood or fibre better than any other glue. While gluing the small delicate valve facings to the body of the valve, keep your fingers perfectly clean, even if this means wiping them on a damp rag hundreds of times while gluing a set of valve facings. If a valve disc has a hole in the center, hold it on the end of an awl while applying the glue. After placing the leather on the glue, immediately press the disc against a warm iron to insure that the leather is perfectly flat. Replace any new facings which have even the tiniest amount of glue on the working surface, and always check each lower facing by trying to pick the leather loose around the edges after the glue dries. to make sure it won't come loose.

Illus. 5-95. Always check new lower valve facings to make certain that the leather is stuck to the wood.

Unleathered wood valve buttons (which mate with leathered seats) rarely need any attention. If they are warped, lap them on fine sandpaper attached to glass, or replace them.

What *Not* to Use for Valve Facings

Although sheepskin is the old standby for reed organ pallet valves and is excellent for valve facings in pressure operated systems such as organ pipe chests, it should not be used in player pianos, for several reasons: air leaks through the edges of sheepskin valve facings, causing a significant loss of suction in a player action, and the suction inside the valve chest causes sheepskin to split and pull apart. It also has the unfortunate property of corroding brass and nickel plated valve seats so badly that in humid climates, the valves often stop working within a short time. Save sheepskin for organ work; don't use it in suction operated instruments other than reed organs.

Many valves in early (pre-1915) player actions, including Aeolian and Standard, have a layer of felt between the leather facing and the wood button or fibre disc. This felt was used to make the operation of the valves quieter, but it had several drawbacks, including its tendency to allow a certain amount of leakage, and to change thickness (with resulting change in valve travel) with absorption and loss of moisture during seasonal humidity changes. Also, the valve felt in many player actions was a favorite food for insects, and in many actions encountered today it is eaten full of holes or is partially or completely gone, replaced by thousands of tiny insect cases and dried eggs. Aeolian and

Illus. 5-96. While early Standard and Aeolian valves contain a layer of felt between the leather and wood, later valves do not have this felt Omit it when releathering valves

Standard both quit using felt in their valves by the late 'teens, and instead glued the valve leather directly to the wood buttons or fibre discs; these valves are no noisier inside a piano stack than the earlier ones with felt are. With the exception of valve boxes mounted close to the front of a piano where the operation of the valves might tend to be noisy (as in a Seeburg G, H or L orchestrion bass drum valve box), felt is not recomended for valves.

Never use sponge neoprene for valves; although this material seems like it should be airtight, it has so much friction that if a valve seats at the slightest angle, it will not slip into the correct position and will continue to leak as long as it is on. Many old player pianos which have been rebuilt and new ones which have been manufactured since the late 1950's with neoprene valve facings and formed neoprene valve buttons are hard to pump because the valves don't seat tightly in the "on" position.

Cleaning and Polishing Seats

Wooden seats are usually in excellent condition, but if you encounter an action with small chips or fragments of

wood missing due to sloppy factory drilling, you will have to resurface them. Fill large voids with epoxy, allow it to dry hard, and then carefully sand the seat with a punching of sandpaper glued to the end of a dowel. In some cases this can be done in a drill press. Careless sanding will make the seat worse than it was, so proceed with extreme caution and test each seat for airtightness with an actual valve to make sure that you are improving matters! Never apply shellac or other sealer to wood valve seats -- it can make them sticky.

Lower valve seats which are faced with leather (Cable Euphona, H.C. Bay) sometimes are still good. Test by mouth with an actual valve, and if you can detect no seepage, leave the old leather in place. More often than not, however, the old leather is rotten and must be replaced. Pick as much of it out as possible by hand, and then clean the old glue from the seats as described in the paragraph immediately above. Make sure the thickness of the new leather is as close as possible to the original to keep from disturbing the valve travel. Upper valve seats faced with leather are usually in the form of gasketed cover plates which can be releathered in one large piece.

Metal valve plates are often corroded from a reaction with tanning chemicals in the leather. Remove light tarnish or corrosion with a rag and metal polish, and heavier corrosion and rust with steel wool. Use extreme caution if you decide to polish them on a buffing wheel, as it is easy to bend them just enough to cause leakage. If nickel plating is flaking loose from brass, have the seats replated if you are sure you can trust your plating company not to bend them while polishing them, or replace them. Or, if you can remove most of the plating by hand polishing, do so and spray the metal with nitrocellulose lacquer to inhibit further corrosion. Always check flimsy stamped metal seats (Simplex, WurliTzer top seats) for flatness by covering the seat with a perfectly flat metal disc and sucking to test for leakage.

Many lower valve seats are made of a small grommet or piece of brass tubing sealed to the wood with thick burnt shellac. Clean the seat with a wad of steel wool, blow the valve chamber out with compressed air, and then renew the burnt shellac sealer around the seat with new burnt shellac or white glue, being careful not to smear glue onto the area where the valve seats. It is good practice to renew this sealer whether it looks good or not, to insure airtight lower seats. If the lower seats are bakelite (Amphion, WurliTzer unit valves), try to press them out from below, and reinstall them with burnt shellac.

Sooner or later you will encounter a player action with metal valve seats which were bent during a previous disassembly. It is nearly always impossible to straighten a bent piece of metal, because of the stretching which occured when it was bent, so you will have to find a set of replacement seats in order to restore such a piano.

Replacement Valve Hardware

Many types of valve discs, seats, stems and other parts are available from supply companies. Reuse old parts when possible, but if fibre valve discs are warped, metal seats are bent or pitted so badly that they can not be made airtight by resurfacing, wire valve stems are corroded so badly that the threads won't hold the leather nuts or wood buttons, or other serious problems exist, obtain new parts. Have the new parts in hand and make sure they are the right size and will work properly before discarding the old parts, since many replacement parts drift in and out of production and may not be available even though they appear in a supply catalogue.

Bakelite Valves and Seats

Most H. C. Bay valves are made of molded bakelite and are usually in good condition. (See Ch. 6 for further information on the H. C. Bay).

Some bakelite outer seats (Kimball and others) unscrew out of the wood and are often in good condition. To replace those which are broken or warped, countersink a large shallow hole in the wood to support a fibre disc as shown in illus. 6-95.

Most bakelite lower valve seats are still in good condition; renew the shellac sealing the bakelite to the wood and check for airtightness. If you encounter a set of bakelite seats which are cracked or crumbled, you will have to make replacements for them out of nylon or delrin rod drilled and turned to the right shape on a lathe.

Adjusting Valve Travel

Most ordinary inside valves should have .040" travel, measured at the stem, although various manufacturers made other recommendations ranging from .028 (Simplex) to .047" or 3/64" (Baldwin), to .062" or 1/16" (Autopiano secondary valves). Measuring travel by observing the space between a floppy valve facing and top seat isn't accurate because the valve disc may be cocked at an angle, showing more travel on one side than the other. An experienced restorer learns to adjust valve travel by a combination of feel and sight, and by watching and listening to the valves and pneumatics operating while testing the stack or other component on the bench. Too little valve travel makes a pneumatic sluggish, while too much causes the valve to "spit," wasting suction; either error will ruin fast repetition at soft playing levels.

Until experience teaches you how to judge travel by eye, ear and feel, use a dial indicator mounted on a rigid stand as shown in illus. 5-97 as an aid for valves with a rigid stem, or use a valve gapping tool as shown in illus. 5-98 for stemless valves. A few rebuilders have constructed elaborate air flow measuring devices for precise adjustment of valve travel, but other equally fine rebuilders obtain equally excellent results simply adjusting travel by eye and ear.

Illus. 5-98. A valve gapping tool which may be inserted into the top valve seat hole to calibrate the travel of a stemless valve. Grind the tips smaller if necessary

Methods of adjusting valve travel vary as much as valves and seats do. Standard valves are adjusted by moving the metal grommets on the stem. Simplex valves are regulated by using various thicknesses of pouch leather for the top faces. Baldwin valves are regulated by inserting or removing paper punchings under the top face. H. C. Bay valves are regulated by sanding. Amphion unit block and Gulbransen valves are regulated by adjusting the thickness of the blotter paper shim for the top seat. And the list goes on. In each instance, there is some way to obtain just the right travel. Refer to Ch. 6 for further information.

Adjusting Valve to Pouch Clearance

One of the most important adjustments in a player piano action is the precise regulation of the clearance between the pouches and valve stems, which should be 1/16". With too little clearance, the action will become hard to pump or will stop working entirely when the pouches shrink the least little bit in response to dry weather. With too much clearance, fast repeated notes will be unresponsive. With use, however, leather pouches gradually form a "doughnut" around the lifter disc or stem, regulating their own clearance to the optimum amount, so it is better to have slightly too much to begin with than too little.

Methods for regulating valve to pouch clearance vary as much as valve and stem configurations do. If you maintain

Illus. 5-97. Checking valve travel with a dial indicator.

original dimensions when replacing valve and gasket leather and install the new pouches with enough dish, the clearance probably will be correct. If one dimension is altered by the introduction of thicker or thinner leather, it might be necessary to alter the clearance. Adjust the length of a fluted wood stem by gently sanding it (perfectly *straight*) or by adding leather punchings. Adjust the clearance in a Standard/Autopiano, old Aeolian or other piano with wooden buttons on the bottom of the valve stems by screwing the button up or down. Adjust Baldwin clearance by adding or removing punchings between the mushroom-shaped valve lifter and the wire stem. Additional examples are shown in Ch. 6.

Outside Valves

Small outside valves or reverse valves—the primary valves of a double valve system—almost always are made with the lower wood button permanently attached to a wooden stem, with the top button lightly glued so it may be adjusted or removed for releathering. In many primary valves, the lower or inside leather facing is not glued to the button.

To disassemble outside valves, place the valve board on supports which hold it up off the workbench far enough to allow the valves to fall loose as you disassemble them. Carefully scrape the old glue or sealer off the top of the stem, and punch the stem through the top button with a pin punch or steel rod of exactly the same diameter as the stem. A tapered punch or one which is too large will break the top button, and a punch which is too small will often break the stem, so take the time to find something of exactly the right diameter. As each valve falls out of the board, loosely reassemble it with its top button. Contrary to the general rule of numbering all parts, it is usually safe to throw all primary valves in a can without keeping them in order, as long as each top button is kept with its own stem.

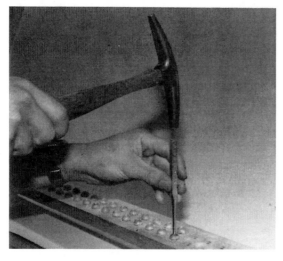

Illus. 5-99. Punching an outside (primary) valve apart, after removing the old glue. The diameter of the punch must be equal to that of the stem

Pry the old leather loose from each top button and gently sand it on 180 grit sandpaper taped to a thick piece of glass. As with any other valve, take pains to keep the button flat, by checking the face as glue removal proceeds. Remove the leather from the bottom face; if it was glued on, scrape the wood with a sharp knife or razor blade, and then sand it by inserting the stem in a hole in a board faced with sandpaper and twisting the valve. Use the thinnest, smoothest split suede calfskin or pigskin for the new valve facings. Usually you will only glue the top facing, but if both of the old facings were glued, glue both new ones. It is even more important here than with larger inside valves to be meticulously neat with the glue so the leather sticks well without having glue on any exposed surface. Press the top faces on a warm iron immediately after gluing, and press the bottom faces against a block of smooth wood with a hole drilled for the stem.

Illus. 5-100. Use a 1/32" thick gauge for adjusting the travel of outside valves. Bevel the ends so they won't disturb the leather

Calibrate the travel of the releathered valves as you install them on the board, as shown in illus. 5-100. Make the gauge 1/32" thick unless a specific service manual recommends otherwise. Insert the gauge under the top button, squeeze the buttons together and spread a drop of hot glue around the top of the valve stem to secure it. If the top button wants to slip on the stem after the tool is removed, leave the tool in place until the glue sets.

Some orchestrions and band organs have large outside valves made of fibre discs attached to wire stems. Treat these as you would floppy inside valves, making sure that the discs are free to wobble without leaking where the stem goes through the leather.

Flap Valves

Flap valves and their seats are made in many configurations; just when you think you have seen every conceivable type of flap valve, another one takes you by

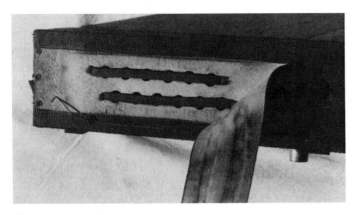

Illus. 5-101. Some flap valves, such as this one in an Apollo electric pump bellows, have strips of felt over the holes to make them quieter

surprise. Some of the more common types include firm leather flaps with a block of wood attached to the moveable end, held tight with a curved "finger" spring (Standard/Autopiano), leather flaps held tight with two or three coil springs attached to one end, with a felt strip running lengthwise down the wooden seat to reduce noise (Ampico, Duo-Art and some coin pianos and orchestrions), aluminum or tin plates backed with blotter paper or thick rubber cloth (Simplex), aluminum discs held against leather seats with one center coil spring (Baldwin), and rubber cloth flaps on leather seats with a music wire spring stretched across one end (Coinola).

To replace ordinary Standard/Autopiano type flap valves, remove the little wooden blocks from the old leather. These are usually tacked *and* glued to the leather. If the springs and any associated hold-down staples are rusty, remove them from the wood, polish, lacquer and re-install them. Clean the wooden seat. Select stiff, airtight, non-stretchy leather with finish on one side and the smoothest possible suede surface on the other; cut it to the size of the old flap, and sand the finish off the end where the wooden block it attached. (Without sanding, the block will not stick to the leather). Reattach the block with hot glue and the original tack or a replacement, warm the glued leather with an iron, and clamp the block until the glue dries. When dry, hook the block on the spring, and

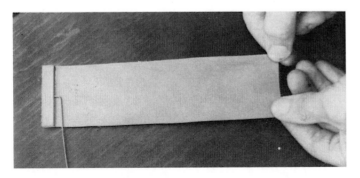

Illus. 5-102. When reattaching Standard type flap valves to the wood, hook the loose end to the spring first, then find the correct position for the glued and tacked end.

move the tail of the flap around, gluing and tacking it in a position where it lays flat without any hint of buckling. If you attempt to glue the fixed end first and then attach the moveable end to the spring, you will usually end up with a buckled, leaky flap valve.

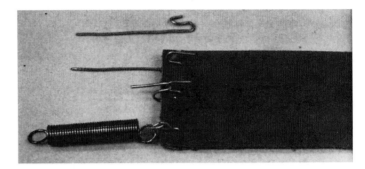

Illus. 5-103. Make little connecting loops like these to attach coil springs to flap valves.

To replace flaps which are attached to coil springs at one end, reuse the original metal clip or make a duplicate. If the original flap had no clip, make a loop of stainless steel wire to connect each spring to the leather, as shown in illus. 5-103. Unlike flap valves with a finger spring, new flaps with coil springs must have the stationary end glued and tacked down first. After the glue dries, gently stretch the two outer coil springs at an angle as shown, locate and drill the position of the screw for one spring, screw this spring down, and then locate and drill the position of the other one so the leather remains flat. If there are three springs, secure the middle one last.

Illus. 5-104. When reattaching flap valves with coil springs to the wood, secure the stationary end first with hot glue and small tacks. Then locate the positions of the small coil springs.

Many flap valves with coil springs lay on soft leather seats with a felt strip running lengthwise to quiet their operation, particularly in reproducing pianos. The underlying leather seat is often rotten even when the flap itself looks good, so replace it and the felt strips if necessary, duplicating the original way of tacking the felt to the wood. Selecting and finding the best leather for Ampico flap valves can be challenging because leather which is soft enough to provide noiseless operation tends to stretch too much. If you find soft leather which appears to be suitable, prestretch it by hand as much as possible without deforming it, to insure that it will not stretch further during actual use, rendering the spring ineffective.

Most blotter paper backed aluminum flap valves are still good, providing that the aluminum is not the least bit bent or buckled. Attempting to replace the old paper just for the sake of replacing it will usually cause the little aluminum tabs to break off, so if the old valve checks out to be airtight, leave it alone. If the aluminum plate is bent, make a new one if you can find and successfully cut similar metal, or if there is room for a conventional leather flap valve with a spring on one end, install that type instead.

Pallet Valves

Finger button pallet valves in home player pianos usually either have a leathered wooden strip supported by guide pins and a spring, or a leathered flat steel spring. Some action cutoff mechanisms are also controlled by a small pallet valve of one of these types. If a pallet has two small pieces of leather, one under the moveable end and another under the fulcrum, replace both pieces. Polish the guide pins, spring and slot, and make sure the valve seats properly by testing it by mouth. To replace the leather on a flat steel spring, clean the spring with steel wool and glue the leather on with PVC-E. Bend the spring or adjust the tension screw if necessary to make it airtight. For both types of finger button pallets, use the usual split suede leather.

Pipe chests in coin pianos, orchestrions and band organs usually control the flow of air to the pipes with the type of pallet valve shown in illus. 5-105. This is the only·type of valve which should be leathered with white alum tanned sheepskin. Use sheepskin of the same thickness as the original, clean the old leather and glue off of the valves and

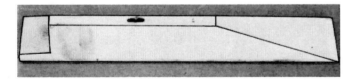

Illus. 5-105. This type of pallet, used in reed organs and pipe chests, is the only type of valve on which sheepskin is the correct leather.

mounting board, check the mating surfaces for perfect flatness. Pallet valves of this type work well as long as they and the mounting surface are perfectly flat, but a little leakage under each valve multiplied by a whole set of valves will cause a band organ or orchestrion to sag and run out of air. Clean the spring slots in the valves. Check the area where the spring presses on each valve. If there is a deep indentation which will cause the valve to bind as it opens, reshape the slot or replace the valve. Then sand the finish off the shiny (non-fuzzy) side of the new sheepskin and glue the valves to it in a row. After the glue sets, trim the valves with a sharp knife. If the pallets originally had leather hinge tails

glued to the wood, apply hot glue to the new tails, running the glue 1/8" under the hinge end of the wood. The hinge will stretch a little, and if the glue doesn't extend under the pallet a little, the pallet will wobble. Press each pallet and hinge into place, and after the glue dries, coat the top surface of each tail with hot glue.

Reed organ pallets are typically slotted for guide pins at both ends, with neither end glued down, and usually have a thick layer of felt between the wood and sheepskin. Instead of gluing individual pieces of felt and leather together, laminate one large piece. Let the glue dry, and then attach the pallets and cut them apart.

Slide, Rotary and Knife Valves

These three types of valves all have one piece of wood which slides against another (or rarely, wood against metal, or metal against metal), and they all must be flat and slippery in order to be airtight and to work freely. Lap the mating surfaces of these valves on progressively finer sandpaper taped to a piece of glass until the surface of the valve is smooth, shiny and flat. Make a thin, wet paste of dry powdered graphite and ethyl alcohol, and rub it into the wood with your finger or an old piano hammer. Burnish it until all excess graphite is removed and the remaining graphite forms a mirror-shiny black surface on the wood. Trying to apply dry graphite to wood is a waste of time, as most of it will disappear when burnished; rubbing the wood with a pencil will add as much clay·and binder as graphite, not providing the necessary lubrication. (An alternate for dry graphite mixed with alcohol is non-oily Dag (R) colloidal graphite sold by piano supply companies. Make sure it contains no oil or grease before applying it to wood).

When a wood knife valve seats on a leathered wood seat, replace the leather—usually with pouch leather, with the fuzzy side glued down—and burnish the unfaced wood with the alcohol/graphite paste. In some pianos you will find that the leather is also coated with graphite; apply the graphite to the new piece of leather *without* alcohol.

BUSHINGS, CUSHIONS AND BUMPERS

Many player piano actions have dozens or even hundreds of cloth bushings, cushions and bumpers which enable parts to work silently. Note the difference between woven action cloth and unwoven felt, and don't substitute one for the other; all bushings are made of action cloth, and if felt is substituted it will pack down and wear out quickly. Many thicknesses and colors of action cloth and felt are available from supply companies, including exact duplicates of most original materials; use the correct material to avoid problems. If a choice must be made between a replacement cushion or bumper which is the right color and the wrong thickness, or the right thickness and the wrong color, choose the latter.

Replacing Bushings

Many old bushings are worn, particularly in wind motors, causing silent parts to knock and rattle. When this occurs, replace all worn bushings, particularly in reproducing pianos. Duo-Art wind motors have adjusting screws on the connecting arms, and these can be used to compensate for a certain amount of wear, but if tightening them to eliminate a knock slows the motor, it's time to replace the bushings. First, push one of the old bushings out of the wood in order to measure it. Then drill out the remaining old glue with a bit exactly the same size as the hole in the wood. Make one trial bushing, temporarily insert it and assemble the shaft or pin to make sure the bushing is snug but permits free movement of the parts. When you find the right thickness and length of the strip of bushing cloth, apply a little hot glue into the hole with a tiny stiff brush, roll the bushing into a tight little coil, insert it (with fine-point medical tweezers if necessary) and let it unroll itself against the glue. Smooth it with a small round tool, and insert the shaft while the glue dries to keep the cloth pressed against the glue. Making your first wind motor crankshaft bushing might be frustrating, but taking the time to do the job over and over if necessary until it is perfect will result in a superior job.

Once in a while you will encounter a Standard/Autopiano or other player action with moth-eaten cloth bushings in the fibre valve stem guides. Rather than replacing the bushings, replace the stem guides if new ones of the right size are available. New replacements have smaller unbushed holes as do quite a few old ones which work just as well as the bushed ones do.

TUBING AND HOSES

Original player piano tubing was made of rubber, but the longest lasting tubing and hoses available today are made of neoprene and are available only from piano and organ supply companies. For maximum life, tubing and hoses should never be stretched over connectors; even the best quality materials crack and split prematurely under these conditions. A snug fit is all that is necessary, and with the

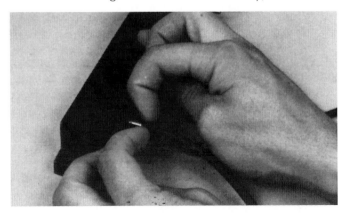

Illus. 5-106. To remove tubing from a nipple, *push*, don't *pull*.

correct fit, hose clamps or sealer are rarely necessary unless an unusual bend in a hose makes it want to come loose, a condition which is better solved by the use of an elbow.

To remove good tubing from a connector, push it off as shown. If you pull, it will hold tighter and you risk damaging the tubing or pulling the connector loose from the wood.

The best tubing is free of any sticky, oily or greasy substance; inferior materials sometimes are sticky, causing tracker bar tubing to become clogged with paper particles and atmospheric dust which passes through the tracker bar.

Several kinds of twill-wrapped hoses are available from various supply companies. The most expensive type is very strong and relatively hard; it lasts the longest but it won't go around corners without kinking, requiring the insertion of elbows in all but the most gentle curves. At the time this is being written, this hose is available only in six foot maximum lengths, resulting in the accumulation of left over pieces too short to use anywhere. It is recommended for coin pianos, orchestrions and band organs. Another type of wrapped hose is softer, so it goes around most corners without additional elbows, and it comes in long coils, so pieces can be cut as needed without waste. It is less expensive and doesn't last quite as long, particularly if stretched any significant amount, but it is perfectly adequate for use in home player pianos and reproducing pianos.

Tubing and hoses are measured by their *inside diameter*. To determine what sizes are needed, measure the outside diameter of the nipples or elbows to which they attach. To find the size of an unknown piece of small diameter tubing, find the fractional drill bit whose non-cutting end fits snugly without stretching the tubing; for a large hose, find a hose connector which fits. Most 9 per inch tracker bars with nipples which fan out into two rows use 9/64" tubing; most with three rows of nipples use 5/32".

When ordering tubing and hoses, check that both ends of a roll are the right size, and that there are no blemishes, slits or gashes. Established supply companies are happy to replace the occasional defective batch that slips through.

What *Not* to Use for Tubing and Hoses

Gray rubber tubing made since the 1940's has too high a content of clay and other fillers, causing it to become hard and to split within a few years of its installation.

Oily or greasy neoprene tubing becomes clogged with dirt; make sure the brand you buy is free of a sticky coating inside.

Small diameters of *automotive neoprene tubing* are too thick to fit into a player piano.

Vinyl tubing, including inexpensive aquarium tubing available from hardware stores, and more expensive tubing made for use in food and chemical processing, turns black and oily within a few years after being attached to brass player piano nipples. In one example, the owner of a fine Steinway Duo-Art grand ended up with sticky black oil all over her white carpet under the piano when vinyl tubing began decomposing within a few years after its installation. Even if transparent vinyl tubing which did not turn oily were available, it looks bad in a player piano.

Soft gummy brown elastic rubber tubing sometimes known as *surgical tubing* turns sticky and literally grows in place as it decomposes after it is a few years old. It is also too thick to fit into most places in a player piano.

Automotive heater hose is always aesthetically incorrect, usually a little too small in diameter, and because of its stiffness and thickness, it frequently crushes fibre nipples and pulls them out of wooden parts.

Radiator hose, like heater hose, is aesthetically in poor taste in a player piano, although in a few instances where the original hose connecting the pump to the stack was very large diameter (2" +) and was molded with a sharp bend, a suitable replacement is not available and the use of flexible radiator hose eliminates the need for a large home-made elbow. Never use automotive hose when player piano hose is available.

Vacuum cleaner hose—either the vinyl or cloth-wrapped variety—is made for vacuum cleaners, not player pianos. Except for the piece which is supplied with new add-on suction boxes, which has to curve around like a snake in order to fit in the piano, it should not be used.

CLEANING AND REPAIRING METAL PARTS

The safest solvent to use for cleaning non-rusty metal parts is odorless paint thinner. Soak metal parts for an hour to loosen hardened old grease, and use 4/0 steel wool for stubborn spots. To clean rusty unplated steel parts, polish them on a fine wire wheel. Rusty nickel plated parts with some of the plating coming loose can be polished by hand with steel wool or on a wire wheel, but they will look far better if you have them replated (see p. 96).

To put a high polish on brass, nickel, steel or other parts, use a buffing wheel with the appropriate compound obtained from a hardware store or piano supply company, using care not to remove any more metal than necessary. After buffing, remove the buffing compound with lacquer thinner, and apply a thin coat of nitrocellulose metal lacquer to inhibit further corrosion.

To clean and polish a tracker bar, remove it from the piano and remove as much of the old tubing as possible by cutting, chipping and scraping without damaging the delicate nipples. In some cases, old rubber cements itself to the brass and turns gooey, requiring great patience to remove it without damaging the brass. After removing all traces of the old tubing, polish the front of the bar on a buffing wheel, wash it in lacquer thinner, blow the thinner out of the holes with compressed air, mask the nipples and the surface which touches the music roll, and apply a thin coat of lacquer to the top, bottom and the ends of the front.

Some player action parts, including some Autopiano and late style Baldwin transmission parts, are brass plated, and by the time you remove the old lacquer and tarnish, most of the brass coating will disappear too. You will have to use your judgement as you proceed, deciding how far to go with polishing these parts.

Few metal player action parts ever break or wear out, but the ones that do can be very difficult to repair. Zinc pot metal alloy was used for Amphion (Ampico) and Baldwin transmission frames, and most of these are riddled with intergranular corrosion, rendering them irreparable. (See Ch. 6). If a pot metal part is neatly cracked into two pieces, epoxy them together in perfect alignment, and carefully drill a hole through the two parts and insert a pin if possible. If a part is warped, cracked and falling apart throughout, it can not be repaired. From time to time these two varieties of transmission frames are available from suppliers, but in most cases the replacement parts don't quite fit, requiring machining to get them to work.

Other metal parts which sometimes need repair or replacement include worn connecting pins in pedal linkages (which are relatively simple to make), transmission gears (some of which are available from supply companies), and an occasional cast iron part which breaks from abuse (which can be welded by a skilled welder). If you are at a total loss for repairing a broken metal part, have a machinist who specializes in small jobs make a new one.

HARDWARE

The hardware in a player piano includes certain parts - wood screws, for example—which are available in ordinary hardware stores, and other parts—such as leather nuts—which are only available from piano and organ supply companies. As with other materials, when it is necessary to replace screws and other hardware, use replacement parts which are identical to the original parts, not something different obtained from a local lumber yard as an expedient.

Screws

With a few exceptions, all player actions are assembled with round or flat head wood screws, with a few parts assembled with oval head screws. Most original screws were either plain steel or were nickel plated, but in some instruments brass or brass plated screws were used, and in others, round head screws were blued with a chemical which turned them black. Blued screws are not commonly available, but large hardware supply companies (including American Piano Supply) sell plain steel, brass and nickel plated screws.

The rebuilder who is a perfectionist uses screws with the

same type of finish that the original parts had: nickel plating, plain steel, or bluing. (Cold bluing is available from gun shops and produces a reasonably acceptable substitute for the original bluing, provided that the screws are polished on a buffing wheel, rinsed in lacquer thinner, blued and then lacquered to prevent almost immediate rusting). While commonly available cadmium plated wood screws are acceptable inside a player action where they aren't visible, they should never be used to replace nickel plated or plain steel screws in a valuable instrument like a coin piano or orchestrion.

In pianos which lived in humid climates, most of the screws are rusty where they were in contact with leather gaskets. Screws which hold gasketed joints together must be tight, and if you are tempted to polish original rusty screws to reuse them, you run the risk of breaking them off when you tighten them. It is false economy to polish and reuse old screws so you won't have to buy the correct new ones. While it might be frustrating to have to interrupt your work to dash off to the hardware store to buy a box of screws during final assembly of a player action, it is far more frustrating to break old screws during final assembly, remove the broken stumps, and repair and plug the holes in the wood without getting sawdust in channels, pouches, valves, pneumatics and other restored parts.

Many player actions have cup shaped washers under the heads of flat head screws which prevent the screw heads from pulling down into the wood after they have been in and out a few times. Always replace any missing or cracked washers.

Screws *Not* to Use

Shopping through a complete hardware store or catalogue, you will encounter all sorts of screws that were never used in player pianos, including fillister head, pan head, binder head, Phillips head, truss head, washer head, drywall, self-tapping and others. Stay with round, flat and oval head wood screws; not only do the other types look bad, in most instances they are simply not the correct fasteners for the job.

Nipples and Elbows

A variety of brass, extruded aluminum and cast aluminum tubing nipples and elbows, both flanged and unflanged, are available from supply companies. In most player actions, original brass connectors may be polished and lacquered, fibre connectors may be cleaned, and lead elbows, if structurally intact and not corroded, may be polished and sealed with shellac, and then these original parts may be reused. If connectors are missing, or if cast lead or pot metal connectors are heavily corroded, cracked or broken, purchase suitable new ones from a piano supply company. Note that many new cast aluminum nipples and elbows are partially or completely plugged with casting sand; always check to make sure they are clean prior to installation. Also, sand or grind off any ridges or burrs left by the casting process which will allow air to seep in between the connector and the hose. Please don't use plastic, cast iron, or other plumbing parts which will make your player piano look like the underside of a toilet!

Leather Nuts

Most threaded adjustable linkages in player actions such as stack pushrods, pedal and accessory control linkages are secured with *leather nuts*, which are invariably rotten. Make it a habit to replace them; new ones are available from supply companies in most of the sizes which were used originally. Check the new ones to make sure they aren't brittle or cracked; if they are, exchange them for good ones. Most leather nuts are supplied with tiny center holes. Drill them out just enough to provide a very tight fit which still allows for adjustment.

Some suppliers sell plastic nuts which are an acceptable substitute in some applications, but beware of plastic nuts which lack the strength of the leather variety. Tiny collars with set screws are also available from organ supply companies, but these are not recommended for threaded wires because the set screws burr the threads, making future fine adjustments difficult.

LUBRICANTS

To lubricate wind motor slide valves, governor knife valves, and other sliding wooden surfaces, use only dry powdered graphite mixed with denatured (ethyl) alcohol to form a paste which will soak into the wood; when the alcohol dries, burnish with your finger or an old piano hammer. Perform this with care to keep from getting graphite all over everything. A substitute for the alcohol-graphite mixture is Dag (R) non-oily colloidal graphite sold by piano supply companies.

To lubricate pumping pedal hinges, transmission shafts, small gears and other metal-to-metal friction points, use SAE 20 electric motor oil or common household oil. Apply one drop on the end of a small screwdriver or toothpick to each moving part, and immediately wipe off all excess. An alternate lubricant used on transmissions in modern Aeolian player pianos is petroleum jelly such as Vaseline. This provides lubrication for a longer time than electric motor oil does, but it tends to accumulate dirt until it turns black and sticky.

To lubricate larger metal parts, such as transmission gears in coin pianos, use grease of medium thickness, thin enough to allow free motion but thick enough so it isn't thrown all over the inside of the piano.

Refer to Ch. 7 for information on servicing and lubricating the electric motors used in reproducing pianos.

COSMETIC REPAIRS

How far to go with cosmetic restoration is, a matter of personal taste. Many owners of player pianos with the original finish in reasonably good condition are perfectly happy with that finish, and do not want to replace it. Many other owners want every single part of a piano to look like brand new, including the whole cabinet inside and out, all of the nickel plating, the finish inside the spoolbox, the piano bottom, etc. You haven't seen a beautiful player piano until you have seen one which looks just like it did the day it left the factory, but a restoration can take up to twice as long if you make every single part look like new as well restoring it mechanically. As a general guideline, invest more time on cosmetic restoration of more valuable instruments.

Wood Finishes

Wood finishes include shellac, lacquer, varnish, and paint. Cabinet and soundboard refinishing are outside the scope of this book, but many player action parts must be refinished during restoration; the appropriate materials and techniques are covered here and in Ch. 4.

Orange shellac and *white shellac* were the most common finishes for interior player action components, including deck boards, pneumatics, pumping bellows and many other parts which are concealed inside the player action. Use shellac of the same color as the original to refinish these parts. To apply a thin coat, wipe it on with a rag; for a thicker coat, use a soft, good quality brush. If you apply it evenly enough you may be happy with the shine after it dries, but shellac often dries irregularly and looks better if rubbed out with 4/0 steel wool.

A *black shellac base finish* was used on many stack cover boards, spoolboxes and other parts which show when the music roll and pumping pedal doors are opened. If old black shellac base paint is checked, scratched or in otherwise poor condition, remove what is left of it by scraping and sanding, and replace it. Most original black player action parts had a semi-gloss finish which can be duplicated with "semi-gloss" or semi-flat black aerosol lacquer or acrylic finish. Do not use gloss black, which shows up every little imperfection in the wood, nor flat black, which turns gray wherever it is touched. When replacing the finish on open pore wood such as mahogany which originally had a perfectly smooth ebony or dark brown finish, you will have to spray on enough coats of sanding sealer to fill the pores in order to create a flat, smooth base for the black finish coats. Apply many thin, even coats and let each one dry; if you try to build up too much at once it will ultimately check. Between coats, scuff the finish with 320 "open coat" sandpaper, and polish the final coat out with fine polishing compound of the type used for producing the beautiful shine on a new automobile paint job.

Enamel, black and in various colors, was used for stacks in some player pianos. Semi-gloss black or appropriate colored aerosol lacquer or acrylic finish provides a reasonable duplicate finish without showing brush and dust marks as brushed-on enamel does.

Varnish stain, a combination of varnish and thick pigment, was used on the front of many stacks and other parts to provide a cheap copy of the finish on the outside of the cabinet. Aerosol *lacquer stain* is available today in a number of wood colors, and if applied carefully, it duplicates the old varnish stain finish.

Metal Finishes

Most original metal parts were either plain steel or brass, or nickel or brass plated steel, or blued steel. After cleaning and polishing steel or brass parts, spray them with a thin coat of good quality clear aerosol lacquer for rust and tarnish protection. If parts were obviously nickel plated and the plating is pitted and peeling loose, have them replated with nickel if you can find a plating company which accommodates small custom orders. New nickel plating provides a beautiful finishing touch for a complete restoration. After the parts are replated, wash them with lacquer thinner with a soft rag, and apply a thin coat of clear aerosol lacquer to prevent clouding and tarnishing. While some technicians favor chrome plating because it never tarnishes, the majority of rebuilders don't like its blue look, compared to the mellow, slightly golden color of nickel. Chrome plating is also more likely to prevent threaded parts from fitting together.

Cold *bluing* is available from gun shops, for bluing screws, flat springs and other parts which were blued originally. Follow the instructions on the container, which usually include buffing each part, cleaning it in lacquer thinner, bluing it and then spraying it immediately with a coat of clear aerosol lacquer to prevent rusting.

SHARPENING TOOLS

Many hobbyists—and professional rebuilders, for that matter—make their work much more difficult because their tools aren't sharp. Keeping a set of screwdrivers, chisels and other tools sharp requires constant maintenance, because these tools wear a little each time they are used. By reshaping a tool properly, it can be maintained for a long time with just a little effort until another reshaping is necessary.

Most new screwdrivers are somewhat wedge shaped so they automatically push themselves out of the screw slots, marring the screws at the same time. A careful mechanic reshapes every new screwdriver on a slow grinding wheel, removing just enough metal to make the blade a little thinner just above the tip so it won't push itself out of the screw. Dip the blade in water to keep it cool while grinding.

Wood chisels and plane blades should also be ground somewhat concave, so a few laps on a whetstone followed by a polishing on a buffing wheel will restore the razor edge. Only after many resharpenings is a complete reshaping necessary.

Keep your awl sharp with a file or by turning it carefully against a sanding disc. Time taken to shape a long slender point on the end in the beginning will save many resharpenings during subsequent use.

Once you start using a small paint scraper to remove old glue and other materials from wood, you will find this tool to be a constant companion during the cleanup phase of restoration *if you know how to keep it sharp!* Clamp the scraper in a vise with the handle pointing up, true the inside of the blade with a new file, turn the scraper over, and file the outside face of the blade a few more times. With experience you will learn to feel when the blade is sharp by the way the file moves over it. Whether or not you learn how to file a really sharp edge on a scraper blade will determine whether this handy tool will be a great help or relegated to the back of a drawer.

If you are serious about player piano restoration, read everything you can find on the subjects of wood, wood finishing, woodworking and tools. After all, fine woodworking comprises a substantial portion of player piano repair!

CHECKLIST OF RECOMMENDED TOOLS FOR THE BEGINNER, ADVANCED HOBBYIST AND PROFESSIONAL

The number of tools acquired and supplies kept in stock are a matter of personal choice. The author knows several individuals who were mechanical hobbyists to begin with, and who possessed a complete workshop full of woodworking tools which would be the envy of any full time professional, who have done an excellent job of restoring just one player piano and have then gone on to other interests. On the other hand, there are full time rebuilders who do good quality work, who take two or three times as long to get the job done with just a few hand tools, even though a well-equipped shop would be much more efficient.

No matter how few or how many tools you feel comfortable with, *buy the best!* Part of the enjoyment of fixing up your own player piano, or restoring one for someone else, is in the time you will spend doing the repair work. Remember when you bought that cheap screwdriver from the bargain table and the blade broke the first time you used it, or the C-clamp which just spread out more and more instead of clamping anything as you tightened it? If you buy cheap tools thinking you will only give them limited use, you will be frustrated from the start and your work will never give you any satisfaction, but once you have purchased fine tools, you will be able to use them, with proper care, for a lifetime.

Necessary Tools for your First Restoration

Owning or having access to a set of good quality ordinary household tools is indispensible for any kind of repair work. If you don't want to purchase all the tools on this list, find a friend who is willing to let you borrow them, and purchase those specialized tools which are not found in an ordinary home workshop.

Hand Tools

Screwdrivers: a complete set, from the tiniest for set screws in transmission gears, to a really huge one for tightening plate and cabinet screws. A small ratchet end offset screwdriver for tight places.

Pliers: several sizes of ordinary pliers, needle nose for handling small parts, round nose for shaping springs, ignition pliers (a tiny version of the familiar "water pump pliers"), medium size locking pliers, and wire-bending "smiling pliers" for regulating backchecks, xylophone beaters, etc.

Wrenches: a set of combination box-end and open-end ignition wrenches from $5/32''$ to $3/8''$ for adjusting small nuts, a set of open-end or combination open-end and box-end wrenches from $3/8''$ to $1 5/8''$, and $6''$ and $12''$ adjustable-end wrenches for adjusting large nuts. Also, a set of hex key ("Allen") wrenches from $1/16''$ to $1/4''$ for set screws.

Hammers: medium size claw hammer, tack hammer, small sledge hammer and small peening hammer.

Chisels: several wood chisels from $1/4''$ to $2''$ wide, for shaping wood, removing old glue and separating old glue joints, and a small cold chisel for opening deformed screwdriver slots in badly rusted screws.

Center punch.

Putty knives, $1''$ and $1 1/4''$, ground as sharp as possible, for separating glue joints, removing glue, etc.

Paint scraper with $1''$ blade, for removing old glue, sealer, etc.

Files: several sizes of mill files for cleaning burrs from small metal parts, sharpening tools, shaping wood, etc.

Utility knife with disposable blades for cutting gaskets, and single edge razor blades by the box of 100 for trimming large bellows.

Small "Exacto" knife with an assortment of small blades for cleaning glue out of little holes.

Hack saw. Side cutter. Scratch awl.

Scissors: a good quality $8''$ or $10''$, for trimming pneumatics, preferably with the handle offset enough so it does not interfere with the edge of the pneumatic being trimmed.

Propane torch, for removing old glue from large surfaces.

Measuring tools: $6''$ and $12''$ steel rulers, $18''$ and $36''$ aluminum rulers, a $12''$ combination square and a steel measuring tape.

Revolving squeeze punch with rotating head, for punching small holes in gaskets and valves.

Compass for making cardboard circles for making pouch and valve facing templates, in lieu of a whole set of tube and arch punches.

Fractional bits ranging from 1/16" to 1/4" in 32nds of an inch, from 1/4" to 1/2" in 16ths of an inch, and from 1/2" to 1" in 8ths of an inch.

Some sort of glue pot: either an improvised double boiler made from a kettle and a glass jar, or an old crock pot, or a thermostatically controlled glue pot, with a supply of small stiff glue brushes.

An iron, preferably a non-steam iron, for heating old glue joints for disassembly, and for ironing bellows cloth, gaskets, pouches, valve facings, etc. to make them stick better.

Clamps: the more clamps, the better. A good beginning variety includes two each of various size C clamps with maximum opening ranging from 1" to 12", and several dozen spring clamps with 2" opening.

Brushes: several old toothbrushes for cleaning greasy parts, 1" paint brushes for applying shellac and other finishing materials, several small glue brushes for hot glue.

A sturdy workbench at least 6' wide, with a medium size bench vise or woodworker's vise. A small swivel vise for holding small parts.

Several dozen containers (cottage cheese or yogurt cups, small cardboard boxes, etc.) for keeping parts sorted while disassembled.

Power Tools

Variable speed reversible 3/8" electric drill.

Stationary belt and disc sander, with at least a 6" x 48" belt and 9" disc.

Air compressor for blowing dirt and sawdust out of channels, valve wells, etc.

Vacuum cleaner. Work light.

Additional Tools for the Serious Hobbyist

The more advanced hobbyist will wonder how he or she got along without the following additional tools, after using them for one job:

Hand Tools

Calipers, inside and outside.

High quality wire cutter for music wire and making new springs.

Pin vise, for holding small drill bits and other tools.

Dial indicator and stand, for measuring valve travel.

Micrometer, for measuring the thickness of springs, piano strings and other objects to the thousandth of an inch.

Tube and arch punches, from 1/16" to 1 5/8" or larger, in 16ths of an inch, and a good punching block.

Hand brace and small hand drill. Hand plane.

Set of high speed woodboring bits (these have a flat blade with a center point) from 3/4" to 1 1/2" for cleaning glue from pouch wells and drilling large holes.

Set of nut drivers. Gear/pulley puller.

Soldering gun, flux & solder, wire stripping tool. Circuit tester or ohmmeter for testing electrical continuity of switches and wiring in reproducing and coin pianos.

Files: round, triangular and flat needle files.

Mitre box and saw, jeweler's saw.

Sets of 1/8" and 1/4" steel number stamps.

Pin punches from 1/16" to 1/4" in 32nds of an inch for driving taper pins out of transmission gears and collars; a center punch for marking holes to be drilled.

Vacuum gauge. Stethoscope.

Suction pump for testing actions prior to installation in the piano.

Test rolls for various instruments as needed.

More clamps, including a few pipe or bar clamps of various lengths, and a set of 88 2" throat spring clamps.

Power Tools

0 - 1/2" capacity drill press with machine vise.

Bench motor with wire wheel, buffing wheel and buffing compound. Bench grinder.

10" table saw with assorted woodworking blades, including a fine tooth veneer cutting blade and a general purpose carbide tipped blade. Band saw.

Hand-held rotary tool ("Moto-tool") for grinding and shaping small parts.

More Tools for the Professional Rebuilder

The efficient professional rebuilder requires, in addition to all of the above, a set of vacuum operated pouch setters for the more common sizes of pouches, a water gauge for determining the precise suction level in reproducing pianos, a complete set of numbered and lettered drill bits, Forstner or multispur bits (for cleaning old pouch wells and drilling new ones) ranging from 3/4" to 2 1/4" in 8ths of an inch, a set of taps and dies, a set of socket wrenches, a set of dado blades for the table saw, a router, a hand held 4" belt sander, a small machine lathe, a 1" wide band sander, a jointer at least 6" wide, a surface planer at least 12" wide for making new pneumatic boards and other parts, a dust collection/exhaust system, and, of course, more clamps!

CHAPTER SIX
Specific Brands

This chapter includes descriptions, illustrations and rebuilding tips for all of the most commonly encountered player actions, along with a few of the rarer ones. It is not intended to be an encyclopedia of every style of every brand of player action ever manufactured, but it does include information for enough different varieties of components to enable the reader to find solutions to most problems encountered in the restoration of any player action. The chapter is divided into two sections, the first devoted to old (pre-1940's) players and the second to modern (post-1950's) ones. Many brands of pianos used a variety of player actions over the years, but those pianos which usually incorporated one brand of player action are listed with each manufacturer. Rare, common and very common player actions are identified; brands not identified as rare or common are somewhere in between. Particular localities sometimes have a high proportion of a particular brand if a piano dealer did a good job of promoting that line.

Many piano manufacturers used more than one brand of player action over the years. Simplex, Pratt-Read, Amphion and sometimes Standard player actions all show up in pianos made by the same company, making it difficult to predict exactly what action will be found in a given piano. To make matters even more complicated, some of the smaller companies used these big name actions and also made their own.

OLD PLAYER ACTIONS

AEOLIAN

Common. Used in Pianola pushup players, many upright pianos and a few grands made by the Aeolian Company, including Aeolian, Steck, Stroud, Stuyvesant, Weber, Wheelock and others, and also Steinway. Foot pumped grand pianos are very rare in the U.S., but more common in Great Britain. Of the remaining examples, many have Aeolian actions. For information on grand pianos so equipped, refer to the section on Duo-Art reproducing pianos on pp. 172–181. The stacks, spoolboxes, expression regulators and other parts used in Aeolian foot pumped grands are very similar to those used in Duo-Art grand reproducing pianos and require the same repair techniques.

Early Pianola actions are large and somewhat cumbersome; the earliest examples have double valves, but by the mid teens only single valve actions were made. The 1920's Aeolian upright player piano action is compact, efficient, and operates on a relatively small volume of suction. From the beginning, Aeolian constructed their player actions beautifully, with the finest quality leather, rubber cloth, tubing, wood, and other materials, and with all parts fitting together perfectly. A few Aeolians were made to play both 65 and 88 note rolls, with two rows of holes in the tracker bar and with a beautifully machined transfer block mounted on the back of the spoolbox. An adapter for the music roll chuck permits it to accomodate either 88 or 65 note spools. Many of these players were also equipped with the "Themodist" expression system, incorporating a divided stack, separate suction regulators for bass and treble, manual controls for precise expression control and accent holes in the tracker bar for playing Themodist rolls. A Steinway or Weber ⁶⁵⁄₈₈ Themodist is considered to be the epitome of the foot pumped player piano by many serious roll collectors.

The stack of the 1920's has two or three tiers of pneumatics which are glued to narrow maple deck boards *and* screwed to thin wooden rails at the open end. Each tier has its own valve and pouch boards, which are assembled without gaskets and then covered over with seal cloth. This provides a very airtight stack which can be restored without any difficult problems, providing that the seal cloth is attached with hot glue. The pump typically has one small reservoir across the front, with the pumping bellows and reservoir all hinged onto one common board like a miniature reed organ pump.

In earlier Aeolian actions, the valves are leather-faced wooden buttons attached rigidly to wire stems. A pouch lifter button is screwed onto the bottom of each stem. The top leather valve facing rests in place but is not glued down, with paper washers inserted under it for calibration of valve travel. The stamped metal valve seats are screwed to the valve board; the bottom seat is sealed to the wood with burnt shellac, and the top seat is screwed down onto a blotter paper gasket. Screwed down over each top and bottom seat is a metal valve stem guide with a fibre insert crimped in place. As in any player action with "identical" valve seats and stem guides, mark the orientation of each part and number everything prior to disassembly. Close scrutiny will show that the metal seats are *not* identical; apparently in some seats the convex shape was stamped in one operation and the four screw holes were punched in a separate operation, causing variation in screw hole locations that will keep the valves from seating properly if the seats are rotated or mixed up during reassembly. In an early action, note whether the upper and lower stem guides have different size holes and reassemble them accordingly. For further information on early style Aeolian cross valves, refer to the Duo-Art information on p. 179.

Later stacks have valves with wooden stems which are larger in diameter than the earlier wire stems. The stem

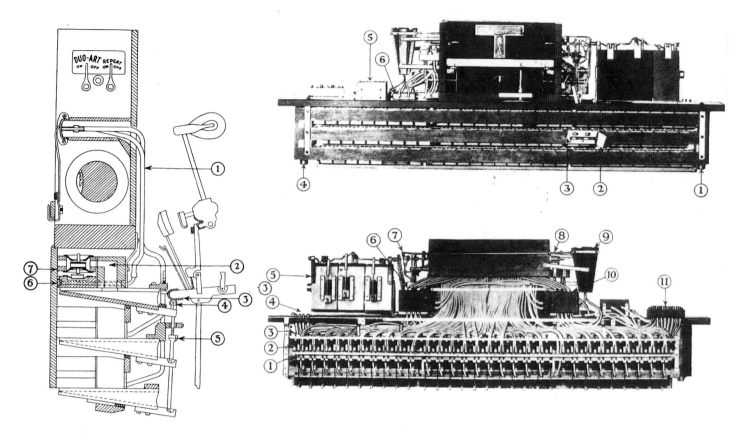

Illus. 6-1. Left: cross section of the Aeolian (Duo-Art) upright stack. Top: front view. Bottom: rear view.

guides are fibre, and the lower portion of each wood valve stem has a threaded wire inserted for the pouch button. The top leather facing and paper punchings are held down with a small fibre washer which can be pried off with a thin blade for replacement of the leather and calibration of travel. Although these parts are probably more uniform than the earlier ones, it is still wise to reinstall them in their original location and orientation.

The aluminum valve seats in later pianos are usually in perfect condition, but earlier nickel plated brass seats are often corroded, particularly if the valves originally were leathered with alum tanned sheepskin. Remove the seats from the deck boards, being careful to pop the sealed lower seats loose without distorting their shape. If necessary, heat the perimeter of each lower seat with a soldering gun to soften the shellac and permit the seat to come loose without bending. Carefully polish the seats with metal polish and lap the seating area on 600 sandpaper. Rinse in lacquer thinner and spray them with a thin coat of nitrocellulose lacquer to retard further corrosion. After the lacquer dries, gently hold a valve on each seat and test for airtightness by mouth. There should be absolutely no perceptible leakage with either high or low suction. If the original valve leather was sheepskin, replace it with suede calfskin of the type used in most later Aeolian actions.

After releathering the valves, polishing and lacquering

the seats if necessary, sealing the channels in the deck and pouch boards, resealing the lower seats to the valve board with burnt shellac, calibrating travel and installing the top seats, run a small bead of glue around each top seat. The deck board is shellacked, so white glue or PVC-E used to seal the top seats may be removed easily during future disassembly. Install the pouch buttons on the valve stems, attach the pouch boards, and adjust the pouch buttons so there is about 1/16" clearance between each button and pouch. Attach the seal cloth with hot glue. The original seal cloth was usually thin cotton rubber pneumatic cloth, sometimes coated with a layer of shellac. Some varieties of modern cloth will deteriorate rapidly if coated with shellac, so its use is not advised. Thin double weight motor cloth may also be used. Whichever cloth you use, glue it only with hot glue.

To gain access to a single valve or pouch for adjustment, cleaning or repair, cut away the seal cloth to expose the valve chamber. Then glue a new patch of single weight cotton rubber cloth over the hole.

Aeolian glued the pneumatics to unusually narrow decks in most upright piano stacks with pouch leather gaskets, requiring each pneumatic also to be screwed to the rest rail (lower tiers) or stop rail (top tier) to help keep them from coming loose. When regluing the pneumatics to the decks, be extra careful to align them properly so the tiny screw

Illus. 6-2. Top: early Aeolian nickel plated brass cross valve plates, brass valve guides with fibre inserts, and valves with wire stems. Bottom: late Aeolian aluminum valve plates, fibre valve guides, and valves with wooden stems. *Photo by Robert Taylor.*

holes in the pneumatics will also line up with the screw holes in the rest or stop rails. Dab a little burnt shellac on each pneumatic before screwing the rest or stop rail in place to help secure the pneumatic to the rail; the screws have almost no strength.

Connect suction to each deck individually to test each note before assembling the stack. Then, after reassembling the lower portion of the stack, remove the spoolbox and other parts from the shelf, attach the shelf to the stack, and install it in the piano, to regulate the pushrods to the piano action. (The piano action should already be regulated). If you wait to regulate the pushrods until after the entire head is assembled and tubed, it will be too late because they will be inaccessable.

After regulating the pushrods to the piano, remove the stack from the piano, remove the shelf, reattach the spoolbox and assemble the whole works. The tracker bar tubing neatly passes downward between the pushrods, and connects to the pouch input nipples located on the back of the stack. Each nipple is contained inside a little countersunk hole in the tubing guide rails. In some stacks, the tracker bar tubing for one deck attaches directly to the pouch input nipples, but each tube for the other deck(s) has an elbow installed at the sharp bend at the guide rail. The original tracker bar tubing was small enough to pass through the holes in the pushrod rail but elastic enough to stretch over the pouch input nipples, two attributes which can be hard to find simultaneously in modern neoprene tubing. The easiest and most durable way to retube one of these stacks is to use small tracker bar tubing from the tracker bar through the pushrod guide rail. Install tracker bar tubing elbows for the deck or decks which did not originally have them, and use short connecting links of slightly larger tracker bar tubing from the elbows to the pouch nipples. The smaller tubing will fit through the tubing guide rail without enlarging the holes and without rubbing on the pushrods, and the slightly larger connecting links between the elbows and pouch nipples will slip over the nipples with ease.

The Aeolian wind motor is large and powerful. The three double pneumatics are held together with large round head

wood screws hidden under seal cloth punchings. Large rubber washers serve as gaskets and spacers between the pneumatics; in many instances, the rubber is still flexible enough to be reused, providing that irregularities are sanded off prior to reassembly. If they are hard and brittle or cracked, replace them with several punchings of thick gasket leather or rubber inner tube glued together. Check the pneumatic hinges for strength and airtightness, and check each port and chamber for airtightness, sealing the wood with lacquer if necessary. Cover the pneumatics with the cloth stopping about ¼" from the hinge. Then cover the hinge area with a large punching of pouch leather as originally covered. Aeolian wind motors are prone to knocking if the cloth bushings for the crankshaft and connecting rods are badly worn; be sure to replace these if necessary with the correct thickness of woven action cloth, not felt. Regulating the slide valves is easy. Simply adjust each one so it uncovers each of its two ports by exactly the same amount. Early wind motors also have three double pneumatics with three slide valves, but the shape is different, with the moveable board of each pair of pneumatics between the two stationary boards and with the open ends facing upward, something like an upside down Gulbransen wind motor. They are no more difficult to rebuild than the later type.

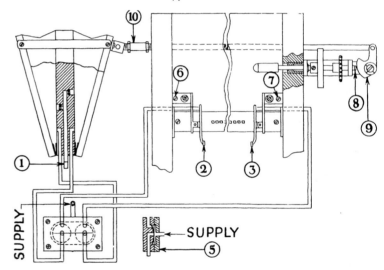

Illus. 6-3. The Aeolian tracking device.

The earliest Aeolian transmissions used in pushup players and early inner players had no automatic tracking device. A manual tracking lever usually moved both spools in unison, providing accurate alignment with no paper edge wear during rewind. To align this system, simply install a roll, loosen the lock nuts and adjust the machine screws at the right side of the transmission frame until the upper and lower spools are in perfect alignment. Tighten the lock nuts.

A few actions built in the early teens have a single tracking pneumatic with one tracking ear; its regulation is obvious.

The most common Aeolian tracking system is the one shown in illus. 6-3. It works very well for rolls of one width— the width to which the tracking ears are set—but if a roll is played which is significantly wider than the distance between the tracker ears, holding them both open, the tracker will stay in the middle position and will not provide correction. In some players, the automatic tracker cutoff mechanism for rewind is redundant, both closing off the tubes which connect the ears to the pneumatics with cutout pouches (#4 in the illustration) *and* cutting off the suction supply from the pump. In players with a constant supply of suction from the pump during play *and* rewind, the cutout pouch block does the job.

Always replace the little leather pads on the ends of the tracker ears. Remove each brass retainer by springing the tabs just enough to slip it off of the arm. If you are doing a fancy cosmetic restoration, polish and lacquer the individual parts, being very careful not to damage the hairlike springs. Then attach new pouch leather on the arms with PVC-E or shellac, and carefully slip the retainers back on.

To regulate the automatic tracking device, insert a roll of average width. Loosen screws #6 and #7 in the illustration and push the ears (or "triggers", in Aeolian parlance) away from the roll. Hold the tracker pneumatic in its centered position, and adjust turnbuckle #10 so cam #9 is centered on shaft #8, as shown in the illustration. Tighten the turnbuckle lock nuts. Then adjust the tracker ears so they are about 1/32" away from each side of the roll while it plays, and tighten screws #6 and #7. Try new and old rolls of various brands to find the best average. If the ears are adjusted to touch the edges of the paper, the tracker will be too sensitive, constantly shifting a little from side to side. 1/32" space will provide a compromise for rolls of slightly different widths.

The original 1925 Duo-Art service manual recommends "By keeping a very loose brake on the takeup spool and a rather slow speed on reroll, the music roll edges will not be torn." Today, this should be modified to read "By removing all brake tension from the takeup spool...". Some rebuilders also disconnect the wind motor accelerator slide valve from the manual rewind lever under the keybed, permanently turning the accelerator valve off. This gives the tempo lever complete control over rewind speed, from reasonably fast down to a dead stop.

AMERICAN PLAYER ACTION

Rare. Not to be confused with Amphion or Ampico actions used in American Piano Company instruments. The American Player Action Co. mechanisms were evidently manufactured for sale to small piano companies who did not build their own player actions. The valves have wire stems, metal seats, and wooden pouch lifter buttons somewhat like Standard/Autopiano valves. Illus. 6-4 shows the unusual design with small pneumatics mounted vertically

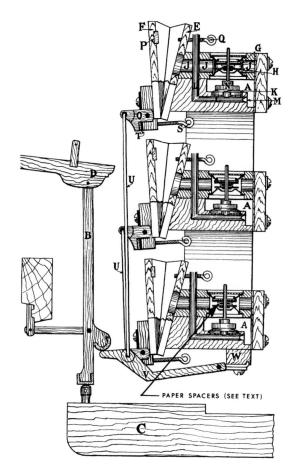

PAPER SPACERS (SEE TEXT)

Illus. 6-4. Cross section of the rare American player action, not to be confused with the American Piano Company (Amphion) or Aeolian-American.

on the back of the three valve/pouch tiers, providing easy regulation of pneumatic travel and lost motion between stack and piano action. To regulate valve travel, insert or remove spacing washers made from various thicknesses of paper front or balance rail punchings.

AMPHION

Very common. The "Amphion Accessible Player Action", as it was called in original factory literature, was manufactured in Syracuse, New York by the Amphion Piano-Player Company and was used in many brands of pianos. Amphion manufactured the player actions for most Ampico reproducing pianos sold by the American Piano Company prior to the Ampico B (see Ch. 7). They also built other reproducing and expression systems, including the Apollo Artecho reproducing mechanism using Artecho rolls, the Dynachord Art Expression Player using the Art Apollo family of expression rolls (Apollo X, QRS Autograph Automatic, QRS red X, and Automatic Music Roll Co. XP rolls - see pp. 188), and a Recordo expression player action, all of which are extremely rare today.

Amphion liked to use cast iron brackets, and you will find them everywhere - supporting the wind motor, con-

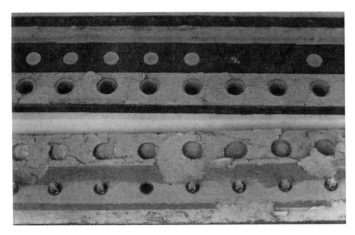

Illus. 6-5. One deck of an early cardboard divider Amphion stack, split apart to show the cardboard.

necting the pumping pedals to the bellows, holding the stack in the piano, etc.

Early Amphion player piano actions have a cardboard divider between the pouch and valve chambers, with the lower valve seats consisting of grommets fastened to the cardboard, and with individual wooden rings glued over the valve chambers for the upper seats. The pouches were rubber cloth and always need to be replaced, requiring splitting of the cardboard divider. Try to separate the cardboard from the pouch board with a sharp knife without damaging the cardboard any more than necessary. If you slice it carefully enough, you might be able to use the old cardboard and grommet valve seats. If the cardboard splits so badly that it can't be glued back together neatly, replace it with appropriate new material and new grommets. Whether you use the original or new cardboard, seal it and the wooden stack parts thoroughly. In many cardboard divider Amphion stacks, the bleeds are nothing more than small holes through the pouch lifter discs. If this is the case, be sure to clean all dirt and lint out of the holes, and punch appropriate holes in the pouches prior to gluing the discs on them. Some stacks have bleed holes in brass tubes which run through a suction chamber in the spool box shelf. Clean these with compressed air; if any bleeds remain plugged, remove the brass tube from the shelf.

If the valves are attached to the fluted wood stems with little round head brads, save the brads and reinstall them when releathering the valves. Without them, the stems will be too rigid, allowing the pouches to trap the valves at an

Illus. 6-6. Amphion valves have an important little round head tack between valve button and stem, to permit wobble for airtight seating of the valve.

angle, causing leakage on the top seats. Calibrate pouch to stem clearance by sanding the stems or adding thin leather or cardboard punchings. Adjust valve travel by inserting blotter paper rings under the top wooden valve seats, sanding the rings as necessary for fine adjustment.

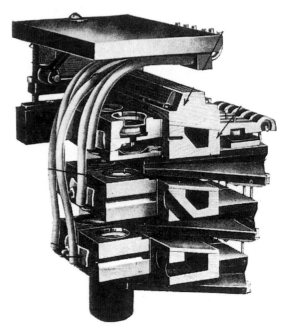

Illus. 6-7. Cross section of the later right side up unit valve stack. Earlier upside down valve stacks are similar but with the decks channelled differently to accommodate the inverted valve blocks.

Illus. 6-8. Left: later right side up Amphion unit valve. Right: earlier upside down valve. In use, the upside down valve is inverted from its position in this photo.

Except for the early cardboard divider stacks, most Amphion actions have unit valve blocks as shown in illus. 6-8. Earlier unit block actions have "upside down valves" with wooden rings for the "top" valve seats, while later actions have the valves mounted right side up with metal top seats. In both styles, the valve blocks are held in place with metal clips and machine nuts. Prior to disassembling a unit valve stack, note where spare valve blocks and solid wood dummy blocks—there are several of each—are located so you will reassemble them correctly. After removing each valve block from its deck, remove the top valve seat. Chip away the hard shellac, and remove the wooden ring from an upside down valve by cutting through the blotter paper ring. Pull the metal seat out of a right side up valve, noting its orientation with mating scratches on the seat and valve block so the seat will fit back into the hole. Cut the old cork gasket off of each block, and carefully sand the gasketed surface—it must be clean and flat. Sand the old shellac

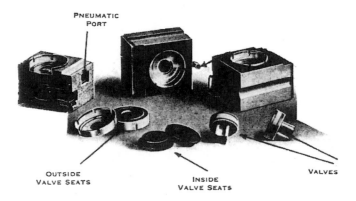

Illus. 6-9. Right side up valves with parts identified.

Labels: PNEUMATIC PORT, OUTSIDE VALVE SEATS, INSIDE VALVE SEATS, VALVES

finish off the sides and front, to expose the glue joint between the pouch block and valve chamber. Separate the pouch block and valve chamber with a sharp chisel, and sand the old pouch leather off of both parts. Blow the sanding dust and old dirt out with compressed air, being careful to clean the bleed, which is located in a channel visible from the back. Mark the orientation of the bakelite lower seat with a tiny scratch on the bottom so you can return it to its original orientation, and push the seat out. Lap the seat on very fine sandpaper taped to glass, chip away any loose old sealer, and reinstall the seat in the block with burnt shellac. Reseal the wood if necessary.

Replace the pouch with a new one made of pouch leather, and glue the block back together, clamping it with padded spring clamps. After the glue is dry, remove the clamps and apply a bead of burnt shellac around the crack between the pouch block and valve chamber, completely filling any voids. After this shellac dries, apply a coat of ordinary shellac to both sides and the front of the block. Releather the valve, reusing the little round head brad to provide stem wobble, and calibrate stem to pouch clearance. Calibrate valve travel in upside down blocks by gluing blotter paper washers as necessary to the wooden rings before gluing them to the blocks with hot glue. Calibrate valve travel in right side up valves by adjusting the position of the top metal seat, and sealing it in place with burnt shellac.

After restoring all of the valve blocks, draw parallel lines on a piece of suede gasket leather and use one valve block to stamp ink impressions on the leather using an ordinary stamp pad. Cut out the individual gaskets, being

Illus. 6-10. Gasket leather stamped with ink impressions of a unit valve block.

meticulously careful about the locations of the holes to avoid leakage, and glue them to the blocks with hot glue. Make sure that none of the gaskets cover the bleed holes.

The pneumatics are glued to the decks in a unit valve Amphion stack with cheesecloth in between, providing easy removal of most pneumatics. Be careful, however, of the occasional stubborn pneumatic which wants to cause the deck board to crack during disassembly. When regluing the pneumatics to the decks, install new cheesecloth, clamping the pneumatics until the glue dries. Be careful not to crush the somewhat fragile hollow deck board with the clamps.

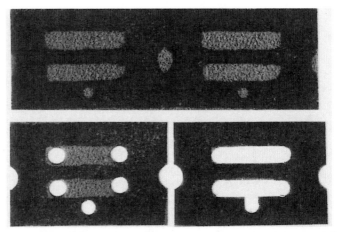

Illus. 6-11. After cutting the leather into individual gaskets, carefully punch both ends of each long hole and then use a sharp knife to cut out the remaining piece of leather.

Apply seal cloth to the ends of each deck board, which usually leak badly through the grain. Install new gaskets between the decks and on the top and bottom cap blocks, and reassemble the decks to the stack feet with the long bolts and nuts.

The Amphion tracking device is a simple double pneumatic with edge-sensing tracker ears. Releather the little valves controlled by the ears and test them for airtightness; adjust the ears a little farther apart than the width of an average roll. The two halves of the pneumatic are held together with large wire staples; keep all of the parts in their

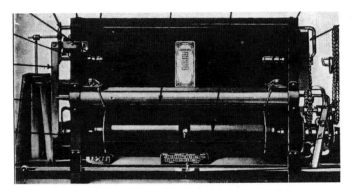

Illus. 6-12. The Amphion tracking device.

original orientation in order to reassemble the pneumatic correctly.

The Amphion transmission frame is made of die cast zinc pot metal, and unfortunately in most pianos this has cracked, warped and fallen apart due to intergranular corrosion. If a transmission frame is broken into two neat parts which will fit together perfectly with no warpage, clean it thoroughly in lacquer thinner to remove the old oil, and

Illus. 6-13. A warped die cast zinc pot metal transmission frame, showing the first signs of intergranular corrosion. A crack at the top has been epoxied.

glue the two parts back together with epoxy, building a little epoxy up around the outside of the break for reinforcement. If a frame is falling apart or warped to the extent that the takeup spool will not spin *freely*, obtain a new one from a supply company. When removing the shafts from the old frame and installing them in the new one, align the keys on the shafts with the keyways in the frame; when pressing the shafts into the gears, support the gears carefully to keep from applying pressure to the frame. Many new transmission frames need filing here and there before the shafts, gears and other parts will fit; sand or file the face which mates with the wood, if necessary, so it lays flat, permitting

Illus. 6-14. The holding screw and levelling screws at each end of the stack make it simple to rough regulate the stack to the piano action After eliminating most of the lost motion with the levelling screws, regulate each individual note with the adjustment screw on the striking finger

Illus. 6-15. The Amphion wind motor Bend each valve wire so the slide valve uncovers the lower and upper port equally as the crankshaft turns

free movement of the shafts after it is installed on the spool-box.

Each end of the Amphion stack is fitted with an adjustable mounting bracket simplifying overall regulation of the stack to the piano. Place the completed stack, without its head, in the piano, and adjust the levelling screws until you arrive at the best average regulation between stack and piano action. Tighten the lock nuts on the levelling screws, secure the stack with the two large holding screws, and regulate each individual pneumatic finger. Then remove the stack from the piano, assemble the head and install the complete stack in the piano. Many Amphion heads are fastened to the stack with a large hinge at each end, facilitating regulation of the stack to the piano with the head swung forward, although this feature is not shown in illus. 6-14.

The Amphion wind motor has cast metal slide valve seats attached to the wooden trunk. Remove these and replace the leather gaskets, gluing the leather to the metal with PVC-E and sealing it to the wood with shellac. As in any other motor in which two pneumatics share one slide valve, regulate each valve so it uncovers or passes each of its ports equally, and the motor will turn smoothly.

The Amphion wind motor governor is one of the best ever made, incorporating a cast iron regulator valve as shown in illus. 6-16. It also includes a small compensating

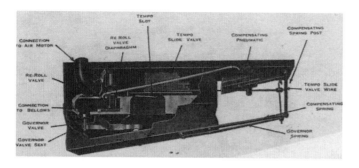

Illus. 6-16. Amphion governor with parts identified

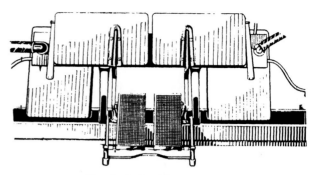

Illus. 6-18. Amphion foot pump

pneumatic which helps it to respond to quick changes in the suction level. The tempo slide valve in many governors is made of celluloid; check to see if it is warped or unstuck from the wood. If necessary, replace it with a new one made of brass, available from supply companies. The accelerator pouch in the governor is mounted on a separate block held by nails. Remember to replace the short piece of tubing which connects it to the outside elbow.

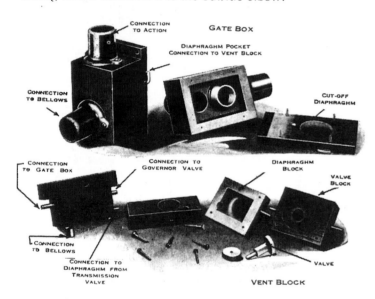

Illus. 6-17. The gate box (action cutoff) and vent block

The action cutoff and wind motor accelerator take the form of large pouches located in the gate box and governor, as illustrated. These two large pouches in turn are controlled by the "vent block" shown in illus. 6-17. A small round brass slide valve on the transmission frame opens a hole during rewind, triggering the vent block pouch which in turn controls the two larger pouches. Most transmission frames have two nipples; the left one is connected to the vent block, and the right one is unused except in early Stoddard Ampico reproducing pianos. Controlling the action cutoff and accelerator pneumatically does away with the jungle of control rods and linkages which are found under the keybed of Standard and many other player pianos.

The Amphion foot pump has the two pumping bellows mounted on the front and two reservoirs on the back, as shown. It is common for the trunk and pumping bellows

boards to split badly during disassembly, and if heat is used to separate the glue joint it also separates the plywood of the bellows board. Be prepared to do major woodworking to repair whatever damage occurs. If the trunk splits badly, reface it with new wood of appropriate thickness, as shown on p. 57. The reservoirs may be rehinged and recovered without removing them from the trunk, but the pumping bellows are so close together that they must be removed. If you remove one, remove both. If one pump practically falls off, you may be certain that the other one will leak if you don't reglue it; if one breaks and splits, you will probably need to remove the other one in order to repair the trunk board properly. Be sure to hinge the pumping bellows securely, as they are subject to a lot of stress.

ANGELUS: see WILCOX & WHITE
APOLLO: see MELVILLE CLARK
ARTEMIS: see STEGER
ARTISTANO: see A. B. CHASE

AUTOPIANO

Common. An affiliate of Kohler Industries, which also controlled the Standard Pneumatic Action Co., and Kohler and Campbell, the Autopiano was a deluxe, well built player action with valves, valve seats, pouch board, pneumatics and fingers, pushrods, wind motor, transmission and other parts almost identical to those of the Standard. The Autopiano stack, wind motor, spoolbox and other parts were used in Welte Licensee reproducing actions marketed in over 100 American piano brands, and the Autopiano was also used as a basis for the American Fotoplayer manufactured by Robert-Morton of Van Nuys, California.

The Autopiano usually has a double valve action, with the primary chest and stack composed of lots of pieces of wood screwed together with hundreds of screws and dozens of gaskets like a double valve Standard stack. Early stacks have both leather valve faces screwed onto long threaded valve stems. These valves tend to be too stiff, so use very thin firm leather in order to have barely adequate wobble for airtight seating. Later stacks have Standard style valves; refer to the Standard section in Ch. 6 for details.

The Autopiano tracking device works on the same pneu-

106

Illus. 6-19. The Autopiano tracking device works the same as the Standard device, although the parts are laid out differently

matic principles as the Standard, using two staggered tracking holes at each side of the music roll and a mechanism with six pouches, but in the Autopiano, the pneumatics stand on end and are connected with wooden links. Refer to the Standard tracker information on pp. 143–145 for a description of the operation of the valves and pouches. Some Autopiano tracking devices have self cleaning bleeds. Each bleed is located in the center of the pouch, with a tiny pin mounted in the pouch well. When the pouch is at rest, the pin sticks through the bleed, keeping it clean. If the pins are removed, the bleeds will be too big.

Some Autopianos contain stamped metal transmission frames and others contain die cast frames. Be careful not to break a cast transmission frame during cleanup and reassembly.

The Autopiano pump, motor governor, pedal pneumatics and other controls are more deluxe than Standard parts, but their restoration presents no unusual problems because everything is screwed and gasketed together, providing easy disassembly.

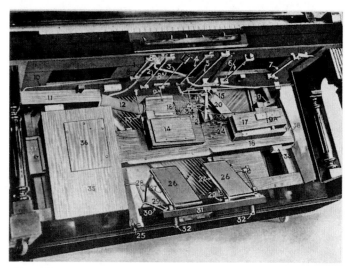

Illus. 6-20. One style of Autopiano pump. Although it is laid out differently from Standard, they are both assembled with lots of screws and gaskets

BALDWIN

Common. Baldwin player actions were installed in pianos manufactured by the Baldwin Piano Co. of Cincinnati and Chicago, including Baldwin, Ellington, Hamilton, Howard, Manualo, Manuola, Modello, Monarch and others. The Baldwin action has several very unique features as described below. Dreaded by many restorers, this action is not really that hard to restore if the right procedures are used, and it is a very airtight, responsive action when rebuilt properly. Its only negative point is the fact that the tracker bar holes are slightly taller than those in some other pianos, causing repetition to suffer slightly in a few rolls with closely spaced repeated notes.

Illus. 6-21. Rear view of a two tier Baldwin stack, showing the long fingers which are glued to the tops of the upside down pneumatics

The stack is made in two or three tiers with each pouch board in back, the valve board in front, and the top and bottom covered with heavy double weight seal cloth. The wire valve stems are horizontal; in some early stacks, they are screwed into small pouch buttons, but in most stacks they are supported at the rear by larger mushroom shaped

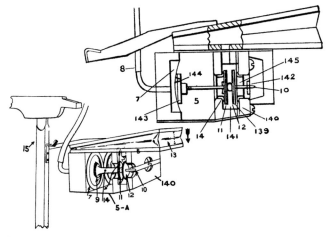

Illus. 6-22. Baldwin pneumatics sit on top of the valve chest, with the open ends facing the front of the piano

turned wooden stem guides which are glued to the pouches as shown in illus. 6-23. Each stem guide has a celluloid bleed in the center of its base showing through a small hole in the center of the pouch, and the bleeds may be accessed for cleaning by pulling the pouch input elbows out of the pouch boards. The pneumatics are glued to the top of each valve/pouch chamber, with the open ends facing forward and with a finger extending over the hinge end and pressing upward on a metal bracket attached to the sticker. With this arrangement, gravity causes the pneumatics to eliminate their own lost motion.

Illus. 6-24. One valve chamber with the pneumatics and upper seal cloth pulled loose.

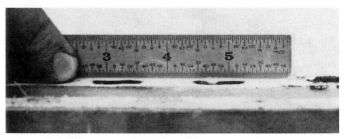

Illus. 6-25. Be very careful not to gouge the wood around the holes when removing the old glue with a scraper.

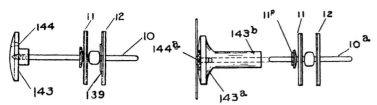

Illus. 6-23. Early Baldwin valves (left) have the valve stem screwed into the pouch button 143, but later valves encountered in most Baldwin pianos (right) slip into a mushroom shaped stem 143a. To calibrate valve travel, add or subtract paper or pouch leather punchings between the outside valve face and rounded wood button, at position 139. To calibrate pouch to valve clearance, add or subtract puchings at 11p.

If most of the old tracker bar tubing is still intact, make a sketch showing its routing through the guide rail. In most actions, there are a few places with three or four tubes tightly squeezed in place and other places where just one or two tubes have extra space, and this will be confusing if you don't make a note of it. After sketching the tubing, remove it and the pouch board elbows.

Remove the head and separate the decks. They are held together with a suction supply manifold on the bass end, a flat wooden plate on the treble end, and several braces connecting the decks to each other. Remove the seal cloth covers from the screw access holes on the suction supply manifold, and keep track of the original placement of each screw in case there are several different lengths.

Mark the locations of the pneumatics on the pouch and valve boards, because you will be removing the old seal cloth, destroying all evidence of the original locations. Number and remove the top valve seat boards, and remove the valves, keeping them in order with their paper calibrating washers in place on the stems. If you are restoring an early stack with the valve stems screwed into smaller wooden pouch buttons, unscrew them carefully without nicking or scratching them.

Usually all of the pneumatics can be removed at once by pulling one layer of the seal cloth off in one long strip with the pneumatics still attached. After removing these parts, you will be left with the pouch and valve boards attached by a number of small spindles, dowels and the remaining seal cloth, with the old pouches and wooden stem guides still in place. Remove the seal cloth by discreetly heating it with an iron or torch a little at a time, and scraping the residue off with a sharp chisel or paint scraper. The decks are

made of poplar, so when scraping the edge of the valve board, be extra careful not to scoop out the weaker areas surrounding the channels or it will be hard to make the stack perfectly airtight. After removing most of the old material and smelly rubber, sand off the remaining glue. Repeat the process on the top and bottom of each deck. This whole operation should be performed outside or with ample cross ventilation to prevent your lungs from acquiring a thorough internal coating of rubber smoke. Once this filthy job is done, the rest of the restoration will be much more pleasant.

Illus. 6-26. The valve board and pouch board are connected by several spools and a number of dowels. Keep these in order!

After removing all of the old seal cloth and glue, number and disassemble the spools and dowels which hold the decks together, number the end frame pieces and knock them apart with a small hammer and block of maple. Number and remove the wooden stem guides from the pouches, being careful not to damage the celluloid bleeds, and sand the old pouch leather off of the pouch boards.

Cut new pouches and punch an appropriate hole in the exact center of each one. Carefully hand scrape the old pouch leather and glue off of the stem guides, and glue each one to a new pouch with hot glue. Make a centering tool as shown in illus. 6-27 which fits snugly into the hole in the pouch board. Insert the tool in the pouch well hole,

Illus. 6-27. Left to right: pouch centering tool, new pouch, valve stem, and another stem glued to a pouch, with pouch board to the rear. To install the pouch, insert the tool through the input hole. Make the point no larger than the bleed hole to avoid damaging bleeds.

apply glue to the rim of the well, and gently lay the pouch & stem guide in place with the bleed slipped over the little pin and with the pouch leather drawn up around the stem guide to keep from dropping it on the glue. Carefully lay the leather in place, distributing the wrinkles evenly until they all disappear. Withdraw the centering tool and proceed to the next pouch. When you are done, reassemble the spindles, dowels, end frames and valve boards to the pouch boards; if you were careful throughout the job, each stem guide will be perfectly centered in the valve well as you peer in from straight above.

Next, apply new medium weight bellows cloth seals to the top and bottom of each deck, using hot glue to attach the cloth just one note at a time and ironing it down as you go. Mix your hot glue the same thickness as for covering pumping bellows, because the heavy seal cloth will soak up quite a bit of glue. Although the usual procedure is to punch holes in gaskets before gluing them down, if you punch the pneumatic feed holes in the seal cloth first, you will drag a lot of glue all over the cloth with the iron. Glue the cloth on first and then cut the holes out with a sharp knife before the glue turns hard.

Again using thick glue—you will find out just how thick within the first few pneumatics—glue the rehinged and recovered pneumatics down to the seal cloth. Press each pneumatic hard against the deck by hand for about ten seconds until the glue begins to set, glue the next pneumatic, and keep going back to the previous three or four pneumatics until they are firmly attached. After the glue has set but before it turns hard, check the inside of each channel carefully and remove any glue which dripped down toward the valve chamber.

It is usually necessary to releather the top valve facings but it is sometimes possible to leave the original pouch leather lower facings intact. Releather the valves as necessary, using PVC-E to secure the leather to the metal valve discs. Turn each deck with the valve wells facing up, and insert and regulate the valves by adding or subtracting paper punchings as shown in illus. 6-23. The valve travel should be $3/64''$, and the clearance between pouches and valve stems should be about $1/32''$, less than in most other stacks. If the valve stems are the early type

which screw into the pouch buttons, be very careful during reassembly not to damage the new pouches.

If ever there is a place not to use white glue, a Baldwin stack is it! It is hard enough to remove the old seal cloth in most Baldwins with the original hot glue, but when you are confronted with one which was previously assembled with white glue you will wish you could chain the previous repairer to your bench to force *him* to remove the cloth and glue for you.

Remove the remaining old seal cloth, glue and leather from the suction supply manifold for the bass end and the flat wood support plate for the treble, repaint them with semi gloss paint, masking off the gasket and seal cloth areas, regasket them, and assemble the stack. Tape over the screw access holes until you have tested the stack and solved any problems; then glue the new seal cloth in place.

Several styles of tracking devices were used in the Baldwin family of player pianos, as shown in illus. 6-28. An early, rarely encountered system has two tracking ears connected to two valves which control the double tracker pneumatic. Somewhat later this system was improved by the addition of the "compound floating triangle" as Baldwin called it— a balanced system of levers which keeps rolls of any width centered. Soon the use of valves was discontinued, with the tracker ears directly admitting air into the two halves of the double tracker pneumatic. All three of these early systems incorporate a latching device and adjusting knob along with the automatic tracking system, permitting the user to override the automatic tracking by locking it into the center position and then manually adjusting the relation of the roll to the tracker bar. (The manual override latch is shown in simplified form as part #414 on the drawing, and the manual adjusting knob is #158). This combination of automatic and manual

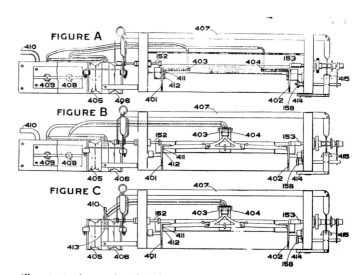

Illus. 6-28. Three styles of Baldwin automatic tracking device. Top: early system with tracking ears controlling valves for double tracking pneumatic. Middle: Floating triangle controlling valves. Bottom: Floating triangle admitting air directly to double tracking pneumatic. The bottom system is the one most commonly encountered.

tracking is a good one, for it provides the advantage of automatic tracking for new rolls with perfect edges, and manual tracking for worn rolls which won't work right with an automatic device. Nevertheless, by sometime in the 1920's, Baldwin discontinued the manual override system, replacing it with a simple tracker bar transposing knob along with the floating triangle mechanism.

Illus. 6-29. Closeup of the floating triangle and pallet valves.

The floating triangle mechanism works beautifully if adjusted correctly, but it can be a nuisance to adjust unless its operation is understood. First, all mechanical parts must be perfectly free to move without any excess friction. This means that the tracker bar tubing must fit where it belongs, out of the way of the moving parts. The two tracking ears pivot on pointed pins and are counterbalanced to provide just a little pressure on the edges of the roll. With the music roll and tracker bar centered on the takeup spool (which usually is not adjustable), the rear point of the floating triangle should be centered between the two metal pallet valves as in illus. 6-29, with each pallet closed. The top of each pallet is bent at a sharp angle and hangs from a groove in the support, and the two pallets are loosely connected to each other with a delicate strip of pouch leather. Replace this leather and the leather pallet facings carefully so there is no tendency for the pallets to be hingebound. When the assembly is held at the angle at which it is mounted in the piano, the force of gravity should be sufficient to pull the pallets tightly shut with absolutely no seepage detectable at the output nipples. If you think it is necessary to bend the body of a pallet to make it seal properly, first consider the use of thicker or thinner pouch leather on its face. If this won't solve the problem, bend the valve *very gently* to keep from ruining it! Each pallet has a tiny tab which comes into contact with the floating triangle; after you ascertain that the pallets seal their output tubes, bend the tabs if necessary so the triangle responds to sideways movement of the music roll as it should. There should be about 1/32" play between each tab and the triangle when an average roll is centered between the sensing ears. Bending the tabs is one of the most delicate adjustments you will ever perform in a player piano, so do this as gently as if you were adjusting the hands of a watch.

Several styles of transmission were used; the following two are the most common: an unusually complex pot metal casting used in early actions having the manual tracker override latch, and an unusually simple stamped

Illus. 6-30. An early Baldwin pot metal transmission hopelessly broken beyond repair. Many modern cast aluminum replacement transmissions require extensive machining before they will fit on the spoolbox and hold everything in alignment.

Illus. 6-31. The beautifully simple later style Baldwin transmission.

transmission frame in later actions. The simplicity of the later style transmission implies that its designers said "let's make this thing as simple as possible after all the problems we've had with the old style!" Unfortunately, most of the early style transmission frames are irreparably warped and broken due to intergranular corrosion, requiring replacement. Replacement early style transmission frames have been available over the years from several suppliers, but the quality has been very inconsistent, with the average new frame requiring quite a bit of additional machining before it will fit in the piano and hold the complex arrangement of shafts and levers in alignment. Before you purchase an early Baldwin with a broken transmission frame, or before you restore one for someone else, find out whether a replacement frame is available or whether you will have to make your own transmission to fit the spoolbox.

Baldwin used several styles of pump, the most common of which is shown in illus. 6-32. With its large unhinged reservoir and complex arrangement of bell cranks and connecting rods, this pump has a somewhat spongy feel compared to the later more conventional pumps. Observe the arrangement of the connecting rods, panels which cover the piano pedal assembly and soundboard, and other parts

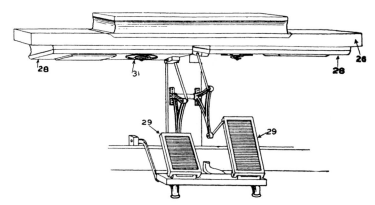

Illus. 6-32. The keybed-mounted pump. Late Baldwin pianos have a more conventional pump.

as you disassemble them, and sketch them if necessary, for you will have a surprising number of parts when you have everything apart. Recovering the pump is no more difficult than any other pump, but you will need large clamps to clamp the new hinges in the pumping bellows while the glue dries. Install a sheepskin punching at each corner of each bellows as Baldwin did originally. The flap valves in most pumps are large leather-faced aluminum discs, held in place by a center screw with a light compression spring and one pin to keep them from rotating. The side of the leather which faces the aluminum is sealed with shellac or lacquer to provide airtightness. These valves open unusually large holes in the bellows, permitting the pedals to return very quickly.

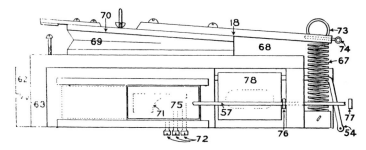

Illus. 6-33. The Baldwin wind motor governor and speed control

The usual Baldwin wind motor governor has several regulating screws (#72 in illus. 6-33) which control the flow of suction through the speed control port. Leave the adjustment of these screws alone during rebuilding, or if you have to remove them to replace a gasket, measure where they are and replace them in the same position. The 1916 service manual, from which the present drawings have been reproduced, gives the following advice regarding the regulation of the governor:

"Governor spring (#67) is correctly regulated when a 2 lb. 4 oz. weight resting at 2 9/16" from the hinge end (18) of the governor pneumatic (69) will just start the moving board (70) of the pneumatic to drop, the box being laid with the pneumatic on its top, and level. This weighting must never be varied from, as it is necessary for steady running with

varying pumping. The speed must never be regulated by the governor, but by the valve slot (71) and regulating screws (72). This is very important.

"These screws when turned in, reduce the speed. When turned out, increase the speed, affecting the tempo at the 40 to 70 portion of the indicator scale. The music sheet should run 7 feet in one minute when the pointer is at 70.

"Should the Governor Spring (67) require correcting, take hold and pull on ring (73) of the spring, pull out pin (74), let spring in or out and replace pin and test by weight."

Over the years, Baldwin governors and wind motors were made in somewhat different configurations and sizes, requiring different weighting of the governor than that prescribed in the 1916 test manual. The above description, however, does clarify the mystery surrounding the difficulty of getting a Baldwin motor to run uniformly if the entire adjustment is attempted with the spring or tempo lever alone, and it makes it clear that the little regulating screws are not intended to provide precise adjustmewnt of tempos at 40, 60, 80, etc. Rather, the screws should be used as a group to regulate midrange tempo after the tempo lever is set to stop the motor at "0", with the spring adjusted so the motor neither races nor slows down during hard pumping.

BAY, H. C.

Common. This two tier action was used in many brands of inexpensive pianos, including the H. C. Bay, Bellman, and Drachman. In most stacks, the valves are made of bakelite with the valve and fluted stem all molded in one piece; no wobble is necessary because the bottom of

Illus. 6-34. H.C. Bay head.

Illus. 6-35. H.C. Bay pump.

Illus. 6-36. Action cutoff pneumatic mounted on top of pump. When the transmission is shifted into rewind, a pallet valve under the transmission actuates the valves shown here, causing the large pneumatic to push the control rod to the left, turning the stack off and accelerating the wind motor.

Illus. 6-37. H.C. Bay stack.

Illus. 6-38. Front of stack with bleed rail and top valve plate removed.

the stem is rounded. (In a few examples, the valves are wooden buttons with fluted stems, as in a Gulbransen). The top valve seats are large gasketed wooden plates held on with many screws, and the bottom seats are leathered. Calibration of individual valve travel is accomplished by sanding the top of the valve; many valves have original sanding marks left by the factory. Regulation of pouch/valve stem clearance is done by placing a thicker or thinner cloth punching on the cardboard pouch disc.

The front of each tier has a removeable gasketed junc-

tion board for the tracker bar tubing; the upper junction board also contains the bleeds for both tiers. Each bleed has a tiny access screw making it possible to clean a clogged bleed without taking anything apart. Note that the screws are for access only, not for adjusting the amount of bleed.

Illus. 6-39. Another view of the front of the stack, showing row of bleed access screws. The valve board and pouch board are glued together along the back, requiring them to be sawed apart for pouch replacement.

Illus. 6-40. Back view of stack with top valve cover plate removed, and one valve removed from its well.

Illus. 6-41. Inside of top valve plate, with two molded bakelite valves.

The Bay stack usually needs new pouches, and the pouch boards are glued to the valve boards around three sides, requiring cutting them apart with a thin veneer cutting blade on a table saw. An intimidating job to the beginner, this is not as difficult as it looks providing that the blade is adjusted perfectly so it doesn't cut into the wrong parts. Before cutting, drill and countersink screw holes, and install and remove the screws which will be used for reassembling the pouch boards to the valve boards with appropriate length #8 flat head wood screws. Measure the thickness of each tier prior to cutting. Sand the boards smooth to eliminate any irregularities caused by the saw blade. Select thin gasket leather which will be added to the valve board, and build up the pouch board with a new strip of wood glued with aliphatic resin glue so *the total thickness of the new wood and gasket equals the thickness of old wood removed by the saw blade.* After the glue dries, drill the pneumatic feed channels and screw holes through the added strip of wood, and sand off any fuzzy wood left by the drill bit. Replace the pouches, seal any wood which needs it, gasket the valve board, and assemble the pouch boards to the valve boards. Next time the pouches have to be replaced, the job will be no more difficult than in most other stacks.

BECKWITH (Sears, Roebuck & Co.)

The Beckwith action was installed in Beckwith pianos marketed by Sears, Roebuck and Co., of Chicago. Other actions were also used by Sears, but the Beckwith action is shown in illus. 6-42. As in a Standard action, the front board of the stack is the pouch board and it comes off by removing a number of screws. The valves also resemble Standard valves with wobbly valve discs held in place on wire stems by force fit collars, and with wooden pouch buttons screwed to the bottom of the stems. The bottom valve seats are fibre discs, the top seats are wood, and each seat has a wooden stem guide screwed over it. As shown in illus. 6-43, each pushrod is threaded into a forked finger on the pneumatic, permitting easy regulation to the piano action by turning the pushrod up or down.

CABLE EUPHONA

The Cable Company of Chicago used this action in Cable, Carola, Conover, Euphona, Kingsbury, and several other brands. The Cable Euphona action was not used in pianos built by Hobart M. Cable in LaPorte, Indiana (Story and Clark), Cable-Nelson in South Haven, Michigan (Everett), Cable & Sons in New York or Philadelphia (Lester) or Fayette Cable (Cable-Nelson); these "other" Cables used Standard, Simplex, Amphion and other player actions.

The two tier Cable action is one of the easiest player actions to restore and to regulate to the piano. The pneumatics face forward, with pull wires connecting them to wooden rocker levers which push up on the piano action. The pouch boards unscrew from the valve boards, simplifying pouch replacement. The valves are celluloid discs, with fluted wood stems rigidly attached. No wobble is necessary because the valve well guides the stem. The top seats are gasketed wooden plates held down with numerous screws, and the bottom seats are leather washers glued to the bottom of the valve wells. The pneumatics are glued to the decks on newspaper gaskets, permitting their removal without damaging them or the decks. In short, everything may be disassembled without damage.

When gluing the pneumatics to the decks, be sure to duplicate the original overhang. If there is slightly too little overhang, the pneumatics will bind on the top valve seat plates. If you replace the leather on the top valve seats with the correct non-splitting calf skin, it is not necessary to glue little pointed fingers of leather up into the holes as the original leather was glued. The pouch board screw heads were originally sealed with beeswax, and it is good practice to replace this during reassembly.

Illus. 6-42. Back view of Beckwith stack.

Illus. 6-43. Closeup of Beckwith stack showing adjustable fingers.

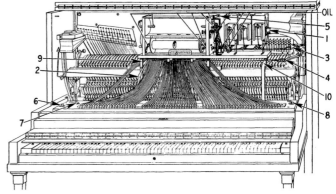

Illus. 6-44. The Cable Euphona upper action, one of the easiest to rebuild and regulate.

113

The only problem in some Cable stacks is the set of short lead tubes which run between the wooden rocker arms, connecting the rubber tracker bar tubing to the pouch boards. Check this carefully for kinks, holes, internal corrosion or other damage, and replace it if it is not in perfect condition. Replacement connectors are available from some supply companies.

CAROLA

Rare. The Carola, not to be confused with the Cable Carola described above, is an unusual action manufactured by Bluthner & Co. of London. It is included here not because it is likely that many rebuilders will ever encounter one, but rather as an example of some of the unusual player actions which it is possible to find. As shown in illus. 6-45, the Carola action featured the "Dodds valve". According to the beautifully printed sales catalogue from which this illustration is reproduced, the "Dodds" valve was "invented and perfected by Mr. Edgar Dodds of the Royal Air Force, during his respites from flying on various Fronts. On his demobilization, Mr. Dodds constructed a complete Player-Piano in which his new idea was embodied and at once demonstrated the practical possibilities, the artistic merit and the unrivalled efficiency of his new valve. So impressed were we with its merits that we promptly opened a Factory in London for the manufacture of this Player on a large scale..."

The wonderful Dodds valve consisted of a bent piece of sheet metal hanging from the flexible, horizontal upper leather valve facing, with the lower valve facing glued to the vertical face of the metal. With each valve housed in an individual unit pneumatic, it was supposed to be much easier to test each note on the bench than in other actions, and the sales pitch in the catalogue would lead the reader to believe that with the introduction of this revolutionary new idea, all other player actions would soon be obsolete. In truth, Bluthner player actions with Dodds valves are practically nonexistent, while the other "extremely complicated" player actions were produced by the tens of thousands, or hundreds of thousands in some

cases, completely oblivious to their supposed obsolescence! Many smaller piano companies, and even some of the larger ones like Bluthner, tried building their own player actions but after a short time decided that it was more sensible to purchase them from a company which specialized in making player actions.

While it is true that some of the best known, commercially successful player actions began as a revolutionary new idea in the mind of an inventor, it is also true that most of the unusual ideas fell by the wayside. The existence of dozens of rare brands of limited production player actions incorporating novel designs is one thing which makes player piano collecting and restoration interesting.

CECILIAN: see FARRAND

CHASE, A. B. - ARTISTANO

Uncommon. The A. B. Chase player action is a remarkable, complex assembly that is removable from the piano in one big, bulky piece. Grand and upright versions were made, and each had a spoolbox which folded under the keybed when not in use - tubing, chain, levers and all!

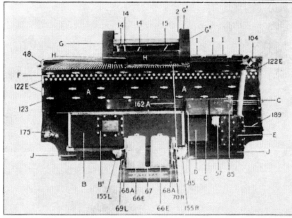

Illus. 6-46. The upright A.B. Chase player action. The grand action is similarly built in one large assembly. In both versions, the spoolbox folds under the keybed when not in use.

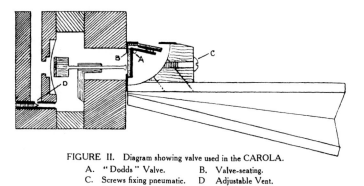

FIGURE II. Diagram showing valve used in the CAROLA.
A. "Dodds" Valve.   B. Valve-seating.
C. Screws fixing pneumatic.   D. Adjustable Vent.

Illus. 6-45. The Carola "Dodds valve," an innovation which never caught on.

Although the player action has its crude points, it works well if properly restored, and is considered desirable because of the high quality of the piano.

Illus. 6-46 shows the upright version. The pouch and valve boards are held together with dozens of small wing nuts (#123 on the photo), simplifying disassembly but causing problems if they are overtightened, ruining the threaded rods. Both the primary and secondary pouches are oval. The pneumatics have so much span that they have thin wood dividers causing the cloth to have two sets of folds. Recovering them is not particularly difficult, but be careful to locate the dividers precisely at the center of the cloth to prevent buckling or wrinkling. Due to the huge span, an original service manual recommends $^5/_{64}''$ travel for the secondary valves! The Chase action has a number of large wooden trunks which convey suction from one part to another; check each one carefully while the action is disassembled, and seal and reglue anything that leaks. Prior to replacing the connecting links of flexible tracker bar tubing, be sure to check every single piece of lead tubing for corrosion or other damage; it is difficult enough to repair a damaged lead tube in the middle of a bundle with the action on the bench, let alone trying to do this after installing it in the piano.

CLARK, MELVILLE - APOLLO

Melville Clark was a pioneer and great experimenter and innovator in the early days of the player piano. His Apollo brand was used on many varieties of player and expression pianos as well as ordinary foot pumped and electric expression pushup cabinet players. One of the most desirable player pianos is the Melville Clark Apollophone, which plays the Art Apollo family of expression rolls (Apollo X, etc.) and contains both foot and electric pumps and a phonograph! The Apollo name was later used on Apollo Artecho reproducing actions manufactured by Amphion, and after the Rudolph WurliTzer Co. took over the Clark factory in DeKalb, Illinois, WurliTzer used the Apollo name on various pianos and players including some which used Recordo rolls. Never make any assumptions about what type of roll an Apollo plays until you examine the tracker bar, player action and expression mechanisms.

The original Melville Clark Apollo apparently underwent an almost continual evolution, with the result that although this brand is not extremely rare, it is very unusual to find any two Clark Apollos which are identical. All parts were precisely made and carefully finished, resulting in neat, beautiful looking mechanisms. Later pianos use more ordinary valves and pouches, but early ones have pouch pneumatics as shown in illus. 6-49. Many of these pianos have leather-faced valves which seat on leather seats, resulting in stacks which are not as

Illus. 6-47. Front and back views of Apollo stack with pouch pneumatics. In the back view, the cover board is removed. *Photo by Jere DeBacker.*

Illus. 6-48. Pouch pneumatic blocks inside the Apollo stack The valves are in two rows, so the little pneumatics are staggered on alternate blocks *Photo by Jere DeBacker.*

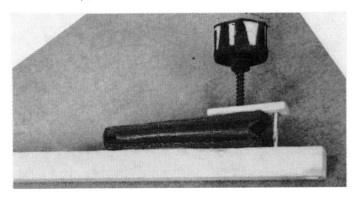

Illus. 6-49. Closeup of pouch pneumatic and valve.

airtight, as most player stacks, but in some pianos with this type of valve, the leakage is overcome by the use of a music roll transmission which is driven by a spring motor instead of the usual wind motor. In pianos with spring-driven music rolls, the pumping pedals are connected to an interesting over-running clutch winding apparatus which slips when the spring is fully wound.

In order for a Clark Apollo to work well, the pouch pneumatics must be absolutely flexible, and valves must seat perfectly. If the old leather is bad, or if the pouch pneumatics are stiff, recover them with the thinnest available pouch leather. If possible, remove the leather from either the valves or the seats, to eliminate leather seating on leather.

If you can't find the bleeds in an Apollo stack, you will find them in a separate wooden chamber located some-where in the neighborhood of the tracker bar.

DOLL, JACOB

This player action has pouches, valves and seats resembling those of a Standard, but the pneumatics face forward and connect to wooden rocker arms under the stack. There is nothing unusually difficult about restoring one.

EUPHONA: see CABLE

FARRAND CECILIAN
(also, early BUSH & LANE CECILIAN)

Uncommon. Used in Farrand, Bush & Lane, Victor and other pianos. The stack was one of the heaviest ever built because it was almost all metal. As shown in illus. 6-50, the valve travel is adjustable by turning threaded parts. Unfortunately, the pouches are contained inside metal chambers which are crimped together with little tabs, and many of the tabs break off when an attempt is made to

disassemble the parts to replace the pouches, particularly if the action is quite rusty. As in modern Aeolian player pianos, the individual units were designed to be replaced, not repaired. Neither the author nor any of his acquaintances have ever replaced the pouches in one of these, so if you decide to purchase one or agree to restore one for a customer, do so with the understanding that pouch replacement will be done on a trial and error basis.

Illus. 6-51. Front view of stack

Illus. 6-52. Back view of stack.

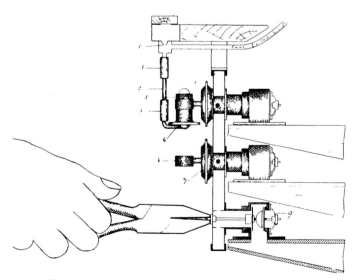

Illus. 6-50. Cross section of the mostly metal Cecilian stack.

Illus. 6-53. Detail of metal Cecilian valve and pouch housings.

GULBRANSEN

Very common. During the 1920's, this action was used mainly in pianos built by the Gulbransen-Dickinson Co. of Chicago—Gulbransen, Gulbransen-Dickinson, and Healy—but it was also sold to other piano companies, mainly in the early years. Three styles were built; the first had a four-tier stack with wider detachable unit pneumatics, the second had the familiar glued together three-tier stack, and the third had three tiers of detachable unit pneumatics. The late style unit pneumatics are almost identical to those of the glued together stack, except they are sepa-

Illus. 6-54. The infamous Gulbransen glued stack with the head and one pneumatic removed.

Illus. 6-55. The late style unit pneumatic Gulbransen stack, easier to repair than the glued version.

rate instead of being mounted on continuous deck boards. The transition from glued decks to detachable unit pneumatics was made somewhere in the neighborhood of Gulbransen piano #250,000 in 1926. The early player action is identifiable by its four tiers; the glued together stack and late unit pneumatic stack look identical when installed in the piano, except the former has 9 screws showing on the front of the stack trunk board, 3 for each deck, while the latter has 160 or 176 small screws, two for each pneumatic.

Many later Gulbransens have just 80 pneumatics, with the last four notes at each end dead. A tag notifies tuners that this was to permit all reproducing piano rolls to be played on the Gulbransen, but it was also a nice way for the factory to reduce the amount of money spent on unit pneumatics by a little more than 9%. If Gulbransen serial number records indicate the actual number of pianos produced, and if at least half of all Gulbransen pianos made in 1926 were players—a very conservative estimate—this practice would have saved the company 100,000 pneumatics in that year alone! (By comparison, in March 1917 the Standard Pneumatic Action Co. produced an average of 800 actions a *week*, consuming over 70,000 stack pneumatics in that time)!

The glued Gulbransen system, which is the most common of the three, deserves the title of "the most airtight player action ever built." Virtually all parts which are gasketed and screwed together in other players are glued together in the Gulbransen. All action parts are made of maple and are well sealed. The valves, pneumatics, wind motor, governor, and other parts are small and efficient, and the internal channels are just large enough to permit the necessary suction flow, eliminating the internal air resilience common to large bulky players; in fact, the main supply hose for the stack is only ¾". The result is a player action which is so tight that you can feel each note play with your feet as you push the pedals down.

Restoring the Stack

To restore the infamous "glued-up" Gulbransen stack, decide whether you would rather try to break it apart and spend hours repairing the damage, or cut it apart on a table saw. Both procedures are described here. In areas with extremely low humidity, many Gulbransen stacks have already begun to come apart, particularly if they previously lived in a humid climate. In this case, it is relatively simple to break the decks off the trunk with only minor damage. In more humid climates in which the hot glue is still strong, there is a greater risk of destroying the trunk board by attempting to break the decks off, so the sawing method is better. The first player piano restoration ever tried by the author was a glued Gulbransen, which split badly during an attempt to break the stack apart in a very damp basement in Chicago. In the dry climate in which he now lives, the author has restored many of these stacks by breaking them apart as described in the first method below, with fine results—player actions which are extremely easy to play, which hold suction as well as new. Note, however, that these restorations were performed with a complete shop full of power tools and that the author has also seen dozens of Gulbransen stacks which were ruined by amateur attempts to break them apart and glue them back together. In no instance should one of these stacks ever be glued back together, and if in doubt, saw the stack apart!

Illus. 6-56. This stack has no pushrods; the piano action has regulating screws built into the stickers.

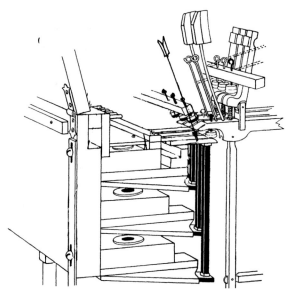

Illus. 6-57. This stack has thin flat pushrods connected to wood fingers (shown by the arrow) which are hinged to a rail with cloth hinges. Other stacks have dowel pushrods with a guide rail in place of the upper fingers.

To break a Gulbransen stack apart which is already somewhat loose, first remove the head, mounting brackets and bleed covers. Three systems of pushrods were commonly used in Gulbransen stacks: pneumatic fingers which push directly on three rows of sticker regulating screws, thin rectangular maple pushrods connected to fingers on

top of the stack, and dowel pushrods. Most pneumatics have built in fingers, but some have the fingers screwed on. If the stack has pushrods, remove them. The slender rectangular pushrods are connected to the pneumatic fingers and upper stack fingers with little buckskin cushions. Slice through the cushions on the pneumatic fingers and try your best to preserve the frail cloth hinges for the upper fingers; you will need to duplicate their precise locations when you rehinge them, and if the original hinges are present it will make this job easier than if you have to make a new scale stick from one of the piano action regulating rails. Lay the fingers and pushrods aside. Remove the pneumatic rest rails, if present, and number and remove the dowels which connect one deck to the next. (Some of the dowel screws will not be removeable until the stack is partially disassembled; remember which ones these are so you can reassemble them in the right order).

Remove the nine large screws from the front of the trunk and the twelve from the back of the three deck boards. Double check to make sure you have removed every screw; just one screw left in place during disassembly can cause a stack to be ruined.

Invert the stack on the bench, measure the span and overhang of the pneumatics, number the bottom row of pneumatics and remove the moveable boards, and number and mark the locations of the stationary boards on the decks. Most, if not all, Gulbransen glued stacks have a tiny pinprick on the deck beside each pneumatic to show its location, but it is a good idea to make more visible marks which will positively last through the sanding of the deck boards.

Illus. 6-58. Moveable boards of lower row of pneumatics numbered and ready to be removed.

Place the stack on a high spot on a concrete floor, with the open ends of the pneumatics facing up. Make a driving block from a piece of hard maple, a little bigger than the end of a pneumatic and long enough to grasp comfortably, with the end grain running lengthwise. Hold the block flat against the end of each pneumatic, give it one *hard* blow with a small sledge hammer, and the pneumatic will pop right off. Keep the working area of the stack directly over the high spot in the floor, and use controlled force; too weak a blow or a crooked block can dent or crack a pneumatic, and too strong a blow will damage the valve stem. By the time you are done severing the pneumatics from the deck, chances are the deck will be quite loose from the trunk board from all the hammering. Examine the glue joint between the deck and trunk, checking for any splitting of either piece. If there is no splitting and if the glue joint is partially loose, give each end of the deck one hard blow with an appropriate size driving block and medium size sledge hammer, and chances are it will come off with only minor tearing and splitting. Wherever small chunks of wood come loose, attach them back where they came from on the deck with masking tape. If the deck remains stubbornly attached to the trunk after one hard blow on each end, attack the glue joint with several thin, newly sharpened putty knives until it comes apart.

Repeat the procedure for the middle and top deck boards. In an average Gulbransen stack in a dry climate, one or two boards come off almost perfectly clean, and the remaining one ends up having several long cracks penetrating the wood. Throughout the procedure, keep every single splinter and chunk of wood, and tape it back to where it came from.

Illus. 6-59. Shearing the pneumatics off of the bottom deck.

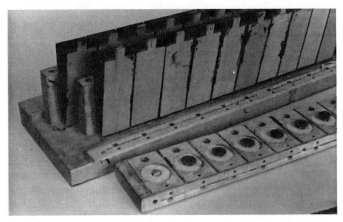

Illus. 6-60. Bottom deck board broken off of trunk, after removing the pneumatics. This method works in very dry climates, but in humid climates major damage can occur.

Separate the top valve seats from the decks, remove the valves and lay them aside.

Reattach all splinters and glue all cracks with aliphatic resin glue, mating the pieces as carefully as possible. This goes for the trunk board, the edges of the decks, the pneumatics and the faces of the decks. Anywhere there is a piece of wood attached to the wrong part, slice it off with a thin knife and reglue it to where it belongs. This can take anywhere from several hours to several days, and it represents the only extra time invested in a Gulbransen over and above an average restoration. Gradually you will reach the point of diminishing returns where little splinters are just too small to slice off and reglue; at this point, go over everything again "with a fine tooth comb" and fill any small voids with epoxy. Be sure to fill even the tiniest voids which occur from one channel to another on the trunk board, and voids between the pouch input channel and pneumatic feed channel on the stationary pneumatic boards.

Illus. 6-61. Voids in the trunk board are filled with epoxy, and the whole trunk is sanded smooth.

After everything is glued and filled, sand the pneumatics, deck and trunk. True the edges of the decks on a jointer, removing an amount of wood equal to the thickness of your best suede gasket leather. Be careful to feed the decks through the jointer in a direction which minimizes chipping; many decks have wavy grain, however, and they chip regardless of the feed direction. If this happens, fill the voids with epoxy and carefully sand it flat after it dries. Drill all seven screw holes all the way through each deck and the trunk board, to accomodate ³⁄₁₆" diameter bolts or threaded rod.

Illus. 6-62. A repaired and sanded deck board, ready to have the pneumatics glued back on.

The pouch input channels on the bottom of the deck boards where the pneumatics glue on are ⅛" diameter. Drill each hole out to ³⁄₁₆" diameter, ¹⁄₁₆" deep, to help prevent the holes from being clogged with glue when the pneumatics are glued in place.

Usually the trunk board needs to have the pouch input channels sealed, due to internal porosity and tiny cracking. To keep the sealer from clogging the bleeds, remove them with a drill bit just large enough to grab the brass without damaging the bleeds. If you do damage the flanges of any of the bleeds, they will leak around the edges, so replace them. Remove the seal cloth from the top edge of the stack, and using a squeeze bottle with a long narrow spout, squirt a generous amount of lacquer into each channel, let it sit for a few minutes, and blow it out with compressed air. This makes a real mess, so use a backboard to keep from splattering lacquer all over everything. When the lacquer dries, check each channel for airtightness by inserting an appropriate drill bit snugly down into the top of each channel just past the bleed port to plug the top end, hold a piece of tracker bar tubing tightly against the lower end of the channel where it mates with the deck, and test by mouth. If you find a leak, seal that channel again. Then remove the bit and check to make sure the channel is not plugged with lacquer; if so, run a long drill bit down into it by hand. When all of the channels are clean and airtight, sand the excess lacquer off the face of the trunk board, reinstall the bleeds and a new piece of seal cloth along the top edge of the trunk. Install leather gaskets for the decks on the trunk.

Illus. 6-63. After sealing all of the channels in the trunk as described in the text, glue firm split suede leather gaskets where the decks will attach.

Some Gulbransen stacks originally had leather pouches, and others had rubber cloth. If you are convinced that available rubber cloth will stay glued and remain flexible for a long period of time, use it for the new pouches, or you can install pouch leather and seal it with two thin coats of thinned Carter's rubber cement. If the leather ever becomes so porous that there is too much bleed, the brass bleed cups can be changed to smaller ones easily without disassembling the stack.

Polish the brass lower valve seats, seal the channels in the wood if necessary, install the pouches, and hinge and

Illus. 6-64. Polish each lower valve seat with a wad of steel wool.

cover the pneumatics. Then glue them to the deck boards precisely in the right place to insure alignment of the small channels. This is no place to practice using hot glue; before you attempt to glue the pneumatics, be sure you know just how thick to mix and apply it so the glue will stick without too much squeezing out. Clamp the pneumatics until the glue has set well, and then test each pouch input channel to make sure the pouch goes up and down freely with no constriction of the channel. If the pouch is slow, insert a paper clip into the hole and pick the glue out. If the pneumatic isn't aligned with the holes in the deck, you will have to do the job over again.

Illus. 6-65. A carefully recovered pneumatic with new pouch and old pouch disc installed, ready to be reglued to the deck.

Illus. 6-66. When clamping pneumatics to the decks, attach strips of wood over the valve wells to keep clamps from digging into wood.

Illus. 6-67. All of the pneumatics for one deck in order, glue pot, iron and clamps ready for gluing.

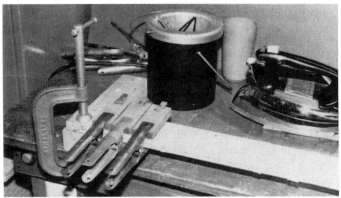

Illus. 6-68. The first three pneumatics are glued to the deck. The deck has been warmed with the iron, and the iron is now warming the next pneumatics. Check the overhang of each pneumatic as you go with a combination square (see p. 73).

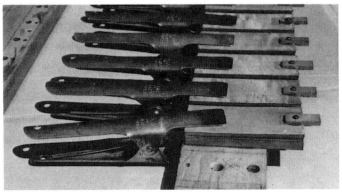

Illus. 6-69. A row of pneumatics neatly glued to the deck in a perfectly straight line. Alignment of the pouch input hole in deck and pneumatic is critical; too little glue will allow air or suction to seep under the pouch, and too much glue will plug the small channel.

Releather the valves, replacing the tiny leather punching between each valve and stem to provide flexibility. Check each valve to make sure the pouch doesn't hold it up off the lower seat, apply a tiny dab of glue to the bottom end of each stem, and insert the valve. Immediately inflate the pouch by blowing through a piece of tracker bar tubing while holding the valve down, to glue the stem to the pouch disc. Although the pouches don't *pull* the valves down as the notes turn off—the valves *push* the pouches down—this glue joint will eliminate any clicking between pouch disc and valve stem, and it will hold the pouch up ready to turn the valve on while still allowing the pouch to have plenty of dish. Calibrate valve travel by gluing a blotter paper ring to the top seat and sanding some of the paper off if necessary. Then glue the seats to the deck.

Regasket and install the bleed covers. Attach the top deck to the trunk, using threaded rod or long bolts with nuts and large washers on the front of the trunk. The washers will keep the nuts from crushing wood, and the nuts will be accessible to tighten the gaskets if necessary in the future without removing the stack from the piano. Tape off all of the holes for the other decks, plug each input nipple with a knotted piece of tracker bar tubing, connect your test pump, and check each pneumatic for good power and

Illus. 6-70. Each stem is attached to the leathered valve button with a tiny leather punching, providing flexibility to allow the valve to seat properly.

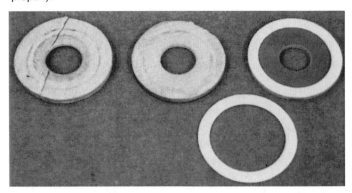

Illus. 6-71. If any wood top seats are cracked or broken, replace them with phenolic seats available from a supply company. Calibrate valve travel if necessary by gluing a blotter ring to the seat, and sand the ring if necessary after the glue dries. Then glue the seat to the deck.

proper repetition. Remove the deck and correct any problems if necessary. Then install the middle deck, and finally the bottom one. It is usually necessary to install the decks in this order to have access to the screws for the bracing dowels. As you install each deck, remember to apply shellac to the trunk board to seal the gasket against leakage. With seven bolts or threaded rods holding each deck to the trunk board, firm suede leather gaskets between the decks

Illus. 6-72. The bottom deck attached to the trunk, ready for testing, with knotted tracker tubing plugging off the input nipples. With the test pump connected to the stack, remove one tube at a time to make sure each pneumatic pops up and down. It is easier to install the spacer dowels between decks if you install the top deck first.

and trunk, and all of the original deck braces in place, the stack is virtually as strong and nearly as airtight as it ever was, plus it may be disassembled at any time for future repairs.

In a stack with slim rectangular pushrods, rehinge the upper fingers with pillow ticking, reattach the finger rail to the stack, and reglue the pushrods with new flexible leather cushions.

Sawing the Gulbransen Stack

If you decide to saw a Gulbransen stack apart instead of breaking it apart as described above, remove the hardware, pushrods and bleed cover, and drill four ¼" diameter holes vertically through the trunk board with a six inch long brad point bit, one hole at each end and one in each of the two spaces between sections of notes. When you reassemble the stack after restoring the parts, you will fasten it together with four 6½" long ¹⁄₁₆" diameter bolts through these holes.

Using a sharp rip blade in a table saw, cut the stack into three pieces, aligning the rip fence so the cuts will be flush with the bottom of the top and middle decks. Be careful not to cut into the pneumatics! Remove the top valve seats, valves and stems, and shear the pneumatics off with the hammer and driving block as described on p. 119. Then rebuild all of the parts as described in the above method, being very careful to seal all internal channels so they are perfectly airtight! In most stacks, you will find places here and there where the pneumatic deck is loose from the sawed section of trunk board, so be sure to reglue or seal these or the notes in the vicinity of the unglued places will cipher.

After gluing the restored pneumatics to the decks and assembling the valves, test each deck by taping off the holes, connecting the deck to a test pump, and uncovering each

Illus. 6-74. The sawed trunk board, showing all of the suction supply and pouch input channels.

hole one by one. Make a tracker bar tubing Y with a bleed in one leg, and attach that leg to the suction supply in order to test repetition of each valve. When every note works perfectly, gasket the saw cuts and reassemble the three sections of the stack with the long bolts, nuts and washers. Install a leather gasket under each washer, and seal around the bolt head and nut with a small bead of PVC-E glue. Test the stack on the test pump once again to make sure the bleeds work right and to find any possible dead notes caused by holes omitted from one of the deck gaskets, and then finish assembling the hardware. Notch the hinged board of the head and change the hinges to longer ones if necessary to accomodate the heads of the four added stack bolts.

The head of a Gulbransen stack is mounted on hinges, and the spoolbox brace is hinged in several pieces, permitting the head to be swung forward when the stack is in the piano by loosening a large thumb screw at each end. When retubing the stack on the bench, swing the head forward to that same position. If you tube it with the head standing straight up, there won't be enough slack in the tubing, and if someone tries to swing the head forward in the piano later, the tubing will stretch or break.

Gulbransen Unit Pneumatic Stacks

To restore a unit pneumatic Gulbransen stack, follow the same general procedure as for restoring a Simplex stack, integrating the above instructions as applicable.

The Wind Motor

Remove the pneumatic fingers, rotary valves and crankshaft from the wind motor, being careful not to lose the tiny coil springs or washers for the rotary valves. Remove the two legs —the flat board on the left side and the 6-channel supply trunk on the right. These were originally glued but usually practically fall off. Remove the screws from the pneumatics and break them off of the common board with a sharp putty knife or chisel. Reglue any splinters or chips right away before they get lost.

With a sharp chisel, pop the two wooden rotary valve

Illus. 6-73. Sawing a Gulbransen stack is a safer method of disassembly in humid environments where the glue is still strong. Just be sure to seal all holes in case any portions of the glue joints happen to be loose.

Illus. 6-75. An unrestored Gulbransen wind motor.

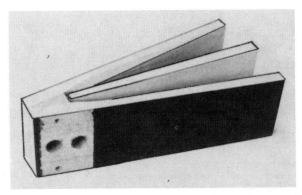

Illus. 6-77. Wind motor pneumatic cleaned and ready for recovering.

seats loose from the right leg. Seal the channels in the leg and the top trunk if necessary. Insert the crankshaft in the bushing which runs through the center of the rotary valve; if the shaft binds or knocks, replace the bushing with appropriate action cloth, not felt, being careful not to drag hot glue where it doesn't belong. This bushing is very important, as it supports the crankshaft and rotary valves. (The left end of the crankshaft is supported by the lower shaft of the transmission). Lap the valve seats on fine sandpaper, and reglue them to the body with Titebond (TM) or equivalent. After the glue dries, check them once more for flatness, lap again if necessary, and burnish them with graphite-alcohol paste. Check the bushings in the pneumatic fingers, and replace them if they drag or knock. Lap the metal rotary valves and make new pneumatic cloth washers.

Illus. 6-78. Top: Gulbransen wind motor pneumatic with old hinge cleaned out of slot. Bottom: New hinge piece glued in place, ready for trimming.

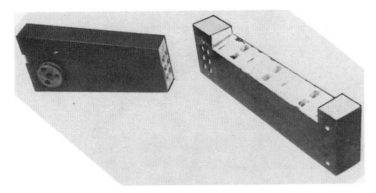

Illus. 6-76. The trunk of the wind motor with the suction supply leg broken loose at the glue joint and the pneumatics broken off.

If the pneumatic hinges are wobbly or rotten, replace them. Clean the old leather and glue out of the slots with a hacksaw blade and install new hinges made of medium weight bellows cloth or leather wrapped with thin pneumatic cloth like the original. After the hinges dry, recover the pneumatics as shown in the illustrations, stopping with the cloth a little short of the hinge, and finishing after the glue dries with overlapping pieces of pouch leather as shown. Replace the seal cloth on the hinge ends of the pneumatics to prevent air from seeping into the channels.

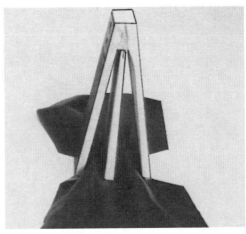

Illus. 6-79. One wind motor pneumatic with the new cloth glued to the ends of all three boards. First hold the center board all the way to the left, to cover the end of the right half of the pneumatic; then hold it all the way to the right, to cover the end of the left half.

Test each half of each pneumatic for airtightness, and *be sure no leakage exists between the two halves!*

Reglue the pneumatics to the trunk, the trunk to the legs, and the fingers to the pneumatics. Test for absolute airtightness of the assembled unit by sucking on each rotary valve port with an appropriate piece of tubing. Then install the crankshaft and rotary valves with their valve guides, coil springs, metal and rubber cloth washers, so there is a little

Illus. 6-80. After the open end dries, hold the center board to the left, and pull the cloth taut on the right stage of the pneumatic. Hold a straightedge on the center board, and slit the cloth with a new single edge razor blade. Repeat this on the opposite side of the same pneumatic.

Illus. 6-81. The cloth is glued all the way around the right stage of this pneumatic and is ready for trimming. After it dries thoroughly, repeat the process for the left stage.

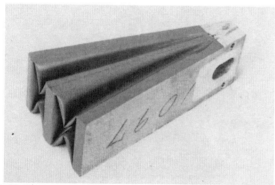

Illus. 6-82. The pneumatic is completely covered, ready to have a small piece of pouch leather glued over the side at the hinge end.

play between each valve guide and valve, with the spring tension holding the valves against their seats.

To set the timing of the rotary valves, loosen the set screws on the valve guides. Draw the middle pneumatic arm straight forward so with the motor standing upright, the bend in the crankshaft is parallel with the bench at dead center. Turn the left valve guide upward until the port at the top is just closed, so any backward rotation of the valve begins to open the port. Tighten the left valve guide set screw. Then set the right valve guide in line with the left one. Rotate the right valve a little one way or the other until the

motor runs as smoothly as possible. Be sure to leave a small amount of right-to-left play in the crank shaft. A Gulbransen wind motor never runs quite as smoothly as more ordinary 6-point wind motors, but the faint "chugging" should be perfectly symmetrical all the way around, with no irregular "loping". If the motor refuses to run evenly, check for binding in the pneumatic fingers or crankshaft bushing, leakage or incorrect timing of the rotary valves.

The Transmission and Tracking Device

Some Gulbransens were made with the simple transmission shown in illus. 6-83; others were made with the "fishing pole" style of automatic tracking device. Rather than rewriting the instructions for this device, the original description and suggestions from the October 1921 shop chart are reproduced in illus. 6-84. Note that in this, as well as in other mechanical automatic tracking devices, the adjustment of paper position relative to the tracking ear ("paper guide" in the illustration) is controlled by bending a small loop in the wire which connects the ear to the mechanism. Making the string longer or shorter than the recommended length, or adjusting the leather nut on the rod controlled by the fishing pole (or "jigger") only changes the angle at which the fishing pole floats; it does *not* regulate

Illus. 6-83. A simple Gulbransen transmission.

Supplement to Gulbransen Shop Chart

The Aligning Transmission (Tracking Device)

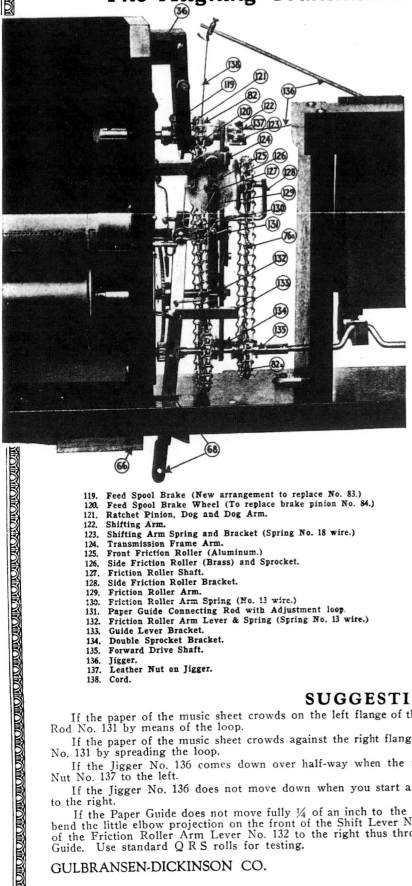

Purpose The purpose of this new device is to keep the music sheet in perfect alignment at all times with the air ducts in the tracker bar. It is not designed with a view to taking care of defective rolls although it will do so to the same extent as any good automatic tracking device.

Operation A music roll is placed in the Spool Box and starts to play. As the Forward Drive Shaft (135) turns, the motion is transmitted by the Sprocket (82A) and Chain (76A) to the side Friction Roller (126) which turns continuously as the music sheet moves forward. By means of the Friction Roller Arm Spring (130) the Front Friction Roller (125) is held against it and on account of the friction it turns. As this front Friction Roller (125) turns, it transmits the motion to its Shaft (127) winding up the Cord (138) and through the Jigger (136) and Shifting Arm (122) moves the Music Roll to the left until it reaches the center, at which time the left edge of the paper comes into contact with a paper guide at the left end of the Tracker Bar. This Paper Guide is attached by a connecting Rod (131) to the upper end of the Front Friction Roller Arm Lever (132). Therefore, when the Paper Guide is moved to the left the Arm Lever (132) is drawn against the tension of the Lever Spring, so that the whole Friction Roller Arm (129) is moved slightly to the left. As this compresses the Roller Arm Spring (130) the Rollers are separated and the Front Roller (125) slips backward as fast as it is turned forward, so that the upper bar of the Jigger plays about half way down. Now, if the paper should move to the left, the Cord would unwind and the music sheet would move to the right. If the paper should move to the right, the cord would wind up still more until the paper reached center, regardless of the position of the paper on the spool.

Proper Condition of Each Part

1. Cord No. 138 should be about 9½ inches long.
2. When Jigger No. 136 is pulled down all of the way there should be fully ⅛ inch play in the right music roll chuck. Leather nut No. 137 determines this.
3. Friction Roller Arm Spring No. 130 should be strong enough to cause friction enough between the Friction Rollers so the Jigger No. 136 will operate, but weak enough so the paper guide at the left end of the Tracker Bar will not curl up the Music Sheet Paper. Strength of Spring is changed by bending.
4. The Paper Guide Connecting Rod with adjustment Loop No. 131, should be adjusted so that the Paper Guide will line up with the left flange of the Take-up Spool so that when the sheet is running forward the paper will not crowd at either end of the Take-up Spool. Bend the loop to lengthen or shorten the Connecting Rod.

119. Feed Spool Brake (New arrangement to replace No. 83.)
120. Feed Spool Brake Wheel (To replace brake pinion No. 84.)
121. Ratchet Pinion, Dog and Dog Arm.
122. Shifting Arm.
123. Shifting Arm Spring and Bracket (Spring No. 18 wire.)
124. Transmission Frame Arm.
125. Front Friction Roller (Aluminum.)
126. Side Friction Roller (Brass) and Sprocket.
127. Friction Roller Shaft.
128. Side Friction Roller Bracket.
129. Friction Roller Arm.
130. Friction Roller Arm Spring (No. 13 wire.)
131. Paper Guide Connecting Rod with Adjustment loop.
132. Friction Roller Arm Lever & Spring (Spring No. 13 wire.)
133. Guide Lever Bracket.
134. Double Sprocket Bracket.
135. Forward Drive Shaft.
136. Jigger.
137. Leather Nut on Jigger.
138. Cord.

SUGGESTIONS

If the paper of the music sheet crowds on the left flange of the take-up spool, shorten the Paper Guide Connecting Rod No. 131 by means of the loop.

If the paper of the music sheet crowds against the right flange of the take-up spool, lengthen the Connecting Rod No. 131 by spreading the loop.

If the Jigger No. 136 comes down over half-way when the music sheet is running true, turn the little Leather Nut No. 137 to the left.

If the Jigger No. 136 does not move down when you start a roll that is true, turn the little Leather Nut No. 137 to the right.

If the Paper Guide does not move fully ¼ of an inch to the left when the re-roll lever is thrown to the right, bend the little elbow projection on the front of the Shift Lever No. 68, to the right so that it will push the Lower end of the Friction Roller Arm Lever No. 132 to the right thus throwing the upper end to the left and with it the Paper Guide. Use standard Q R S rolls for testing.

GULBRANSEN-DICKINSON CO.   October 1, 1921

Illus. 6-84. The Gulbransen automatic tracking device

the relationship between the tracking ear and the position of the music roll.

The Pump

The Gulbransen pump is neat and compact, with an action cutoff pneumatic on the front of the left reservoir, and the wind motor governor on the front of the right one. The action cutoff pneumatic manipulates a series of levers which close the action cutoff valve in the left end of the trunk, and open the accelerator in the right end. Note the orientation of both parts of the wind motor speed control valve, as shown in illus. 6-85, for correct reassembly. When you break the four bellows off of the trunk you will find a piece of seal cloth between the right hand reservoir and the trunk. Note its position and be sure to replace it. Replace the rubber cloth on the accelerator valve and the pouch leather on the action cutoff, copying the original

configuration of felt, action cloth, etc., and be sure that both of these valves wobble enough to seat perfectly.

When rebuilding the action cutoff pneumatic, break the unit apart to replace the rubber cloth pouch, which is always stiff. If there is a little wooden lever connecting the pouch to the valve, be sure to center it properly in the valve well when you replace the delicate cloth hinge.

It is very difficult to cover the Gulbransen wind motor governor neatly with the bellows attached to the trunk because of the small space between the hinge end of the governor and the trunk, so hinge and cover the governor with the bellows off of the trunk. Make sure the governor valve wobbles a little without leaking, in order to regulate the suction flow properly. Replace the patch of pneumatic cloth inside the reservoir which is located behind the channels connecting the governor to the tempo control valve;

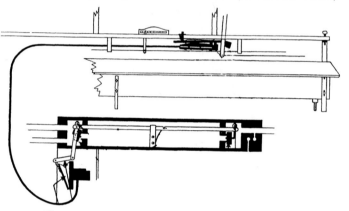

Illus. 6-86. Cutaway view of action cutoff mechanism.

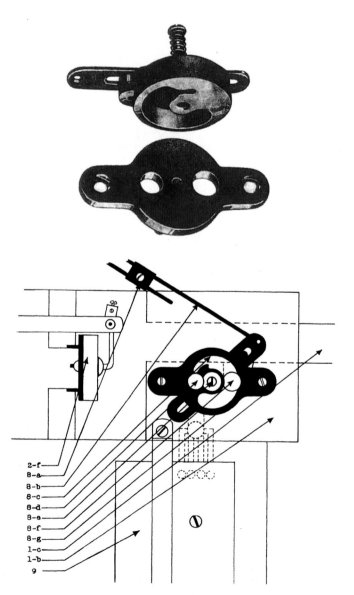

Illus. 6-85. Correct orientation of the tempo valve.

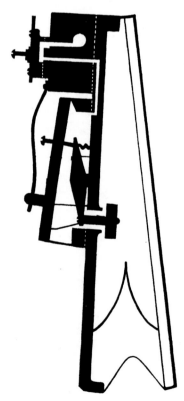

Illus. 6-87. Cross sectional schematic of wind motor governor.

this seal prevents seepage from the reservoir into the wind motor.

After reassembling the trunk, regulate the action cutoff and motor accelerator to the common linkage so one valve completely opens and the other completely closes within the range of movement of the cutoff pneumatic, and see that everything works freely so the return spring on the connecting rod is able to hold the accelerator valve tightly shut.

An original service manual gives the following advice for regulating the governor: "Before adjusting the motor governor always be certain that the feed spool brake is not too tight; see that all moving parts of the Motor are free, the rotating valves in time, and the valve seats free from oil and well graphited…. Next see if the motor stops when the tempo indicator registers 0, but moves when the indicator pointer is at 10. If the brake, the motor and the tempo valve are not in proper adjustment, the motor governor cannot be adjusted satisfactorily.

"If the motor drags, or goes too slow for the tempo indicated, either there is insufficient power reaching the motor or there is excessive friction in the motor or transmission…. The general speed of the motor may be increased by turning the governor spring regulating screw to the right or 'in'.

"If the motor races, or speeds up under heavy pedalling, turn the governor regulating screw to the right or in a quarter turn at a time. If this has no effect possibly air is leaking through the right gate valve allowing the bellows to act directly upon the motor. In turning the governor regulating screw inwardly, push the governor bellows collapsed and feel the opening at the lower end. As the governor regulating screw is turned in farther this space will increase. It should not be over a quarter of an inch or the pedal touch will be effected.

"If the motor slows down under light pedalling, turn the spring regulating screw inwardly a quarter turn at a time. If this causes the motor to race under heavier pedalling, turn this screw out again, and turn the regulating screw out a quarter turn at a time.

"If the motor balks, or stops completely while playing, especially noticeable under hard pumping or with a large roll, the governor valve probably closes and chokes off the power from the motor. Turn the regulating screw out a half turn and the governor spring regulating screw in a half turn. If this does not overcome the trouble evidently the valve is sticking against the valve seat. Place a small quantity of talcum powder in the motor exhaust tube nipple, move the tempo lever to the right and pump. The powder will absorb any moisture on the valve seat."

The sustain pneumatic is a huge unit pneumatic with two pouches and valves contained within a glued together compartment. Break this apart to replace the pouches and valve leather, and as in the action cutoff valve, if the valves are supported by hinged wooden arms, be sure to rehinge the arms so the valve stems end up perfectly centered in the valve wells.

HARDMAN PECK

The stack has three tiers, with the pouch input elbows inserted through three individual front valve box covers; the valves move vertically and have metal top and bottom seats something like Aeolian. Keep all of the valve parts oriented correctly and in the right order. The Hardman has a six point wind motor with see-saw pneumatics similar to Aeolian. The wind motor governor is mounted on the head, left of the spoolbox. Most Hardman actions have a single tracking pneumatic and single tracker ear which tends to damage rolls during rewind.

HIGEL, OTTO

The earlier Higel "Metalnola" action is pictured in illus. 6-88. Although the manufacturer promoted it as "The Player Action of the Future," the intricate die cast valve chambers suffer from warping and cracking; inspect a player piano with this action thoroughly before purchasing it or agreeing to restore it for a customer.

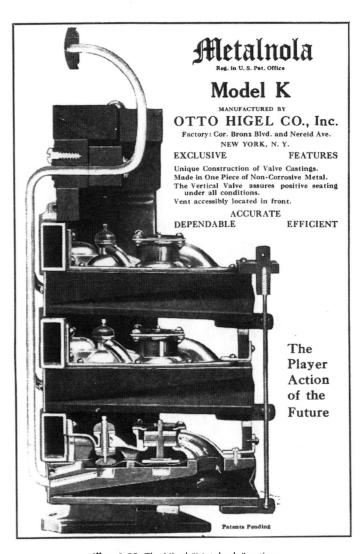

Illus. 6-88. The Higel "Metalnola" action.

What the future actually held for the Otto Higel company was a completely redesigned, more conventional action made of wood. A unique feature was the unit pouch system, with little wooden pouch blocks clamped in place with metal brackets, as shown in illus. 6-89. Each pouch block is glued to the lower valve seat; illus. 6-90 shows, from left to right, an assembled pouch and valve seat, a separated pouch and valve seat, two valves and an assembled unit as viewed from the valve seat. When replacing the pouch leather, be careful not to stretch it too tight around the sides of the block. This will cause the pouch to push the valve stem upward at an angle, cocking the valve and causing it to leak on the outside seat.

Illus. 6-89. The inside of the later style Higel stack, with unit pouch blocks held in place by metal brackets.

Illus. 6-90. Higel pouch blocks, valve seats and valves removed from chest.

The inside of the valve chest is faced with a pouch leather gasket to provide an airtight seal for the unit blocks; each block fits over two guide pins. Replacing this gasket is no small task, because all of the guide pins must be removed and then all the screw holes and valve well holes must be cut out, and the pins must be relocated in their original holes. Illus. 6-91 shows the inside of the chest with three pouch blocks removed. Two of the valves are removed, showing their guide pins, and one valve is in place. The valves are very similar to Pratt-Read valves, except that in the Higel, both valve faces are leathered. To calibrate valve travel, sand the wooden valve button or use thicker or thinner leather. Illus. 6-92 shows the pneumatic deck side of the valve chest. The gasket toward the top conducts tracker bar atmosphere signals to the

pouches; the narrow wooden strips hold the valve guide pins in place. In one action restored in the author's shop, the decks appeared to have been glued to the valve chest at one time but had been broken loose and then reattached with black automotive gasket compound. Traces of this show in the photograph. The stack was reassembled with deck gaskets to facilitate future disassembly.

Illus. 6-91. Inside of chest, showing three pouch blocks and two valves removed, with the right hand valve still in place in its well.

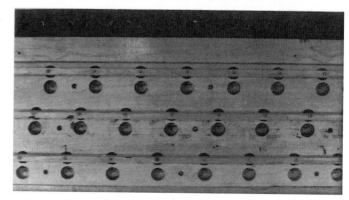

Illus. 6-92. The pneumatic deck side of the Higel stack after removal of decks.

KIMBALL

Common. Found only in pianos manufactured by the W. W. Kimball Co., including Kimball, Whitney, Hinze and others. The usual Kimball player action is fairly straightforward, with the pneumatics glued to the bottom of the pouch boards, and the valve boards screwed to the top. Most of the parts are painted black, and the screw heads and top valve seats are sealed with beeswax. The unusual feature of the Kimball stack is the lower valve seat, consisting of a pneumatic cloth washer covering a felt washer, held in from the bottom by a fibre washer glued into a shallow oversize hole which is countersunk under each valve well. In illus. 6-93, #17 is the valve, "D" is the pneumatic cloth seat, and the felt and fibre washers are shown in cross section under "D". The bakelite top valve seat, "F", (called the "regulating valve cap" in the manual from which this illustration was taken) is threaded into the wood, permitting easy regulation of valve travel. In several Kimball stacks restored by the author during the 1970's, the pneumatic cloth seats were still soft and airtight, but if the rubber cloth is hard or if the felt is motheaten, replace the seats. Replacement fibre discs are available from suppliers. Make new seats of appropriate felt and thin rubber cloth like the original; they are among the most airtight valve seats ever made.

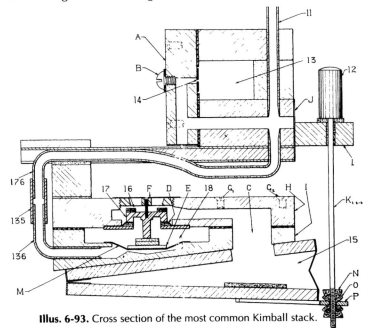

Illus. 6-93. Cross section of the most common Kimball stack.

Kimball bleeds are located behind short, large diameter machine screws ("B" in the illustration) which are screwed in place with rubber gaskets. The rubber washers are invariably brittle and decomposed, so replace them with leather ones.

The Kimball automatic tracking device has a pair of pneumatics controlled by four staggered holes in the tracker bar, something like the Standard device. Many Kimballs have no automatic tracking device, but instead have a manual tracking lever located in the key slip. Regulate this so the average roll is centered on the tracker bar when the lever is at its midpoint.

Some very early Kimball players had unit pneumatics made almost entirely of bakelite, shown in illus. 6-94. In

Illus. 6-94. Early bakelite Kimball unit pneumatics warped and cracked beyond possible repair.

one example seen by the author, every single unit was cracked and warped beyond possible repair. Other early pianos have the conventional Kimball stack, but have the pump glued to the keybed, making the pump very difficult to restore.

Later Kimballs have the pouches located in the top pneumatic boards, and the lower valve seats are metal rings.

Illus. 6-95. Late style Kimball with metal lower valve seats. Top: threaded bakelite top valve seats sealed with beeswax. Middle: To replace a number of broken bakelite seats, the wood is drilled for installation of new phenolic seats available from a supply company. One valve with wobbly stem attached is shown next to a new top seat. Bottom: When drilling for new top seats, care must be taken to keep from drilling into suction feed channel.

LAUTER

The Lauter-Humana player has unit valve blocks with seal cloth on the front as illustrated, with a channelled manifold board feeding suction to the valves. Early stacks have three tiers; later ones have four. Break the valve blocks apart, remove and clean the bleeds, replace the pouches, clean and reseal the inner metal seats, releather the valves, and reassemble. Sand lightly on all sides, blow out gently with compressed air, and glue a new gasket on the back and new seal cloth on the front.

In the four tier stack, the exceptionally short, wide pneumatics have oblong holes near the hinge end, causing the wood to crack easily when the pneumatics are removed from the decks. The wind motor has six huge formed rubber cloth pouches connected to rocker arms. Replace the pouches with pouch leather, seal the leather well with several thin coats of dilute rubber cement, and after reassembling the motor, adjust the throw of each pouch in relation to the rocker arm so the pouch is centered between the extreme limits of its motion.

129

Illus. 6-96. Unit valve from a Lauter Humana, glued together and broken apart.

LESTER

The Lester Piano Co. of Philadelphia manufactured player pianos with various actions, including Standard, Simplex, Pratt-Read and possibly others, but they also made their own two tier player actions. Each pneumatic tier has its own individual valve chest, but in some stacks, the two valve chests share a common pouch board, so all of the parts must be aligned perfectly before screwing the pouch board in place. The valves are secured to wire stems with force fit collars. Some Lester stacks have oval pouches; others have round pouches. Watch for heavy corrosion on the metal valve discs which holds the valve facings crooked and prevents them from wobbling. Remove corrosion by slipping a single edge razor blade between the leather face and metal disc, dragging the blade out against the plate. Otherwise, the Lester action poses no unusual problems.

Illus. 6-97. One style of Lester player action installed in a Fayette Cable piano.

PRATT-READ

Very common. Used in dozens of piano brands, Pratt-Read actions were deluxe, heavy, well designed, well built, and very airtight, with almost all parts made of maple. Cross sections of three styles are shown in illus. 6-98, 99 and 100.

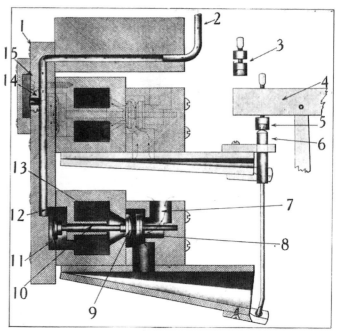

Illus. 6-98. An early, seldom encountered Pratt Read stack with the pouches in front. The pneumatics and valves come off of the pouch board in large sections.

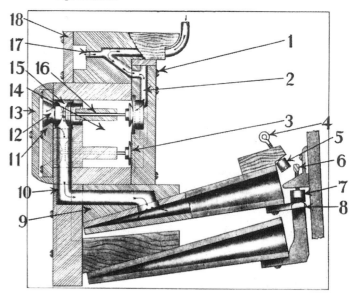

Illus. 6-99. Pratt Read stack in which the pneumatic decks are attached with screws and may be removed easily.

Some stacks are screwed together and pose no unusual difficulties in restoration. Others have the two deck boards glued to the trunk board; one of these, from a fine Packard piano, is shown here. To restore the glued stack, remove the head, the various boards screwed to the front

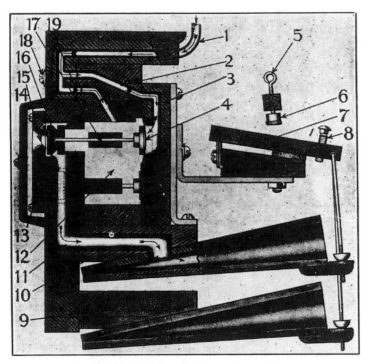

Illus. 6-100. Another Pratt Read stack, this one having the decks glued to the trunk board, requiring sawing for disassembly.

of the stack, and the valves. Remove the lower deck by cutting the trunk on a table saw (illus. 6-102), but first, drill a series of screw holes up through the bottom of the trunk board between channels (shown inverted in illus. 6-101) to be used during reassembly. The saw blade will remove more wood than the thickness of a leather gasket, so build the cut area back up with a strip of maple of appropriate thickness. Drill the channels out after the glue dries.

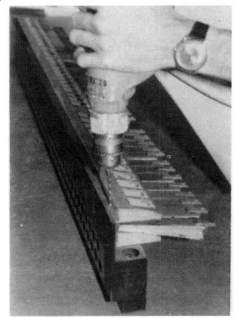

Illus. 6-101. Drilling holes in the glued stack prior to cutting it apart. These will later be used for screwing the stack together. Space them between internal channels.

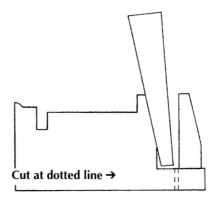

Cut at dotted line →

Illus. 6-102. Remove the bottom row of pneumatics, the valve cover and valves, and any other parts attached to the front. Make sure there are no screws or other hardware in the path of the saw blade. Lay the stack on its front on a table saw against the rip fence, and cut the trunk at the dotted line to remove the bottom deck. *Power tools are inherently dangerous; if you are inexperienced in their use, have an expert make this cut.*

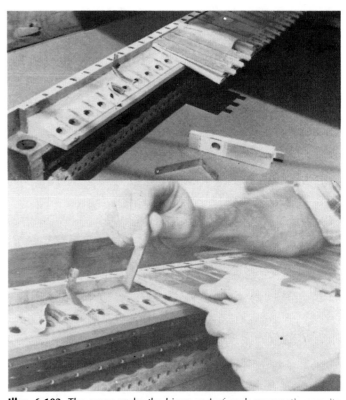

Illus. 6-103. The space under the hinge end of each pneumatic permits room for insertion of a prying tool as shown in these two pictures. The pneumatics in this stack were glued to the decks with pouch leather gaskets, simplifying their removal.

In this stack, the pneumatics are glued only to a small bevelled area of the deck board, making it easy to remove them with a small prying tool as shown.

Although a number of different tracking devices were used in Pratt-Read actions, the one shown here wins the prize for "most complex automatic tracking device." The paper edge sensing holes float sideways in slots in the tracker bar, pulled inward by the smaller two tracking pneumatics until they meet the edges of the roll. At this

131

Illus. 6-104. Bottom deck sanded and ready for new strip of wood to replace material removed by saw blade in excess of thickness of leather gasket. (The total thickness of the new strip of wood and gasket should equal the thickness removed by the saw).

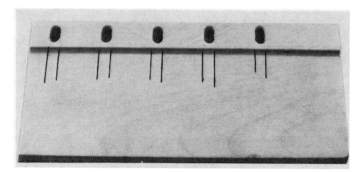

Illus. 6-105. Pencil lines are drawn on the bottom deck to show the locations of the pneumatic feed channels, the new strip of wood is glued on, and the pneumatic feed channels are drilled out.

Illus. 6-106. After the pneumatics are rehinged, recovered and reglued to both decks, the repaired and gasketed bottom deck is ready to be screwed to the rest of the stack. Remember to shellac the wood which mates with the gasket for a more durable airtight joint.

point, the two larger pneumatics align the roll with the tracker bar. Although the system looks like a "Rube Goldberg" contraption, it is made beautifully and tracks perfectly with rolls of any width, and also incorporates a manual transposing lever!

Illus. 6-107. Two views of the reassembled stack with new leather nuts on the pushrods, ready to be installed in the piano and regulated. The line from one side to the other, about an inch above the bottom on the front view, is the added gasket where the stack was cut apart.

Illus. 6-108. Front and back views of the 10-pneumatic wind motor. Each front board pivots in the middle and is attached to two small pneumatics; each slide valve covers and uncovers two ports.

Illus. 6-109. Front and back views of the automatic tracking device, which compensates for wider and narrower rolls by moving the edge sensing holes in the tracker bar.

PRICE AND TEEPLE

Price and Teeple player actions were installed in pianos made by that manufacturer, including Price & Teeple, Schaeffer, Carleton, Rembrandt, Symphonola and others. The unique design of this very heavy stack has the pneumatics attached to brackets mounted on steel rods, with large diameter rubber tubes connecting the pneumatics to the valve chest. There is nothing unusually difficult about restoring this action, but beware of breaking off the pneumatic bracket screws when attempting to regulate the stack to the piano action. Test them while the player action is disassembled, and apply a little penetrating oil or heat to help remove the screws. If they show any signs of rusting, replace them prior to reassembling the action.

Illus. 6-110. Price and Teeple stack, showing valve chest under head, with tubing from valves to pneumatics. The pneumatics unscrew easily from the bracket, but the machine screws which secure the brackets to the rods break off if rusted.

SCHULZ

Common. Found in pianos built by the M. Schulz Co. of Chicago (Schulz, Brinkerhoff, Maynard, Werner, Walworth, Bradford, Irving and others) as well as pianos made by other companies.

The most commonly encountered Schulz player action is deceivingly simple appearing from the outside. Inside the plain, neat looking stack, however, lie tiny pouch pneumatics instead of pouches (illus. 6-111), and therein lies the difficulty of restoring one of these. Restoration takes more work than the average player action, but a well-restored Schulz is a fine, very responsive instrument. Because of the precision required in restoring and adjusting the pouch pneumatics and valves, it is strongly recommended that you restore several easier players before tackling this style Schulz.

After disassembling the stack, number the moveable boards of the pouch pneumatics, cut them off and unhook them from the valves and lay them aside. Cut the stationary boards of the pouch pneumatics from the decks with a very sharp chisel. Note that the valves work upside down from most valves, and are off in the "up" position. Re-

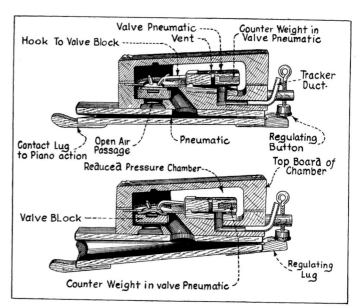

Illus. 6-111. Cross section of Schulz stack with pneumatic in "on" and "off" positions.

Illus. 6-112. One deck with top cover removed.

Illus. 6-113. Closeup of Schulz pouch pneumatic and valve. The glued pneumatic board is very thin; handle it carefully.

move the inside valve seats, which are usually made of cardboard but sometimes of fibre; remove the valves. Replacement seats and valves are available from suppliers.

Number and mark the position of the playing pneumatics, remove them, clean and rehinge them. Due to the lost motion regulating screws on the front of the stack, it is important for the pneumatics to have strong hinges; if you plan to cover them with polylon, use inside and outside hinges. Recover the pneumatics, and reglue them to the valve boards. Clamp the pneumatics while the glue dries. Although illus. 6-111 shows one pneumatic feed hole, in some stacks, each pneumatic has two feed holes, one on each side of the atmosphere intake slot for the valves, labelled "open air" in the illustration. If the pneumatics are not glued absolutely tight to the deck/valve chest, the suction feed holes will leak across into this slot. After the glue dries, check each channel and remove any glue which squeezed into the vicinity of the valve well.

Remove the hooks from the pouch pneumatics, and re-cover the pneumatics with "Schulz pouch cloth," a material made specifically for covering tiny pneumatics, or with zephyr skin. These little pneumatics must be perfectly flexible and airtight, so be careful to use just the right amount of glue! Duplicate the original method of covering, with no inside hinge, a little span between the two boards at the hinge end, and then with an external piece of twill tape holding the hinge together. Cut out the hole in the hinge end for the hook prior to gluing on the twill tape outer hinge. After the glue dries, cover each bleed with masking tape and test each pneumatic for air-tightness, making sure that you don't get a false indication of leakage due to tape which isn't stuck down well or isn't airtight. Reinstall the hooks, but leave the masking tape over the bleeds until later.

If you plan to releather the original valve buttons, check very carefully for warpage, sand them perfectly flat, and face them with leather which will provide the correct travel. Seal the valve wells and the inside of each valve chest if necessary, and place the valves in the wells. Check the new fibre valve seats for flatness —in some batches, quite a few are warped —and temporarily press each one in place to check the travel, making adjustments to the valves if necessary.

Thread each top valve seat and valve on each hook, hold the stationary board of the pouch pneumatic and valve seat in place, and see that the weight of the move-able board of the pneumatic with its lead insert is sufficient to pull the valve up to the seat. Position the pouch pneumatic perpendicular to the long dimension of the deck so the pouch input hole isn't obstructed, and when you have found the correct position, mark it on the deck. Regulate the hook by bending it, so the pneumatic at rest is 1/8" open. To avoid breaking the pneumatic or loosening the hook in the wood, use two pliers or small wire bending pliers.

Glue each pouch pneumatic to the chest with hot glue, clamping the pneumatic so the glue joint will be airtight; after the glue dries, test once again through the input nipple for airtightness. When the pneumatics test perfectly airtight, remove the masking tape. Fine regulate the hooks to center the valves, to adjust the seating of the valves and to adjust the rest positions of the pouch pneumatics. Then glue the valve seats in place.

The cover boards which enclose the top of each valve and pouch board are made of 1/8" thick poplar, and they will leak seriously unless you seal them well. After the sealer dries, regasket them and assemble them to the valve boards. Tighten the screws just enough to make the stack airtight for now, but don't seal the gaskets and don't turn the screws down hard yet. Test the stack with your

Illus. 6-114. Looking up at bottom rear of a late Schulz stack prior to restoration. Most of the pneumatics have fallen off of the bottom deck due to the original seal cloth having been replaced with polyethylene in a previous unsuccessful amateur repair attempt. The pouch blocks are visible where the pneumatics are missing.

test pump, and make a list of any notes which are sluggish or which have other problems. Remove the valve cover and make minor corrections, bending the hooks as necessary to correct valve problems. Reassemble and test again. When every note works perfectly, remove the valve covers, seal the gaskets and install the screws tightly, for the last time.

Other sources recommend gluing the valve seats first, the pouch pneumatics second and the stack pneumatics third, but by gluing the stack pneumatics to the decks/valve chests first, any glue which runs into the valve wells can be cleaned out. By regulating the pouch pneumatic hooks prior to gluing the valve seats down, it is easier to bend the hooks and to find the best locations for the pouch pneumatics, lessening the need for further regulation after everything is glued together. Regardless of the method used, however, it is unusual for the stack *not* to need minor regulating of the hooks after initial testing.

The late style Schulz stack is more ordinary, with square valves and wobbly stems, metal inside valve seats and fibre outside seats, as shown in illus. 6-114. The pouches are mounted in removeable wooden blocks and

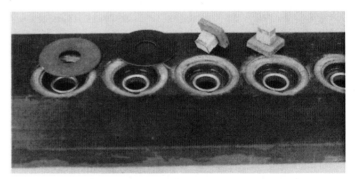

Illus. 6-115. Top of late style Schulz deck board, with (left to right) old top valve seat, new replacement phenolic top valve seat, and two valves.

held in place by the tracker bar tubing elbows which go all the way through the deck board into each pouch block. After the pouches are installed, the bottom of each deck is covered with seal cloth, and the pneumatics are then glued on. This stack was used in full size uprights as well as the smaller studio uprights of the late 1920's.

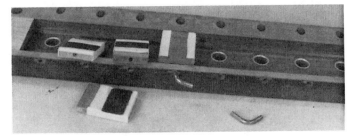

Illus. 6-116. Bottom of pouch board with pneumatics and seal cloth removed. One releathered pouch block is installed, and several more are ready.

Illus. 6-117. An unrestored pouch block with fibre valve lifter in place.

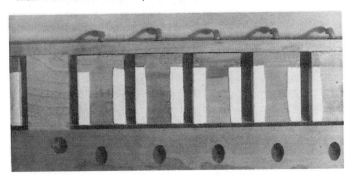

Illus. 6-118. Pouch blocks installed in bottom of pouch board, ready for new seal cloth. Each block is held in place by the tubing elbow; a small collar of burnt shellac is placed on the end of each block prior to insertion of elbow, to insure airtight connection. After seal cloth is glued in place and pneumatic feed holes are cut out, pneumatics are glued on.

Several types of tracking device were used, the most unusual one having two "centering discs" which ride on *the inside of the music roll flanges,* during play, as shown in illus. 6-119. These take the place of tracker ears which feel the edges of the music roll in other automatic trackers. If one of the spool flanges pushes on a centering disc, the disc opens a small valve which admits air into one of the tracking pneumatics, adjusting the position of the roll. The centering discs are lifted away from the roll during rewind. In a simpler version, there are no pneumatics; cen-

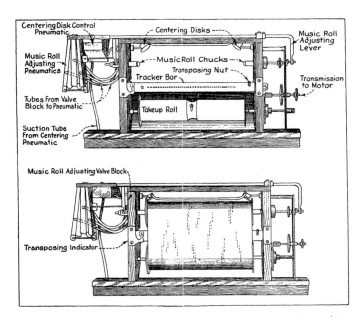

Illus. 6-119. Drawings of Schulz centering disc automatic tracking device.

tering discs or fingers simply push the roll to a centered position during play. In rewind, the centering device lifts out of the way, and a brake prevents the spool from wandering sideways.

Some Schulz players have a ten-point wind motor with five double teeter-totter pneumatics. Be careful during restoration to keep everything in alignment, so the pneumatic cloth isn't wrinkled after reassembly.

The Schulz pump presents no unusual problems. When recovering the teeter-totter pneumatics which control the action cutoff and motor accelerator, use an inside hinge in one and cover the other with no inside hinge and with a little extra span across the outside. This way, when they are attached to each other they will have the necessary flexibility and won't fight each other, wrinkling the cloth.

Illus. 6-120. Unrestored Schulz pump with dangling broken hoses. The teeter totter pneumatic holds the action cutoff and wind motor accelerator positively in play or rewind.

Illus. 6-121. The Simplex unit pneumatic in various stages of manufacture.

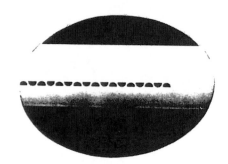

Illus. 6-122. The Simplex tracker bar is characterized by half-round holes.

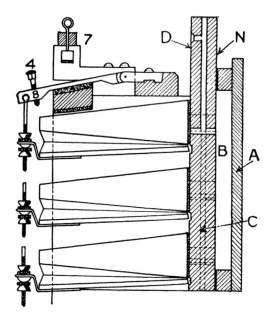

Illus. 6-123. Cross section of the Simplex stack.

SIMPLEX

Very common, second only to Standard in terms of numbers of different piano brands in which it was installed. The Simplex Player Action Co. of Worcester, Mass., not only sold their unit pneumatic player actions to piano manufacturers, but even solicited business from piano technicians, who had only to send in seven measurements and a scale stick of the piano action to have a new player action custom made. A Simplex action may be identified by the "trapezoid tracker" bar, which provides a somewhat greater margin for error in mistracking of the rolls before the holes become misaligned.

The Simplex unit pneumatic in its various stages of manufacture and assembly is shown in illus. 6-121. The pouch is located in a thin wedge shaped board glued to the bottom of the valve chamber. The lower valve seat is a metal insert, and the top seat is a contoured metal washer held in place with burnt shellac.

To restore a set of Simplex pneumatics, disassemble the stack, number and remove the pneumatics. If the pneumatic fingers line up properly with the pushrods—if they were not put together crooked during a prior repair job—leave the old burnt shellac in place which sealed the metal fingers to the pneumatic boards and keep the pneumatics and fingers in order so the fragments of old shellac will mate. It is not necessary to scratch a number on every finger, if you number the first one in each row and then thread all of the fingers in order on a piece of mechanic's wire. If you must clean the old shellac off of the fingers and boards because of crooked prior assembly, plan to make any sideways adjustment of the fingers

which might be necessary during reassembly of the stack to align them with their pushrods. This will make reassembly of the fingers and pushrods much more time consuming, and you will risk stripping the screw holes for the stack cover board, as the stack will have to be reassembled and tested one row of pneumatics at a time, with the cover installed and removed once for each tier. In some Simplex stacks, you might think that every finger is installed in the same exact place on each pneumatic; in others, it will be obvious that the fingers are located in different places. In any case, it is smart to keep everything in order.

Measure the span and cut the moveable boards off of the valve chambers. If the top valve seats have cheesecloth secured with beeswax, remove the cheesecloth for reuse. Carefully scrape all of the old burnt shellac from around the top valve seats and heat them with a small soldering iron until they practically fall out with no prying, and put them in a can of alcohol overnight to dissolve the remaining shellac. The least amount of prying will ruin these valve seats, as you will see if you forcibly pop one loose and then hold it on a flat surface.

Remove the valves and lay them aside. Peel as much of the old cloth and gasket material off of the pneumatics as possible and sand the pneumatics clean. Sand the old sealer off of the wood inside the pneumatics, only in the area where you will install the inside hinges. Be extremely careful to sand all surfaces flat, removing the glue without removing any wood, particularly on the gasketed hinge end where any rounding of the wood will ruin the airtight connection with the suction supply and pouch input channels. If the pneumatics were sanded carelessly once before, set up guides on your disc sander table to sand the gasket end of all pneumatics flat, or they will stick out every which way when you reassemble the stack. Sanding will expose the glue line between the pouch block and valve chamber. With a newly sharpened chisel or felt and leather cutting knife, break these two pieces apart. If the chisel is sharp and you place it precisely on the glue line, most of the blocks will separate with minimal chipping.

Scrape the old pouches out of the wells with a narrow chisel, or clean them out on a drill press, and renew the sealer inside each pouch well and underneath it, on the top inside surface of the pneumatic. Perfect airtightness of the pouch well is extremely important; any seepage through the wood will seriously hurt repetition, because the top and bottom of the pouch well (the inside of the pouch chamber and the inside of the pneumatic, respectively), are always in opposite states of suction and atmospheric pressure. (When the pneumatic is off, atmospheric pressure in the pneumatic will bleed into the suction under the pouch, and when the note is on, suction from the pneumatic will bleed into the atmosphere under the pouch). When sealing the insides of the pouch wells, be careful not to get sealer on the rim of the well, as this will cause the pouch to come unglued later. Renew the sealer in the valve chambers.

Replace the pouches. Some Simplex actions contained pneumatic cloth and others contained pouch leather; use whichever material was originally used or be prepared to change the bleeds. Test each pouch for airtightness and flexibility —if the pouch is crooked when it inflates, it can push the valve up at an angle. Reattach each old cardboard pouch disc (or an identical replacement) to the new pouch with a small drop of glue at the center only, to permit maximum flexibility of the pouch.

Glue the pouch boards to the valve chambers with hot glue, clamping them with padded spring clamps until the glue dries, and lightly sand off the excess which squeezes out. Make sure the little bridge of wood between the pouch well and pneumatic feed hole is glued tight, to prevent leakage.

Simplex pneumatics were originally covered with no inside hinges, but you will have stronger pneumatics which are just as flexible if you install inside hinges. After the hinges dry, cover the pneumatics as they were covered originally, with the cloth overlapped *only* ¼", on the

side of the pneumatic just in front of the hinge, as shown in illus. 5-72. Use just enough glue to hold the layers of cloth tightly together; if any glue oozes inside, the pneumatic will be hingebound. Note that the cloth strips must be wider than the span of the open end of the pneumatic in order to cover the sides completely.

If you were able to leave the old burnt shellac on the fingers and the pneumatics where the fingers are mounted, reattach the fingers to their original pneumatics with a little additional burnt shellac, making sure that the shellac squeezes out all the way around. The remains of the old shellac will show you the precise location of each finger. If you haven't already learned not to use hot glue for sealing metal to wood, learn it now! The hot glue will stick neither to the finish on the pneumatic nor the finger and will flake off after it dries. It will add no strength to the finger, and some of the little flakes will probably end up in the valves. If you cleaned the old burnt shellac off of the pneumatics and fingers, don't install the fingers yet.

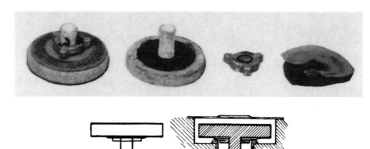

Illus. 6-124. One style of Simplex valve. Subtle variations exist, but they all contain a pneumatic cloth punching between the wood and lower pouch leather facing which is invariably bad even if the leather still looks good.

Turn your attention to the valves. The valve button and stem are one piece of wood, as shown in illus. 6-124; due to the geometry of the pouch disc, valve and seats, no wobble is necessary. Always releather the valves; even though the valve leather frequently still looks good, between each lower leather facing and the valve button is a slightly smaller rubber cloth punching which is always bad, requiring replacement of the leather as well. Gently pry the little aluminum fastener off the stem with a thin blade. Sand the old glue off of the button. Punch a hole slightly larger than the valve stem in a piece of fine sandpaper and glue it over a hole in a piece of wood; insert the valve stem in the hole and rotate the valve back and forth to clean the lower face. Make new rubber cloth and lower leather facings of the same diameter as the original ones, and glue them in place with very thin hot glue. Insert each valve in its repouched and recovered pneumatic, make sure the pouch doesn't hold the valve up off the lower seat, and suck on the suction supply hole in the back of the pneumatic to test for airtightness of the lower seats and facings.

Lay the top valve seat in place, and see what thickness of thin pouch leather will be required so the valve will have just the right amount of travel, accounting for a few thousandths of an inch of hot glue. Glue the top leather facing in place, recheck the travel, and seal the top seats back in place with burnt shellac. If you seal the original or new cheesecloth dust covers over the top valve seats with beeswax, wait until the burnt shellac is dry—this takes anywhere from several days to several weeks, depending upon the surrounding humidity.

Draw parallel lines equal to the height of the pneumatics on a piece of gasket leather, and stamp ink impressions of the pneumatics adjacent to one another between the lines, using a stamp pad and one pneumatic, as shown in the Amphion section of this chapter. Separate the gaskets with a knife, and punch the holes out with appropriate tube or squeeze punches. Careful punching will insure an airtight piece of leather between the suction

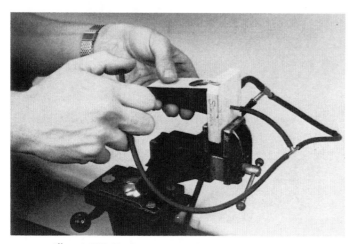

Illus. 6-125. Testing a pneumatic on a suction test block.

supply and pouch input holes. Glue the gaskets in place; use hot glue if the pneumatics are covered with rubber pneumatic cloth, or PVC-E if they are covered with polylon or bilon.

Test each pneumatic on a jig, with a bleed inserted in one leg of the tracker bar tubing, as shown in illus. 6-125. Each pneumatic should snap up and down on low suction, with no excessive valve spitting. Correct any problems.

Regasket and seal the front stack cover board, and repaint it if necessary. Install the flanged fingers on the stack, and then assemble the stack, one row of pneumatics at a time. Install the top row of pneumatics first, making sure that each one is flat against the trunk board as you tighten the two screws. Apply shellac to the board several pneumatics ahead, to seal the gaskets. Tape off all the rest of the holes on the outside of the stack, attach the cover board and test this row with your test pump, correcting any problems. Turn the stack upside down and install the pneumatic fingers on this row if you haven't already done so, checking each pushrod for squareness as you seal the finger in place with burnt shellac. Remove the stack cover, install the middle row of pneumatics and repeat the procedure. Then repeat the whole thing again for the bottom row.

The Simplex automatic tracking device uses two tracking ears connected to a friction drum and clutch; its operation and adjustment are described in illus. 6-127, reproduced from an original service manual. The fishing pole, or "lever shift wire D", as it is called in the illustration, is mounted toward the left of the back of the spoolbox. The friction wheel—actually a small wooden drum—and the pinion bar "F" take the place of the two right angle friction wheels of the otherwise similar Gulbransen device.

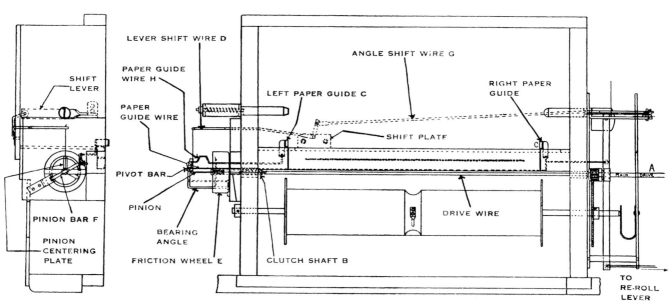

THE SIMPLEX AUTOMATIC TRACKER

is the simplest and most efficient of any of the many devices of this character. It is purely mechanical, has no pneumatics and is operated by a positive constantly active force that operates the music roll. It is the nearest trouble-proof of any tracker we have knowledge of.

The four principal parts are the

Main drive shaft	A
Clutch drive shaft	B
Paper guides	C
Shifter wire	D

The main drive is the wire in the center of the gear frame passing under and back of the tracker bar, and is constantly revolved by a chain and sprocket driven by the wind motor.

The extension of this shaft through to the left side of spool box is called clutch drive shaft. This shaft is pinned universal joint fashion to main drive shaft and slides back and forth with the main drive shaft for the purpose of connecting the drive shaft to the clutch shaft when playing the roll and to disconnect it in re-rolling.

The clutch drive shaft is made up of ten parts, clutch shaft and bearing, friction wheel, pinion centering plate, spring, pinion bar, pinion, pivot bar, and bearing angle.

Paper guides are made up of seven parts, right and left guides with two pins, springs, guide wires, also paper guide release wire connected on the gear shifter.

Shifter wire is made up of four parts, shift lever angle, shift wire, lever shift wire, transmission cord.

The operation of the tracker is as follows: When a roll is being played the drive shaft A is revolving the clutch shaft B at the same time revolving the friction wheel E which in turn revolves the pinion bar F, the pinion being pinned to this bar. This bar revolving winds up the cord which is fastened to lever shift wire D and as the cord is wound around the pinion the shift wire is pulled downward which through proper connecting parts causes the music roll to move towards the left. This is brought about only when the right hand edge of the music sheet touches the right side paper guide.

When the music roll moves far enough to the left for the left edge of the music sheet to touch the left side paper guide the friction is eliminated between the pinion bar F and friction wheel E, and while the friction wheel E continues to revolve in the same direction, the pinion bar F will revolve in the reverse direction, allowing the transmission cord to unwind and raise the lever shifter wire arm D and move the music sheet towards the right side through the action of the spring and connecting parts. The result is that after the paper guides are once set in proper location the music sheet when operating alternately touches first one side or the other and is corrected in its location as it gets out of line with tracker first to one side or the other.

SUGGESTIONS

If the average roll tracks over to left side, make left side guide wire longer by bending at H and if the roll tracks to the right side too much make the same guide wire shorter by bending at the same place, H.

To set the paper shifter, wind the cord around the pinion until almost two-thirds down the full length of the cord and if paper tracks to left, turn buttons in shift wire G to left; if paper tracks to the right, turn buttons to the right.

Care should be taken to see that the drive wire A is connected well to clutch shaft B, but not too tight to cause friction. Clutch shaft and pinion should be oiled in its bearings occasionally but put no oil on friction wheel or pinion bar F.

See that all connecting parts work freely.

Illus. 6-127. Description of the automatic tracking device reproduced from original Simplex literature.

Many Simplex pedal pneumatics and other controls were glued together with no gaskets to make a more airtight action. Break them apart like the stack pneumatics, to replace internal pouches, reseal the wood, releather the valves and perform other necessary repairs.

In the early years, Simplex made a deck board stack which is crude and difficult to make airtight. This type of stack was evidently leaky from the day it was new, judging by the huge pump that goes with it. Each deck has a thin valve chamber made of a sandwich of three layers of wood glued together. The middle layer of each sandwich is drilled and slotted for the valves and their suction supply channels, and this layer is covered over with very thin wood on the top and bottom which forms the upper and lower valve seats. The valves are slid into position through the slots at the edge of the board; each valve has a thin cloth tab glued between the valve button and one leather facing, with the other end of the tab glued to the seat board. (Without the tabs, there is nothing to prevent the valves from scooting around sideways). Releathering the valves involves tearing the little tabs out, replacing them and gluing them to the seats with thin wedges inserted through the supply channels. If one of these stacks has lived through wide ranges of humidity, the valve chamber sandwiches leak, requiring tricky regluing to make them airtight again. This type of player action is restorable, but at best it does not perform as well as most other players.

STANDARD

Very common. The Standard Pneumatic Action Co. was an affiliate of Kohler Industries, which also controlled Autopiano, and Kohler and Campbell. Standard player actions were used in well over 100 different piano brands and are by far the most commonly encountered player actions today in most parts of the country where player pianos were common in the 1920's. Standard and Autopiano stacks, are almost identical, so the following discussion of these parts pertains to both brands. Many of the illustrations in Ch. 2 show Standard components.

Illus. 6-128. Left: Standard suction supply manifold mounted on keybed. Right: Back of stack which mates with suction manifold.

To remove the entire stack and head from the piano in one heavy assembly, disconnect the two control wires for the transmission and tempo pointer at the right end of the stack, remove the spoolbox brace screw from the plate, remove the one very long vertical screw (or two horizontal screws) holding the right end of the stack in the piano, and remove the four oval head screws from the left front of the pouch board which hold the stack to the suction supply manifold.

After removing the whole assembly from the piano, the head and primary valve chest come off by removing assorted mounting screws and a row of screws which connect the primary chest to the secondary pouch board. Disassembly will be obvious as you proceed; keep track of where each group of screws comes from. It is very important in an Autopiano or Standard stack to mark and repair stripped screw holes as you proceed because of the large number of screws and potential abundance of leaks if dozens of screws are stripped. The screws connecting the head to the secondary pouch board are particularly important, because if they are loose—which they frequently are —only a slight amount of leakage into the pouches will be amplified into a gross amount of valve leakage.

Illus. 6-129. Some of the flanged fingers must be removed to gain access to screws which hold the finger rail to the top of the stack. Remove the pushrods from the pneumatics, remove the flanged finger rail from the stack, and temporarily reattach the loose fingers to the rail to keep them in order.

The flanged finger rail is usually attached to the stack with screws located under some of the flanges. Remove only those flanges which cover these screws, and after removing the finger rail from the stack, temporarily reattach the loosened flanges on the rail to keep them in order. The flanges are glued to the rail but usually pop loose with no damage. Remove the old leather nuts, polish the pushrods and install a new top leather nut on each one.

Remove the secondary pouch board from the front of the stack to gain access to the deck board screws, and remove the decks from the valve board. As in a Simplex, the pneumatic fingers in a Standard are metal and are screwed to the wood and sealed with burnt shellac. Number the fingers and both boards of each pneumatic during disassembly in order to reassemble everything where it came from. Some Standard pneumatic fingers have action cloth or leather inserts which keep the pushrods from clicking on the fingers. If these are motheaten, replace them, bending the end of the finger open just barely enough to replace the insert and then bending it shut again.

After rehinging and recovering the pneumatics and regluing them to the decks, test each pneumatic for airtightness, and remove excess glue from the suction supply channels. Then regasket the edge of each deck. By replacing the gaskets after regluing the pneumatics, you won't run the risk of having excess glue ruin a gasket. Reattach the fingers to the pneumatics, sealing them with enough burnt shellac that a little squeezes out around all sides and through the little hole in each finger. This will add a surprising amount of strength to the two screws holding each finger on its pneumatic. Without the shellac, you can count on a few of the fingers breaking loose after playing a few dozen rolls vigorously.

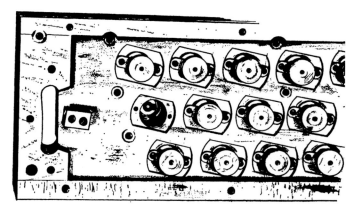

Illus. 6-131. The Standard secondary valve chest with front pouch board removed.

Illus. 6-130. The top valve seats and outer stem guides may be seen peeking out from behind the hinges of these pneumatics. The condition of the top valve facings—invariably rotten—may be inspected through these holes

Number the valve plates, mark their orientation and remove them and the stem guides from the valve board. A simple way to mark the orientation is to scratch a line across one end of each stem guide and valve plate onto the wood. To avoid bending the lower plates, which are sealed in place, heat the perimeter of each plate with a soldering iron to melt and loosen the old sealing wax or shellac. Check the plates for corrosion and warpage, and lap them on fine sandpaper and spray on a thin coat of nitrocellulose lacquer if necessary. Early style valves have a layer of felt between the top leather face and supporting disc, but later ones do not. The later actions work just as well, just as silently, they are easier to regulate and less susceptible to moth infestation. The top (outside) valve facings nearly always need to be replaced in a Standard/Autopiano; when you replace them, check the fibre discs for warpage. Lap them until they are flat or replace them, and releather the discs *without* felt. Always check new replacement valve discs for flatness before leathering them; many new ones are warped nearly as much as the old ones.

Save the original bottom valve facings unless they are rotten; regulating the valves after replacing the bottom

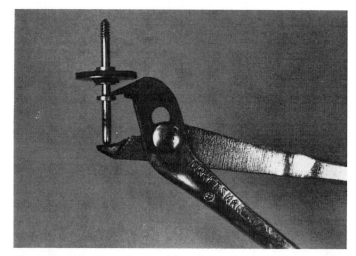

Illus. 6-132. Regulate valve travel by moving the stem grommet with a modified ignition pliers. If any grommets are loose, replace them with new ones.

facings involves a lot of extra work. If the bottom facings are still good, and if there are felt or action cloth punchings between the leather and the metal backing plates, pull the felt out of each valve with tweezers or a hemostat, and press the stem collar which is above the metal backing plate down a little to eliminate the gap, using a tool made from small ignition pliers as shown in illus. 6-132. Leave the stem collar below the lower valve facing alone. Always check for lumpy corrosion between the lower facings and metal backing discs, and scrape it out with a single edge razor blade.

If the lower facings must be replaced, pull the two upper collars off of the stem with the modified ignition pliers. If you remove them carefully enough, they might be tight enough to reuse; if not, obtain new ones from a supply company. Use the same tool to calibrate valve travel during reassembly. In some Autopiano stacks, the top valve facings are screwed onto threaded portions of the stems; with this style of valve, be sure that the valve leather is flexible enough to provide sufficient valve wobble but airtight enough so it doesn't leak around the stem. The original service manual says to regulate the secondary valves to $1/16"$ travel; this unusually large amount of travel is necessary for valves with felt punchings because they are so spongy, but if you releather the valves without the felt, set the travel at $3/64"$. After regulating the travel, seal the metal seat in place with burnt shellac. A little shellac should ooze out around the valve plate, but make sure none runs anywhere near the area which touches the valve. Check the stem guides for moth damage; if necessary, rebush them or replace them with new fibre guides from a supply company.

Many Standard/Autopiano secondary pouches still look good but have insufficient dish, and attempts to regulate the valve stem pouch buttons to the pouches will be to no avail. With inadequate pouch dish, the pouches will either hold the valves up off the lower seats, or if the buttons are screwed up far enough to eliminate this, the pouches will not have enough travel to press the valves against the upper seats. Regardless of how good the pouch leather looks, replace it if there is insufficient dish or if there is any chance that the pouch wells are packed with dirt. Also, it is not uncommon for a pouch input channel to nearly intersect another pouch well, causing a note to play when its neighbor does, so check every pouch well carefully and renew the sealer as necessary. After replacing the pouches, test each pouch by mouth for airtightness, holding your finger over the bleed in a single valve stack.

Thread the pouch buttons onto the valve stems, using a straightedge to calibrate them as shown in illus. 6-133. Their precise adjustment depends on the thickness of the new gasket leather and the amount of pouch dish, but usually the buttons protrude $1/8"$ beyond the rim of the valve board, *with the valves held against the inside seats.*

Illus. 6-133. Regulating the pouch buttons.

Temporarily assemble the pouch and valve boards, tape over the screw holes, and clamp the suction supply manifold or a large flanged hose connector to the suction supply opening. Lay the stack with the pouch board down, tape over the pouch input holes, and apply suction to test each valve for tightness. As you check each valve for the right travel and test it for tightness, hold your finger over the pneumatic feed hole, and listen carefully for leakage on the top seat. Correct any problems, and remove the pouch board.

Assemble the deck boards to the valve board, attach the pouch board, and test the stack once more, making sure that each pneumatic repeats quickly and positively. In a double valve stack, hold a short piece of tracker bar tubing on each pouch input channel to alternately apply suction and atmosphere with your mouth. When you are satisfied with each note, install the flanged fingers and pushrods. Use thin action cloth punchings between the leather nuts and pneumatic fingers like the original ones, and tighten the leather nuts so they are just barely snug, not so tight that they make the pneumatic feel stiff as it moves throughout its range.

When testing the Standard/Autopiano stack without the head, you might encounter a few "leakovers"—notes which play along with adjacent ones. These ciphers are often caused by the absence of the head screws, and they cease to be a problem once the head is attached.

Restore the primary valve chest if the action has one, replacing all gaskets, valve leather and pouches, sealing the pouch wells and channels if they are not airtight, repairing stripped screw holes, etc., and set the travel at $1/32"$, per the original service manual. For further information on releathering and calibrating the travel of primary valves, refer to p. 90. Many Standard/Autopiano primary pouch boards have far deeper wells than the desired amount of pouch dish; if this is the case, carefully dish the pouches all the same amount without touching bottom.

If the original lead tubing is corroded or damaged, remove it. Either plug the holes with dowels and redrill them for $5/32"$ OD tracker bar nipples, or drill the holes out to $7/32"$ and install a set of $7/32"$–$5/32"$ reducing nipples, to accomodate ordinary neoprene tracker bar tubing.

After restoring all the parts, reassemble the primary chest, tape off the output and input holes, (or tie off the input holes with knotted tracker bar tubing, if you have installed brass tubing nipples), connect the chest to the test pump, and test each valve for repetition.

As in most player pianos with flanged fingers which play the piano whippens, the Standard stack should be regulated to the piano with the primary valve chest, head and stop rail removed. Place the stack in the piano, and see if moving the whole stack up or down will take care of a substantial part of the lost motion between the fingers and whippens. If necessary, insert dense cardboard shims under the right end of the stack and under the suction supply manifold at the left, raising or tilting the stack to roughly regulate it. Then test each finger as shown in illus. 6-134, regulating the capstan until just a tiny amount of lost motion exists. After the capstans are regulated, install the stop rail, connect your test pump to the stack, and play each note by opening the pouch input hole. Adjust the stop so the backcheck catches the hammer at the same place as it does when you play the key by hand.

Illus. 6-134. Top: A homemade hook used for regulating stack flanged fingers to piano action. Bottom: Using the hook and a capstan wrench to regulate the flanged finger capstans. Install and regulate the stop rail after regulating the capstans.

Apply a thin coat of shellac to the secondary pouch board where the gasket touches it, let it dry until it is tacky, and install the head (and primary chest) in the piano.

Illus. 6-135. A late two tier double valve Standard stack ready to be installed in its mission oak Foster piano. (Most Standard and Autopiano stacks have three tiers with larger pneumatics.) All leather nuts and cloth punchings have been replaced. The fingers and stop buttons have been regulated to the piano, and the primary valve chest and head are installed. This same stack is shown in illus. 4-8.

The Wind Motor

The Standard/Autopiano wind motor has five pneumatics glued to a mahogany-faced trunk, and it is common for the mahogany to split when the pneumatics are removed. Remove the broken pieces of mahogany from the pneumatic boards, reglue them to the trunk and sand it smooth, or sand the mahogany completely off and replace it.

Some Standard/Autopiano transmission frames are made of stamped metal and others are made of die cast pot metal, with thick cloth bushings holding some of the shafts to eliminate the need for precision machining. Be careful not to break a pot metal transmission while cleaning it.

Illus. 6-136. Five-point wind motor of a double valve Standard player action, installed in the Foster piano. This spoolbox has a stamped metal transmission frame.

The Tracking Device

The Standard tracking device is one of the most sophisticated pneumatic mechanisms in any player piano. Its operation at first might seem difficult to understand, but it is just an assembly of interconnected pouches and valves, and unless you know how it works your chances will be slim of getting one to work right.

The tracker bar has two staggered paper edge sensing holes on each side of the roll, as shown in illus. 6-137.

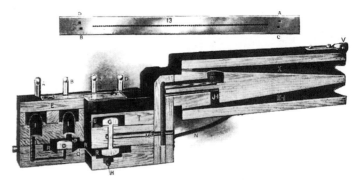

Illus. 6-137. Cutaway drawing of the Standard automatic tracking device.

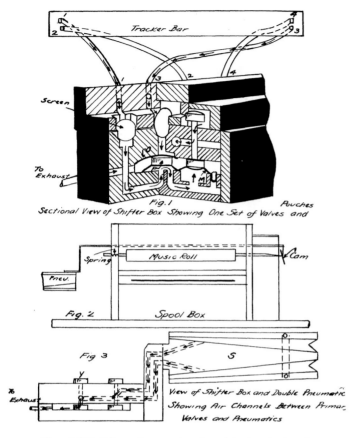

Fig. 1
Sectional View of Shifter Box Showing One Set of Valves and Pouches

Fig. 2 — *Spool Box*

Fig. 3 — *View of Shifter Box and Double Pneumatic Showing Air Channels Between Primary Valves and Pneumatics*

Illus. 6-138. Schematic representation of the Standard tracker.

The valve box contains two primary valves, two inside valves and six pouches - two primary pouches, two overhead pouches and two cutout pouches. Each primary valve admits atmosphere or suction to half of the tracking pneumatic; each primary valve is controlled by a primary pouch with a bleed. Each inside valve is glued to a cutout pouch which opens and closes the channel from one outer tracking hole to one primary pouch. Above each inside valve is an overhead pouch, with a bleed, which is connected to one of the inner tracker holes. The inner and outer tracking holes are cross connected to the primary valves, so the outer left and inner right holes control one valve, while the outer right and inner left holes control the other. The following paragraphs describe all possible states of the valves, pouches and pneumatics.

1. If all four tracking holes are *closed*, the overhead pouches are *up*, the cutout pouches are *open*, the primary pouches and valves are *down*, and both halves of tracking pneumatic have suction. (Although the cutout pouches open the passageway from the outer tracker hole to the primary pouch, the outer tracker hole is covered with paper, so the primary pouch remains down).

2. If all four tracking holes are *open*, the overhead pouches are *down*, the cutout pouches are *closed*, the primary pouches and valves are *down,* and both halves of the tracking pneumatic have suction. (Now although the outer tracker holes are open, no atmosphere reaches the primary pouches because the cutout pouches are blocking the passageways).

3. If the two inner tracking holes are *closed* and the two outer holes are *open*, the overhead pouches are *up*, atmosphere travels from the two outer holes to the primary pouches, lifting them and the primary valves, so both halves of the pneumatic have atmospheric pressure.

In the first three conditions described above, the system is balanced because the tracking holes on both sides are balanced. In the following conditions, the tracking holes are imbalanced, causing a response from the tracking pneumatic.

4. If one inner tracking hole is covered and the other three holes are open, one overhead pouch will permit its valve and cutout pouch to lift, admitting atmosphere to one primary pouch, lifting the primary valve and admitting atmosphere to one half of the tracking pneumatic. The other half of the pneumatic still has suction, creating an imbalance and recentering the roll.

5. If both inner tracking holes are covered and only one outer hole is opened, that outer hole will feed atmosphere to one primary pouch, lifting the valve and admitting atmosphere to one half of the pneumatic. The other half of the pneumatic still has suction, creating an imbalance and recentering the roll.

In other words, as long as both inner tracking holes are covered by the roll, the outer holes are connected to the primary valves and they control the pneumatic. As long as both inner holes are open, both outer holes are shut off by the cutout pouches. If one inner hole is covered by the roll, by definition the opposing outer hole must be open, causing one cutout pouch to open *and* to feed atmosphere to its primary pouch.

To get a better feel for how this complex unit operates, remove a properly working one from a piano, remove the primary valve dust cover and apply suction. With all four nipples open, both primary valves will go down, and the pneumatic will remain centered. With all four nipples closed with your fingers, the primaries will stay down and the pneumatic will also remain centered.

With only the two nipples for the inner tracking holes covered, the primaries will go up and the pneumatic will remain centered. You can now manipulate the pneumatic by alternately opening and closing the nipple for each outer hole.

With all four nipples open, opening and closing the outer hole nipples will have no effect on the pneumatic, but if you alternately open and close the nipples for the inner tracking holes, the pneumatic will respond.

If you have a properly working tracking device and you

don't remember how to connect the tubes after you put the unit together, apply suction, and open and shut each nipple one at a time with your finger, *leaving the other three open*. Opening and closing two of the nipples will have no effect on the pneumatic; the other two will cause it to move. The two which cause it to move are for the inner tracking holes. Find the nipple which causes the pneumatic to pull the roll to the left when you close it, and tube it to the right inner tracking hole. Tube the other one to the left inner tracking hole. Tape over the two inner tracking holes, and find the remaining nipple which causes the pneumatic to push the roll to the left when you close it. Tube this one to the right outer tracking hole, and by the process of elimination—you guessed it—tube the last nipple to the left outer hole.

If a Standard tracking device refuses to work properly after you carefully seal the channels, repair stripped screw holes, and replace all of the gaskets, valve leather and pouches with new leather ones, you either have a leak somewhere or the pouches are not dished properly. Double check to make sure none of the holes for mounting screws are causing the problem. If it still doesn't work, check the pouches, particularly the cutout pouches. Are the valve buttons perfectly centered? Is there just enough dish for each cutout pouch to open the channel, but little enough so the cutout pouch has no wrinkles? Are the working areas of the cutout pouches perfectly free of glue so the valves can seat properly? Are the overhead pouches dished properly, or do they have a little glue on the working surface, causing them to cock the valves at an angle? If the valves and pouches work as they should but the pneumatic refuses to remain centered, are both halves of the pneumatic and the pneumatic gasket perfectly airtight? A leak in one half of the pneumatic or into one channel in the gasket will cause the pneumatic to pull off in one direction. If everything seems airtight but you can't seem to find the problem, replace the cutout pouches again, using a little more or a little less dish. At the moment the job might be frustrating, but once you get an old Standard tracker to work properly, it will last for a long time providing that you clean the paper dust out of the screens and tracker bar tubes regularly.

The Standard tracking device underwent several subtle but important changes. In earlier actions, the weight of the pneumatic pulls the tracking cam down during rewind, permitting the spring in the left hand spool chuck to push the roll to the right, causing paper wear. In later examples, a spring helps to hold the tracking pneumatic up, counteracting the spring in the chuck. In still later examples, the orientation of the cam is reversed, so the weight of the pneumatic counteracts the chuck spring. The tracking holes in the tracker bar are tubed differently, depending on the position of the cam, as shown in illus. 6-139.

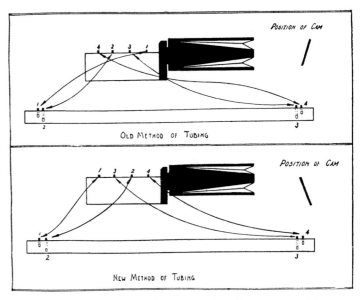

Illus. 6-139. Old and new orientations of tracking cam and tubing.

The Pump

The left reservoir of a Standard pump contains an accent pneumatic, labelled the "expression pneumatic" or "crash valve" in the original service manual. During ordinary pumping, this pneumatic has no effect, but when a pumping pedal is given a quick push, the momentary higher suction in the trunk pulls the large valve in the pneumatic shut, closing the reservoir off from the rest of the player action. The pneumatic opens immediately after the accented note plays, reconnecting the large reservoir to the system. The author has seen many orphaned Standard crash valve pneumatics which were removed by previous technicians who thought they would take more work to restore than they were worth. The crash valve is an important part of the Standard system, however, because it provides the only means of obtaining a quick accent. Restore it and put it back in the pump where it belongs!

Illus. 6-140. The Standard pump. A: action cutoff. B: wind motor governor. C: tempo control and motor accelerator.

The hinges of Standard pumping bellows were usually reinforced with rope. When rehinging the bellows, replace the rope as described on p. 66.

The Standard is a real workhorse, easy to play and very responsive. A double valve Standard repeats faster and better than most other player pianos at softer playing levels and with somewhat damaged rolls which mistrack slightly. The Schulz and Gulbransen have a reputation for being superior because they are so hard to rebuild that every single restoration detail has to be done perfectly or they won't work at all. On the other hand, it is possible to get many Standards playing by simply covering the pneumatic and bellows, leaving the rotten old leather gaskets, pouches and valve facings in place; consequently, most Standards in existence work, but don't work very well. If every part of a Standard action is treated as carefully as the parts of the more difficult actions are, a Standard will give any player a run for the money.

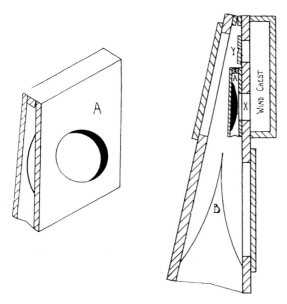

Illus. 6-141. The accent pneumatic or "crash valve."

STARR

Made by the Starr Piano Co. of Richmond, Indiana, and used in Starr, Remington and other pianos made by that company. The player action is tight and well built, with pneumatics and decks both made of maple. The stationary board of the pneumatic resembles that of a glued Gulbransen with its suction feed channel, and pouch well, but the pouch input channel exits through the back of the pneumatic instead of through the deck. The rest of the action is completely different from the Gulbransen, with metal top valve seats. There is nothing unusually difficult about restoring one.

STEGER ARTEMIS

This action was used in Steger, Artemis and other players made by the Steger Piano Co. of Steger, Illinois. The stack of the 1920's has unit pneumatics with pushrods for the lower two decks and metal fingers for the top deck. The pouch board is on the front of the stack. Each valve hangs vertically from a zephyr skin tab which is glued between the wood valve button and inside leather facing; the valve has an adjustable threaded stem with a tiny wood pouch button. The inside seats are wood; the outside seats are rectangular aluminum plates, gasketed to the chest with various layers of blotter paper and pouch leather which control the valve travel. The pneumatic screws onto the outside of the aluminum plate, with another leather gasket; the two long pneumatic screws plus two shorter ones hold the valve plate to the stack. The natural tendency of the valve is to hang at a slight angle, since the zephyr skin tab is not over the valve's center of gravity. If the zephyr skin tabs are stretched, replace them so the valves are centered on their seats. In some examples, the original inside valve facings appear to be in new condition, with no signs of flaking or deterioration, but the leather is so porous that the piano could not have been very airtight when it was new. When releathering the valves, choose new leather which is as smooth as possible, and be sure it slides on the valve seat enough to pull tight when suction is applied. Some Artemis players which work well otherwise will not build up suction at

Illus. 6-142. An Artemis pneumatic, valve and valve plate.

the beginning of a roll because the friction between the inner valve seats and leather valve facings prevents the valves from sliding into position. The only way to get one with this problem started at the beginning of the roll is to pump without the roll on the tracker bar, until all 88 notes play at once. Then draw the roll leader over the bar, causing the valves to seat one after the other from the center outward. Once they are seated, the piano will play until you stop pumping.

STORY AND CLARK

Used in pianos made by the Story and Clark Co. of Chicago, Illinois. As shown in the illustrations reproduced

146

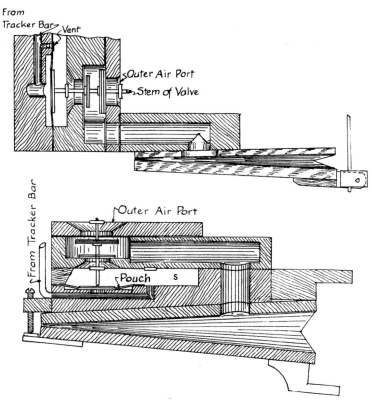

Illus. 6-143. Two styles of Story and Clark stacks.

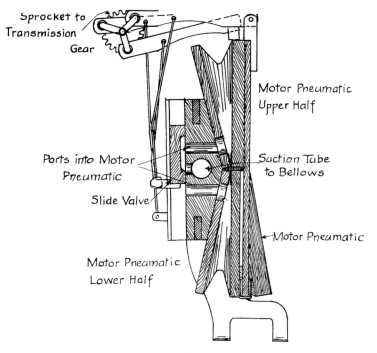

Illus. 6-144. Cross section of Story & Clark 6-point wind motor.

here from the 1924 service manual, two styles of stack were used—one with vertical and the other with horizontal valve seats. The valves are the same in both styles; the horizontal version, called the style "M", has regulating screws on the front as shown in illus. 6-143, for regulating lost motion between the pneumatics and piano action, as

in a Schulz. The Story and Clark wind motor has six pneumatics in three pairs. In some pianos, each connecting board is fastened only to the top pneumatic of each pair, with a hook connecting it to the lower pneumatic, coupling the two pneumatics without wrinkling the cloth. In others, each connecting board is screwed to both pneumatics, causing the cloth to wrinkle unless the pneumatics are hinged, covered and glued to the trunk precisely as they were. A better way to rebuild this style of motor is to make new moveable pneumatic boards, drilling the tiny screw holes in the pneumatics for the mounting boards after the pneumatics are glued to the trunk. Be careful to drill only part way through the pneumatics, to avoid getting sawdust inside.

STRAUCH

Two tier stack similar to Lester, with Standard-like valves, round metal lower valve seats sealed in place, and oval pouches. The valve shown here has a stem guide which is nailed in place on the deck, but many stacks have the guides screwed in place. As in a Standard, clean the corrosion out from between the lower leather valve face and metal backing disc.

Illus. 6-145. Valve, valve seat and stem guide from Strauch stack.

WILCOX AND WHITE ANGELUS

Uncommon. Made by the Wilcox and White Company of Meriden, Connecticut, this action in various forms was installed in "Symphony" and other player reed organs, a variety of pushup piano players, some of which also contain organ reeds, and player pianos, including early Knabes. Instead of pneumatics, the stack has large rectangular pouches glued in wooden frames, with thin wooden plates glued to the pouches. Each pouch has a large wire crank which converts the sideways movement of the pouch into up and down movement of the pushrod. The soft wood pouch frames are glued into slotted soft wood rails which practically fall apart in some stacks, and which stubbornly resist disassembly in others. Proceed carefully, be prepared to make new wooden parts if necessary, seal the pouches carefully with thinned liquid rubber cement, seal all of the wood with lacquer to make it airtight, and use only hot glue or liquid hide glue for reassembly. Watch for corroded zinc valve backing plates in this action.

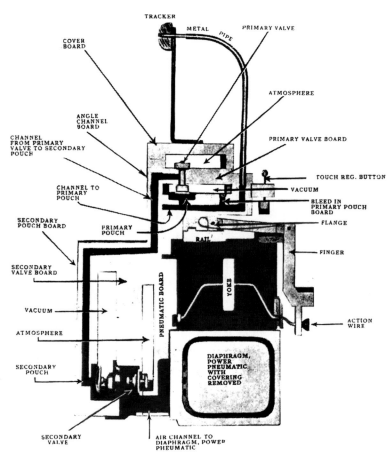

Illus. 6-146. Cross-section of the Wilcox and White stack.

WURLITZER

The Rudolph WurliTzer Co. marketed a complete line of regular and automatic musical instruments—home player pianos, coin pianos, orchestrions, band organs, pipe organs, etc., - and the automatic instruments have a variety of different player actions. Although most home player pianos have the third style of player action listed below, it is possible that the other styles, used in coin operated pianos and band organs, were also installed in some home instruments, so all five commonly used stacks are described here.

The earliest stack was used in band organs and coin pianos built for WurliTzer by the Eugene DeKleist Co. of North Tonawanda, New York, and it continued to be used after WurliTzer acquired the DeKleist Co. It has a valve chest on top of the stack, with horizontal brass inside and outside seats, and with channels conducting suction from the valves down to the pneumatics through the front board. The valves are made of two wooden buttons faced with leather and connected to each other with a small piece of string to provide flexibility for seating. Each wood button has a wire stem which fits into a stem guide in the brass seat, and the bottom stem is threaded for a wooden pouch button. If you encounter a stack with these valves, check that the string has not shrunk, pulling the two wood buttons together and eliminating the flexibility required for seating. In some cases it is possible to pull the two parts apart gently, just enough to provide a little wobble, without breaking the old string. It is very important in one of these stacks to number and mark the orientation of the valve seats; the screw holes were not drilled uniformly, and if the seats are mixed up or rotated from their original orientation, the valve chest will not be tight.

The second commonly encountered stack has valves similar to those in the first type, but with vertical seats. Instead of being in one valve chest, the valves are in the individual pneumatic tiers, and the front of the stack is the pouch board. The outside seats are wood, but the inside seats are the old brass plates. Delicate conical springs are used on the stems to help the wobbly two piece valves seat on the inside seats; be extremely careful not to damage them. This type of stack has celluloid bleeds; check them carefully for damage, and replace them with brass bleed cups unless they are in perfect condition.

The third WurliTzer stack is the type encountered in most home player pianos; a somewhat similar stack was used in band organs, but it was rarely if ever used in coin pianos. This stack has two tiers of pneumatics, with each tier having its own valves and pouches. The outer valve seats are metal plates sealed in place with burnt shellac, and the inner seats are bakelite inserts (or rarely, stamped metal plates). Each valve has a leather-faced fibre lower disc with a fluted wood stem attached to the bottom and a thick threaded brass stem coming out of the top. The top leather-faced fibre disc is threaded onto the brass stem so it wobbles without leaking around the stem. The pouch board is glued to the bottom of the valve board around the perimeter. The channels from the valves to the pneumatics go down through the bottom, and the pneumatics are glued to the pouch board, making it impossible to get at the pouches. To replace the pouches in this stack, remove the pneumatics, outer valve seats and valves, and drill up through the bottom for countersunk flat head screws which will be used for reassembly as in an H. C. Bay. Carefully saw around the perimeter to remove the pouch board. Build up the area where wood was removed by the saw with a new strip of wood and a leather gasket, seal the wood and lower valves seats if necessary, replace the pouches, reassemble the stack and glue the pneumatics back on. Releather the valves, making sure that the top face can wobble, install them, adjust the travel, and seal the top valve seats in place.

The fourth type of WurliTzer stack, used in all varieties of coin pianos and band organs, has the same valves and seats as the third, but they are located in individual unit blocks with the pouches installed from the bottom and covered with fibre or dense cardboard. After repouching these blocks, glue new cardboard over the bottom and bevel the edges of the cardboard to help keep it from

Illus. 6-147. The WurliTzer unit valve. The pouch is glued in from the bottom, held in with a retainer ring, and the bottom is then covered with cardboard or fibre and a layer of rubber cloth.

splitting loose. Then glue rubber pneumatic cloth over the cardboard to seal it and to help prevent it from splitting loose.

The fifth WurliTzer stack, used in late instruments including home player pianos, incorporates "four in one" pot metal valve castings. Most of these castings are now cracked beyond repair; if you find a home player piano with a few good castings, save them for someone who needs them to restore a more valuable band organ or orchestrion.

In some home player pianos, the pump has a metal rod bracing it to the keybed; to remove this pump from the bottom of the piano, loosen the rod and slide it downward into the pump.

Illus. 6-148. Unit valves installed on the stack in a 44 note WurliTzer Pianino coin piano of the 1920's.

MODERN PLAYER PIANOS

Since the late 1950's a variety of modern spinet and console player pianos have been made by Aeolian, Kimball, Universal, WurliTzer, and others. Most of them, including those with foot and electric pumps, have a very compact stack under the keyboard, with tracker bar tubing running around the ends of the keyboard (usually) or through the keys (rarely). Many modern players have plastic unit valves which are not considered to be repairable, since replacement valves are available economically. If

the day comes in the future that restoration is desirable and the plastic parts are no longer available, rebuilders will have to figure out how to disassemble and reassemble the plastic for replacement of pouches and valves, without shattering the plastic into bits. For now, buy replacement parts.

With the exception of Aeolian players, the others have small electric gear motors to play and rewind the music roll, controlled by electronic circuit boards for tempo control, automatic rewind, shutoff, and in some cases, replay. At the time this is being written, the main problems which occur in these other brands are failure of the gear motors and electronic components. While the electronic circuits are rather simple, their repair is beyond the scope of this book. Kimball has gone through a number of design changes, and gear motors for the earlier spinet players of the 1960's are no longer available. If this obsolescence spreads to other players, the technician of the future will also have to learn how to replace "lifetime bearings," small nylon gears and motor windings in the gear motors, as well as learning to substitute new parts for obsolete transistors, diodes, potentiometers and other electronic parts.

AEOLIAN

Modern players built by Aeolian Pianos, Inc., of Memphis, Tennessee, have been sold under many names, including Hardman, Hardman Duo, Duo-Art (not to be confused with the Aeolian Duo-Art reproducing piano of earlier times), Musette, Pianola, and a variety of catchy names designed to capitalize on the ragtime fad of the 1970's—the Sting, Entertainer, Cabaret, etc.

The Hardman Duo of the late 1950's was designed more like an old player piano than anything to come along since. It has a fairly conventional wooden stack located above the keyboard, resembling the old Standard stack more than anything ever made by Aeolian or the American Piano Company. The metal valve plates were sealed with a material which tends to flake and get into the valves; if you rebuild one, number and remove all of the plates and clean all of the old sealer out of the channels, valve wells, off the valves and plates. This stack was assembled with cork gaskets which pull apart during disassembly; replace them with leather to make future disassembly easier.

Sometime around 1960 Aeolian changed from the Standard-like wooden stack to an Amphion-like stack, with narrow wooden decks and plastic unit valves, mounted under the keyboard. The foot pump, electric suction box and volume control, automatic sustaining pneumatic and action cutoff are also in the bottom. Above the keyboard are the head with an ordinary five point wind motor, governor and speed control, and Standard-like automatic tracking unit, and the split hammer rail pneumatics, automatic rewind pneumatic and shutoff mechanism. The players made during the 1970's are much harder to pump than a well-restored old player, but Aeolian appears to be trying to improve the quality of the pianos and make the player actions work better at the time this is being written. Although the plastic unit valves are meant to be replaced and not repaired when they go bad, Aeolian is to be commended for using interchangeable valve blocks of the same dimensions for over twenty years, as well as interchangeable parts for most of the other components of the player actions, so new parts can be used to repair older pianos. They also have kept detailed service manuals in print and have provided service clinics to piano technicians to make it easier for those who do not repair player pianos to tune and service their instruments.

Unit Valve Blocks

Older unit valve blocks were made of orange or red plastic. They have the fluted plastic valve stems glued to the neoprene valve buttons, and these often come unglued, requiring replacement of the whole block. Since sometime in the mid 1960's the blocks have been made of clear plastic, and the stems and valve buttons are pinned together, with a certain amount of wobble but not enough to prevent many valves from leaking, making the actions hard to pump. Early valve blocks have a tiny bleed hole formed in the plastic, which tends to clog with paper lint and dust because of the thickness of the bleed channel; later blocks have brass bleed cups which are easier to clean out by pumping the tracker bar.

To replace a unit valve block, split it into three pieces—the pouch block, valve chamber and top valve seat—which will then come off the wooden deck with a minimum of damage to the wood. Scrape the wood flat and clean, and glue a new block in place with Duco cement. Press it against the wooden deck for a few minutes, and then apply a piece of masking tape across it and several neighboring valves on each side. This will keep it from sagging until the glue dries. Never glue the blocks to the wood with epoxy or any other glue which will cause the wood to split next time the valve is removed.

Illus. 6-149. Modern Aeolian unit valve blocks.

Automatic Shutoff

Over the years, various schemes have been used for automatic shutoff. Older pianos have a main power switch under the keybed, wired in series with a small microswitch with a finger which drops into a slot in the takeup spool after the roll is done rewinding, shutting off the motor. This system works well as long as the finger is resting on top of the spool where it belongs. Unfortunately, many owners remove the takeup spool, which comes out simply by pushing it to the left a little, and then put it back in with the finger underneath, preventing the piano from being turned on. This caused so many problems for Aeolian that they finally abandoned its use.

In subsequent shutoff systems, the main power switch is on the left side of the spoolbox, with a shutoff pneumatic mounted on its left side. Several methods have been used for controlling the shutoff pneumatic. In the first system, the shutoff switch is a larger finger which drops into a slot in the takeup spool. Instead of controlling a microswitch, this finger operates a pallet valve, sending an atmosphere

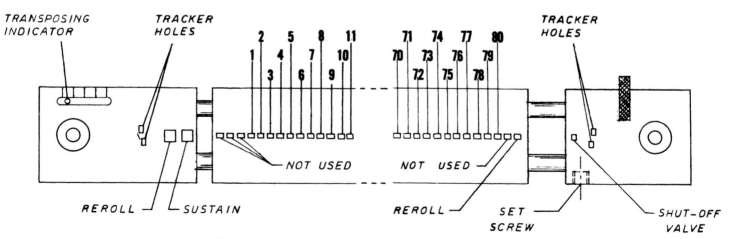

Illus. 6-150. Modern Aeolian player piano transposing tracker bar, showing positions of rewind and shutoff holes. An earlier system did not have the extra shutoff hole at the right side, as explained in the text.

signal to a unit valve which applies suction to the shutoff pneumatic.

The next system never worked reliably. The shutoff pneumatic is connected directly to the rewind pneumatic, but with a bleed in the line. In theory, when the end of the music roll opens the rewind holes in the tracker bar (the large hole to the left of the sustaining pedal hole, and the rightmost hole in the group of playing note holes, as shown in illus. 6-150), the rewind pneumatic quickly snaps shut, but the shutoff pneumatic doesn't because of the bleed. After the roll is done rewinding, it uncovers the tracker bar, this time long enough for the rewind pneumatic *and* the shutoff pneumatic to work. In many pianos so equipped, adjusting the size of the bleed either causes the piano to shut off at the moment it switches into rewind, or not shut off at all.

The system in use at the time this is being written has an extra tracker bar hole for shutoff, between the right rewind hole and the right tracking holes, as shown in the illustration. It is connected to a valve block which powers the shutoff pneumatic, and it works reliably.

Tracking Device

The Aeolian tracking device works the same as the old Standard device, with a double pneumatic, two primary valves, two inside valves and six pouches. Unfortunately, it is assembled with cork gaskets which split during disassembly, sometimes requiring replacement when it is necessary to gain access to the pouches. Although most examples work right when brand new, some malfunction within a few months, requiring careful replacement of the pouches and gaskets. If you find this necessary, be careful not to strip the screws holding the bottom pouch board to the rest of the device. If the pouches are the least bit asymmetrical, or if they have too much or too little dish, the tracking device will not work. Some trackers have gross misalignment between the pouches and valves; either plug and redrill the screw holes for correct alignment, or replace the whole unit.

Wind Motor and Governor

Many wind motors made in 1960's and 70's developed small cracks in the slide valve seating area, particularly in pianos located in dry climates. If a wind motor "lopes", fill the cracks with thin poplar shims as in shimming a soundboard, remove every trace of glue, sand the surface perfectly flat and apply graphite.

If a wind motor seems to be fairly tight in a well-used piano, but won't run fast enough, regardless of the setting of the tempo control and governor spring, and with the top spool brake clean and adjusted properly, remove the front cover of the governor to see if the tempo control orifice is clogged with dirt. If so, clean it out with a thin blade, being careful to preserve the original shape of the orifice.

Volume Control

In pianos with an electric suction box, a three-level volume regulator is mounted on top of the box, controlled by a knob in the spoolbox. On the right side of the front of the reservoir is a lever which pushes on a slide valve in the regulator. To regulate minimum playing level, adjust the position of the collar on the shaft so that with the volume control knob in the soft position, the piano plays as softly as possible without missing any notes. At this point, some owners still think the piano is too loud. If so, regulate it even softer on the basis that simple rolls will play softly, but complicated rolls will miss many notes, requiring the control knob to be turned up to medium.

Miscellaneous Problems

Many Aeolian players have a wooden support under the left side of the spoolbox which is supposed to be glued to the keybed. This almost always breaks loose, allowing the spool shelf to sag; after tuning the piano, or any time you notice that the support is loose, apply a little Titebond or equivalent on the bottom of the support and wedge it into the correct position.

Aeolian transmissions are lubricated at the factory with a thick coating of Vaseline, which turns gummy after a few years of use. Any time you have the front off, check the top spool brake; if necessary, remove it and clean the friction pad in lacquer thinner to remove the sticky buildup.

A number of transmissions were drilled with holes slightly too small for the shafts. If you encounter one with shafts which refuse to turn, remove it from the spoolbox, disassemble it, and drill the shaft holes out enough to slip the shafts in easily without excess play.

If the gears don't mesh properly, check the position of the takeup spool in relation to the tracker bar, and then check the position of the large brass gear on its shaft. This gear is prone to slipping sideways, causing the gears to miss or to clash.

Many other servicing procedures are discussed in the Aeolian service manual, available through the manufacturer or Vestal Press.

KIMBALL

In older modern Kimball players, the valves are housed in large plastic blocks glued to the wooden pneumatic decks. These blocks come unglued when the wood shrinks and swells with humidity changes. If you encounter a piano with loose but otherwise good valve blocks, install leather gaskets to help them stay stuck to the decks.

Later Kimballs have single unit valve blocks which may be disassembled for servicing or replacement of the neoprene pouches or valves. Before attempting to make any repairs to an older Kimball, find out whether replacement parts are available.

UNIVERSAL

The Universal player piano was developed and marketed as a higher quality alternative to other brands. Designed by people experienced with the best features of all the old player pianos, the Universal is one of the easiest player pianos to pump because it incorporates an electric motor for the music roll. To date its main problems are with the electronic circuitry. Early instruments also had a problem with the pneumatic control which starts the music roll after suction is built up in the system.

Some pianos seem to have the top spool chucks installed so the music roll is not perfectly parallel with the tracker bar. While this causes no problems with most single tune rolls, the left side of some large medley rolls uncovers the rewind hole half way through, switching the piano into rewind prematurely. This problem may be solved by holding the "roll forward" button down during play.

WURLITZER

Most modern WurliTzer players have solenoids to play the piano action, with a small suction box used only to apply suction to the back of the tracker bar. Inside the tracker bar ports are little plungers connected to microswitches which make contact when holes in the roll allow the suction to pull them back. Unfortunately, the little plungers malfunction with the least accumulation of paper dust, requiring frequent cleaning. Also, the tracking device has an electric motor which constantly pushes the roll alternately to the left and right in response to a paper edge sensing double pole microswitch. This wears out both sides of music rolls faster than in most other player piano. For several years in the early 1970's, WurliTzer also made a limited number of pneumatic player pianos; these are of higher quality and they work better than the pianos with solenoid actions.

Illus. 6-151. An Aeolian console player piano of the early 1980's.

CHAPTER SEVEN
REPRODUCING PIANOS AND EXPRESSION PIANOS

This chapter begins with a general description of reproducing and expression pianos, followed by general information appropriate to all grand pianos, electric piano motors and wiring, and lock and cancel mechanisms. Then each of the major reproducing and expression piano systems is discussed in detail, including how it works, a tracker bar layout, rebuilding hints, and how to regulate it. With each discussion of a specific brand, other literature is recommended. This literature contains detailed information which is "required reading" for the restorer, but it would be redundant to reprint it all here. Obtain all applicable literature and *learn every word* prior to restoring a reproducing piano. Throughout the chapter, most information pertains specifically to grand reproducing pianos unless otherwise stated, since most reproducers are in grands, although here and there specific reference is made to uprights. By referring to the appropriate recommended literature as necessary, you will be able to translate the information to upright pianos as well.

Reproducing pianos use special rolls and contain extra mechanisms which enable them to closely imitate the playing of human pianists. The three systems which survive today in large numbers include the "Welte-Mignon" (introduced in Germany in 1904), the Aeolian "Duo-Art" (introduced in the U.S. in 1913), and the American Piano Co. "Ampico" (introduced in the U.S. in 1914). From the early 1900's until the late 1930's, most of the world's finest pianists—both classical and popular—recorded their performances on specially-equipped recording pianos, with a few new rolls being issued into the early 1940's. After a musical selection was recorded, the master roll was edited, and special expression "coding" was added to the margins of the roll so it would play back the original performance as accurately as possible. While there were other important reproducing systems—the Hupfeld DEA and Triphonola, Philipps Duca, Angelus Artrio and Apollo Artecho, these exist today in such small numbers that it is a rare occurrence to see one, let alone to own or restore one.

The stack in a reproducing piano is divided into bass and treble, with separate suction regulators for each half. Each suction regulator has pneumatic mechanisms which can raise or lower the suction quickly, slowly, smoothly, or suddenly as controlled by the marginal perforations in the music roll. Reproducing pianos do have their musical weaknesses, the primary one being the inability to strike several notes at different volume levels simultaneously on the same half of the keyboard, but all of the major systems are capable of playing beautiful music with realistic expression, from the softest whisper to the loudest crash, with perfectly smooth transitions as well as sudden volume changes, providing that the piano as well as the player action is meticulously restored and regulated.

It can not be overemphasized that every detail of the mechanism must be just like new in order for a reproducing piano to work. For example, if just one of the more than 1,300 cloth bushings in a grand piano action is just a little too tight, the piano will not play as softly as it should. If the strings are not level where they come out of the agraffes, if the hammers are not voiced, if all of the dampers do not lift precisely at the same moment, if one suction channel in a deck has a leak, if one pneumatic is hingebound, if one regulating screw or wire is out of adjustment, if the valve travel is not uniform, if a pump bearing is a little loose, if the pump covering material is too stiff or not stiff enough, if the motor cushions have deteriorated, or if any one of 10,000 other things is wrong, the performance of a reproducing piano will suffer. By now it should be obvious that the wise beginner should be well-versed in proper restoration techniques for player pianos before attempting to restore a reproducing piano.

While some player action rebuilders do not work on pianos, leaving piano restoration to a piano technician, the finest reproducing piano restorations have always been done by technicians who fully understand both pianos and pneumatic systems and who have sufficient keyboard training to play the piano at least well enough to know if it is regulated right, and to hear when everything is working just right. The performance of the piano and reproducing action are closely tied together, and it is more difficult for two people who separately restore the piano and player action to make a reproducing piano sound as good as one person who understands every facet of the entire instrument.

Reproducing pianos use wind motors to drive the music rolls, with the exception of the Ampico B, which uses an electric motor. On the premise that "if the Ampico B has an electric motor, all other reproducing pianos should too," some restorers who have experienced difficulty in getting wind motors to run smoothly have removed them from Duo-Art and other reproducing pianos, substituting electric motors in their place. Such alterations not only destroy part of the originality of a piano which is capable of working perfectly with properly rebuilt original parts, but they also alter the playing characteristics of the reproducing action. For example, in a Duo-Art, when the piano is playing loudly the spill valve is completely closed, and the only air which enters the pump between playing notes is the air which comes through the wind motor. In order to substitute an electric roll motor for the wind motor, an additional spill valve must be provided in order to keep from stalling or overheating the pump motor, and this additional spill valve by definition must alter the expression characteristics of the reproducing action. If you have trouble getting wind motors to run smoothly, learn how to restore wind motors! If you are more interested in innovating than in restoring, direct your designing and engineering talents toward something other than irreplaceable antiques.

EXPRESSION PIANOS

Expression pianos also have automatic volume regulators which act in response to marginal perforations in the music rolls, but they do not have a divided stack. With the entire stack playing at the same volume level, solo and accompaniment effects are more limited than in reproducing pianos, but a well regulated expression piano can nevertheless produce remarkably good music. The most widespread system in the U. S. was the Recordo, made in many different styles by many different piano companies. Others were the Art Apollo, Solo Art Apollo, Cable Solo Carola, and in Europe, the Empeco and Hupfeld Phonoliszt.

GRAND PIANOS

So far, this book has dealt exclusively with vertical player pianos, but most reproducing pianos and many expression pianos are grands. Many piano rebuilding techniques are the same for grands and verticals, but the grand action, damper action and keyboard are different and take much more time to regulate properly. For best results, study grand action regulating until you know every detail from memory, in order to diagnose and correct action problems.

Most grand reproducing pianos have a hammer rail lift mechanism like that of the vertical piano, with a pneumatic which lifts the hammer rail in response to its perforation in the music roll. As in any grand piano, the hammer shanks should not touch the rail when the rail is down; regulate the height of the rail so there is approximately ⅛" space between it and the hammers at rest. After the action is completely regulated, adjust the lift pneumatic so it lifts the hammers to 1" from the strings. It is very important to regulate the dampers perfectly in a reproducing grand; the keys drop a little when the rail lifts, and in doing so they will lift some of the dampers off the strings if the dampers are not regulated right.

Classical music demands quick, positive operation of the automatic sustain mechanism. For the fastest possible response of the sustaining pneumatic, regulate its pushrod

so there is just 1/16" lost motion between it and the damper lift rod or lever, and regulate the stop screw so the pneumatic just barely lifts the wedge dampers clear of all of the strings.

Removing and Installing Grand Piano Player Actions

If you attempt to remove the reproducing action from a grand piano which is standing on its legs, by the time you are done, you will wonder why anyone ever bothered to build a grand reproducing piano. This job is far easier if you stand the piano on its side. Not only do you avoid the risk of bodily harm or damage to delicate but heavy parts by dropping them, but you also avoid the unpleasant experience of having fifty years of dirt, oxidized lead, black paint chips and pieces of brittle rubber accumulate in your mouth, nose and under your eyelids. In some small grands, the stack can not be removed with the legs in place, so the piano must be on its side for disassembly.

To tip a reproducing grand on its side, place a regular padded grand skidboard up on blocks just high enough so the bass edge of the cabinet will touch the skidboard before the drawer or other parts touch the floor. In some instances it is necessary to have several helpers lift the piano several inches off the floor in order to remove the pedal lyre. When tipping the grand down to the skidboard, use more helpers than you would for an ordinary piano because of the weakness of most reproducing grand double legs; keep as much weight as possible off the back and treble legs while tipping. Once the bass keyboard corner of the piano is resting on the skidboard, proceed as in tipping an ordinary grand, but recheck during every stage of the move to make sure the blocks under the skidboard remain stable.

Before tipping a Duo-Art grand on its side, remove the spoolbox and other parts of the player action from the cavity behind the fallboard.

Before removing the player action from the bottom, sketch the routing of hoses and tubing (including the crowded tracker bar tubing connected to the primary valve chest in an Ampico, if it is still in place). This differs from one piano to the next, and since the restoration job will take weeks as a full time job, or months if you do it in your spare time, your job of installing the hoses, elbows and tubing will be much easier if you have a reminder of where they all went. Remove the whole player action from the piano, so you can do a good job of cleaning the soundboard, beams, etc. In most pianos, major repairs and possibly refinishing will be necessary, and the time to do this is while the player action is out.

After refinishing, rebuilding and regulating the piano, and restoring the player action components and testing them individually on the bench, stand the piano on its side again for installation of the player action. This makes it easier to align the stack pushrods and insert them into the slot in the bottom of the keybed, in pianos without flanged fingers on the stack, and it is also far easier to install the tubing and hoses with the piano in this position. In many Ampico grands of 5'4" or shorter length, the parts are squeezed into such a small space that the tracker bar tubing connecting the primary valve chest to the stack will kink unless it is looped just right. Beware of cumulative bunching of the tubing, requiring you to remove it and start over with another scheme. When you are done installing all of the tubing, recheck each piece connected to the primary chest to make sure none is kinked.

To install a stack which has poppet wires held in alignment by a guide rail which is screwed down to the top of the keybed behind the piano action, remove the guide rail, secure the poppets in a more-or-less straight line with masking tape, install the stack, remove the tape, and then feed the poppets into the guide rail one at a time as you reinstall it after standing the piano on its legs.

After all of the components, hoses and tubing are installed, stand the piano on its legs for final regulating. Every time you stand a grand reproducing piano on its legs, recheck the legs for loose glue joints and cracked wooden parts. The author knows of more than one instance in which an ordinary grand piano fell off both front legs into the lap of a tuner, and while he has never heard of anyone being killed or seriously injured by a falling reproducing piano, the possibility of this happening is quite real, particularly in a piano with a cracked or an unglued leg! If you must work under a reproducing grand with weak or wobbly legs, protect yourself by strategically placing padded concrete blocks or other large solid objects under the perimeter.

Although it may seem like a lot of energy is expended in standing the piano on its side for removal and installation of the player action, even more time and discomfort are involved in performing these jobs with the piano on its legs. After the player action is installed and the piano is standing up, if you find it necessary to remove a large component, have a helper support the component while you remove the screws. It is helpful when removing a pump or stack from under a piano to support the part with your knees while removing the screws, inserting boards or large books under your feet if necessary, and then lowering the part to the floor by gradually straightening your legs until they are flat on the floor.

Making a New Belly Cloth

An important finishing touch on any grand reproducing piano is the belly cloth which covers the mechanisms below the soundboard. Not only does the belly cloth keep the mechanisms cleaner and make the bottom look neater to most people, it also softens the subtle mechanical noises which emanate from even the most carefully restored instrument. The easiest way to fit the cloth to the piano is with the piano on its side; if you postpone the job because you just can't wait to hear the piano play after installing the player action, you will become intimately acquainted with your floor and the piece of cloth as you crawl under the piano and out again ten or fifteen times.

Obtain a piece of black vinyl coated material, a sufficient number of black snap fasteners, and a set of small snap setting tools (usually a small concave anvil and a punch) at a fabric store. Whether or not the original belly cloth still exists, the bottom of the piano usually still has the male portions of the snaps attached around the perimeter. If not, replace them; the holes in the piano should be obvious. If you still have the original cloth, use it as a pattern to cut the new fabric a little oversize; some old belly cloths either were stretched too tight to begin with, or have shrunk sufficiently that some of the snaps no longer reach where they should.

With a helper, hold the new material up to the bottom, flush with the long straight bass side of the cabinet and the straight line of snaps on the keybed or stack cover, making sure that the material is large enough to cover everything and reach all of the snaps on the piano. Mark the position of one of the middle snaps on the long straight side of the cabinet on the cloth, and install the mating portion of the snap on the cloth. Attach the cloth to the piano with this one snap, gradually work your way toward the treble side and tail end of the cabinet, adding one or more snaps each time. After installing all of the snaps, trim the perimeter of the cloth to the desired size.

Ampico grands typically have several cloth covers - the usual belly cloth under the soundboard, and a separate cover for each group of tubing which hangs down from the back of the drawer, one on each side of the pedal lyre.

ELECTRIC MOTORS, WIRING AND SWITCHES

Most reproducing and expression pianos have an electric motor with wiring running around the inside of the cabinet to the power cord and the switch. Either service the motor yourself, or take it to a reliable motor technician who enjoys and is good at working on old motors. A complete servicing includes disassembling, cleaning and lubricating the bearings, cleaning the starting switch and checking it for positive opening and closing without excessive sparking, checking the wire leads for broken strands of wire and damaged insulation, checking for excessive end play, reliable starting, overheating, binding and other problems.

Many motors are misdiagnosed by novices as having a burned out starting winding when there is actually nothing more wrong than a stuck starting switch in need of cleaning. Starting switches come in all shapes and sizes, and if the contact points are burned or worn, reshape them if there is enough metal left, or have a machine shop make new parts if necessary. Electric motor shops rarely want to make new starting switch parts, but a good machinist can copy anything made of brass. The switch must work freely; if it fails to close just once, the next time the motor is turned on it will just sit and hum, and will burn out if it isn't turned off almost immediately. It is possible for a motor to overheat to the point of catching something on fire before blowing a circuit breaker or fuse, so don't take chances on the starting switch.

It is very important to figure out whether the motor originally had grease or oil as a bearing lubricant. Most piano motors use oil, sometimes described in old service manuals as "non-liquid" oil, a type of oil held in suspension in thicker grease which would release the oil as needed, to keep it from dripping out of the motor. One of the fastest ways to burn out a perfectly good old motor is to pack oil holders with grease. If the old lubrication holders attached to or built into the end bells had wicks, this is a sure sign that it was designed for oil. Unless a motor has grease cups, use oil! With the motor on the bench, grasp the shaft and try to pull it up and down, perpendicular to its axis, to test for worn bearings. If the shaft is loose in the bearings, the motor might overheat, and the oil will run out, possibly dripping into the windings, harming the insulation.

Check the armature for end play. For maximum efficiency, the fibre end play washers should hold the armature in the same lateral position in which the magnetic field pulls the armature while running. If the fibre washers permit excessive end play, remove them and turn the motor on long enough for the field winding to pull the armature into the magnetically centered position. Note this position in case the starting switch has springs which will push the armature out of position after you turn the motor off. Turn it off and insert the appropriate number of fibre washers at each end to keep the armature in this position with about 1/32" end play. Extra fibre washers of the correct size are available from electric motor repair shops.

By all means, if you service the motor yourself, don't drop any of the parts! The slightest bend in the armature will render the motor useless.

Inspect the electrical wiring in the piano. Remove the covers from the plugs, switches and junction boxes or "condulets", and check the ends of the wire for broken strands or bad insulation. Electric wire is one item *not* to preserve for the sake of originality if the insulation is going bad! Replace it if necessary with the correct wire according to your local electrical code, using the correct type and size of wire and accepted procedure for splices and for fastening it to switches and plugs. Disassemble the main power switch and check it for wear and broken parts. If the switch is bad, you will have to use your ingenuity to repair it or find an electrically suitable substitute which will fit into the original housing.

Many Ampico pianos originally had a ground wire between the motor case and pump casting, to prevent the buildup of static electricity. If you decide to connect the green grounding wire of a three wire power cord to the motor frame, have a competant motor technician check the motor carefully for internal shorts to the frame. Many old motors with an internal short which seem to run perfectly on two wires will become too hot to touch in a few seconds if a grounding wire is added; if this is the case, have the motor rewound or the defect repaired. In light of the fact that the on/off switch in many reproducing pianos could conceivably become hot if a short develops in the motor or wiring, safe practice dictates the addition of a green grounding wire from the switch housing all the way to the third prong of the plug on the power cord, although antique restoration aesthetics contradict this.

The correct size of the motor pulley is very important in any motor-driven piano. A common practice over the years was to install a larger motor pulley to turn the pump faster as the system became leakier, but leaving an oversize pulley on the motor in a restored piano puts unnecessary stress on the motor and pump. According to original service literature, Ampico rotary pumps should turn from 110 to 120 rpm, and Duo-Art rotary pumps should turn from 120 to 125 rpm. This dictates a motor pulley between 1¾" and 2" OD. Very small motor driven pumps, such as those in most Melville Clark Apollo X pianos, turn somewhat faster, and very large pumps like the remote Duo-Art 6-bellows "steamboat pump" turn much slower.

LOCK AND CANCEL MECHANISMS

Many reproducing pianos have "lock and cancel" holes for turning certain mechanisms on and off. If a function is controlled by a lock and cancel mechanism, a short perforation at one tracker bar hole switches it on, and a short perforation at another different tracker bar hole switches it off. This eliminates the necessity of punching long extended holes (or "chain perforations") in the music rolls which would weaken the paper. In many instances, several locking holes are cancelled by one cancel hole. Lock and cancel mechanisms take many different forms. In the Ampico A intensity mechanism, for example, each intensity pneumatic is controlled by a small outside valve which, when momentarily turned on by a short hole in the roll, admits air under its own pouch through a bleed hole, locking the valve on. When a short cancel hole is punched, the cancel mechanism applies suction to the bottom of the intensity valve pouch, overpowering the weak atmosphere signal, pulling the pouch down and turning the valve off again. In the Welte Licensee expression mechanism, for another example, each locking valve has one pouch underneath which switches the valve on, and another on top which switches if off again.

THE AMPICO

The Ampico was marketed by the American Piano Company in their own pianos: Mason & Hamlin, Chickering, Knabe, J. & C. Fischer, Marshall & Wendell, Franklin, and Haines, as well as several English and European brands. A few Ampicos were made to special order in Steinway and other grands, but these were not production items. Three major versions of the Ampico player action were made and installed in upright and grand pianos, including the Stoddard-Ampico, the Ampico A and the Ampico B, in that chronological order. The first two were installed in uprights and grands, but the model B was made in grands only. Each of the three major versions have slightly different expression coding in the music rolls, and the "B" mechanism is radically different from the other two, but any of the rolls can be played on any Ampico with passable results.

Within the major versions of the Ampico (Stoddard, A and B), a number of subvarieties were made. A foot pumped upright version was called the "Marque' Ampico; this was made in both early Stoddard and later Ampico A versions. A small studio upright was marketed beginning in 1927, and the spinet Ampico was introduced in 1938, just a few years before the end of the original player piano era. For further information about the various models and brands, refer to the *Encyclopedia Of Automatic Musical Instruments* (Bowers), *Player Piano Treasury* (Roehl), and *Re-Enacting the Artist* (Givens).

The three Ampico systems may be identified by the novice by a few simple external clues. The Stoddard has a control switch labelled "soft," "normal," and "loud." Many Stoddards have two replay knobs in the drawer (or spoolbox) which move in slots as the roll plays; by adjusting the position of the knobs, the operator can select a certain portion of a roll to be repeated over and over. The Ampico A has a control switch labelled "subdued," "medium" and "brilliant," and the tempo knob slides from side to side, starting at "0." The Ampico B tempo control knob rotates, starting at "50."

Ampico A and B music rolls may be identified by a few simple clues. Original A and B roll labels are shown in illus. 7-1. Note that the earlier B labels are identical to A labels but with stars in the lower corners. Many recut rolls have confusing labels; if in doubt as to the identity of a roll, unwind the leader to check the expression perforations. B rolls have telltale amplifier holes very close to the edges, and holes 1 (1B) and 98 (1T) are always punched simultaneously.

During the transition period between the model A and B, a number of Ampico grands were made with model A stack, expression mechanisms and pump, but with a model B drawer. One collector has noted that at least half of the Ampicos which he has seen in the Eastern U. S. with B drawers have A components underneath! Since a

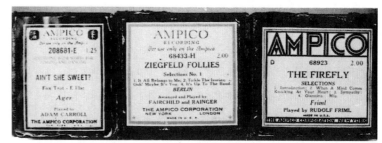

Illus. 7-1. Left to right: Ampico A, early Ampico B and later B roll box labels.

full model B is worth substantially more than a model A with a B drawer, it is extremely important to look underneath before purchasing a piano with a model B drawer. The A and B components under the soundboard are completely different and are easily identified after a brief glance at the illustrations in service literature.

THE STODDARD-AMPICO

Relatively scarce today, this was the earliest mass-produced major version of the Ampico. It is described in detail in several Vestal Press reprints: "Stoddard-Ampico Upright Views," stock #C-31, which describes earlier instruments with Auto Pneumatic Co. player actions, and "1919 Inspectors' Instruction Book with 1920 Supplement," stock #C-11, describing later ones with Amphion actions. The expression mechanisms work on the same principles as the Ampico A; rebuilding techniques are basically the same, and regulating procedures are explained in the 1919 manual. The main difference between regulating a Stoddard and an A is that the Stoddard has timing screws for adjusting the speed of the slow and fast crescendos. Slow crescendo and slow decrescendo should each take eleven seconds; fast crescendo and decrescendo should each take two seconds.

THE AMPICO A

The Model A Ampico is by far the most common version of the three. Prior to restoring one, obtain a model A test roll and the following literature, which contains complete explanations of the various mechanisms: "The Ampico Reproducing Piano—1923 Inspector's Reference Book," (Vestal Press #C-1—this beautiful 18 p. manual contains pictures and detailed explanations of the components of an upright Ampico, but the descriptions of the expression mechanisms, pump and other parts are equally applicable to the grand), "1925 Expression Tubing for Grand, 280-C (#C-6—a complete tubing diagram for grand Ampicos of this vintage), "How to Rebuild the Model A Ampico" by David Saul (#T-3), "Ampico Tubing Diagram—Upper Action, 235-C" (#C-12, useful only for uprights), and "Ampico Foot-Blown Print

(#C-13X, useful only for certain models of the Marque' Ampico).

The Ampico A Expression System

The Ampico A has four control switches in the drawer (or spoolbox, in an upright): the modifying switch, which can be set for subdued, medium or brilliant playing; the sustaining pedal switch, which permits or prevents the sustaining pedal from working automatically from the roll; the automatic cutout switch, which turns the automatic expression on and off for Ampico and 88-note player piano rolls; and the repeat switch, which causes the piano to replay the roll or shut off after rewinding.

The Ampico stack is divided into treble and bass, each half having an identical set of automatic expression regulating mechanisms. (Exceptions are certain Marque' Ampicos, which have an abbreviated expression system). Each expression mechanism has three intensity pneumatics which, in various combinations, produce seven suction levels, and a crescendo mechanism which can slowly or quickly increase or decrease the suction. ("Crescendo" is a musical term meaning "gradual smooth increase in volume level").

The Ampico A tracker bar is laid out according to the following list. In this and all other tracker bar layouts, or "tracker scales," as they are usually called, the word "on" denotes a function which is "locked" (switched on) by a short perforation and "cancelled" (switched off) by a different hole in the tracker bar. (Refer to the introductory information on lock and cancels on p. 156). For example, in the following scale, short perforations at holes 2, 4 and 6 lock their respective intensities on until they are turned off by the common cancel hole 7. In original Ampico service literature, the last eight tracker bar holes in the treble are numbered 1T–8T, from the right margin inward. These numbers are included in parentheses.

```
 1 (1B)   Slow bass crescendo (decrescendo when released)
 2 (2B)   Bass intensity 2 on
 3 (3B)   Sustaining pedal
 4 (4B)   Bass intensity 4 on
 5 (5B)   Fast bass crescendo/decrescendo
 6 (6B)   Bass intensity 6 on
 7 (7B)   Cancel bass intensities, holes 2, 4 & 6
 8-90     Playing notes, low B through high A
91 (8T)   Rewind
92 (7T)   Cancel treble intensities, holes 2T, 4T, & 6T
93 (6T)   Treble intensity 6 on
94 (5T)   Fast treble crescendo/descrescendo
95 (4T)   Treble intensity 4 on
96 (3T)   Hammer rail up
97 (2T)   Treble intensity 2 on
98 (1T)   Slow treble crescendo (descrescendo when released)
```

Locking holes 2, 4 and 6 control the bass intensities, providing seven steps of volume, and hole 7 cancels all three of them. Similarly, locking holes 97, 95 and 93 control the treble intensities, cancelled by hole 92. Hole 1—which is not a locking hole, causes the bass to play gradually louder and louder in a slow crescendo. After hole 1 is closed, the bass becomes gradually softer in a decrescendo. If hole 5 is opened together with 1, the crescendo occurs quickly; if 5 is opened by itself after a crescendo, the bass decrescendos quickly. (In other words, 5 increases the speed of the crescendo and decrescendo). Likewise, 98 produces a slow treble crescendo, 98 + 94 = fast treble crescendo, closing 98 produces a slow treble crescendo, and opening 94 after 98 is closed produces a fast decrescendo. Holes 3 and 96 are chain perforations, not lock and cancels, operating the sustaining pedal and hammer rail, respectively.

As shown in illus. 7-2, the intensity pneumatics are connected to a common lever arm which pushes down on the valve stem, trying to push the valve shut. Connected to the bottom of the valve stem and opposing the intensity pneumatics is the spring pneumatic which receives suction from the crescendo pneumatic through tube #13. With no expression holes punched in the roll, the suction in the spring pneumatic and intensity pneumatics is balanced so the regulator valve is open just enough for the piano to play as softly as possible. When atmosphere is admitted to one or more of the intensity pneumatics, or when higher suction is fed to the spring pneumatic, the regulator valve opens, and the half of the stack controlled by that regulator plays louder.

When no crescendo holes are open, the crescendo pneumatic controls the minimum playing level of its half of the stack by feeding a precisely regulated amount of suction to the spring pneumatic. This "minimum intensity" is adjusted manually so the half of the stack controlled by that expression mechanism just barely plays without missing any notes, by turning screw #31 in illus. 7-3. When the slow crescendo tracker bar hole is opened, the slow crescendo valve mounted on top of the pneumatic slowly feeds more suction into the pneumatic, which pulls up against its spring, gradually feeding higher suction into the spring pneumatic and producing a slow crescendo. When the slow crescendo hole is closed, atmosphere is gradually admitted into the pneumatic, producing a slow decrescendo. When the fast crescendo hole is opened with the slow crescendo hole, suction is admitted into the pneumatic faster, causing it to collapse faster, producing a fast crescendo; if the fast crescendo hole is opened after the crescendo hole is closed, atmosphere is admitted to the pneumatic more quickly, producing a fast decrescendo. The operation of the crescendo mechanism and its valves is described in detail on pp. 8, 11-14 and 68-69 of the 1919 manual, and on p. 7 of the 1923 manual.

While the crescendo mechanisms are used for slow and fast crescendos and decrescendos, most of the volume changes are handled by the intensity pneumatics. Note that these pneumatics are "off" when they have suction and "on" when they have atmosphere. Each intensity

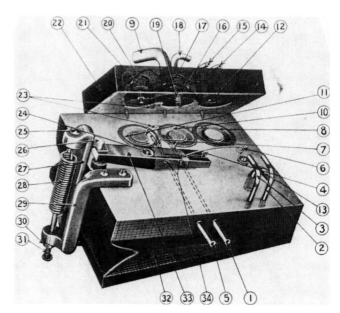

Illus. 7-3. The Ampico A crescendo mechanism, one for the treble and another for the bass.

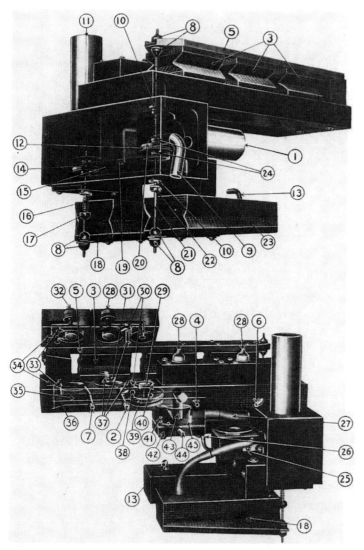

Illus. 7-2. The Ampico A has two of these intensity mechanisms, one for the treble and another for the bass.

pneumatic is controlled by a small outside valve called the "intensity valve"; when this valve is down (off), the pneumatic has suction. Each intensity valve has an inside valve called the "lock valve." When a short intensity hole passes the tracker bar, it admits atmosphere under the intensity valve pouch, and as soon as the valve goes up it feeds atmosphere through a bleed under its own pouch, locking itself on and feeding atmosphere to the pneumatic. This permits the spring pneumatic to push the regulator a little farther open, causing half of the stack to play louder. When a short cancel hole passes the tracker bar, the cancel valve feeds atmosphere under the three lock valve pouches, lifting the lock valves which feed suction under the intensity valve pouches, turning the intensity valves off. The three intensities have seven possible combinations, providing seven volume levels. From softest to loudest, these are: all off, 2, 4, 6, 6 + 2, 6 + 4, and 6 + 4 + 2. (4 + 2 provides the same level as 6. The numbers for the bass intensities are given, but the treble works the same

way). A complete description of the intensity mechanism appears on pp. 8-11 and 67-68 of the 1919 manual, and p. 9 of the 1923 manual.

Two other important mechanisms are a part of each intensity mechanism: the re-regulator valve and pneumatic, and the finger button expression control. When the modifying switch is set at subdued, the re-regulator pneumatic (#18 in illus. 7-2) partially closes off the port between the main expression regulator valve and the stack, decreasing the loudness of the higher intensities without altering softer playing. Its operation is explained on pp. 9-10 of the 1923 manual. The finger button expression control (#45 in illus. 7-2) is a pouch which gradually decreases the suction to the intensity pneumatics as the finger button is pushed farther and farther down, causing the appropriate half of the stack to play louder; its action is described on p. 10 of the 1923 manual. These mechanisms are significantly different in the Stoddard-Ampico, as explained on p. 28 of the 1919 manual.

Late Ampico A intensity mechanisms have a small pneumatic added which decreases the playing volume slightly when the sustaining pedal operates. When the pedal lifts the dampers off the strings, less force is needed to play the piano at the same volume because the pneumatics do not have to lift the dampers. The little pneumatic, shown in illus. 7-4, compensates for this subtle volume difference.

The Amplifier

The amplifier pneumatic is mounted on the pump and connected to the spill valve spring. When the modifying lever is in the "subdued" or "normal" positions, the

Illus. 7-4. When the sustaining pneumatic takes the weight of the dampers off of the keys, the stack plays slightly louder than it should. This little pneumatic pushes on the spring pneumatic when the sustaining pneumatic operates, lowering the suction a little to compensate for the lighter action weight.

amplifier pneumatic does not work, and the pump suction remains at 15". When the modifying switch is in the "brilliant" position, it admits air under the pouch in the "amplifier control box," lifting valve #11 and connecting the amplifier pneumatic to suction from both halves of the stack, as shown on p. 18 of the 1923 manual. The control box also contains a pair of check valves which prevent higher suction from one half of the stack from feeding back into the other half when the two halves are playing at different levels. When the piano plays softly, the spill valve remains at 15", reducing the strain on the pump motor, but when the music roll calls for louder playing, the stack suction goes up, pulling the amplifier pneumatic farther shut, increasing the spring tension on the spill valve and raising the available pump suction level.

Automatic Expression Cutout Block

The purpose of this mechanism, shown in illus. 7-5, is to block the expression hole signals from the tracker bar to the expression mechanisms when ordinary 88-note player piano rolls are played; it is turned on and off by the "automatic on/off" switch in the drawer.

The Ampico A Stack

The Ampico A has a double valve stack, with a separate primary valve chest. The stack is an ordinary Amphion unit valve stack, as described on p. 103. Prior to about 1924, grand stacks had upside down valve blocks, and pushrods which went through a guide rail attached to the piano. From about 1925 on, the valve blocks were right side up, and the pushrods had flanged fingers, simplifying

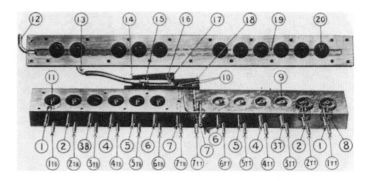

Illus. 7-5. The automatic expression cutout block, which blocks the expression holes in the tracker bar for playing 88-note player piano rolls. Note that sustaining pedal hole 3B has no cutout pouch, because the sustaining pedal operates with both Ampico and player piano rolls.

installation of the stack in the piano. For a short time after the valves were turned right side up, they had the wooden outer seats and blotter paper gaskets of the upside down valves, but soon the design was changed, incorporating metal outer seats pressed into place.

In some Ampicos, residual suction in the stack causes the last playing note to play again after the piano goes into rewind. To prevent this, some Ampico stacks have two extra unit valves, one for each half, mounted in positions in the stack where there are no pneumatics. Each of these valves has the output channel cut open, so when the valve turns on, it dumps a large amount of atmosphere into the stack. Their pouch input tubes are teed together and are teed into the line connecting the cutoff primary valve and the large action cutoff pouch in the pump suction supply manifold. At the moment the piano switches into rewind, these two blocks instantly bleed sufficient atmosphere into the stack to prevent the last note from playing again.

Late A grand stacks have a lost motion compensator similar to the one on an Ampico B stack. When the hammer rail pneumatic lifts the hammer rail, the keys go up a

Illus. 7-6. Bottom view of 1928 Chickering Ampico A with keybed cut out to accomodate flange finger stack. Earlier pianos with a poppet wire stack have only a small slot cut out of the keybed where the pushrods enter.

Illus. 7-7. The stack which fits into the piano in the previous illus. The arrows point to two of the lost motion compensator pneumatics which lift the rail on which the flanged fingers rest.

little in back, and the lost motion compensator lifts the flanged fingers of the stack, preventing lost motion from occurring between the stack and piano action as it does in earlier pianos.

The Drawer

The A drawer contains a maze of tubing which is understandable if you consult David Saul's "How to Rebuild the Model A Ampico," and the grand tubing chart labelled "280-C...1962 redrawn by Harold Malakinian," (Vestal Press #C-6). Copies of this chart printed after 1984 are correct, but prior to this time it has the secondary valves for the rewind and play pneumatics incorrectly identified; actually, the rewind ("reroll") valve is toward the *front* of the drawer, and the play ("repeat") valve is toward the *rear*. (These are the inside valves contained in the valve box which is attached to the side of the tracking pneumatic). The earlier Vestal Press tubing chart labelled "revised 1970 by D. Lavric" is basically the same, containing the same mistake plus the following additional ones: in the right margin, the line reading "6 Pedal" should read "7 Automatic Cut Out," and the line reading "7 Automatic Cut Out" should read "6 Pedal." Also, the tracker bar in the drawer has an extra hole for 83, which should actually be the one connected to the junction block on the right rear of the drawer labelled "note 83." Another change which will make the grand tubing print more easily understandable is to change the label for the rear primary valve in the "reroll/repeat primary valve box" from "reroll" to "action cutoff." There is no primary valve for the reroll pneumatic. Note that the drawing in the Saul manual is a top view, while the grand tubing print is a bottom view.

Automatic Rewind, Replay and Shutoff

The rewind/replay/shutoff systems were completely different in upright and grand pianos, and a number of subtle design changes were incorporated over the years.

Uprights

The Stoddard-Ampico system used in upright pianos is clearly described on pp. 34 and 42 of the 1919 manual. It is the only system in which both nipples on the transmission frame are used. Viewed from the front, the left nipple controls the pouch in the "universal vent block," and the right nipple is teed into the line connecting the spoon valve and the shutoff primary valve. (Note that this primary is an *inside* valve). The later upright system is described in detail on pp. 14-15 of the 1923 manual. An important difference between upright and grand systems is the fact that when the roll is done rewinding in the upright, the spoon valve on the takeup spool *closes* a port, but in the grand, the music roll *opens* a port in the takeup spool. In the upright, the play pneumatic primary valve is an inside valve, while in the grand, it is an outside valve. As shown on p. 14 of the manual, the upright system has three reroll cutout pouches, labelled "Fig. H" and "Fig. I." The tracker bar rewind tube 8T is connected to the rewind valve #23 only when all three cutout pouches are pulled up.

Pouch #29 is pulled up by suction from the bleed in the universal vent block, only when the transmission is in the play position, with the left hand nipple closed. (The right hand nipple is not used). When the transmission is already in rewind, this pouch closes, preventing the rewind pneumatic from working.

Pouch #30 is pulled up as long as the "automatic cutout switch" is on, in the position for playing Ampico rolls. When the switch is off, for playing 88-note player piano rolls, pouch #30 closes, preventing the rewind pneumatic from working.

The cutout pouch in Fig. I is pulled up as long as the spoon valve is open, causing valve #26 to lift, applying suction to the top of the pouch. (Valve #26 also applies suction to the pouch for the play pneumatic valve or the pouch for the shutoff pneumatic valve, depending on the setting of the repeat switch J). When the spoon valve closes, this pouch closes, preventing the rewind pneumatic from working.

The three cutout pouches are safeguards to prevent the piano from going into rewind unless it has just finished playing a roll and is ready to rewind. By preventing the rewind pneumatic from working once the transmission is already in rewind, and when the spoon valve closes after the roll is done rewinding, the rewind pneumatic can't come on at the same time the play pneumatic is trying to put the transmission back into play.

Grands

All Ampico A grands have at least one "reroll cutout" pouch located in the right compartment of the drawer, as shown in the "drawer tubing connections" drawing in David Saul's rebuilding guide. Some grands have two reroll cutout pouches instead of one, with both mounted in one longer block. In addition, some grands have a separate "roll starting cutout" pouch located in the left compartment, as shown in the 280-C grand tubing diagram. As mentioned above, these pouches work completely differently than the three pouches in an upright.

In all model A drawers, the valve for the rewind pneumatic is a lock and cancel valve. It is is locked on by the nipple attached to the transmission frame, and it is cancelled by the "reroll cutout" pouch. The rewind valve has no primary; the rear primary valve marked "reroll" in the grand tubing prints is only for the action cutoff and wind motor accelerator, and it is not connected to the valve for the rewind pneumatic.

When the tracker bar rewind hole 8T opens at the end of a music roll, it activates the rewind valve, causing the rewind pneumatic to shift the transmission into rewind. This opens the left hand nipple in the transmission frame which *locks* the rewind valve on, holding suction on the rewind pneumatic all through rewind to keep the transmission from slipping back into play. It also activates the rear primary valve which controls the main action cutoff, and wind motor accelerator. (The right hand nipple in the transmission frame is not used).

If the repeat switch is "on," at the moment the repeat hole in the takeup spool opens at the end of rewind, it activates the "repeat primary" valve, which does two things: it closes the "reroll cutout" pouch, blocking the signal from the transmission frame nipple to the rewind valve, cancelling the rewind valve and turning the rewind pneumatic off, and it simultaneously activates the repeat secondary valve, causing the repeat pneumatic to push the transmission back into play. Without the rewind cutout pouch, the replay and rewind pneumatics would fight each other, preventing replay.

In grands with two "reroll cutout" pouches mounted in one block in the right side of the drawer, one pouch is the regular reroll cutout already described, and the other is connected to the "automatic" switch. When the switch is on, in the position for playing Ampico rolls, the pouch raises, permitting the automatic rewind to work; when the switch is off, in the position for playing 88-note rolls, the pouch blocks tracker bar tube 8T, preventing the automatic rewind from working.

The "roll starting cutout" pouch, shown in the left side of the drawer in the grand tubing print, permits the shutoff valve to work only when all of the following conditions are met: the repeat switch is "off," the takeup spool hole is uncovered at the end of rewind, and the rewind pneumatic has suction in it. This prevents the piano from shutting off at any time other than the very end of rewind.

Some grands have just one reroll cutout pouch, some have a single reroll cutout pouch plus the roll starting cutout, others have the double reroll cutout pouch alone,

and still others have all three pouches. It is likely that other designs were used as well. If a grand has a spoon valve and the associated parts shown in the 1923 manual, then it works like the upright system.

Restoring the Ampico A

The Expression Mechanisms

Ampico A expression mechanisms pose no unusually difficult problems in restoration; detailed instructions for restoring the various expression mechanisms are included in David Saul's "How to Rebuild the Model A Ampico," Vestal Press #T-3. During disassembly, note and sketch the orientation of every part. Try to pop the phenolic or metal lower valve seats loose, and reseal them with burnt shellac. After releathering the regulator and re-regulator valves, install the collars on the stems to permit a little valve wobble, and be sure the various leather nuts, metal nuts and cloth washers are in the right order and face the right way. If any of the intensity pneumatic boards are rotated or mixed up, the screw holes will no longer line up with those in the lever arm and mounting base, causing the pneumatics to wrinkle and distort. If the pneumatics are already distorted due to poor quality prior rebuilding, make new ones of exactly the same dimensions. After covering them, drill the mounting holes in the stationary boards and attach them to the body of the expression mechanism. Then attach the lever arm to its mounting block, mark the positions of the lever arm screw holes in the moveable boards of the pneumatics, and drill the new holes. Be careful to drill only part way through the wood, to avoid getting sawdust inside the recovered pneumatics.

When each intensity mechanism is completely reassembled and tested, hold the regulator valve closed by pressing down on the valve stem, and adjust the leather nuts for the lever arm so the arm is parallel to the mounting board for the pneumatics. With the valve still closed, adjust the stop collar #22 so there is $3/16$" space between it and the valve stem guide #10. Still holding the valve closed, adjust the leather nuts for the spring pneumatic so the distance between the inside edges of the pneumatic boards at the open end is exactly $7/8$". This is the *inside* span, not the *outside* span of the pneumatic.

When restoring the automatic expression cutout block, note that although hole 3B, sustaining pedal, has a pouch well in the cutout block, it has no pouch, because this function works on 88-note as well as Ampico rolls. The "cancel pneumatic" has a hinge spring which often pulls the moveable board off to one side, preventing the pad on the pneumatic finger from closing the nipples. When you recover this pneumatic, install new inside and outside hinges. After it is covered, bend the legs of the hinge

Illus. 7-8. Top: These intensity pneumatics are wrinkled and stiff because the boards were mixed up during recovering. Bottom: The same intensity pneumatics after re-recovering, using new boards and drilling new screw holes during reassembly.

Illus. 7-9. Two views of a beautifully restored crescendo unit.

spring if necessary so they don't pull the moveable board off to one side.

Installing a Test Block

Regulating the expression in an Ampico requires taking suction level readings with a gauge. Although this may be done easily enough by pulling a tube off here and there and connecting it to your gauge as required, a more convenient way to check suction levels is to install nipples in the bass and treble sides of the stack or primary valve chest and in the action cutoff block of the pump, and tube

these nipples to a handy little test block mounted in an easily accessible location under the piano. Make a plug for each test nipple by inserting a ½" long dowel flush with the end of a 1" long piece of tubing; seal the end of the dowel with burnt shellac or glue to prevent seepage.

The Drawer

The four control switches in the drawer are made of pot metal, as is the usual Amphion transmission frame described on p. 105, all of which are nearly always warped beyond use. Replacement parts are available from several suppliers. Check new switches for airtightness, correct alignment of the channels in "on" and "off" positions, and for flatness of the mounting surfaces, correcting any flaws

Illus. 7-10. The inside of an Ampico model A drawer.

as necessary. It is imperative that the spools in an Ampico turn absolutely freely without any binding due to a warped transmission, due to the fragile condition of many valuable original Ampico music rolls; the top spool brake is necessary to keep the roll from stopping while the paper tightens itself during loud passages toward the end of the roll, but most rebuilders remove the rewind brake.

In all Ampicos, upright and grand alike, it is very important for the rewind and play pneumatics to be as flexible as possible and for the valves and pouches to work perfectly, with no binding or excess friction in any any of the mechanical parts, for the rewind/play/shutoff system to work reliably.

The Wind Motor Governor

Restoring the governor is straightforward, but be sure to replace the celluloid tempo control orifice if it is warped or cracked. New brass plates are available from several suppliers. If the celluloid is still good, seal around the edges for airtightness, or you will not have reliable control of the music speed.

The Pump

The Ampico A rotary pump has four bellows, with a cast iron front facing the pulley, a wooden suction manifold connecting the four bellows on the back, and a suction "distributing and muffler block" containing the action cutoff, spill valve and amplifier pneumatic assembly on top, as shown in illus. 7-11. The back manifold has a round access door, removable with two wooden turn latches. In this discussion, "back," "front," and "top" are used as they apply to an upright pump, because this is the orientation of the pump during disassembly and reassembly on the bench, and this is how the pump is shown in the 1923 manual.

Illus. 7-11. The suction distribution block, action cutoff, spill valve and amplifier assembly of the Ampico A pump. The board on which these parts are mounted is sometimes cracked beyond repair; it has been replaced in the pump in this photo, insuring that the pump will once again be as airtight as possible.

The iron front supports the crankshaft with two large ball bearings, and the connecting rod spider is supported on the crank by two smaller ball bearings. Each pumping bellows has a cast iron bracket which holds the connecting pin for the connecting rod. Three types of connecting rods were used: solid wooden rods with cloth-bushed holes, wooden rods with spring-loaded wedges which automatically compensated for a certain amount of bushing wear, and cast iron arms with cone bearings. In the solid wooden rods, always replace the bushings with new action cloth for a snug fit; with any wear at all, these bushings will knock. The cast iron rods are like those of a Duo-Art pump, described in the Duo-Art section on p. 180. The wooden rods with spring-loaded tightening wedges are the most common of the three types and are notorious troublemakers, so they are the type discussed in the following section.

To disassemble the pump, remove the suction distributing block and amplifier pneumatic assembly from the top. Mark the orientation of the back wooden suction manifold and remove it, number the bellows, their connecting pin brackets, and connecting rods. Make sure your numbers and other marks will be easily visible after the parts are cleaned and polished, for it is extremely important to put all the parts back exactly where they came from to avoid knocking and the notorious "Ampico pump

thump." Remove the large nuts holding the brackets to the bellows, remove the brackets from the bellows, and then remove the brackets and connecting rods from the pump. Hold the crankshaft inside the pump with a suitable wrench and unscrew the flywheel in the direction opposite the arrow on the front casting. Slip the crankshaft assembly with the connecting rod spider still attached out of the back of the pump. Then remove the front casting from the bellows and separate the four bellows from each other.

To remove the connecting arm spider from the crankshaft, remove the two machine screws which hold the flat square cast iron cover on the spider. Remove the cover to expose the nut inside. In many Ampico pumps, this nut has a left hand thread even if the pulley has a right hand thread. Remove the nut, and slip the spider off of the crank.

In most pumps, the two large ball bearings in the front casting and the two small ones in the connecting spider (one in a Duo-Art) are filthy, and they feel gritty as they turn. Even if all of the old hardened grease is cleaned out of the bearings, the balls are in a deteriorated condition with minute metal particles flaking off, so it is a good practice to replace them with new sealed ball bearings which are available from any bearing supply company. The crankshaft support bearings in most Ampico and Duo-Art rotary pumps are identified by the number 1203 (or 203), having an outside diameter of 40 mm, an inside diameter of 17 mm, and a thickness of 12 mm, although some pumps have 10 mm thick thrust bearings. The smaller crank bearings are usually number 1200 (or 200), with an outside diameter of 30 mm, an inside diameter of 10 mm, and a thickness of 9 mm. While these are usually available from any good bearing supplier, obtain replacements before doing anything to the original bearings which might damage them.

The large bearings are usually tightly pressed into the front casting. Remove both sets of metal and felt oil seals from the slots in the casting, and remove any metal spacing washers or rings, noting their positions for reassembly. Some pump castings have a shoulder inside the hub which controls the position of the larger bearings, but others simply have a large hole bored all the way through. If the latter is the case, note the exact depth of each bearing in the casting. Between the two bearings is a metal sleeve which permits the flywheel to be tightened without squeezing the inner races of the two bearings together. With a small pin punch, slide this sleeve to one side. Lay the casting in a horizontal position on your bench, insert the punch between the sleeve and the casting until it reaches the outer race of the bearing which faces downward, and give the punch a firm tap with a medium size hammer. Move the punch to the opposite side of the bearing and tap it again. Keep moving the punch back and forth, all the way around the outer race, and you will gradually drive the bearing out of the casting. After it comes out, turn the casting over, and it will be simple to remove the other bearing. Throughout the operation, support the casting solidly to eliminate the risk of breaking it.

If you encounter a bearing which is loose in the casting, shim the new bearing with thin brass shim stock as necessary to prevent knocking. Loctite might work, too.

To install the new large bearings in the casting, place the bearings in a freezer until they are well chilled. Clean the casting, and heat it with a propane torch, moving the torch in a circular motion around the hub for a few minutes. Apply a little oil to the outside of one bearing, and press it into place as quickly as possible to take advantage of its slightly smaller size while it is still cold. Press only on the outer race! In a pump casting with a bearing rest shoulder, press the bearing all the way in until it stops on the shoulder. In one with the same diameter hole drilled all the way through, press the bearing in to its original position as recorded in your notes. Some bearings are extremely tight, and in lieu of a huge bearing press must be driven in with a hammer and an appropriately shaped driving block which won't chip the outer race. Tap on one side and then the other to keep from wedging the bearing in crooked. Turn the casting over, insert the spacing sleeve, and install the other bearing. Freezing the bearings and heating the casting only makes a tiny difference, but it *does* help at least to get the bearings started in the holes without undue force. Press the smaller bearings into the connecting spider; these usually go in with gentle tapping. Again, never apply pressure to the inner race! Wash the felt oil seals in lacquer thinner, clean the metal caps, and reassemble them.

It is extremely important to rehinge and recover the bellows in an Ampico pump so they are aligned exactly as they were originally. If you sand any wood off the sides of the bellows, alter the shape of the hinge wedges, or hinge the moveable boards at the slightest angle, the pump will be guaranteed to thump. Check the flap valves and seats for airtightness. In some pumps, the flaps are still usable but the seats are rotten. If you replace the flaps, be careful not to distort the shape of the springs and metal clips. The new flap valve leather must have two important attributes: it must be soft enough to conform to the silencing felt strips which run lengthwise down the center of each flap, but it must stretch lengthwise as little as possible. If necessary, clamp the leather down overnight with a slotted wooden block over a thick piece of wire to form the lengthwise hump, and then prestretch the leather manually before installing it. Note that the leather for covering the bellows must be cut wider than the span of the open end in order to cover the sides completely.

After hinging and covering the bellows, replace the cloth or leather covering the area where the bellows are attached to each other with new material of the original thickness, so the screwholes in the sides of the bellows will line up with the front casting and back manifold. Assemble the four bellows, and attach the front casting with its new bearings. Clean the crankshaft, connecting spider and connecting rods. Check the wooden manifold which goes on the back of the pump for airtightness, and reseal the inside if necessary; replace the gaskets. Check the back edges of the four bellows (which mate with the back manifold) for flatness; major leakage will occur if the back does not lay flat on all four bellows. If the edge of one bellows seems lower than the others due to careless prior rebuilding, build it up level with the others with a layer of pouch leather. Recover the amplifier pneumatic and re-gasket the various cover plates or replace the seal cloth access covers for the inside flap valves. If the board which supports the amplifier pneumatic and action cutoff block is cracked, or if the screw holes are stripped, make a new one. A number of important screw holes are in locations where it is impossible to plug them with new wood, and if any of the long screws which hold the action cutoff block are stripped, they will permit serious leakage.

The spring-loaded wedges in the connecting rods do their job only if everything is in perfect alignment. Keep all parts of the connecting rods in their original order and orientation. Replace the connecting rod bushings with piano action cloth of the correct thickness. Observe where the cloth was originally glued down and where it was not glued, and duplicate this with the new bushings. Replace the cloth spacing washers. The bushings were originally lubricated with graphite grease, and the wedges with graphite, and these are still the best lubricants. Never use oil or grease on the wedges! After assembling the crankshaft, connecting rods and brackets, install the back of the pump and the board on which the amplifier pneumatic is mounted, but do not install the action cutoff block yet. Secure the pump to your bench, and temporarily connect a motor to it. With all of the suction ports taped off, gradually pull down on the amplifier pneumatic, and listen for knocking or thumping. If the pump was not damaged by a previous restoration and if you did everything carefully, the pump should turn silently without the faintest suggestion of a thump.

There are many causes for a knocking Ampico pump, including bellows covering material which is too stiff or not stiff enough, worn bushings, bad bearings, or one bellows which is not as airtight as the others. Bellows covering leather which is too thick and stiff can cause the connecting spider to lag behind and then catch up with a thump, once per revolution of the crank, instead of shimmying silently four times per revolution as it should. Leather which is too thin will pop in and out as the bellows open and close. One leaky bellows can cause the pump to speed up for part of each revolution. If all of these possible causes are ruled out, and the pump still has one or more muffled thumps with each revolution of the flywheel, the problem is most likely caused by misalign-

Illus. 7-12. The spring loaded wedges in these Ampico pump connecting arms were designed to prevent knocks from occurring, but if any part of the pump is reassembled crooked, the connecting arms will twist as the crank turns, causing the wedges to knock. Installing stronger springs will only make matters worse. Some pumps have plain connecting arms without the wedges.

ment of the connecting rod pins. The purpose of each connecting rod wedge is to press the connecting links snugly against the pins, taking up any lost motion as the bushings or pins wear. Unfortunately, if any part of the pump is installed at the slightest angle, skewing the two connecting pins for one rod, the pins will push the connecting links together, squeezing the wedge out a little, and then release them, allowing the spring to pop the wedge back in, once per revolution. This is the primary cause of "pump thump." Contrary to recommendations in earlier literature, installing stronger springs for the wedges will aggravate the problem, not solve it, as the stronger springs will simply cause louder thumps as they push the wedges back in harder. If you suspect the wedges of thumping, place the pump on your workbench, tape off the nipples and spill valve, turn the flywheel slowly by hand with your eye focused on one wedge, and watch for a tiny movement coincident with the thump. The wedge can thump with $1/32$" of movement or less, so analyze the situation carefully, and you will find the culprit or culprits. Loosen the nuts which hold the connecting rod bracket on the pneumatic, and you will see that the old "footprint" in the wood causes the bracket to twist when the nuts are tightened. Pull the bracket off of the bolts, but leave it attached to the connecting rod. Clean the wood, and apply a thin layer of epoxy to the footprint, levelling the surface with a flat blade. Apply a thin film of oil to the bracket to keep it from sticking to the epoxy. Place the bracket on the bellows, and gently secure the nuts, squeezing the epoxy to conform to the bracket without

forcing the bracket into the old footprint, which will twist it again. After the epoxy dries, tighten the nuts. If you perform this carefully so the bracket puts no twist on the connecting rod, the thump should be gone.

Restore the action cutoff block, with a new cutoff pouch and new gaskets; be sure your gasket leather is thick enough to accomodate the metal screen if one is present. Seal around the output nipples, and attach the box to the pump.

Ampico actions contain a number of pot metal or lead hose elbows which are almost always badly corroded. If the inside surface is crumbling or flaking, replace the elbow. If the inside and outside are still smooth, paint the inside with a liberal coating of shellac to inhibit future corrosion. Replacement elbows are available from several suppliers. If you obtain aluminum elbows, grind the burrs and casting marks off the outside so the hoses will be able to make an airtight connection, and clean the casting sand out of the inside. Note that most Ampico and Duo-Art hoses are $1\frac{1}{16}$" ID; 1" hose has to stretch too much, and $1\frac{1}{8}$" is too loose.

Marque' Ampico pianos contain an ordinary Amphion foot pump, as shown on p. 106.

Regulating the Ampico A

Before attempting to regulate the reproducing action, make sure the piano action, keyboard, damper action and pedals are regulated as perfectly as possible. If you do not play the piano, have a friend who is proficient at playing classical music try the piano for you, to check for unevenness and other problems.

Adjust each pedal pneumatic so it has a little lost motion before it begins to push on the pedal linkage. Without this lost motion, there is chance that the sustain pneumatic will hold the dampers off the strings slightly, or that the hammer rail pneumatic will hold the hammers a little above their correct resting place. Adjust the stop in the sustain pneumatic so it lifts the dampers until the wedge dampers just clear all of the strings, and adjust the stop in the hammer rail pneumatic so it lifts the hammers to 1" from the strings.

If the stack has a lost motion compensator, adjust it so when the hammer rail pneumatic collapses, the flanged fingers just barely follow the motion of the keys without pushing on them.

Your test roll should have a set of instructions listing the purpose of each test and what adjustments are to be made. These instructions are also included on pp. 3 and 5 of the 1923 manual. Many of the tests simply verify whether mechanisms—lock and cancel valves, pedal pneumatics, etc.—are working or not, but a few tests require adjustments to be made. As in regulating a grand piano action, the finest regulating job can only be done by going through the entire regulating procedure several times, as certain adjustments have an effect on others. It is a good idea to check the markings on the roll for the tempo test, since many modern rolls have gross inaccuracies in the length of paper which is supposed to be between the beginning and ending marks. Regulate everything listed in the manual and on the test roll as carefully as possible. The complete regulating procedure is not repeated here, but the following information summarizes the main suction level settings basic to the correct reproduction of the music, assuming that all of the other mechanical adjustments are set correctly. In the following paragraphs, and the original service manual, instructions are given for connecting a vacuum gauge to tubes pulled loose from the player action; if you installed a test block during rebuilding, connect the gauge to it instead.

Medium setting: pull one of the treble note playing tracker bar tubes loose at the back of the drawer and connect it to your suction gauge. Put the test roll on the tracker bar, set the tempo at "0," turn the automatic switch off, turn the modifying switch to "medium" and turn on the motor. With the treble finger button held all the way down, the suction should be 20". If the suction is too low, tighten the spring which connects the amplifier arm to the spill valve; if it is too high, loosen the spring.

Subdued settings, treble and bass: with the suction gauge still connected to a treble note playing tracker bar tube, the test roll on the tracker bar with the tempo set on "0," and the automatic switch turned off, turn the modifying switch to "subdued." Turn the motor on, hold the treble finger button all the way down, and the gauge should read 10"–12". If it is too low, turn up nut #17 on the treble re-regulator valve stem, shown in illus. 7-2; if it is too high, turn the nut down. Reconnect your suction gauge to one of the bass note playing tracker bar tubes, and adjust the bass re-regulator nut as necessary. If adjusting the nut has no effect, the re-regulator valve or the unit valve block for the re-regulator pneumatic is not working.

Brilliant setting: with conditions the same as in the above examples but with the modifying switch set at "brilliant," press the appropriate finger button all the way down. The gauge should read 27"–30". If it is too low, turn up the screw in the moveable board of the amplifier pneumatic; if it is too high, turn the screw down.

Minimum intensity settings, treble and bass: during the repetition test on the test roll, with the automatic switch turned on, adjust screws #31 on the treble and bass crescendo pneumatics so each half of the stack plays as softly as possible without missing any notes.

If all of the mechanisms in your piano work right, and the piano crashes when it should, including all the way through the wild note-capacity test toward the end of a full-length test roll, the final test of your restoration and

piano regulating is the minimum intensity test; if every note plays extremely softly during the repetition test, you have done a good job. After adjusting the minimum intensities as carefully as possible with the test roll, play a number of music rolls and readjust them if necessary. While the test roll serves as a general guide, real music rolls are what matter. If you can't get the piano to play softly enough without missing some of the notes, go back and check the regulation of the piano action, stack and other parts.

THE AMPICO B

The model B Ampico is a completely re-engineered version of the Ampico reproducing system, with each mechanism redesigned to have as few moving parts as possible. Consequently, although the B operates according to very sophisticated pneumatic concepts, most of the mechanisms are very simple with few parts to get out of adjustment. The style B action was installed only in grand pianos.

Prior to rebuilding a B, obtain a copy of the 1929 service manual (Vestal Press #C-21X) and David Saul's *The Model B Ampico Reproducing Piano—An Illustrated Rebuilding Guide* (#C-2), a model B test roll and a note compensation test roll. (These test rolls are discussed later in this section, under Regulating the Ampico B). The

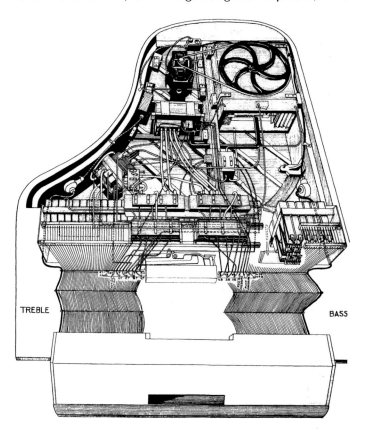

Illus. 7-13. The Ampico B mechanism.

1929 manual contains complete descriptions of how the model B works, and the Saul rebuilding guide contains large, clear photographs of most of the important pneumatic mechanisms in their disassembled state, plus important detailed rebuilding and regulating information which is not duplicated here. While the author of the present volume does not endorse some of the materials and techniques recommended in the Saul book, that book contains valuable information and photographs which are not duplicated here.

The Expression System

Upon first glance, the expression mechanisms look so different from those of the model A that it is hard to imagine any connection between the two, but in fact the two systems do have a lot in common, as a comparison of the A and B tracker scales illustrates.

0	(0B)	Amplifier trigger pneumatic
1	(1B)	Blank
2	(2B)	Bass intensity 2 on
3	(3B)	Sustaining pedal
4	(4B)	Bass intensity 4 on
5	(5B)	Shutoff
6	(6B)	Bass intensity 6 on
7	(7B)	Cancel bass intensities, holes 2, 4 & 6; cancel bass sub intensity, hole 00
8-90		Playing notes, low B through high A
91	(8T)	Rewind
92	(7T)	Cancel treble intensities, holes 93, 95 & 97; cancel treble sub intensity, hole 00
93	(6T)	Treble intensity 6 on
94	(5T)	Fast crescendo/decrescendo
95	(4T)	Treble intensity 4 on
96	(3T)	Hammer rail
97	(2T)	Treble intensity 2 on
98	(1T)	Amplifier and crescendo pneumatic
00		Bass and treble sub intensity valves on

The model B Ampico was compatible enough with the A that either A or B rolls could be played on either type of piano with passable results. There is sufficient difference between the two types, however, that each roll produces musically better results when played on a piano with its own system. The 1929 manual begins with a list of over 20 major differences in the design and construction of the two systems; the following paragraphs summarize some of the most important changes without repeating that entire list.

The model B stack is divided into bass and treble, with separate intensity regulators for each half. Each intensity regulator has a large rubber cloth pouch which controls the suction flow by covering and uncovering holes in a grid with a rolling movement, as shown in Fig. 3 of the 1929 manual. This pouch replaces the regulator valve of the Ampico A intensity mechanism. The lock and cancel intensity valves which are controlled by the intensity holes in the tracker bar are simpler than those in the A, and they vary the loudness of the stack by metering precisely regulated atmosphere to the bottom of the pouch, as shown in Fig. 4 of the manual. An additional intensity,

the sub intensity, is controlled by hole 00 at the extreme right side of the tracker bar; this hole locks bass and treble sub intensities on, while holes 7 and 92 cancel them individually.

Each half of the stack has a "spill unit" which admits a small amount of atmosphere to the stack as long as the piano plays softly, to permit the regulating pouches to do their job at very low playing levels. When intensity 6 is turned on, the spill unit for that half of the stack closes. This mechanism is shown in Fig. 18 of the manual.

The B action is equipped with a manual control called the "first intensity adjuster," (fig. 5 in the manual). Pulling the handle out admits slightly more atmosphere to the bottom of each regulator pouch, reducing the softer intensities without effecting the louder ones. Also built into the first intensity adjuster is the "sustaining pedal compensator." When the sustaining pedal comes on, the compensator admits slightly *more* atmosphere under the expression regulator pouches, reducing the stack suction level a little to compensate for the fact the the stack pneumatics do not have to lift the weight of the dampers when the pedal is on.

The model B has one pneumatic, connected to the pump spill valve spring, which serves as the entire crescendo system as well as a three-stage amplifier. Holes 98 and 94 cause the pneumatic to act as a crescendo pneumatic which effects the entire stack by gradually closing or opening the spill valve. Hole 0 controls a trigger pneumatic which, when used in various combinations with 98, cause the crescendo/amplifier pneumatic to latch in one of three positions, providing three ranges of suction as shown in fig. 10 of the manual. The first level, or "normal," causes the pump to produce a range of 5" to 20" of suction, depending on the setting of the intensity valves. The "1st Amplification" stage pulls the spill valve farther shut, causing the pump to produce from 7" to 28," and the "2nd Amplification" stage causes it to produce from 10"-40". When hole 0 opens, it automatically activates the fast crescendo valve, causing the crescendo/amplifier pneumatic to move to its latching position quickly. The manual clearly explains the sequencing of holes 0 and 98 necessary to latch the pneumatic in its various positions.

Although B pianos do not use hole 1 in the tracker bar because holes 98 and 94 control the crescendo for the entire stack, B rolls have a 1 hole punched simultaneously with every hole 98 in order for B rolls to operate both crescendo mechanisms in A pianos.

Subduing Switch

Not mentioned in the 1929 manual is the "normal/subdued" switch and mechanism which is part of many Ampico B's. When the switch is set at the "subdued" position, the mechanism reduces the higher playing levels without distorting the expression or reducing the softer levels. It accomplishes this by admitting a precise amount of atmosphere from chamber J directly into chamber C of illus. 4 in the 1929 manual, bypassing the 2, 4, and 6 intensity orifices. It also contains a bleed which feeds a small amount of suction into chamber C. At higher suction levels, the atmosphere from the subduing mechanism prevents the regulator pouch from opening as far as it normally does, reducing the louder playing levels. At lower levels, however, the bleed in the device applies just enough suction to the bottom of the regulator pouch to keep the minimum intensity from dropping below its normal level. The mechanism contains two sets of channels, bleeds and cutouts, one set for the treble expression regulator and the other for the bass. Two different subduing mechanisms are shown in figures A-1 and A-2 of David Saul's rebuilding guide. The first type is in a separate housing located under the soundboard; it has a lever which mechanically opens and closes the bypass channels and bleeds. The second type is built into the first intensity adjuster, and it contains spring loaded cutout pouches which open the bypass channels and bleeds when suction is applied.

The Stack

The Ampico B system has a single valve stack, with unique "ball bleeds" providing excellent repetition at low suction levels, without primary valves. Each valve chamber has two bleeds, as shown schematically in fig. 17 which is reproduced here from the manual. At rest, only the small #70 bleed is open. When the tracker bar hole opens, the pouch pushes the valve up very quickly because there is very little bleed. However, before the valve reaches its top seat, the ball reaches its own top seat, opening the #60 bleed. Now, with both bleeds open, when the tracker bar hole closes, the valve drops very quickly because of the extra large bleed. Just before it hits the lower seat, the ball closes the #60 bleed.

The ball bleed system works very well as long as the balls and the inside of their bleed containers are not sticky, corroded or worn. Unfortunately, ball bleeds which are sticky from an accumulation of cigarette smoke or atmospheric pollution, or worn from use, cause serious repetition problems. It is very important to clean the ball bleeds as described on p. 28 of Saul's book, rinsing them several times in acetone or lacquer thinner to eliminate all residue. It is equally important to use good quality neoprene tubing in all Ampico B restorations, as even the best quality vinyl tubing can give off sticky vapor which will accumulate inside the bleed chambers. If "Sil-Glyde" is used for sealing pouches as recommended in the Saul book, it might possibly give off a sticky vapor, eventually causing ball bleeds to stick. To be on the safe side, use only a *very thin* coating of liquid rubber cement to seal

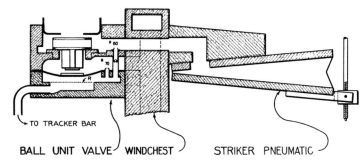

Illus. 7-14. Schematic drawing of Ampico B valve, showing cross section of ball bleed.

the pouches. If well-cleaned ball bleeds persist in sticking, the balls may have worn the containers. Obtain new replacements if possible.

As in the late style Ampico A, the B stack is equipped with a lost motion compensator mechanism which keeps the flanged fingers lightly touching the bottom of the keys when the soft pedal is on.

No matter how carefully a piano action and player stack are rebuilt, some notes require a little more suction than others to barely play at the softest possible volume level. In the Ampico A and other reproducing pianos, the minimum playing level must be regulated high enough to accomodate those notes, at the expense of others which then play a little louder than necessary. In more expensive Ampico B pianos—Mason & Hamlin, Chickering and Knabe—each stack pushrod (or "poppet wire") can be adjusted to regulate the maximum opening of its pneumatic at rest. When a pneumatic is all the way open, it has more power than when it is partially collapsed. If one note needs a little more power, its poppet wire can be regulated so the pneumatic is fully open at rest; if another note needs a little less power, its poppet wire can be regulated to hold the pneumatic partially closed at rest. With each pneumatic individually regulated, the sub intensity can be set lower than would otherwise be possible, producing a very uniform pianissimo. In pianos with this type of stack, the expression regulators and intensity valve blocks are mounted directly on the stack, as shown in fig. 15 of the manual.

Less expensive Ampico B pianos—Marshall & Wendell, J. & C. Fischer, Symphonique, etc.—were equipped with a flange finger stack more like that of the late style Ampico A grands, without the indidually adjustable poppet wires. In a piano with this type of stack, the expression regulators and intensity valve blocks are mounted separately, behind the stack.

Gaskets

The Ampico B is one player action in which it is accepted practice to use cork gaskets instead of leather, because all gasketed components are assembled with compression springs which hold the parts tight during seasonal humidity changes without having the gaskets shellacked to the mating surfaces. In fact, some gaskets are covered with thin rubber cloth to prevent the cork from sticking to the mating wood, permitting easy disassembly without the total destruction of gaskets which usually occurs in the model A. If you must use cork for its authentic look, be sure to obtain material which is airtight. Note, however, that the finest professional restorers use leather.

The Drawer

Like the stack and expression mechanisms, the model B drawer has unusual features, including an electric roll drive motor, the capacity to play large "jumbo" rolls which play as long as 30 minutes, a brake which completely stops the takeup spool periodically to tighten the paper during rewind, and a mechanism which slows the roll before it finishes rewinding to preserve the end tab and leader. The operation of the drawer is explained in detail in the 1929 manual, and the repair and adjustment of the various components are covered on pp. 9-23 of Saul's rebuilding guide. Excessive sparking of the governor contacts—a common problem—is an indication that the governor resistor is open; check the resistor and replace it if necessary.

Regulating the Ampico B

The model B test roll contains the usual tests for regulating the expression devices and for checking whether or not the mechanisms are working properly. The "Note Compensation" test roll simply plays sequences of notes at the minimum intensity level, to aid in adjusting the individual pneumatic poppet wires in stacks so equipped. Obtain a copy of each roll, preferably reproduced from the original master rolls. A variety of different test rolls have been marketed for the Ampico B in modern times, including at least one which combines tests for both A and B models, but a good copy of the original B test roll without the A tests mixed in is easier to use. The instructions are reproduced here from the original B test roll because the 1929 service manual does not include them and because many recut test rolls exist without any instructions. The following introductory paragraph is by Dave Saul:

"All text is reproduced here exactly as it appears on the original test roll, including page numbers, etc. The marks for adjusting pallet number 1 during rewind may not be present on recut versions of this test roll. On the original, they are black, filled-in rectangles about ½" square, making them easy to observe when the roll is in motion during rewind. The length of the first and second note perforations for each note in the MINIMUM PERFORATION TEST

differ by only one increment of paper advance 1/30" or about .033" in this case. The same is true for the intervals between perforations in the MINIMUM BRIDGE TEST. Because of this, only a roll cut from a master, using the original punch size and paper advance, will produce meaningful test results. These tests often mislead users into believing that valves are at fault when the problem is really in a worn out or poorly regulated piano action. When Ampico pianos were new, this was undoubtedly less of a problem, but things have changed quite a bit since then. As all qualified restorers know, the one-sentence instruction at the beginning of the test roll regarding piano action regulation has to be taken very seriously if good results are to be obtained." (D.S.)

Tempo 85

70403
TEST ROLL
For use with
SERVICE MANUAL
1929

Before testing the Ampico Mechanism make sure that the piano action is in proper regulation

All page notations refer to Ampico Service Manual 1929 All tests should be made at Tempo 85

EXPRESSION CODE

BASS	TREBLE
0 Amplifier	0 "Sub"
1 Blank	1 Slow Crescendo
2 No. 2 Intensity valve	2 No. 2 Intensity valve
3 Loud Pedal	3 Soft Pedal
4 No 4 Intensity valve	4 No 4 Intensity valve
5 Shut Off	5 Fast Crescendo
6 No 6 Intensity valve	6 No. 6 Intensity valve
7 Cancel valve	7 Cancel valve
	8 Reroll

First Intensity adjuster is set to middle position.

STOP

TEMPO TEST—Tempo 85

Paper should travel from first to last chord (8 1/2 ft.) in one minute For tempo adjustment see Page 43

0 feet
1 foot
2 feet
3 feet
4 feet
5 feet
6 feet
7 feet

(large mark here on roll)

If roll slows down during rewind with repeat switch on between this mark and the one 3 feet further on, do not change adjustment of pallet No 1.

8 feet
8½ feet

STOP

TRACKER TEST

All perforations should be over the center of the tracker bar holes when the tracker pneumatics are in the central position. The roll should shift evenly to both sides when the tracker ears are operated by hand. For tracker adjustment see Page 56.

(large mark here on roll)

If adjustment of reroll slow-down is necessary, have roll standing still (tempo at zero) at this point Adjust Pallet No 1 so that the reroll speed pneumatic just opens. For explanation of Pallet No. 1, see Pages 52 and 53

STOP

SLOW CRESCENDO TEST

The crescendo pneumatic should start to collapse when the first chord is struck, be fully collapsed at the second chord and fully open as the third chord is struck Explanation of the Slow Crescendo Mechanism is found on Page 23

(large mark here on roll)

If roll slows down during rewind with repeat switch on between this mark and the one 3 feet further back, do not change adjustment of Pallet No 1

STOP

FAST CRESCENDO TEST

The crescendo pneumatic should start to collapse when the first chord is struck, be fully collapsed at the second chord and fully open at the third chord. Explanation of the Fast Crescendo Mechanism is found on Page 23

STOP

AMPLIFIER AND PUMP PRESSURE TEST

This test is to show that the Amplifier locks and cancels to various positions as indicated by the perforations. Connect gauge to pump test tube Check the pump pressure and amplified pressures at the points indicated Make each test at 85 tempo For explanation of the Amplifier Mechanism see page 19

NORMAL

Pump pressure should read between 15" and 21".

STOP

FIRST AMPLIFICATION TEST

Gauge should read between 21" and 29".

STOP

SECOND AMPLIFICATION TEST

Gauge should read between 30" and 40"

STOP

CANCEL FROM SECOND TO FIRST AMPLIFICATION

Gauge should read between 21" and 29".

STOP

CANCEL FROM FIRST AMPLIFICATION TO NORMAL

Gauge should read between 15" and 21".

STOP

NORMAL TO SECOND AMPLIFICATION

Gauge should read between 30" and 40"

STOP

CANCEL FROM SECOND AMPLIFICATION TO NORMAL

Gauge should read between 15" and 21"

STOP

INTENSITY VALVE TEST

The "Sub" valve and Intensity valves should operate as indicated by the expression perforations.

First Intensity
Sub Intensity

First Intensity
Second Intensity
Third Intensity
Fourth Intensity

STOP

INTENSITY VALVE LOCK & CANCEL TEST

The "Sub" valve and Intensity valves should lock and cancel as indicated by the expression perforations. Connect gauge to treble and bass test tube The interval between the steps should increase gradually except between the sixth and seventh steps. For explanation of the intensity valve operation see Page 12.

Sub Intensity
First Intensity
Second Intensity
Third Intensity
Fourth Intensity
D 4 Intensity
Fifth Intensity
Sixth Intensity
Seventh Intensity

STOP

MINIMUM PERFORATION TEST

Set the First Intensity Adjuster to a point where generally the first notes play softly and the second notes play distinctly If any particular second note does not speak distinctly inspect the Ball bleed unit for bleed leakage etc. For explanation of the First Intensity adjuster see Page 12 For explanation of the ball bleed unit see Page 34.

STOP

MINIMUM BRIDGE TEST

With this same setting of the First Intensity Adjuster, the third note hole should produce a tone practically as loud as the first The second note hole should produce a tone loud enough to be distinctly heard. If either of these conditions are violated, inspect the Ball Bleed unit for stopped-up bleeds, etc.

STOP

PEDAL PRESSURE TEST

Connect gauge to pedal pressure test tube Gauge should read between 15" and 19"

STOP

SOFT PEDAL TEST

The hammer rail should start to raise at the first chord, be fully raised at the second chord and back to rest at the third chord.

STOP

SOFT PEDAL LIFT TEST

The second chord struck at the No 3 Intensity with the hammer rail raised should sound with the same loudness as the first chord struck at the No. 1 intensity with the hammer rail at rest. For explanation of the Soft Pedal see Page 29.

STOP

LOUD PEDAL TEST

The chord struck with the dampers raised should not sing through the second pedal perforation. For explanation of Loud Pedal operation see Page 27.

STOP

LOUD PEDAL COMPENSATION TEST

The second chord struck with the dampers raised should sound about the same loudness as the first chord struck with the dampers at rest. The compensating screws are correctly set at the factory. Do not readjust these screws. Look elsewhere for difficulty. For explanation of Loud Pedal Compensation adjustment see Page 28.

STOP

Reroll and Repeat Test.

Reroll should slow down at point between indications on treble side of music roll. For explanation of Reroll operation see Page 49 For explanation of Repeat operation see Page 53

(end of roll)

Due to the relatively simple mechanical design of the Ampico B, there are fewer adjustments than in the model A and other reproducing pianos, as seen by comparing the instructions reproduced above with those in the 1923 A manual. The pump spill valve settings at the normal and two amplification levels are "built in" and are dependent upon the characteristics of the spill valve spring. In the unlikely event that this spring is damaged or missing, borrow an original one for comparison in selecting or making a replacement. If two identical extension springs are hooked together end to end, they will stretch equally as more and more pull is applied; use this test to find a suitable replacement. The correct expression curve of the Ampico B is dependent upon the spill valve spring, so don't settle for anything less than a perfect duplicate.

The note compensation test roll is only to be used after everything else in the piano and player action is regulated as perfectly as possible. As stated in the 1929 manual, *Never adjust the openings of the striker pneumatics until AFTER the piano has been tuned, the piano action regulated and the hammers voiced.*

THE DUO-ART

The Duo-Art was manufactured by the Aeolian Piano Co. and was marketed in their own Weber, Steck, Stroud, Wheelock, and Aeolian pianos as well as in Steinways. The cabinet and keyboard of a Duo-Art grand is extended, with about 6" of extra length between the fallboard and front edge of the pinblock, to accomodate the spoolbox, wind motor and associated parts. Special Steinway pianos with room for Duo-Art player actions were purchased wholesale from Steinway by the Aeolian Co. and were retailed only by Aeolian dealers; they did not even appear in Steinway sales literature.

Duo-Arts were made in upright and grand versions; due to the location of the roll mechanism and other components, most Duo-Art grands have a system of levers mounted in the keyslip for rewind, tempo, motor on/off, and manual control of expression. Of all the major electric reproducing pianos, the Duo-Art is the only one in which the levers permit precise manual control of expression for those who wish to put their own expression into the music.

Three basic varieties of Duo-Art grands exist: early, late

and very late. Early grands have a "temponamic" knob for both tempo and manual control of the accompaniment level, and have the body of the stack mounted between the pushrods and the *back* of the piano. Late grands have separate controls for tempo and accompaniment level, with the body of the stack between the pushrods and *front* of the piano. Early and late grands have most of the tracker bar tubing routed between the keys, through junction blocks which are attached to the bottom of the key frame. Very late grands have all of the tracker bar tubing routed around the ends of the piano action and have all of the control levers in the spoolbox. Despite these differences, the expression mechanisms are basically the same in all Duo-Art pianos, so all Duo-Art rolls are compatible with all pianos.

Illus. 7-15. The Duo-Art spoolbox, wind motor and associated parts are located between the keys and the pinblock, thus requiring the keys to be of extra length compared to regular grand piano keys.

A relatively small number of foot pumped Duo-Art pianos were made, and a few had both foot and electric pumps. Some of these pianos have complete expression systems, while others have only one accordion pneumatic and suction regulator. If you restore one of these, make careful notes of the original tubing scheme as you disassemble the player action.

Before restoring a Duo-Art, obtain the following materials: a copy of the original test roll with instructions, the 1925 service manual (#C-30X), 1927 service manual (#C-3), How to Rebuild the Duo-Art by Mike Kitner (#T-5), Preliminary Instruction Pamphlet (#C-34X), upright tubing print (#C-22X, useful for early uprights only), and 1927 Export Supplement to Service Manual (for combination foot-pumped/electric models, #C-35X). Refer also to the old Aeolian section in Ch. 6.

The "Duo-Art" name is used by the Aeolian Co. on certain models of modern player pianos; these are *not* reproducing pianos, and the information presented here does not apply to them.

Illus. 7-16. Late (left) and early (right) Duo-Art grand stacks. *Photo by Robert Taylor.*

Illus. 7-17. Left: pouch board for Duo-Art stack. Right: closeup of pouch buttons in late style grand stack showing divider which permits the bass and treble halves of the stack to operate at two different suction levels. *Photo by Robert Taylor.*

How the Duo-Art Expression System Works

Unlike the Ampico and Welte, the Duo-Art does not have identical expression regulators for the bass and treble. It does have a divided stack and two identical-looking regulators, but one feeds suction to the entire stack all the time for the "accompaniment" playing level, and the other feeds additional "theme" suction to the

bass, treble, or both, as controlled by holes 3 (bass theme) and 92 (treble theme). The expression box contains flap valves which permit accompaniment suction to enter both halves of the stack, while preventing higher theme suction in one half of the stack from feeding back into the other half. Tracker bar holes 4-7 control the loudness of the accompaniment regulator, while holes 88-91, 3 and 92 control the theme regulator.

1		Rewind
2		Sustaining pedal
3		Bass theme
4		Accompaniment intensity 1
5		Accompaniment intensity 2
6		Accompaniment intensity 4
7		Accompaniment intensity 8
8-87		Playing notes, low C# through high G#
88	(7T)	Theme intensity 8
89	(6T)	Theme intensity 4
90	(5T)	Theme intensity 2
91	(4T)	Theme intensity 1
92	(3T)	Treble theme
93	(2T)	Shutoff/play
94	(1T)	Hammer rail

As shown in illus. 7-18, each suction regulator—accompaniment and theme—has a four-stage "accordion pneumatic," with each stage able to collapse twice as far as the previous one: $\frac{1}{16}$", $\frac{1}{8}$", $\frac{1}{4}$" and $\frac{1}{2}$"; all possible combinations of the four stages produce fifteen different suction levels in the regulator, plus the minimum intensity level which occurs when all four stages are at rest, for a total of sixteen basic suction levels. These are identified as 0 and 1-15.

The accompaniment accordion, controlled by holes 4-7, regulates the position of the knife valve in the accompaniment regulator, which feeds suction into the entire stack at all times.

When theme intensities 88-91 are punched, the theme accordion pneumatic adjusts the position of the knife valve in the theme regulator, but this has no significant effect on the stack until theme holes 3 or 92 are punched, opening large pouch valves inside the expression box which admit theme suction into the bass and treble halves of the stack, respectively. (When theme suction is desired in both halves of the stack, holes 3 and 92 are opened simultaneously). Because the theme holes in original rolls are punched in the form of two tiny side-by-side elongated perforations, they are known as "snake bites."

While it might seem at first glance that only sixteen playing levels can be produced by the Duo-Art expression box, the system is actually far more sophisticated than it appears. For one thing, it takes a different setting of the accordion pneumatic to play one note at a given loudness than it does to play several notes simultaneously at the same loudness, as demonstrated by the test roll. For another, the accompaniment and theme regulators interact with each other, so there are many subtle "in between" levels produced by combinations of accompaniment and theme accordion settings. Other very subtle musical effects are produced when snakebites are punched without any theme intensities (momentarily coupling the theme regulator pneumatic to the stack), and when theme intensities are punched without any snakebites (adding a little load to the pump, or pulling the spill valve a little further shut), both of which occur regularly in classical music rolls.

Duo-Art On/Off Switch

Holes 4-7 and 88-92 each have two holes in the tracker bar. The upper holes are used by Duo-Art rolls for the eight intensity valves which operate the accordion pneu-matics, as designated in the above tracker scale; the lower holes are used by 88-note rolls for the four lowest and four highest playing notes. The tracker bar tubes for these holes are connected to cutout pouch blocks which are controlled by the Duo-Art on/off switch. With the switch in the on position, the tubes for the upper holes are connected, and the tubes for the lower holes are blocked; in the off position, the reverse is true. Earlier pianos with 88-note stacks have two sets of eight cutout pouches; later pianos with 80-note stacks do not play the four lowest and highest notes automatically, so they have only one set of eight cutout pouches, with the lower row of eight tracker bar holes left unconnected.

The Duo-Art on/off switch has a third setting, between

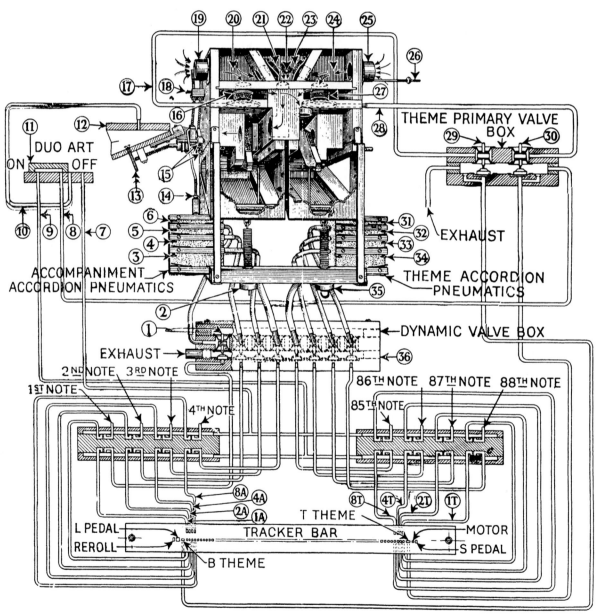

Illus. 7-18. Schematic representation of the Duo-Art expression system, showing the upright style expression regulator with its two four-stage ac-cordion pneumatics.

174

on and off, as indicated by the little arrow on the name plate. In this position, the piano responds to the bass and treble snakebite perforations in "Themodist" music rolls when the player pianist manipulates the accompaniment and theme loudness controls. (In earlier pianos, tempo and accompaniment loudness are both controlled by the "Temponamic" knob; in later pianos, accompaniment loudness is controlled by its own lever similar to the theme lever.)

Crash Valve

The expression box in late style Steinway and other large Duo-Art grands incorporates a "crash valve" which bypasses the expression regulators, feeding full pump suction to the stack whenever all four theme intensity holes are punched simultaneously. The shaft which connects the theme accordion to its knife valve has a lever which opens the crash valve pallet only when intensity 15 is reached, causing a dramatic difference between the already loud level 14 and maximimum level 15.

Grand Modulator

The grand modulator contains a regulator pneumatic and knife valve, and a bypass pouch. When the dynamic lever on the key slip is set at "soft," the bypass closes, and the pneumatic regulates the pump suction, diminishing the loudness of higher intensities without effecting soft playing; when the lever is set at "normal" or "dance," the bypass opens and the modulator has no effect. The modulator also contains the action cutoff for rewind.

Soft Pedal Control

Tracker bar hole 95 controls the hammer rail lift in upright *and* grand Duo-Art pianos. In addition to the hammer rail lift pneumatic, some grands have a huge pneumatic which shifts the piano action sideways, duplicating the action of the una corda pedal. It might appear that since a concert piano does not have a hammer rail lift, connecting the action shift pneumatic to hole 95 would more accurately reproduce the playing of the artist. The truth of the matter, however, is that music roll editors considered hole 95 to be part of the expression system and used it far more than most pianists *ever* used the una corda pedal. Concert pianists use this pedal mainly for altering the *tone quality*, not the loudness, of the music, and a careful observer will note that most live pianists use it only 1/100th the amount that it is used by Duo-Art music rolls. When the action shift pneumatic is connected to hole 95, the striking points of the piano hammers become worn completely flat, ruining their voicing prematurely.

Connect the hammer rail lift pneumatic to hole 95, as shown in the 1925 grand tubing diagram, and connect the action shift pneumatic—if present—to operate when the dynamic lever is set at the soft position.

Restoring the Duo-Art

The restoration of the old Aeolian player action is covered in Ch. 6, and the Duo-Art reproducing action is covered comprehensively in the rebuilding guide by Mike Kitner. The most difficult part of restoring a Duo-Art is breaking the expression box apart, as described on pp. 4 and 5 of the Kitner guide.

The basic tubing scheme of grand Duo-Arts is shown in the 1925 grand tubing print. Before disassembling a grand piano, note any minor variations in the control tubing attached to the key frame junction blocks.

Illus. 7-19. An unrestored Duo-Art grand expression box, with the accordion pneumatics decomposed into a heap. Disassembly will produce a large number of small parts; sketch or photograph them as necessary to facilitate correct reassembly. *Photo by Robert Taylor.*

Illus. 7-20. A grand expression box carefully cut open, with new theme pouches and crash valve pouch installed. For ease of future servicing, glue a pouch leather gasket to the perimeter and partitions of the section to the left in the photo, prior to reassembly. *Photo by Robert Taylor.*

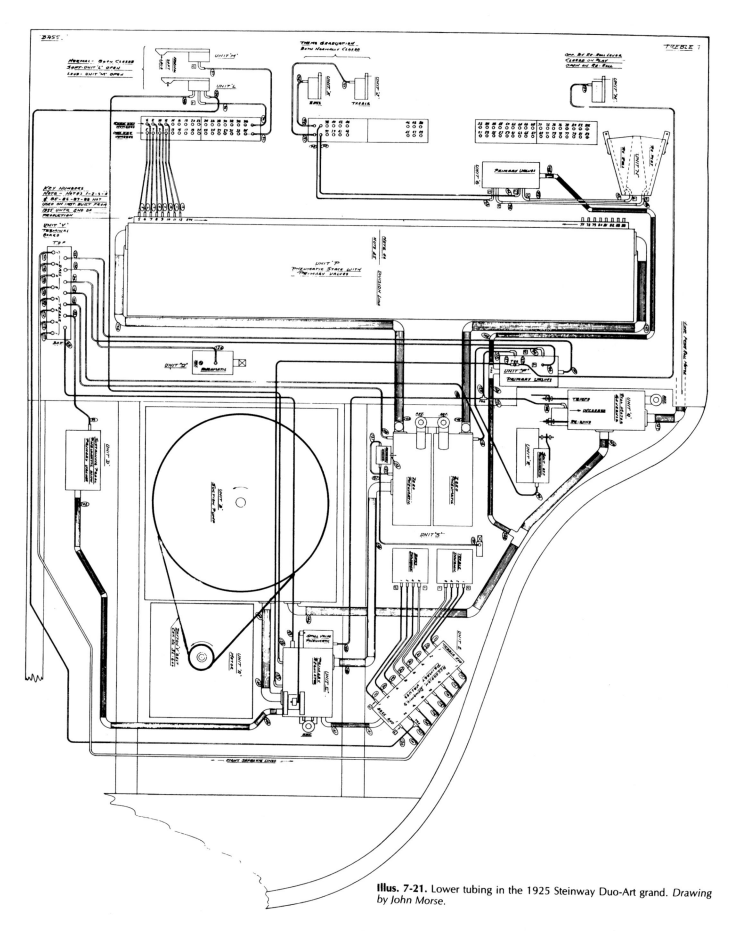

Illus. 7-21. Lower tubing in the 1925 Steinway Duo-Art grand. *Drawing by John Morse.*

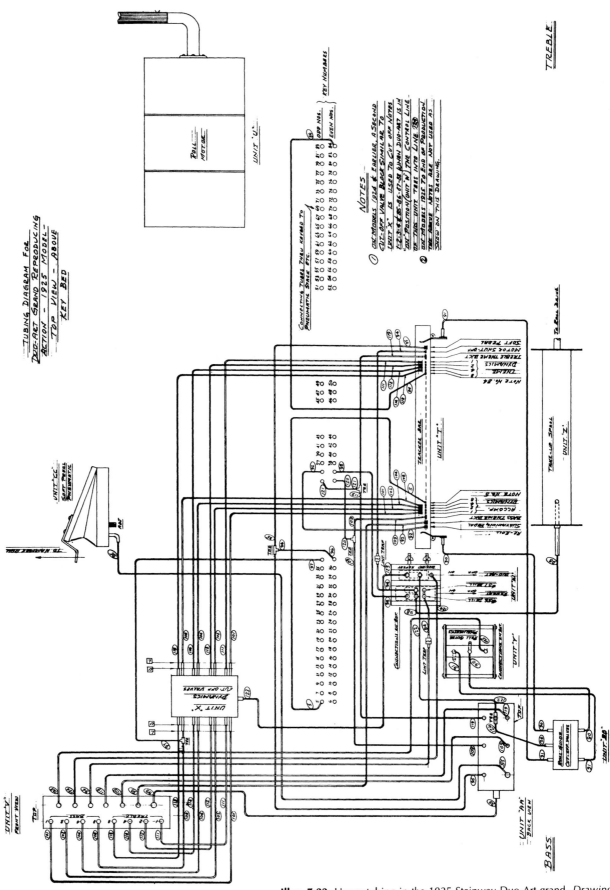

Illus. 7-22. Upper tubing in the 1925 Steinway Duo-Art grand. *Drawing by John Morse.*

177

Illus. 7-23. Top view, top half of expression box. Flap valves 21 and 23, illus. 7-18, are in the center compartment toward the bottom of the picture. *Photo by Robert Taylor.*

Illus. 7-24. Expression boxes, assembled and disassembled, showing just a few of the many parts. *Photo by Robert Taylor.*

Illus. 7-25. The two sections of the expression box reassembled with a thin gasket between. For insurance against leakage, glue a ½″ wide thin rubber pneumatic cloth seal around the gasket. *Photo by Robert Taylor.*

The tubing of pre-1918 upright pianos is shown in the upright tubing print C-22X.

Later uprights have one junction block with sixteen connections on the left side of the spoolbox shelf (#11, illus. lower right illus. 6-1), and another smaller one with four connections on the right side (#4, same illustration). Every 1920's Stroud upright examined by the author conforms to the following scheme, but if you rebuild a piano in which the original tubing is still intact, sketch it just in case it differs. (Incidentally, the Pierce Piano Atlas numbers for upright Stroud and other Duo-Arts are wrong. If you encounter a date rubber stamped on the piano or player action, make note of it as this is your only guide to the age of the piano).

Left Junction Block

Front row, left to right:

1 From tracker bar 91 to pouch for theme intensity valve 1
2 From t.b 90 to pouch for theme intensity valve 2
3 From t b. 89 to pouch for theme intensity valve 4
4 From t b 88 to pouch for theme intensity valve 8
5 From t b. 7 to pouch for accomp. intensity valve 8; teed to "dance" pallet under keybed
6 From t b 6 to pouch for accomp. intensity valve 4
7 From t b. 5 to pouch for accomp intensity valve 2; teed to pallet on hammer rail pneumatic
8 From t b. 4 to pouch for accomp intensity valve 1; teed to pallet on hammer rail pneumatic

Back row, left to right:

1 From tee in t b. tube 92 to treble theme lever pallet under keybed
2 From tee in t.b. tube 3 to bass theme lever pallet under keybed
3 From 2nd nipple back from front of Duo-Art on/off switch, to pneumatic which brings up accompaniment level for 88 note rolls
4 From treble theme primary valve to treble theme pouch in expression box
5 From bass theme primary valve to bass theme pouch in expression box
6 From t b. 94 to input of hammer rail pneumatic valve; teed to soft lever pallet valve under keybed
7 From t b. 2 to input of sustaining pneumatic valve
8 Suction supply from expression box to theme primary valve box

Right Junction Block

Left to Right:

1 From tracker bar 1 to input of rewind valve
2 From left rear hole of repeat switch to input of play (repeat) valve
3 From right front hole of repeat switch to input of shutoff valve, teed to tracker bar 93 through tee with built-in constrictions
4 Suction supply for automatic tracking pneumatic, plugged off in some pianos

Repeat Switch

Left front: to hole in takeup spool, teed to right rear
Left rear: to r.h. junction block tube 2
Right front: through tee with built-in constrictions, to r h. junction block tube 3 and tracker bar 93
Right rear: to hole in takeup spool, teed to left front

Illus. 7-26. End view of late style stack. The end plate screws are several different lengths. *Keep them in order! Photo by Robert Taylor.*

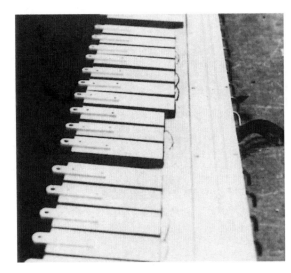

Illus. 7-27. Steinway and Weber grand stacks typically have pneumatics of three different lengths for bass, tenor, and treble. *Photo by Robert Taylor.*

The Stack

Grand Duo-Art stacks have metal (early) or wood (late) end plates screwed to the decks and stop rails with the screws of several different lengths. Be sure to check for stripped screws so you can repair the wood while the stack is apart.

Some stacks have two sizes of bleeds to compensate for pouches with different porosity. When you replace the pouch leather and seal it with rubber cement, open the holes of the smaller bleeds to the same size as the larger ones with an appropriate diameter piece of music wire sharpened to a point.

See p. 72 for information on stack pneumatic hinge springs.

Illus. 7-28. Duo-Art pneumatic hinge springs have a habit of slipping out of the pneumatics. Replace them with new identical phosphor bronze springs (usually #22 Brown & Sharpe wire gauge). Dip the ends in shellac just prior to installation to help prevent this problem. *Photo by Robert Taylor.*

Cross Valves

Earlier Duo-Art pianos have stamped metal valve plates with cross shaped cutouts, as shown in the Aeolian section of Ch. 6. These have a notorious reputation for leaking, but they work as well as any other valve seats providing that they and the stem guides are kept in order and in the correct orientation during restoration. The cross shaped holes and four perimeter screw holes were punched in two separate operations, so if the plates are turned or mixed up during reassembly, the top and bottom holes and stem guides will no longer be aligned, preventing the valves from seating. Releather the valves with the same type of split suede leather as Duo-Art used originally; this has proven to be the best material for valve facings, and it is the choice of professional rebuilders. Never use sponge neoprene facings on Duo-Art valves.

If cross valve seats are corroded badly, attempt to polish them without bending the surfaces on which the valves seat. Once they are bent, you will have to locate replacement valve seats, which are available only inter-

mittently from specialty suppliers. To polish them, lay a wooden pouch button from the bottom of one of the valve stems upside down in the valve plate, and press on this as you lap the plate on 600 sandpaper on thick glass. By pressing on the wood button, you will not risk springing the corners of the cross shaped hole.

The Pump

Most original Duo-Art crankshaft support bearings are somewhat gritty, with the surfaces of the balls pitted, so it is better to replace them than to attempt to clean them. The procedure is the same as that used for replacing Ampico pump bearings as described on pp. 164-165. In Duo-Art pumps which turn counterclockwise, the pulley and the nut on the inside end of the crankshaft usually have left hand threads.

Most Duo-Art rotary pumps contain cast iron connecting rods with cone bearings, as shown in illus. 7-29. After

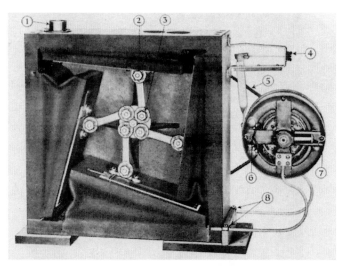

Illus. 7-29. A Duo-Art rotary pump with cone bearings.

Illus. 7-30. The Duo-Art "steamboat pump," found in early Steinway uprights and in remote cabinets which were usually located in the basement under early grand pianos.

Illus. 7-31. The smaller Duo-Art tugboat pump, which was used in earlier Stroud and other upright Duo-Arts. A similar but smaller version was used in early combination electric/foot pumped player pianos.

a lot of use, the balls wear indentations into the conical faces of the connecting posts and nuts. If the indentations are equal all the way around, the bearings will work without knocking, but if there is uneven wear, it will be impossible to adjust the cone nuts to permit free motion of the connecting rods without knocking. Overtightening worn out cone bearings will only accelerate the wear, put excessive strain on the electric motor, and sometimes cause the balls to break. If necessary, have a good machinist turn down the nuts and posts just enough to remove the wear. If too much metal is removed from the faces of the cones, it will be impossible to tighten the nuts, and the posts will have to be replaced.

After cleaning the bearings and obtaining new balls, apply a little grease to each ball and the race of the bearing to hold the balls in place during assembly. Tighten the cone nut to eliminate all play in the connecting arm without binding, and add the washer and lock nut. Hold the cone nut with a thin wrench while you tighten the lock nut, and recheck the connecting arm for knocking or binding. If the threads on any of the posts are damaged to the point that the lock nuts can not be tightened, have a machinist make new posts.

Restoration of the large six-bellows Duo-Art steamboat pump is described in detail in Mike Kitner's rebuilding guide. A smaller four-lung version of this pump was used in early Aeolian Co. upright pianos (Steinway uprights usually had the steamboat pump), also mounted with the crankshaft parallel to the back of the piano, but with a large enough pulley that no countershaft was necessary.

The motor pulley in most Duo-Art pianos is 2″ in diameter. Use a ³⁄₈″ V belt, making sure that it doesn't run in the bottom of the pulley. If so, obtain a new pulley of the correct diameter which fits the width of the new belt, and save the original pulley.

Regulating the Duo-Art

All Duo-Arts are regulated with the same basic test roll, and since basic regulating procedures are covered thoroughly in the Kitner work as well as the "Preliminary Instruction Pamphlet" and the 1925 and 1927 manuals, complete instructions are not repeated here.

Note that the theme and accompaniment springs in some expression boxes are different. If you suspect that they are mixed up, hook them together end to end and pull on them to see which one is stronger. The stronger one goes on the theme regulator.

When regulating the minimum intensity of each regulator, set the theme regulator one degree louder than the accompaniment regulator. The following description from

p. 11 of the 1925 manual explains what "one degree" is: "After setting the accompaniment properly,...make the theme adjustment. The setting of the theme is dependent upon the setting of the accompaniment as, no matter where the latter is set, the theme must be one degree louder. Naturally, the conception of one degree will vary with the individual, but a uniformly safe rule to follow is to have the theme pneumatic collapse one eighth of an inch more than the acccompaniment pneumatic."

Earlier printings of this book recommend that the expression in a Duo-Art piano can be "polished" by regulating the hex head screws that control the amount of travel of the "1," "2," and "4" stages of each accordion pneumatic to compensate for the characteristics of an individual piano. As pointed out by David Saul in an article in the May/June 1993 AMICA Bulletin (Volume 30, Number 1), this is not a desirable thing to do, as altering one stage will throw all stages into the wrong relationship with each other, making the expression response curve wrong. Always regulate the travel of the accordion pneumatics to exactly $1/16$", $1/8$", $1/4$" and $1/2$" as recommended in all original factory service literature.

If you must change something, try adjusting the tension of the regulator springs by a small amount, and then reset the zero levels. Always make sure that if one spring is stronger than the other, the stronger one is on the "theme" regulator. If the springs have been replated, there is a chance that they might have been damaged by hydrogen embrittlement, necessitating their replacement. If this is the case, try to find an identical-model piano, and copy the springs from its expression mechanism.

As in any reproducing piano, the test roll only provides a starting point for the minimum intensity settings. For precise regulation of each individual note, as described on p. 169 in the Ampico B section, regulate the maximum open position of each pneumatic by adjusting the leather nuts and action cloth washers on the pushrods. After you have regulated the player action as carefully as possible to the test roll, perform the final regulating by playing a large number of original music rolls. If necessary, it is better to set the minimum intensity so the piano drops out one or two notes in twenty rolls than to boost it for the sake of those one or two notes—unless you are making a recording of the piano, of course.

WELTE-MIGNON

The Welte company of Germany produced orchestrions and organs ranging in size from large to immense, and by comparison, their reproducing pianos were small, hence the name "Welte-Mignon." Four main varieties of Welte-Mignon reproducing pianos were produced, two in Germany and two in the U.S. The "original Welte," also known as the "red Welte," was the first reproducing piano, introduced in 1904 in Germany, and made in grand and upright pianos as well as keyboardless uprights and vorsetzers. Red Welte rolls are $12\frac{7}{8}$" wide and have a hole spacing of about 8 holes per inch. The second version was the "original Welte" built by the Welte-Mignon Corp. of New York City beginning in 1906, using standardized $11\frac{1}{4}$" wide rolls with holes spaced 9 per inch, made in grand and upright pianos and vorsetzers. The third major version was and is by far the most common in the U.S. —the Auto Deluxe Welte Mignon, better known as the Welte "Licensee," manufactured by Kohler Industries of New York City, using rolls $11\frac{1}{4}$" wide with holes spaced 9 per inch. The last version was the German "green Welte." The first three versions all use the same basic tracker scale, but the green Welte scale is entirely different. Of the four systems, the grand piano version of the Auto Deluxe Welte "Licensee" is the only one with a drawer; the others have the spoolbox and associated parts above the keyboard like a Duo-Art.

The German-made Original Welte-Mignon ("Red Welte")

Original "red Welte" instruments have a slow moving pump resembling a small version of a Welte orchestrion pump. Several feeder bellows are mounted in a row, with metal rods and bell cranks connecting them to the crankshaft. The pump is turned by a direct current motor, and a pair of lock and cancel holes in the tracker bar turn a motor resistor on and off for louder and softer playing. Holes 1 through 8 of the tracker scale are the same as those in the "Licensee" scale below, 9 and 10 operate the motor resistor, and 11 through 100 are the same as 9 through 98 of the "Licensee" scale.

The stack valves in original German Welte instruments are wooden buttons mounted on wire stems which are threaded into discs glued to the pouches. It is extremely important to handle these valves carefully; since they are rigidly attached to the stems, any crooked sanding, poor centering of the stem holes in the new pouches, or other careless work will result in extremely leaky valves.

If you restore a Welte or other German instrument with an open container of mercury, eliminate the mercury; it is extremely toxic, and its vapors can accumulate to a toxic level in a small enclosed space. For authentic restoration, leave the body of the mercury switch in place, but wire around it to an appropriately rated concealed miscroswitch. If mercury has spilled all over the inside of the instrument, dust the mercury particles with zinc oxide, which will amalgamate with the mercury, reducing the danger to your health as you collect it; then vacuum the instrument well with a high power vacuum cleaner, venting the exhaust outside, and discard the filter after you are done. Spilled mercury may also be collected safely with an eye dropper.

The American-made Original Welte

A unique feature of this instrument was its turbine suction box in place of the usual motor-driven bellows pump. The expression mechanisms were similar in design to those of the original German instrument, as shown in illus. 7-32. The tracker scale, test roll and regulating procedures are similar to those for the Welte-Mignon "Licensee."

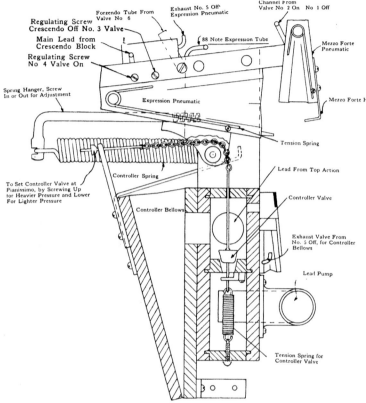

Illus. 7-32. The American made original Welte expression mechanism.

The Welte-Mignon "Licensee"

The Auto Deluxe Welte-Mignon "Licensee" action was manufactured by the Auto Pneumatic Action Co., which also made Autopiano player actions, and was related to the Standard Pneumatic Action Co. It was marketed in over 100 brands of pianos in America, and the typical installation has earmarks of something which was added to a piano rather than the mass-produced look of a typical Ampico or Duo-Art action.

While it is unusual to find two identical Welte-Mignon Licensee pianos, the player actions generally follow the design shown in the original service manual (Vestal Press #C-4) and tubing chart (C-8). Obtain both of these plus a test roll with instructions prior to restoring a Welte Licensee. The service manual currently in print as this is written does not have the illustrations which appeared in some versions, but all necessary illustrations are included in the tubing chart.

Like the Ampico A, the Welte Licensee has a pair of identical expression mechanisms, one for treble and one for bass, as shown in illus. 7-33. The regulator valve in each "governor pneumatic" is controlled by the "expression pneumatic;" the position of the expression pneumatic is controlled by the crescendo valve, forzando on and off valves and mezzo-forte pneumatic from perforations in the music roll.

1 Bass mezzoforte off	90 Blank (shutoff in some
2 Bass mezzoforte on	instruments)
3 Bass crescendo off	91 Sustaining pedal on
4 Bass crescendo on	92 Sustaining pedal off
5 Bass forzando off	93 Treble forzando on
6 Bass forzando on	94 Treble forzando off
7 Hammer rail down	95 Treble crescendo on
8 Hammer rail up	96 Treble crescendo off
9-88 Playing notes, low C	97 Treble mezzoforte on
through high G	98 Treble mezzoforte off
89 Rewind	

In most Welte Licensees, play (repeat) and shutoff are controlled by a sensing finger which falls into a slot in the takeup spool, operating a pallet valve. In a few instruments, the tracker bar has an additional hole between 1 and 2 for this function.

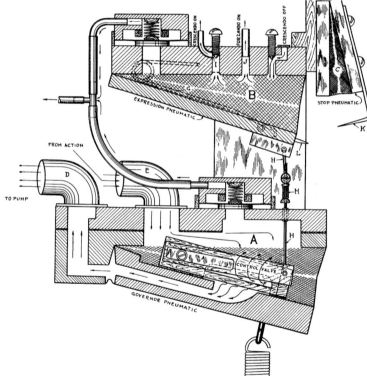

Illus. 7-33. Welte Licensee expression mechanism.

The farther the expression pneumatic closes, the louder its half of the stack plays. The crescendo valve is a lock and cancel valve. When on, it admits a small amount of suction to the expression pneumatic, slowly pulling the pneumatic closed, producing a crescendo in the music; when off, a small amount of atmosphere is admitted to the pneumatic, producing a decrescendo. The mezzo-forte or mf pneumatic, labelled "stop pneumatic" in the diagram, is also controlled by a lock and cancel valve. When on, its brass hook K provides a reference point for the wandering expression pneumatic at a medium volume level. The mf pneumatic is very important, as it provides the only reference point for the expression system other than minimum (fully open) and maximum (fully collapsed) positions of the expression pneumatic. Although forzando on and off holes in the tracker scale appear to be lock and cancels, they are not. Instead, the forzando on valve is a non-locking valve which applies full suction to the expression pneumatic, pulling it rapidly·shut to the loudest playing level; the forzando off valve admits full atmosphere to the expression *and* governor pneumatics, allowing them to fall open quickly to the minimum intensity level.

The crescendo valve by itself produces a very slow crescendo; the forzando on valve, when turned on for more than a split second, produces a very rapid one. For crescendo effects in between these two extremes, the roll locks the crescendo valve on and then operates the forzando on valve in short momentary pulses, creating crescendos of intermediate speed or small sudden increases in the volume level, as required by the music.

The sustaining pedal valve has two modes of operation. With the Welte switch turned on for playing Welte rolls, the pedal is controlled by a lock and cancel valve from holes 91 and 92, whether or not the sustaining pedal switch is turned on or off. With the Welte switch turned off for playing 88-note player piano rolls, the pedal is controlled by a non-locking valve from hole 3 if the sustaining pedal switch is turned on, and it does not operate if the pedal switch is turned off.

Restoring the Welte Licensee

The Stack

The Welte Licensee stack is the same as an Autopiano or Standard stack; see the rebuilding instructions in Ch. 6.

Illus. 7-34. Welte grand stack with small primary valve chest attached directly to secondary pouch board.

Some Weltes have a small primary valve chest attached to the front of the secondary pouch board as shown in illus. 7-34 instead of having a completely separate primary valve chest. If the inside facings of the secondary valves must be releathered, regulating the secondary valve travel accurately is more difficult in a Welte than in an Ampico or Duo-Art because of the pressed-fit valve stem grommets, particularly if the valves contain layers of felt like early Standard and Autopiano valves do. As in a Standard, eliminate this felt if you have to take the valves apart, to make the valve travel less spongy. If the original inside valve facings are still airtight, leave them in place but remove any lumpy corrosion from between the facings and the metal backing plates.

Illus. 7-35. This pushrod assembly, shown upside down, is separate from the stack. The lead tubing goes through the wooden rail closest to the keybed, preventing the tubing from rubbing on the pushrods. After installing the pushrod assembly in the piano, the stack is installed, with the pneumatic fingers aligned with the bottom of the pushrods. Other pushrod systems were also used.

The Expression Mechanism

If any part of a Welte expression mechanism leaks, it will be impossible to regulate the expression pneumatics so they consistently do what they are supposed to do. Check each component for seepage and correct the problem before assembling anything. Covering the tunnel-like governor pneumatics so they are straight, airtight, and flexible can be quite a challenge for a beginner; the sequence shown in illus. 7-36, etc.is one way of doing this critical job so the pneumatics turn out right.

Welte lock and cancel valve blocks are made of maple, and they give the appearance that if you correctly replace the valve, pouch and gasket leather they will automatically work properly. Nevertheless, getting them to work right consistently can be quite tricky. Before reassembling a valve unit, check both pouches to make sure they are airtight. The smallest pinhole will prevent the valve from locking and cancelling. As you reassemble each valve unit, place the valve stem in the wooden button attached to the lower pouch, and make sure that the lower valve facing seats properly. If the pouch has less dish, or if the

Illus. 7-36. The three parts of the Welte governor pneumatic, sanded, painted and ready for reassembly. Left to right: the *hinge block*, the *moveable board*, and the *stationary board*.

Illus. 7-37. The moveable board, showing suction channel.

Illus. 7-38. Step one: Glue a piece of fuzz back bellows cloth to the hinge block. This piece forms the hinge between the hinge block and moveable board.

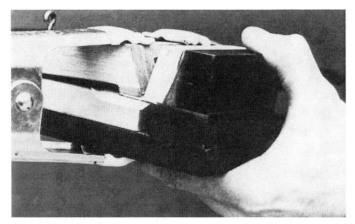

Illus. 7-39. Step two: Temporarily attach the hinge block and stationary board to the mounting board, to provide correct alignment, and glue the moveable board to the piece of hinge material.

Illus. 7-40. Step three: Remove the clamps and the mounting board. These photos show two views of the hinge block and moveable board hinged together after the glue is dry.

Illus. 7-41. Step four: Cover the remaining three sides of the tunnel with motor cloth. Do not overlap it over the hinge.

Illus. 7-42. Step five: With the stationary board attached to the mounting board, attach a folded hinge made of pillow ticking.

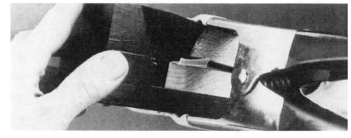

Illus. 7-43. Step six: Attach the hinge block to the mounting board, and glue the moveable board to the pillow ticking hinge on the stationary board. If everything to this point has been done carefully, the alignment of all three parts will be perfect.

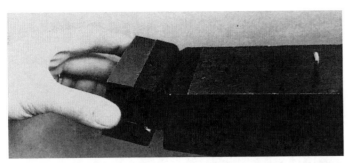

Illus. 7-44. Step seven: Remove the mounting board once more, and cover the open end and sides of the governor pneumatic with motor cloth. Do not lap the cloth over the hinge end of the pneumatic.

Illus. 7-45. Step eight: Attach a separate outside hinge made of motor cloth to the area indicated by the pointer, covering the end of the moveable board and the fuzz back cloth hinge.

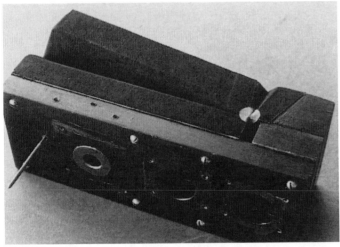

Illus. 7-46. Step nine: Apply a pouch leather punching to each corner of the hinge where the various pieces of cloth meet (since they do not overlap), and install the unit on the mounting board for the last time. The governor is now ready to have the regulator valve and other parts installed.

gasket leather is thinner than the original, the pouch will hold the valve up off its seat. Make sure the lower valve face grommets are spread apart just enough to permit adequate wobble. Thread the stem into the upper pouch, making sure that the top valve face is able to seat on the

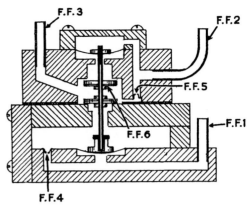

Illus. 7-47 One of the unit valve blocks from the expression mechanism. Although it is a carefully made valve, it can cause problems if every adjustment is not exactly right.

top seat. See that the valve has a scant $1/16''$ travel; adjust the position of the top face on the stem, if necessary, by moving the grommet or adding pouch leather washers. Press the valve block against its mounting surface without screwing it down, and test to see that it locks and cancels properly. Close off the output nipple; with this open to atmosphere, the valve will not lock on reliably even if there is nothing wrong with it. When you open the input to the lower pouch momentarily and close it again, the valve should pop up and stay up without leaking. If it won't stay up or if it leaks, turn it a little farther into the upper pouch. If it won't shut off completely when the input to the upper pouch is opened momentarily, the lower face is not seating.

The mezzoforte hooks on the expression pneumatics and stop pneumatics must be smooth and well lubricated. Replace the pouch leather on the blade of the large hook on the stop pneumatic, gluing it with PVC-E, and rub the leather with graphite. The original service manual recommends applying a little graphite and grease (graphite grease works well) so the hooks slip loose the moment suction is released from the stop pneumatic.

The Drawer

Many Welte parts are plated with an extremely thin layer of brass which will disappear with any more than the very gentlest polishing. While a layer of corrosion looks bad, so does a set of parts with half of the brass polished off, so be careful!

The rewind and play pneumatics in the Welte drawer are just barely powerful enough to move all of the linkages and associated parts for the manual rewind lever, the wind motor accelerator slide valve, the transmission, the rotary valve mounted on the automatic tracking pneumatic which blocks the four tracking tubes, and the rotary valve in fig. 15 in the tubing chart. When rebuilding the drawer, check the bushings for the main rod which runs through the back of the drawer to the pneumatics, and replace them if they are tight, loose or sticky. A loose bush-

Illus. 7-48. Left side of drawer, containing wind motor and control switches and levers.

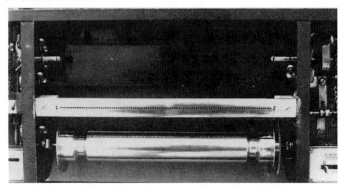

Illus. 7-49. Music roll compartment.

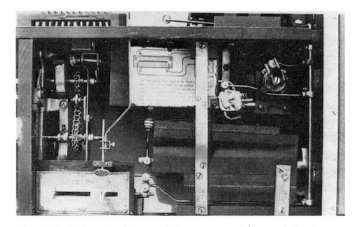

Illus. 7-50. Right side of drawer. Die cast pot metal transmission frame is at the left, the wind motor governor is the large pneumatic toward the right, and the tracking device is under the printed instruction sticker. The rewind and replay pneumatics are not shown. All linkages must work as freely as possible, with no extra lost motion, or the rewind and replay will not work properly.

ing is just as bad as a tight one, as it will introduce lost motion into the linkage, preventing the rotary switches from turning far enough. Shim the supports for the manual rewind control as necessary so the control knob will slide from side to side under its own weight if the block on which it is mounted is tipped.

Carefully inspect the condition of the lead tubing mounted on the keybed above the stack. The ends are often corroded where the rubber tubing was connected; if there is any question about the condition, replace it all.

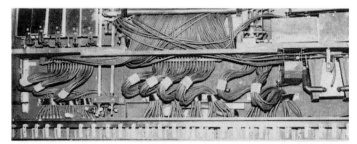

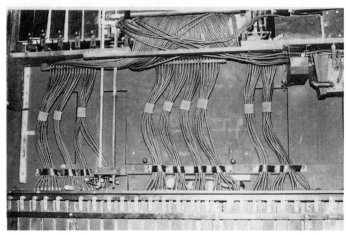

Illus. 7-51. Bottom view of piano with drawer closed (top) and open (bottom). The bottom covers are not on the drawer in these photos.

The Pump

Welte Licensee pumps have noiseless flexible straps connecting the crankshaft spider to the four bellows. The original straps were often made of canvas folded over and over on itself and soaked in shellac; replace these with rubber impregnated canvas belting material. New connecting straps made of leather, even the strongest, toughest cowhide, will be the first thing to wear out in the player action. Duplicate the length of the original straps; if the new ones are too long, the bellows will be too far shut, decreasing their pumping capacity, and if the straps are too short, the bellows will open so far that the leather will puff in and out.

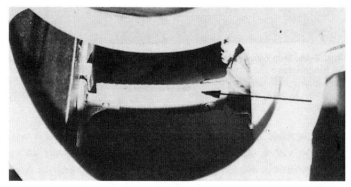

Illus. 7-52. Closeup of pump, with rubber impregnated canvas connecting strap showing between spokes.

Regulating the Welte

Because of the floating expression regulators, the Welte depends on the timing of the expression holes in the music rolls and the correct speed of the music roll more than any other reproducing system does in order to express properly. Although quite a number of superb rolls were made, quite a few others are just "so-so" unless the wind motor, governor and all other parts are regulated as perfectly as possible.

The first thing to adjust when regulating the expression mechanism is the upper spool brake in the drawer! Make it just tight enough to keep the music roll from fluttering as it unwinds from the supply spool. Then check the spring on the wind motor governor. The flexible end *must not touch the moveable board of the pneumatic*, except when the pneumatic is at rest with no suction in it. In many pianos, this spring is no longer its original shape, because a long-forgotten tuner bent it in trying to make the wind motor run faster after the player action was worn out and leaky. If you find this spring has a number of old bends, be careful not to break it.

Illus. 7-54. The complete Welte Licensee mechanism installed in the piano.

Illus. 7-53. One side of the expression system, showing the governor pneumatic at the right, the expression pneumatic at the left with its adjustable bleed assembly for regulating the crescendo speed, and mezzo-forte pneumatic at the bottom left.

To regulate the governor, set the tempo pointer at 0 and cover the tracker bar with a blank portion of the test roll. Regulate the leather nuts on the rod connecting the tempo slide valve to the tempo lever so the wind motor stops with the pointer at 0 and just begins to move at 10. Disconnect the governor spring, and set the pointer at 80. Adjust the regulating screw on the moveable board of the pneumatic so the paper moves about the same speed that it does at 10 with the spring in place. Reconnect the spring, and adjust the leather nuts on its connecting link so exactly eight feet of paper pass the tracker bar in one

TEST READINGS

Pianissimo   Bass, 4 to 6 inches
               Treble, 5 to 7 inches
To vary according to weight of piano action.

Crescendo Pneumatic at Mezzo
Forte Hook.
               Bass, 16 to 18 inches
               Treble, 17 to 20 inches

Fortissimo or Full power, 25 to 35 ins.
According to size of room and brilliancy of piano. This should be increased to about 50 inches for concert or recital purposes.

Illus. 7-55. Recommended Welte Licensee suction levels.

minute with the pointer at 80. Repeat this entire routine several times until you are certain that the wind motor speed is correct. If the wind motor won't do the same thing twice in a row, either something in the transmission or motor is binding, the upper spool brake is gummy, something is wrong with the governor knife valve, pneumatic or spring, or something is wrong with the suction supply. Persist in troubleshooting until the problem is solved and the motor is dependable; the entire Welte expression system depends on it. In the words of one old timer, "When regulating a Welte, a speed of 80 means just that. It doesn't mean 79.9 and it doesn't mean 80.1!"

After ascertaining that the speed is correct, adjust the bass mf hook so it is 7/16" from the blade on the pneumatic with the pneumatic at rest. Adjust the treble mf hook 1/2" from the pneumatic blade. Then proceed with regulating the expression mechanism as explained in the service manual. Some of the timing settings have an effect on others, so keep repeating the tests until everything works precisely as it should.

EXPRESSION PIANOS

Most expression pianos do not have a divided stack, but they do have automatic mechanisms for playing loud and soft, and many expression rolls have "hand played" arrangements.

Art Apollo

The Art Apollo piano was designed and manufactured by Melville Clark, and rolls using this expression system were made under a number of different names, including Apollo X, Art Apollo, and QRS Autograph Automatic. Other brands of pianos also use these rolls, including the Price & Teeple Art Symphonola, the Amphion Dynachord Art Expression piano, and the Seeburg X which uses style XP rolls, a coin operated version issued by the Automatic Music Roll Co.

1	Full pump suction to stack	7–92	Playing notes, low B to high C
2	Sustaining pedal	93	Bass hammer rail
3	Expression soft	94	Treble hammer rail
4	Expression loud	95	Accent
5	Rewind	96	Play
6	Shutoff		

Illus. 7-56. One style of Art Apollo stepping mechanism; the two opposing pneumatics turn the ratchet wheel, which adjusts the regulator pneumatic in response to tracker bar holes 3 and 4. *Photo by Jere DeBacker.*

Some pianos have an extra hole at one or both ends of the tracker bar; if in doubt, find the true position of hole 1 by pulling an X roll over the tracker bar and centering it with the two manual tracker alignment holes on the leader. Holes 3 and 4 operate a stepping expression mechanism which has four levels. Some Melville Clark Apollo pianos have a four position ratchet slide valve with two opposing pneumatics which push it back and forth; others have a rotating pinned wheel. Amphion actions have a ratchet slide valve. Some Seeburg X pianos have a complicated mechanism with several opposing pairs of pneumatics and slide valves which force each other to act in sequence in response to holes 3 and 4. Most, if not all, rolls in the Art Apollo family were made by adding expression coding to QRS player piano rolls.

Hupfeld Phonoliszt

The Phonoliszt expression system was used in expression pianos as well as in the Phonoliszt-Violina, a reproducing piano and violin player. Although this system looks simple, it is capable of very effective results.

1	Low F	39	Mezzo forte
2–34	Low G to D#	40	F#
35	Sustaining pedal	41	Crescendo
36	E	42	G
37	Soft	43	Bass hammer rail
38	F	44–77	Notes G# to high F

Illus. 7-57. Expression regulating mechanism for a Hupfeld Phonoliszt piano. This piano also formed the basis for the remarkably lifelike Phonoliszt-Violina piano and violin playing machine.

Recordo

The Recordo name began as a brand name for expression rolls produced by the Imperial Music Roll Co. for use on expression pianos with the following scale:

1	Bass hammer rail		
2	Mandolin (rarely)	94	4th intensity
3	Sustaining pedal	95	3rd intensity
4	Play	96	2nd intensity
5	Rewind	97	1st intensity
6–93	Playing notes, low A through high C	98	Treble hammer rail

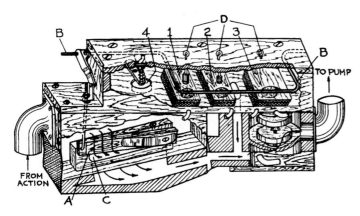

Illus. 7-58. Standard Pneumatic Action Co. Recordo expression regulator, incorporating three pneumatics which open the knife valve to three increasingly louder positions, and a bypass valve (#4) which feeds full pump suction to the stack. This mechanism has only five levels (0, 1, 2, 3 and 4) because each pneumatic overrides the previous ones

Over the years, many piano companies manufactured pianos which played Recordo rolls, each company manufacturing its own expression mechanisms which differed from those of other brands. Many brands of Recordo music rolls were also produced, including Aria Divina, Imperial Automatic Electric, International for Expression Pianos, Melodee Expression, Pianostyle for Expression Pianos, QRS Recordo, Recordo, Recordo Red Label, Rose Valley Recording, U. S. Auto-Art, Vocalstyle Home Recital Series, Vocalstyle Reproducing and Vocalstyle Reproduco.

The first Recordo rolls, made from approximately 1915 to late 1923, used the four intensity holes in combinations for ten or twelve expression levels. From late 1923 to January 1926, the four holes were used only for five expression levels, with each higher intensity overriding the lower ones. From January 1926 to February 1930, the four holes were used in sixteen combinations for rare expression mechanisms with sixteen intensity levels. Each type of roll produces good musical results only in pianos with expression mechanisms for which it was designed, and in some pianos, it is necessary to disassemble the expression mechanism in order to figure out which system it really is.

Themodist and Other "Snakebite" Expression Pianos

The simplest "expression piano," marketed as the Aeolian Themodist Pianola, the Angelus Melodant, the Hupfeld Solodant Phonola, and probably under other names as well, simply has bass and treble theme snakebite holes in the left and right margins. The stack is divided, and each half has a suction regulator with bypass valve feeding it suction from the pump. Each half of

the stack normally has regulated suction, but when a snakebite perforation occurs, the appropriate bypass valve opens, feeding full pump suction to that half of the stack, causing an accent. Themodist-type pianos are not true expression pianos because they lack an electric pump and other automatic features, but they do have more expression capability than ordinary player pianos. Duo-Art reproducing pianos will play Themodist roll accents automatically, (with the manual levers used for adjusting theme and accompaniment volume levels), with the "Duo-Art on/off" lever set at the middle (arrow) position (pre-1925 pianos) or in the "off" position (post-1925 pianos).

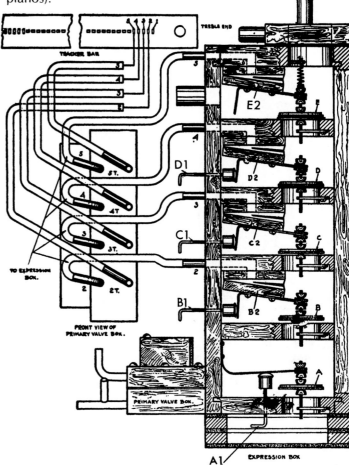

Illus. 7-59. Cross section of the Artistone 5-level Recordo expression box, incorporating a "leaker" system. The pump and stack are connected to this box, which admits more or less atmosphere into the system to make the piano play softer or louder. The bottom of the box is a large felt-covered atmosphere inlet. With no expression holes punched in the roll, all of the pneumatics collapse, providing the maximum atmosphere leakage into the system and thus the softest playing level, regulated by A1 at the bottom. When an expression hole opens in the music roll, its pneumatic drops open, closing off the leak to the extent determined by the adjustment of regulating screw B1, C1, or D1; each successively higher pneumatic closes the leakage further, causing successively louder playing levels. The top pneumatic, E2, has no regulating screw and provides the loudest playing level. This system and the one in the previous illustration are just two of the many Recordo systems manufactured by various piano companies.

CHAPTER EIGHT
COIN PIANOS
AND
ORCHESTRIONS

Illus. 8-2. Joseph Cossolini repairs the veneer on one side of the WurliTzer where it attaches to the back.

Coin operated pianos and orchestrions are the rarest and most valuable of all automatic pianos, and like reproducing pianos, they deserve the very finest restoration, with attention paid to every little detail. Orchestrions are desirable collectors items, and as such, alterations and over-restoration are just as bad as poor quality restoration. This means that if an original part had a semi gloss black finish, highly polished gloss black lacquer is wrong. If a metal part was nickel plated, chrome plating is wrong. If a rough iron casting was painted silver or black, any kind of plating is wrong. If the lead in a leaded glass window had gold or copper colored paint, then gold plating is wrong. Substitution of parts different than the original is wrong; this goes for changing a coin piano to play a style of music roll other than the one it was designed to play, adding a computer tape player to the existing music roll mechanism, replacing a coin mechanism or motor with a modern one, adding extra instruments which the piano originally did not have, installing parts from another brand of coin piano, etc. An exception to the rule of originality, however, is that regardless of what material a pump was covered with, it should be recovered with leather.

Unlike many reproducing pianos, which were given fine homes, pampered, and then preserved carefully after the novelty wore off, most coin operated pianos received

Illus. 8-3. Soundboard expert Warren Groff checks the position of the plate for the WurliTzer after regluing the back posts, installing a new soundboard and pinblock, and reattaching the bridges. The completely restored orchestrion is shown on p. 3.

Illus. 8-1. The back of a tall WurliTzer orchestrion which fell apart during disassembly in the author's shop. The only usable parts were the back posts and bridges.

extremely hard use in commercial locations, and most of them have already been "restored" several times. Screw holes in player actions are stripped, stuffed with toothpicks, stripped again, and moved to new locations, piano action parts are totally worn out, with slots in the wood where center pins have eaten beyond the cloth bushings, metal spoolbox and pump parts are worn, requiring machine work to be done, soundboards are concave instead of convex, 6/0 tuning pins are loose, pinblocks have been doped so heavily that fine tuning is impossible, etc. Besides the effects of hard use, the poor quality of old repairs make it even more time consuming to restore a coin piano to new condition. At least 75% of the repairs made to coin operated instruments up to the time this is being written have subtracted from their value rather than adding to it, and as the years have passed, a higher and higher percentage of orchestrions restored by the author had been restored badly as recently as five or ten years earlier. Before you begin the restoration of a valuable coin piano or orchestrion, learn everything you can about it, visit other collectors who understand what competent work is, and make sure that your repairs will add to rather than subtract from the instrument's value.

Coin and rewind mechanisms, organ pipe chests, percussion actions, lock and cancel mechanisms, spool box transmissions, multiplexing devices, pumps and other parts were made in so many varieties that to cover even the major varieties of the major American brands—Link, Marquette (Cremona), National, Nelson-Wiggen, North Tonawanda, Operators (Coinola, Reproduco), Peerless, Seeburg, Western Electric and WurliTzer,—and European brands—Hupfeld, Imhof & Mukle, Philipps, Popper, Weber and Welte—would take take a book much larger than this one. Rather than devoting a large amount of space in this book to detailed technical information of interest only to a few advanced, specialized collectors, this chapter includes general information on tuning, regulating and getting coin pianos and orchestrions to work right, along with tracker scales for the more common instruments.

Restoration Standards

Every motor-driven piano has a spill valve, usually located on the suction reservoir, which admits or spills atmosphere into the system when the suction goes higher than a certain preset level. A general guideline for airtightness in a coin piano or orchestrion is that with the correct pulley on the motor—usually no larger than 1¾" or 2", the suction reservoir should pull shut with one or two revolutions of the pump crankshaft, and it should remain fully collapsed, spilling a generous amount of air into the system during the entire time the piano plays. In a large orchestrion, the suction reservoir may pulsate a little when the bass drum pneumatic plays, but otherwise, it should remain pulled all the way shut. Likewise, the pressure reservoir in an instrument with pipes should open completely with one or two revolutions of the crankshaft and remain fully inflated during the entire roll; if it collapses during fully scored musical passages and then has to work its way open again, the system is leaky. (A band organ pump should be able to inflate the pressure reservoir fully within one revolution of the crankshaft if everything is airtight). Small Seeburg coin pianos should be able to play with two of the four pumping bellows disconnected, although few other instruments have this much built-in reserve. Under no circumstances should it be necessary to use a larger motor pulley or add a suction box to the existing pump in order for the piano to play loudly.

Extra Instruments—How they Work

In most coin pianos and orchestrions, the extra instruments simply duplicate the playing of the piano. In some machines, the piano has a shutoff mechanism in the note playing range of the extra instruments, which allows the xylophone or pipes to play solos when desired. The note range of each instrument and where it is coupled to the piano are obvious by looking at the connections on the valve chests. Each extra instrument is turned on either by a chain perforation in the roll, or by a lock and cancel mechanism. The music rolls are orchestrated to turn the extra instruments on and off at appropriate times during the music.

Usually, a pipe chest has a pallet valve for each note; a suction operated pneumatic mounted on the outside of the chest pushes on a pin which opens the pallet, admitting air into the pipe. The pneumatic receives suction from the valve well of the associated note in the piano stack; when the piano note plays, the pipe plays along with it. Regardless of whether the piano is playing softly or loudly, the piano stack suction level is ample to operate both the piano and the pipe chest pneumatics. Two methods of turning the pipes off are used: a slider mounted below the pipe feet which blocks the passage of air from the pallet valve to the pipe, or a large valve which turns the pressure supply to the pipe chest on and off. In both systems, the pneumatics and pallets work regardless of whether the pipes have air pressure or not.

Three common methods are used for playing a xylophone along with the piano. In the first method, used in most Seeburg xylophones and WurliTzer bell actions, the xylophone or bell action has a large outside valve for each pneumatic, with each pouch input tube connected to a piano valve well. When the piano note plays, suction from the piano valve pulls the xylophone pouch and valve down, connecting suction to the xylophone pneumatic. The suction level in the piano stack must at least equal that in the xylophone valve chest for this system to work. In the second method, used in Cremonas, Western Electrics, and some Coinolas, each xylophone note has an inside valve. Between the piano stack and the xylophone valve chest is an interface with a spring loaded pouch valve for each note. Each spring loaded pouch normally covers a hole which is tubed to the input of the xylophone valve; suction from the piano stack valve pulls the spring loaded pouch down, playing the xylophone note. In this system, the piano and xylophone valve chests can operate at two different suction levels, permitting the loudness of each instrument to be regulated individually. In the third method, used in only a few Seeburgs and Coinolas, each xylophone note has an inside valve, and each pouch input tube is teed to the piano stack tracker bar tube. This system only works if both sets of pouches—piano and xylophone—are airtight, with exactly the right size bleeds in the piano and no bleeds in the xylophone valve chest. Because of the delicate balance of getting two pouches to turn on and off simultaneously from one tracker bar hole, and the fact that the two valve chests must always work on the same suction level, prohibiting individual regulation of each instrument, this system was rarely used. In all three systems, the xylophone is turned on and off by an action cutoff valve connected between the suction supply and xylophone valve chest.

In orchestrions with pipes *and* xylophone, suction from the piano stack valve is connected to the pipe chest pneumatic and the xylophone, using one of the first two methods described above for operating the xylophone valves. In some orchestrions—Seeburg H roll and Operators (Coinola) O roll instruments, for example-the pipes or xylophone play solo by means of a mechanism which turns the piano off in the note range of the extra instruments.

Reiterating Mechanisms

Some xylophones and most snare drum actions have reiterating, or repeating, pneumatics. The reiteration speed of the pneumatic with built in pallet valves depends mainly on the weight and length of the beater and it is not readily adjustable. Other styles with slide valves usually have several adjustments on the slide valve and pneumatic, allowing the speed to be adjusted to an extent. Loudness is regulated by adjusting the mechanism as well as the suction level. When restoring a reiterating xylophone, make each part of each pneumatic as uniform as possible in order to assure uniform reiteration.

Illus. 8-4. The repeating mechanism on a Seeburg H orchestrion snare drum. Each time the pneumatic collapses, it pushes the little valve shut, turning itself off. A spring pulls the pneumatic open, which turns it on again. This type of mechanism can be made to play soft and loud according to the expression in the music roll, if enough time is spent with every little adjustment.

Lock and Cancels

All sorts of lock and cancel mechanisms are used in orchestrions, to avoid having groups of extended chain perforations in the music rolls. Some have mechanical hooks and latches, others have pneumatics which push slide valves back and forth, and still others have sophisticated combinations of valves and pouches which hold each

other on. Test each lock and cancel mechanism on the bench prior to installing it in an orchestrion, and regulate it for quick, positive latching and unlatching.

Pressure Pumps

Any instrument with organ pipes must have a source of air pressure to play them; most WurliTzer orchestrions have two separate pumps connected to the same crankshaft, one for suction and the other for pressure, but most other orchestrions have combination pumps.

Most combination pumps—Seeburg and Cremona, for example—have the bellows out in the open, with stiffeners glued to the inside of the leather which prevent it from puffing in and out. Each bellows has two flap valves (in large pumps, two *sets* of flap valves). The inside flaps are connected to a common suction chamber leading to the suction reservoir, and the outside flaps are boxed in with a common pressure chamber connected to the pressure reservoir. The atmosphere pulled into the system through the suction-operated player mechanisms and suction spill valve is captured and blown into the pressure reservoir for playing the pipes.

A less common type of combination pump—used in Coinolas with pipes—is simply a rotary pump with the front and back boxed in to capture the pressure exhausted through the usual flap valves. In this type of pump, stiffeners are unnecessary because the pressure on the outside of the bellows always exceeds the pressure inside, even while the crankshaft pushes them shut. This prevents the leather from puffing in and out.

It is very important to install the stiffeners in pumping bellows neatly and to glue them tightly to the leather to prevent them from peeling loose and to prevent the leather from popping in and out. In a large pump, begin by splicing leather to make one piece long enough to go all the way around each bellows. Feather (or "skive") the splice areas by pressing the leather down on a stationary belt sander with a block of wood prior to joining them so the thickness of the splice doesn't exceed the thickness of the single piece of leather. Draw a center line from one end of the leather to the other, and using the original materials as a guide, glue the stiffeners to the new leather. If the old stiffeners are in excellent shape, clean and reuse them, but if they are cracked or torn, replace them with new ones made of appropriate fibre material or wood. After the glue dries, fold the leather as it will be when the bellows is shut, and bind the long seam between each pair of stiffeners with a strip of thin leather, which will keep them from peeling loose. If the leather bulges around the corners as you glue it on the bellows, wet it and iron it until it pulls down flat. Always use hot glue; if you use the right kind of chrome tanned garment leather and glue it correctly, you will not be able to pull it loose after the glue dries.

Electric Motors

Like reproducing pianos, most American coin pianos originally had 1200 rpm electric motors. (The speed on the nameplate ranges from 1150 to 1200, but the true no-load running speed is usually close to 1200). A higher speed motor—1800 rpm or faster—is wrong, and it puts undesirable strain on itself as well as the pump. A general rule when replacing an incorrect motor pulley is to find one which will drive the mechanism just fast enough to play the music the correct speed. For information on servicing old electric motors, see pp. 155-156.

Rewind/Play and Coin Mechanisms

Coin pianos were made to be used "on location" to earn their owners a profit, and if the rewind/play or coin mechanisms didn't work perfectly, the pianos didn't earn their keep. Many private collectors restore the musical parts of their coin pianos but stop short of restoring the automatic rewind, play and coin mechanisms because these are not as important for home use. An instrument is not completely restored, however, unless it reliably starts when a coin is inserted, shuts itself off at the end of each song, and rewinds and switches back into play without fail.

A common problem with automatic rewind and play mechanisms is that even when the spool brakes are tightened excessively, the paper jumps away from the tracker bar at the moment that it changes direction, opening the tracker bar holes to atmosphere and causing the transmission to jump back and forth from play to rewind until the end of the paper comes off the spool. The usual cause for this is excessive play between the drive pins and the sockets which are attached to the spools. Since the spool brakes act on shafts in the transmission, not the spools themselves, no amount of brake tension will prevent the paper from buckling out if the spools continue turning a little after the shafts stop. Replace the drive pins and sockets if necessary, leaving just enough play to permit the takeup spool to be adjusted sideways and the feed spool to be removed for changing the roll.

Coin chutes and mechanisms often have several problems at the same time, making it difficult to diagnose them. If your coin mechanism doesn't work reliably, open the cabinet and deposit one coin after another until you find a problem. Solve it and deposit more coins until the next problem becomes evident. Some ratchet-type accumulators contain fine hairpin and coil springs, and if these are deformed or the wrong strength, find an identical mechanism which works right to see what the springs should look like. Most coin switch mechanisms originally had a piece of very flexible braided wire connecting the movable blade of the switch to its supporting binding post to provide electrical continuity, eliminating sparking be-

Illus. 8-5. A coin mechanism from a Cremona orchestrion. Note the important little piece of flexible braided (not stranded) wire which connects one binding post to the moveable blade of the knife switch.

tween the blade and post. In many pianos, the connecting wire is either missing—causing deformation of the knife or support where the arcing occurs—or it has been replaced with the wrong wire which is far too stiff, requiring such a stiff spring that the coin will not reliably trip the switch. In either case, obtain a piece of braided wire from an electronic supply house and install it in the switch.

The real test of a coin mechanism is to deposit 100 coins in a row. If it works without fail, it will probably work thousands of times. If not, it will malfunction within a short time.

Regulating, Tuning, and Voicing Orchestrions

Putting the finishing musical touches on an orchestrion makes the difference between a noisy rattletrap and a beautiful musical instrument. Most people expect an orchestrion to sound bad, and the typical response to a nice sounding, well regulated, tuned and voiced orchestrion is "I never imagined one of those could sound so good; I thought they were *supposed* to sound out of tune." While there is nothing particularly complicated about these finishing touches, they do require an understanding of music and a good ear for pitch, tone quality and shades of loudness, in addition to the mechanical ability to know what to do in order to arrive at the correct sound. A passable job may be done by a technician who tunes with an electronic tuning device, but the job is not finished until fine tuning and voicing is performed by someone with musical as well as mechanical ability.

Finding the Correct Pitch for Tuning

Most orchestrions were tuned to A-435 pitch, 20 cents flat of the A-440 standard in use today. Tune the piano and other instruments to 435 unless it is obvious that the instrument was originally tuned to 440. Most orchestrion xylophones have the pitch stamped on one bar; the original pitch of violin pipes can be approximated by setting the tuning slides half way down in their slots and raising the pressure to just below the point at which the harmonic freins can not be regulated to keep the pipes from overblowing (see the section on voicing and tuning violin pipes below).

Tuning Keyboardless Pianos

Small keyboardless pianos such as the Seeburg style L, KT and others may be tuned two different ways. One is to stand in front of or beside the piano, on a step stool if necessary, and to reach down in to play the whippens by hand. A passable tuning job can be done by tuning one note at a time to an electronic tuning aid; the more time spent compensating for inharmonicity, as described in *Piano Servicing, Tuning and Rebuilding*, the better the piano will sound. If the piano has a spoolbox in front of the piano action (Seeburg L, Western Electric X, etc.) reach behind it. If the piano has extra instruments in front of the action—the xylophone, tambourine, etc. in a Seeburg KT or the drums in a KT Special—remove these prior to tuning.

Fine tuning a piano by ear produces better results, but it is difficult to play octaves, fifths and other intervals in a keyboardless piano if a lot of other parts are in the way of the piano action. The second way of tuning is to use a test and tuning roll which has a section of unisons and octaves. Disconnect the roll drive by removing a cotter pin or other mechanical part, set any expression devices to the loudest setting, wind the test roll through by hand, and play the unisons and octaves for tuning by playing the tracker bar holes with your fingers. The disadvantage of this method is the motor noise in the background as you tune.

The piano in a large keyboardless European orchestrion such as a Hupfeld, Weber, Philipps, etc., slides out of the back of the cabinet for tuning and servicing. Have enough helpers to keep it from tipping over, remove the screws or bolts which hold it in the cabinet, slide it out, and lean it against the wall, unless it has its own 4-wheel carriage built in. When reinstalling the piano in the cabinet, be careful to align the whippens with the stack pushrods to avoid breaking them.

Illus. 8-7. The piano in large Hupfeld, Weber and other European orchestrions slides out of the back of the cabinet for easy tuning and servicing.

Pipes

If an orchestrion has only one or two ranks of pipes, they are usually wooden flutes or violins. Tuning and voicing them involves adjusting the air pressure, adjusting the flute pipe stoppers or tuning shades, and adjusting the violin tuning slides and harmonic brakes or "freins." Each of these adjustments depends on the other, so it is necessary to do each several times. Never blow on pipes by mouth; the condensation will corrode the inside of metal pipes and raise the grain in wooden ones, altering the speaking characteristics.

If flute pipes have caps screwed on, remove each cap and blow out the inside of the pipe and the cap with compressed air. If the cap is glued on, blow down through the

Illus. 8-6. A small keyboardless piano like this Seeburg L can be tuned by opening and closing the perforations of a test roll, or by reaching down from the side to lift the whippens by hand.

mouth of the pipe to remove as much dirt as possible, without breaking the cap off. The smallest speck of sawdust or other foreign matter will prevent a pipe from speaking properly. Check all parts of the pipe carefully for unglued seams, and reglue them if necessary. The body of the pipe must be airtight in order for it to work. If the pipe has a stopper, replace the leather, sanding the new leather if necessary for a snug, airtight fit. If the stopper is a little too loose, it will fall down into the pipe in dry weather; if it is a little too tight, the pipe will crack in humid weather. After cleaning, repairing and refinishing if necessary, install the flute pipes on the pipe chest. Providing that the original dimensions of a flute pipe and the opening in the toe have not been altered, the only thing to be regulated is the air pressure. This is controlled by adjusting the spring tension on the pressure reservoir and the position at which the spill valve opens or the regulator valve in the reservoir closes. Set the pressure as high as possible without causing the pipes to chirp or overblow.

Wooden violin pipes have a "harmonic brake" or "frein" attached to the front of the mouth. After the violins are roughly tuned with the tuning slides approximately half way down in the slots, adjust each frein so the pipe produces as clear a tone with as much harmonic content as possible without overblowing or sounding fuzzy. If many of the violins overblow regardless of the adjustment of the freins, lower the air pressure ½" and try voicing them again. Then fine tune each pipe, adjusting the frein again for the brightest possible tone, and fine tune them once more.

Large orchestrions have ranks of reed pipes—clarinet and others—which are trickier to voice and tune correctly. Unlike most pipe organ and band organ reed pipes, which have "beating reeds" (with the reed tongue beating against the edges of the shallot), most European orchestrions have "free reeds" (with the tongue passing in and out of the shallot as it vibrates). Each pipe usually has two adjustments: the voicing slide and the tuning wire. As their name implies, the slide or collar at the top of the pipe is primarily for voicing, while the wire is primarily for tuning, although each has an effect on the other. If the reeds are in excellent condition, tune them by gently tapping the wires up or down. If a reed does not speak, or sounds different from its neighbors, check for dirt between the reed and shallot, and make sure the little wedge holding the reed in place is tight. *The shape of the reed is critical; don't do anything which might bend the reed, as the slightest stretching of the metal will ruin it!* If you have problems with reeds, hire a fine pipe organ technician, or send the pipes to a pipe maker before experimenting, not after you have ruined them!

The tuning of any piano with pipes involves a certain amount of compromising, because the treble octaves of a piano have far more inharmonicity than the pipes, requiring the treble piano notes to be tuned sharper. Since few aural tuners can set the same identical temperament on a piano and two sets of pipes separately, the best sounding tuning job will result from tuning the temperament of each instrument with a stroboscopic tuning aid (i.e. Conn or Peterson), as described in *Piano Servicing, Tuning and Rebuilding*. First set the temperament on the piano with the tuning aid and fine tune the rest of the piano by octaves by ear, using the usual tuning checks. Then set the same temperament on each rank of pipes with the electronic tuner, and tune the rest of the pipes by octaves by ear, double checking the tuning with the electronic tuner. When two pipes are almost in tune with each other, one can pull the pitch of the other toward it, giving the false impression that both pipes are in tune. To insure against this happening, check each octave by ear and with the electronic tuner. The resulting tuning job will be a piano well in tune with itself, a rank or ranks of pipes in tune with each other, and a minimal amount of compromise between the two. This sounds far better than compromising the tuning of the piano or the pipes just for the sake of having each pipe perfectly in tune with its piano note.

Percussion Instruments

Most original rosewood xylophones were tuned fairly well and are still reasonably well in tune. If you encounter one with a heavy coat of varnish on the bars and find that it is seriously out of tune, remove the varnish with paint stripper and retune the bars, using a stroboscopic electronic tuning aid. To make a xylophone bar flatter, remove a little wood from the sanded area toward the middle of the back of the bar where some wood was removed originally. To make it sharper, sand each end of the bar equally where it was originally sanded on the ends. After sanding, allow the wood to cool to room temperature, and recheck the tuning. If you proceed slowly, you will improve matters. It is possible to distort the harmonic series of a bar by sanding indiscriminately, so check your progress frequently with the tuner. Never attempt to retune an A-435 xylophone to A-440 just for the sake of bringing it up to modern pitch; just be sure to tune the piano to the pitch of the xylophone.

Steel orchestra bells are usually still well enough in tune unless they are so rusty that they must be replated. If you have to get them replated, use nickel only—*never chrome*—and be prepared to tune them by sanding some of the plating off of the tuning areas toward the middle of the back and the ends of the bars. Do this as carefully as possible to prevent the new plating from peeling loose. The metal will become quite hot, altering the tuning, so allow each bar to cool completely and then recheck the tuning. After you are done, rinse the bars in lacquer thinner and apply the thinnest possible coat of nitrocellulose lacquer to inhibit future dulling and corrosion. Steel orchestra bells in an orchestrion, particularly those played by reiterating pneumatics—are so loud that they are extremely offensive if they are not retuned after having them replated.

Drums and Traps

Before regulating the drum playing mechanisms, check the drums. Skin drum heads change with the weather, becoming loose and floppy in humid periods and drying out until they break in extremely dry periods. Plastic heads do not change dimensions with humidity changes so they require less maintenance, but if you still have any unbroken skin heads in an orchestrion, leave them in place and take care of them, for authenticity. Over a long period of time, through many humidity changes, skin heads become tighter and tighter if you do not take up the slack each time they get loose. It is common in old drums for the heads to have lost all of their "collar"—the area which bends around the shell of the drum—preventing any further adjustment with the tension rods. If this is the case, dampen both heads thoroughly and tighten the tension rods evenly until there is about ⅜" collar on a bass drum or ¼" on a snare drum. Then suspend the drum with the heads positioned horizontally, with a well wrung out damp rag wadded into a ball touching the middle of each head. This will cause the moisture to leave the head concentrically from the rim inward, leaving the skin evenly tensioned with no wrinkles.

Regulate each single stroke drum, cymbal and triangle beater so that if you push the pneumatic to its fully closed position, the tip of the beater *just clears* the striking surface of the instrument. If the beater touches the surface of the instrument when you hold the pneumatic shut, it will muffle the tone just like a blocking piano hammer mutes the tone of the strings. Test each instrument pneumatically, and bend the beater wire or adjust the stop screw so the beater hits the instrument and then rebounds away from it. For example the triangle should produce a clear sustained "ting," not a short "chink." Some bass drum and tympani beaters will bounce against the head when regulated properly if the tracker bar hole is left open, but they will play correctly from the music roll because the holes are very short, permitting the beater to rebound from the head just after it strikes, without bouncing.

Regulate a reiterating snare drum or wood block beater so it plays the instrument as gently as possible on low suction (when the expression device turns the drums on soft, if the piano has one), and so it plays a single tap when a single hole is punched in the music roll. A reiterating snare drum mechanism tends to be horribly overbearing, so spend as much time as necessary to make the drum as subtle as possible. *The drums in an orchestrion should be in the background of the music, not the foreground!* Most orchestrion snare drums have some sort of damper which

prevents the snare from rattling against its head in sympathetic response to the piano and other instruments when the drum is not playing. Play loud chords on the piano to make sure the damper does its job, because a sympathetically rattling snare is very annoying. Seeburg orchestrions have this damper mounted on a pneumatic (two pneumatics in the KT Special) which pulls the damper away from the head when the drum plays. WurliTzer orchestrions have the snare suspended in a frame which normally hangs away from the drum, and a pneumatic pushes the whole snare assembly against the drum when the beater plays. Coinolas simply have a small spring loaded piece of wood which presses against the snare all the time, bouncing away when the beater works.

Balancing the Loudness of the Instruments

Most orchestrions have separate suction regulators for the piano and drums, permitting the loudness to be balanced. In many orchestrions, the rewind mechanism operates on the same suction level as the piano, and the main spill valve on the suction reservoir must be set so the rewind mechanism works reliably. In Seeburgs, for example, this is around 20". After regulating this level, regulate the piano suction regulator if there is one, bringing the maximum playing level down to the loudest volume which is pleasant for the room in which the piano is located. (In many instruments, there is no separate regulator, so you have to live with the piano playing at whatever suction level is required by the rewind mechanism).

Next, turn the expression mechanism on soft, and adjust the piano soft regulator so the piano plays softly without missing any fast repeated notes. In some instruments, there is such an abrupt change between the loud and soft playing levels of the piano that the music sounds silly; if this is the case, bring the soft level up or the loud level down a little until there is a noticeable but not too extreme change in loudness when the expression device operates.

If the percussion suction line has its own regulator for loud playing, adjust this so the drums play well but not too loudly in relation to the piano and pipes. Most orchestrions also have individual stops which regulate how far each percussion pneumatic opens in the off position. Regulate these open limit stops to adjust the relative loudness of each drum to the others. Then adjust the setting of the percussion soft regulator (if there is one) so the drums just barely play when the expression is on soft. After setting all suction levels in the instrument, recheck the operation of the reiterating snare drum pneumatic on soft and loud playing, single taps and sustained rolls.

Many collectors enjoy listening to their orchestrions with the front doors open because they enjoy the loudness as well as the mechanical action. This tends to make the

Illus. 8-8. Orchestrions contain some of the most sophisticated mechanisms of all pneumatic instruments. This expression regulator in a Hupfeld Pan Orchestra is probably the most complicated mechanism ever devised for any automatic musical instrument. Every part must work freely and must be adjusted perfectly in order for the instrument to perform properly.

pipes much louder than the piano, and if the piano is regulated to play loudly enough to match the pipes with the doors open, the hammers will regularly break strings. If your coin piano or orchestrion breaks strings frequently,

turn the suction down and learn to enjoy the music with the front doors partially or completely closed.

MODERN ORCHESTRIONS

As the value of original orchestrions has risen over the years, building new orchestrions from old 88-note player pianos has become more and more popular. To satisfy the demand for components, several supply companies have manufactured 10-tune spoolboxes, coin mechanisms, xylophone and orchestra bell actions, pipes and pipe chests, and drum actions for conversion use. While a homemade orchestrion can be just as much fun to watch and listen to as an old one at a much lower cost, the addition of modern parts to an old player piano does not make it a valuable antique. More than one modern homemade orchestrion has been purchased by an unsuspecting buyer who thought it was an antique, particularly at auctions. To avoid disappointment, study *Player Piano Treasury* by Harvey Roehl, *The Encyclopedia of Automatic Musical Instruments* by Q. David Bowers, and other literature prior to buying an orchestrion, so you will be able to recognize the difference between an original orchestrion and the product of a modern hobbyist.

TRACKER SCALES

Coin pianos and orchestrions use music rolls of all sizes and shapes. Some instruments use standardized "A" or "G" rolls which were made by several companies, while others use a unique roll style not used by any other instrument. Nearly 150 different coin piano and orchestrion tracker scales were collected by the author for the earlier book *Treasures of Mechanical Music;* WurliTzer alone had over ten different roll styles just for their coin operated instruments, not including band organs or pipe organs! The following pages include scales for the more common American coin pianos and orchestrions. Note that earlier sources, including *Rebuilding the Player Piano* and some scales published by orchestrion roll manufacturers, include many significant mistakes such as transpositions of lock and cancel perforations for extra instruments, incorrect expression controls, and other errors which cause an instrument to miss many of the musical effects scored into the rolls. The following scales have been verified by watching and listening to many music rolls on each instrument.

Any function listed as "on" or "off" is a lock and cancel. Any musical function (i.e. "sustaining pedal," "hammer rail," etc.). *without* "on" or "off" remains on only as long as the hole is punched. "General cancel" cancels all registers. "Play" denotes the hole which shifts the piano back into the play mode after rewinding; earlier sources call this "repeat," "replay," or "rewind to play." "Shutoff" denotes the hole which either turns the piano off after the end of a song, or subtracts one credit from a coin or pushbutton accumulator mechanism. Odd fractions of an inch for tracker bar hole spacing are measurements of actual tracker bars, accurate to enough decimal places to enable a machinist to make a correctly spaced bar.

A Rolls

11 ¼" wide, 6 holes per inch. Used by Seeburg, Western Electric, Nelson-Wiggen, Cremona, Coinola and dozens of other coin pianos with mandolin and sometimes one additional instrument.

1	Hammer rail or low suction expression control
2	Sustaining pedal
3	Play
4–61	Playing notes, C through A
62	Extra instrument (pipes or xylophone)
63	Rewind
64	Mandolin
65	Shutoff

Some A rolls are identified with the letter A and a roll number, but others have the number only. Some early A rolls were called "S" rolls; the "S" stood for "Seeburg."

The extra instrument, if present, is usually either a rank of flute or violin pipes or a xylophone, either single stroke or reiterating. Some A rolls are specially arranged with many short holes in the treble for a single stroke xylophone. These rolls are frequently identified as "xylophone rolls" or have the word "xylophone" incorporated into the roll title, as in Clark Orchestra Roll 898, "Xylo-Pep."

A Rolls
(Keyboardless pianos)

Seeburg style L, Western Electric C, Coinola Cupid and some other small cabinet pianos have only 54 playing notes for the 58 note holes in the roll. The lowest bass note is B, and it is coupled to the next higher B on the stack so that both notes play at once from hole 15. The second bass note, C, plays from hole 4, the third note, C#, from hole 5 and so on. The last 5 treble notes are missing in this piano, so the 5 highest note holes in the tracker bar are coupled down an octave on the piano. The highest 13 piano notes, E, F, F#, G, G#, A, A#, B, C, C#, D, D# and E are played from holes 44 through 56, respectively. Holes 57 through 61 are coupled to holes 45 through 49, as follows: 57-45, 58-46, 59-47, 60-48, and 61-49.

Small keyboardless Nelson-Wiggen coin pianos such as the style 8 have a 58 note piano which requires no octave coupling

Large keyboardless pianos such as the Seeburg K and Western Electric X use the same piano back made by the Haddorff Piano Co. of Rockford, Illinois, as the Link 2E which has 61 playing notes tuned from G to G Because the A roll has only 58 playing notes, the lowest three piano notes have no pneumatics, and the piano is tubed as follows: Lowest notes: G (not used), G# (not used), A (not used), A# (hole 4), B (hole 5), C (hole 6) . Highest notes: F (hole 59), F# (hole 60), G (hole 61)

A Rolls
(National Calliope)

The 53-note National calliope has a note range from C to E Unlike the Tangley CA-43 (see below) in which the extra notes in the music roll are coupled together in the bass, the National has them coupled in the treble For this reason, an A roll which sounds excellent on a National typically sounds bad on a Tangley, and vice' versa. The high treble notes in the National are coupled as follows: E (44, not coupled), F (45 and 57), F# (46 and 58), G (47 and 59), G# (48 and 60), A (49 and 61), A# (50), B (51), C (52), C# (53), D (54), D# (55), E (56).

A Rolls
(Nelson-Wiggen Style 8)

The Nelson-Wiggen style 8 cabinet piano has two extra instruments, xylophone and bells, both of the reiterating type. Some examples were tubed to play A rolls, and others were tubed to play G rolls In the A roll version, each time hole 62 calls for an extra instrument, one instrument plays At the end of hole 62 an alternating mechanism pushes a switch valve over so the other instrument will play next time.

A Rolls
(Seeburg Pianos)

Many Seeburg coin pianos, including styles E with xylophone, and cabinet L, have the hammer rail pneumatic teed to the mandolin, and have a suction regulator which is controlled by hole 1 In late Seeburg A roll pianos having a three way (soft-medium-loud) volume control knob, hole 1 operates in conjunction with the control knob in determining various combinations of the hammer rail pneumatic and regulator pneumatics on the suction distribution box

A Rolls
(Tangley Calliaphone)

The 43-note Tangley Calliaphone model CA-43 has a note range from F to B. The two highest notes, A# and B, are not played automatically, leaving 41 notes which are played from the 58 notes of the A roll. These are coupled in the bass as follows: F, lowest note (tracker bar holes 9 and 21), F# (10 and 22), G (11 and 23), G# (12 and 24), A (13 and 25), A# (14 and 26), B (15 and 27), C (4, 16 and 28), C# (5, 17 and 29), D (6, 18 and 30), D# (7, 19 and 31), E (8, 20 and 32), F (33, not coupled), F# (34)...up to the highest note A (hole 61).

A Rolls
(Western Electric Selectra)

The Western Electric Selectra tune selecting device depends on hole 61 to find a certain song. Special Selectra A rolls were cut with a long hole 61 between songs.

G and 4X Rolls

Early G roll instruments such as the Seeburg styles G, L orchestra and early KT have pipes as their extra instrument(s). Early Automatic Music Roll Co. and some Columbia/Capitol rolls are arranged for pipes, with elongated treble note holes. Later instruments such as the late KT, Nelson-Wiggen 4X, 5X and others, have a single stroke xylophone 4X rolls, introduced by the Clark Orchestra Roll Co. in 1923 are similar to G rolls but are arranged for single stroke xylophone with many short alternating holes to make the xylophone busier. From 1923 on, most Auto-

matic Music Roll Co. and many Capitol G rolls also hve 4X-style xylophone arrangements The xylophone lock and cancel holes of the 4X roll are in the same place as the flute lock and cancels of the G roll Many late Clark 4X rolls rarely or never play the violin pipes and tympani beaters. Most collectors prefer to use Automatic and Columbia/Capitol G rolls with pipe arrangements on their instruments with pipes, and Clark 4X and similar rolls on instruments having single stroke xylophones.

G Rolls
(Seeburg G)

11¼' wide, 6 holes per inch Very early G rolls were called SS rolls

1	Hammer rail	33	Shutoff
2	Sustaining pedal	34	Tympani
3-14	Bass notes G#-G, octave coupled	35	Bass drum & cymbal
		36	Tympani
15-26	Continuation of note scale, G#-G	37	Violin pipes off
		38	Play
27	Flute pipes off	39	Violin pipes on
28	Rewind	40-63	Treble notes G#-G
29	Flute pipes on		
30	Snare drum	64	Mandolin
31	Normal suction, piano and drums	65	Triangle
32	Low suction, piano and drums		

The roll has 48 holes devoted to playing notes: 3-26 and 40-63 Seeburg G and L Orchestra piano stacks have 60 pneumatics, with each of the 12 lowest playing notes on the roll playing 2 pneumatics in octaves

G Rolls
(Keyboardless Orchestrions)

Seeburg, Nelson-Wiggen, and Western Electric keyboardless G roll orchestrions use the same piano back as the Link 2E which has a total of 61 notes, tuned from G to G The lowest three piano notes in these non-Link orchestrions have no pneumatics and are not used. Because the lowest G roll note is G# and because the lowest three piano notes are unused, there are only 10 octave coupled bass notes, beginning with low A# and ending with G. Holes 3 and 4 are not coupled From bass to treble in chromatic order, the tubing is: G (lowest piano note, not used), G# (not used), A (not used), A# (hole 5), B (6), C (7), C# (8), D (9), D# (10), E (11), F (12), F# (13), G (14), G# (3), A (4), A# (5), and so forth in chromatic sequence to the top treble note G (63).

G Rolls
(Seeburg KT)

Most KT's do not have a lock and cancel for piano expression, so holes 31 and 32 are unused. In KT's with one valve controlling both tambourine and castanets, these two instruments play together from hole 30 (snare drum). In KT's with two separate valves, the tambourine plays from 30 and the castanets from 35 (bass drum). Early KT's, made before about 1920, have one rank of pipes (flute or violin) as the extra instrument, and later KT's have a xylophone with 22 notes, from G to E. The lowest three piano notes are not used; there are only ten octave-coupled bass notes.

1	Hammer rail	33	Shutoff
2	Sustaining pedal	34	Unused
3-26	Playing notes G#-G,	35	Unused, or castanets (see text above)
27	Extra instrument off	36	Unused
28	Rewind	37	Unused
29	Extra instrument on	38	Play
30	Tambourine and castanets, or tambourine alone (see text immediately above)	39	Unused
		40-63	Treble notes G#-G
31	Unused	64	Mandolin
32	Unused	65	Triangle

G Rolls
(Seeburg KT Special & E Special)

The KT Special and E Special have more percussion instruments than there are holes in the G roll to play them, so several instruments are coupled together, while others alternate with each other, depending upon the setting of a multiplex switch which is controlled by the hammer rail perforation (hole 1) The following scale is for machines with a 2-instrument multiplex switch

1	Hammer rail and percussion multiplex switch	32	Low suction
		33	Shutoff
2	Sustaining pedal	34	Tympani and tambourine
3–26	Playing notes G#-G	35	Bass drum and cymbal—
27	Xylophone off	36	Tympani and castanets
28	Rewind	37	Drum lights off
29	Xylophone on	38	Play
30	Snare drum;	39	Drum lights on
30 + 1	= wood block	40–63	Treble playing notes G#-G
31	Normal suction	64	Mandolin
		65	Triangle

The next development in the evolution of the KT Special was the standard larger cabinet with a rectangular stained glass window and a bulky top trimmed with dentil molding. The cymbal is mounted over the bass drum and is played by an extension of the bass drum beater, but each of the other percussion instruments has its own separate valve The wood block has a reiterating beater instead of a single stroke beater This would seem to suggest that Seeburg intended to tube the wood block to play the reiterating snare drum part alternately with the snare drum, switched by the multiplex switch. The castanets would then logically be tubed to some other single stroke instrument, perhaps one of the tympani beaters or the tambourine. The bass drum and cymbal would always play from hole 35.

The final version of the KT Special has a multiplex switch with two input and four output channels, switching two separate tracker bar holes from two instruments to two others. The snare drum, wood block, tambourine, one tympani and the bass drum/cymbal beater each have their own separate valves, but the other tympani, triangle and castanets are all connected to one valve. Enough instruments in existence are tubed to the following scheme to suggest that it might be the way Seeburg originally tubed them:

Later machines with a 4-instrument multiplex switch use the following scale:

30	Snare drum; 30 + 1 = wood block
34	Tympani
35	Bass drum and cymbal; 35 + 1 = tambourine
36	Tympani, triangle and castanets
65	Tympani, triangle and castanets

G Rolls
(Miscellaneous Orchestrions)

Large Nelson-Wiggen and Western Electric orchestrions with more drums and traps than related holes in the roll have a multiplexing device which functions like the one in the Seeburg KT Special. The Nelson-Wiggen 5X has 20 large marimba bars, from G to D, playing at 8' pitch—the same pitch as the piano Other Nelson-Wiggen orchestrions have as many as 28 small xylophone bars, playing at 4' pitch—an octave higher than the piano

Hupfeld Helios Rolls

11⅝" wide, 26 holes per 10 cm. Used by Hupfeld Helios orchestrions.

1	Oboe (or clarinet) on	37	General cancel
2	Cymbal	38	F
3	Bass drum	39	Soft expression
4	Short hole: Violine on	40	F#
	Long hole: Violine and cello on	41	Piano off
		42	G
5	Snare drum	43	Shutoff
6	Xylophone (and in later models, lotus flute) on	44-69	Piano notes G# to A
		70-74	Bell notes E, F#, G, G#, A
7	Snare drum	75	Mandolin on
8-12	Bell notes B, C, C#, D, D#	76	Short hole: Viola on
13-34	Piano notes E, F#, G# to D#		Long hole: Viola and aeoline on
35	Sustaining pedal	77	Flute on
36	E	39 + 43	= Rewind

Larger Helios orchestrions have many ranks of pipes which are controlled by multiplexed tracker bar holes Refer to Bowers' *Encyclopedia* and Reblitz' and Bowers' *Treasures of Mechanical Music* for further information.

Link A Rolls

12" wide, 6 holes per inch, endless Used by Link orchestrions

1	Hammer rail down	12	Left wood block beater
2	Hammer rail up	13	Front pipes or xylophone on
3	Unused	14	Cancel pipes, xylophone and mandolin
4	Sustaining pedal		
5	Tambourine shaker	15	Rear pipes on
6	Left snare drum beater	16	Bass drum
7	Middle snare drum beater	17-65	Playing notes G to G
8	Right snare drum beater	66	Shutoff
9	Triangle	67	Mandolin on
10	Tom-tom (tambourine beater)	68–70	Unused
11	Right wood block beater		

This roll was used by keyboard orchestrions styles A and AX and the style 2B cabinet orchestrion. The lowest 12 bass notes are octave coupled, with two notes per hole. One style AX has a 12 note treble octave coupler turned on and off by a lock and cancel. If a Link orchestrion using style A rolls has a pneumatic expression device mounted on the pump, it is connected to holes 1 and 2 as in the RX roll (see below). If you restore a Link A roll piano having some or all of its original tubing intact, note the tubing connections, as other variations probably exist. For example, hole 68 might be used to turn the mandolin off in some rolls or instruments.

Link RX and C Rolls

12" wide, 6 holes per inch, endless Used by Link coin pianos with mandolin and sometimes one extra instrument.

1	Expression loud (see below)
2	Expression soft (see below)
3	Hammer rail up (or xylophone or pipes on; see below)
4	Sustaining pedal
5–65	Playing notes G to G
66	Shutoff
67	Xylophone or pipes on (teed to hole 3 in some pianos)
68	Mandolin on
69	Cancel mandolin, pipes, xylophone (see below)
70	Unused

RX rolls usually have popular or theatre music; C rolls have classical arrangements. The expression controls and mechanisms varied over the years According to Ed Link, the people who built the instruments in the factory sometimes tried new ideas, which explains some of the variations The following text describes several instruments examined; there are probably other variations as well.

Early style C Piano

The scale is the same as the RX scale listed above, except for:

1 Full suction (quick release for 2)
2 Low suction (end of perforation: gradual crescendo back to full suction, unless released by 1)
3 Hammer rail up
67 Pipes on
68 Mandolin on
69 Cancel pipes, hammer rail, mandolin

Early style 2E Piano

1 Full suction (quick release for 2)
2 Low suction (gradual cresc. back to full, unless released by 1)
3 Teed to 67, xylophone on
68 Mandolin on
69 Cancel mandolin and xylophone

This piano has no hammer rail movement. Another 2E has no suction regulator, but instead has a hammer rail pneumatic which is raised by hole 2 and which gradually drops back to normal after the end of 2, unless hole 1 causes it to fall back quickly.

Late style 2E Piano (or 2EX)

1 Accent (full pump suction to stack); quick release for 2
2 Hammer rail up, low suction (gradual crescendo when released, unless 1 appears)

Marquette (Cremona) M Rolls

11¼" wide, 9 holes per inch Used by Cremona orchestrions

A Counter for tune selector mechanism (chain perforation in middle of each tune)
B Unused
C Play
D Play hole for selector mechanism

1	Shutoff	16	Flute pipes on
2	Unused	17	Flute pipes off
3	Hammer rail up	18	Piano treble off
4	Hammer rail down	19	Piano treble on
5	Triangle	20	Mandolin on
6	Low suction for piano and drums	21	Mandolin off
7	Normal suction for piano and drums	22	Sustaining pedal
8	Snare drum	23	Tambourine
9	Piccolo or xylophone on	24	Castanets
10	Piccolo or xylophone off	25-88	Playing notes A to C
11	Tympani	E	Fast forward or rewind hole for selector mechanism
12	Bass drum and cymbal	F	Rewind
13	Tympani	G	Unused
14	Violin pipes on	H	Shutoff
15	Violin pipes off		

Holes C, 1 and F are the same as the play, shutoff and rewind holes in an ordinary instrument and are used by Cremona instruments having no automatic tune selecting mechanism, and by selector-equipped instruments when the knob is turned to "R" For details of the operation of this mechanism, see p 504 of *The Encyclopedia of Automatic Musical Instruments* or p 223 of *Treasures of Mechanical Music*

Large Cremona orchestrions contain three extra instruments: flute pipes, violin pipes and piccolo pipes in the style K, and flute pipes, violin pipes and xylophone (or bells) in the style J When the piano treble is turned off in one of these instruments, one of the three other instruments will always be turned on The style 10 cabinet model Cremona orchestrion, which also has a piano treble mute, has only two extra instruments—violin pipes and flute pipes—and some musical passages requiring the piccolo or xylophone might turn the piano treble off when neither flute nor vic¹⁻ are on. If this occurs, teeing "flutes on" to 16 and 9, and "flutes off" to 17 and 10 will prevent occasional silent sections in the music

The style 10 keyboardless orchestrion has 58 piano notes, C to A. The lowest 11 bass notes are tuned an octave below their normal pitch to provide the full bass sound of an 88 note piano The correct tubing of the 58 notes to the 64 note-playing holes of the M roll is unknown If you locate an instrument with its original tubing, carefully note the connections and correct tuning of the bass

Mills Violano Rolls

The Violano operates electrically, with no pneumatic parts, so it is not included here See *The Mills Violano-Virtuoso* by Mike Kitner and Art Reblitz, published by The Vestal Press.

National Rolls

12" wide, 6 holes per inch Used by the National coin pianos.

1	Chest suction vent	69	Sustaining pedal
2	Hammer rail down	70	Low suction
3	Hammer rail up	71	Normal suction
4–68	Playing notes A to C#		

These rolls are for the National Automatic Music Co. coin piano with ferriswheel music roll changer; each roll has only one tune. A pallet valve rides on the surface of the paper At the end of the tune, a large rectangular hole is punched, allowing the pallet valve to open, tripping the rewind mechanism.

North Tonawanda Pianolin Rolls

6 ⅝" wide, 8 holes per inch, endless Used by North Tonawanda coin pianos.

1	Shutoff	4	Sustaining pedal
2	Mandolin	5-48	Playing notes F to C
3	Hammer rail	49	Pipes off (chain perforation)

The lowest 13 notes are connected to flute pipes; the upper 31 are connected to violin pipes.

Operators O Rolls

11¼" wide, 9 holes per inch. Used by Coinola and Empress orchestrions.

A	Play	13	Pipes on, swell shutter open
1	Tympani	14	Bells or xylophone on
2	Bass drum and cymbal	15	Low suction, piano and drums
3	Tympani	16	Normal suction, piano and drums
4	Wood block, reiterating	17	Bells or xylophone off
5	Snare drum, single tap	18	Shutoff
6	Snare drum, reiterating	19	Pipes off, swell shutter closed
7	Triangle	20-31	Playing notes E to D#, octave coupled
8	Sustaining pedal	32-85	Continuation of note scale, E to A
9	Hammer rail down	86	Tambourine, reiterating
10	Hammer rail up	87	High pump suction
11	Mandolin off	88	Crash cymbal
12	Mandolin on	B	Rewind

The pipes or xylophone play 24 notes, A#—high A, from holes 62 to 85. A thick felt muffler drops between the piano hammers and strings to mute the piano notes in this range, allowing the extra instrument(s) to play "solo."

In Coinolas having two ranks of pipes with separate lock and cancel mechanisms, the flute pipes are controlled by holes 13 and 19, and the violin pipes from 14 and 17 In the style SO, both ranks of pipes turn on and off together from holes 13 and 19, and the xylophone is controlled by 14 and 17 Some early Coinolas have a set of harmonium reeds which are controlled by 13 and 19

Original Coinola orchestrions have a snare drum expression lock and cancel controlled by 15 and 16 but do not have a suction regulator controlled by this lock and cancel for the piano Many O rolls, however, have these expression holes punched even when the drums are not playing, like the expression holes for the piano in G, H and M rolls The roll arranging department evidently thought holes 15 and 16 had an effect on the piano Hole 87, found only in late O rolls, controls a pneumatic which closes the spill valve on the suction reservoir in large Coinola orchestrions, increasing the overall suction level to the entire instrument

Keyboard style Coinola orchestrions and the cabinet style SO have the lowest 12 notes on the roll octave coupled in the piano, with a total of 78 playing notes on the piano for 66 notes in the roll Cabinet style Coinola orchestrions do not have the lowest 12 notes, so holes 20 through 31 play one note each In fact, some Coinola cabinet style orchestrions are made around the same Haddorff 61 note piano plate as the Link 2E, Seeburg KT, etc , and they have no piano notes at all for the last octave of solo notes, leaving these notes to be played only when the solo instrument is turned on Holes 86, 87 and 88 are used only in late O rolls and late orchestrions.

Operators OS & NOS Rolls

11¼" wide, 9 holes per inch. Used by Reproduco theatre and mortuary piano/organs.

A	Vox humana on, flute off	11	Treble hammer rail up
AA	Play	12	Treble hammer rail down
B	Viola on, quintadena off	13-82	Playing notes, A to F#
1	Hammer rail	83	Quintadena (or violin pipes) off
2	Sustaining pedal	84	Quintadena (or violin pipes) on
3	Swell shades closed	85	Tremolo
4	Swell shades open	86	Mandolin
5	Piano on (muffler off)	87	High pump suction
6	Diapason on	88	Shutoff
7	Flute on	C	Xylophone on
8	Flute off	CC	Rewind
9	Diapason off	D	Vox humana, viola and xylophone off
10	Piano off (muffler on)		

If a Reproduco is tubed to this original tracker scale, the piano is rarely used. Only in the few rolls where holes 5 and 12 are punched, the hammer rail and sustaining pedal holes 1 and 2 are also used. Very few instrument s have a mandolin or high pump suction device.

200

Most Reproducos in existence have 61 flute pipes, divided into 24 stopped "diapason" pipes (12 behind the soundboard and 12 inside the cabinet) and 37 open flute pipes, plus 37 quintadena pipes inside the cabinet Holes A, B, C and D are not punched in the tracker bar in most of these instruments, with holes AA (play) and CC (rewind) in the same locations as they are in a style O machine.

Some NOS rolls for theatre use are perforated to play at half the normal speed, providing about twice as much playing time per roll.

Peerless 44 Rolls

8¼" wide, 6 holes per inch, endless. Used by the 44-note keyboardless Peerless coin piano

1–5	Notes F to A	10–42	Notes C-G#
6	Shutoff	43	Hammer rail down
7	A#	44	Hammer rail up
8	B	45–48	Notes A-C
9	Sustaining pedal		

The continuous 44-note chromatic note scale from low F to high C is provided by holes 1-5, 7, 8, 10-42 and 45-48, in that order

Peerless D Rolls

11¾" wide, 6 holes per inch, endless Used by the keyboard style Peerless D.

1 Playing note C (displaced from hole 9 by sustaining pedal)
2 Hammer rail down
3 Hammer rail up
4–8 Playing notes G to B
9 Sustaining pedal
10–69 Playing notes C# to C

Holes 4 + 6 = shutoff. The pneumatics for low G and A are connected to a T-shaped lever This lever allows each note to play separately, but when both pneumatics are activated simultaneously, the T transfers their motion to the shutoff valve instead. The stack in the Peerless D is below the keyboard, and it plays the piano by pushing up on the back ends of the piano keys. To prevent bystanders from defeating the shutoff by holding the low G and A piano keys up at the front end, these two keys are cut in half and connected with hinges; if a key is depressed by hand, it will play the piano action, but if the front end is held up, the hinge will allow the stack to push up on the back end (and T shutoff lever) anyway, turning the piano off

Peerless O Rolls

1 Unused?
2 Cymbal
3 Tympani, reiterating
4 Bass drum
5 Left snare drum beater
6 Middle snare drum beater
7 Right snare drum beater
8 Note C (displaced from hole 16 by sustaining pedal)
9 Hammer rail down
10 Hammer rail up (canc. by 9); low suction (canc. by 16)
11-15 Playing notes from low G to B
16 Sustaining pedal
17-76 Playing notes C# to C
77 Shutoff
78 Rewind (or hole 94) in some rolls
79 Violin pipes off
80 Violin pipes on
81 Flute pipes off
82 Flute pipes on
83 Castanets
84 Mandolin off
85 Play
86 Castanets
87 Triangle
88 Mandolin on
89-97 Unused (94 is used for rewind in some rolls)

Some Peerless O roll orchestrions have a 66-note piano stack, from G to C, playing from holes 11-15, 8 and 17-76 in that order. Other Peerless orchestrions have a full 88-note stack with the bass and treble octave coupled as follows: Piano keys 1 to 10 are coupled to keys 13 to 22 respectively, keys 11 and 12 are not coupled, and keys 77 to 88 are coupled to keys 65 to 76 respectively.

The holes labelled "unused" in the above tracker scale may have been used in special rolls made for the Peerless photoplayer which may have had more effects than the O roll orchestrions did.

Philipps PM Rolls

(WurliTzer Mandolin PianOrchestra Rolls)

8⅞" wide, 4 holes per centimeter. Used by Philipps and large keyboardless WurliTzer orchestrions.

1	Bassoon (or clarinet) on	51	Blank (shutoff in very early rolls)
2	Clarinet (or viola) on	52–76	Notes C-C
3	Shutoff	77	Swell shutters open
4	Snare drum	78	Swell shutters closed
5	Sustaining pedal off	79	Cello on
6	General cancel	80	Violin pipes on
7	Tympani	81	Flute on
8	Tympani	82	Piano hammer rail down
9	Triangle	83	Bass drum and snare drum expression loud
10	Bells on	84	Tambourine
11	Unused	85	Bass drum and cymbal
12	Mandolin on	86	Castanets
13	Sustaining pedal on	87	Piccolo on
14–27	Playing notes C to C#	88	Xylophone on
28	Rewind		
29–50	Notes D-B		

In many WurliTzer Mandolin PianOrchestras, the hammer rail operates with the swell shutters; many rolls have no holes punched in position 82.

Seeburg H Rolls

15¼" wide, 6 holes per inch Used by Seeburg model J and H orchestrions Very early H rolls were called SSS rolls

A	Unused	46	Castanets
1	Hammer rail	47	Low suction, piano and drums
2	Sustaining pedal	48	Normal suction, piano and drums
3–14	Playing notes E to D# (see below)	49	Snare drum
15–34	Playing notes E-B	50	Bass drum and cymbal
35	Flute pipes off	51	Tympani
36	Flute pipes on	52	Tympani
37	Rewind	53–86	Treble playing notes C to A (solo section)
38	Violin pipes off		
39	Violin pipes on	87	Mandolin (very early rolls only)
40	Piano treble off	88	Triangle
41	Piano treble on	B	Unused
42	Play		
43	Xylophone off		
44	Shutoff		
45	Xylophone on		

The Seeburg H piano accompaniment section runs from low G up through B above middle C. The piano solo section runs from C above middle C to high A The pipes play from the 34-note treble piano solo range, with the violin pipes always playing an octave below the piano, from middle C up. Some H orchestrions have flute pipes of the same pitch as the violins, but most H's have piccolos which play an octave higher than the violins, the same pitch as the piano. The 22-note xylophone is the same pitch as the piano and runs from C two octaves above middle C to high A

Bass octave coupling: The piano notes, in order from the lowest upward, are coupled to the following holes: G (hole 6), G# (7), A (8), A# (9), B (10), C (11), C# (12), D (13), D# (14), E (3), F (4), F# (5), G (6), G# (7), A (8), A# (9), B (10), C (11), D (12), D# (13), E (14) and so on. The lowest three notes on the music roll, E to F#, play one bass note each The next 9 notes, G to D# (holes 6-14) are coupled to play in octaves. Some MSR instruments (see the MSR scale below) have low F and F# coupled, and other variations may also exist.

The mandolin was never used except in very early rolls This is evidently because more H rolls were probably sold to photoplayer owners than H orchestrion owners, and photoplayers use hole 87 for swell shutters. Hole 46 plays single stroke castanets in the H orchestrion, but it also plays a reiterating tambourine in photoplayers, so it is frequently punched for the reiterating mechanism.

Seeburg MSR Rolls

These rolls, made for use on photoplayers and mortuary organs, are the same as style H rolls except for the following differences:

A	Bass pipes on, piano off	44	Swell closed
2	Style R only: vox humana	46	Tambourine and castanets
38	Violin or quintadena pipes off	87	Swell open
39	Violin or quintadena pipes on	B	Bass pipes off, piano on

Two arrangements were used for the swell shutters In one system, a ratchet mechanism opens and closes the shutters in four distinct steps, in response to holes 44 and 87 The ratchet slide valve controls three pneumatics which push the shutters open against a large spring; when none of the pneumatics is collapsed, the spring holds the shutters closed In the other system, the shutters are "balanced" with no return spring, so they stay in any position to which they are opened. One large pneumatic pushes them open, and an opposing one pushes them shut. Short pulses in positions 44 and 87 cause the pneumatics to move the shutters a little at a time, and long slots in these positions cause them to close or open fully.

Seeburg XP Rolls
(See the Art Apollo scale on p. 188.)

WurliTzer Pianino Rolls

5½" wide, 10 holes per inch. Used by keyboardless WurliTzer Pianino coin pianos.

1	Shutoff	6–49	Playing notes F to C
2	Hammer rail up, mandolin on	50	Snare drum
3	Rewind	51	Sustaining pedal
4	Hammer rail down, mandolin off	52	Flute pipes on, violin pipes off
5	Violin pipes on, flute pipes off		

A mechanism in the spoolbox switches the roll back to play after rewind.

A few Pianinos have two ranks of pipes and xylophone. Some rolls might turn the xylophone on with holes 5 + 52, and off with holes 2 + 4. However, other rolls seem to ignore the xylophone if tubed to this scheme, but play it effectively if 2 + 4 turn it on and 4 + 51 turn it off.

If a Pianino is tubed to the above layout, the violin pipes usually play when the snare drum is playing, and the flutes play when it is not If you prefer the opposite, reverse tubes 5 and 52

WurliTzer 65-Note Automatic Player Piano Rolls

9⅝" wide, .1227" hole spacing. Used by WurliTzer keyboard style coin pianos and orchestrions.

1	Shutoff	7–71	Playing notes A to C#
2	Hammer rail up, mandolin on	72	Violin pipes off, flute pipes on
3	Hammer rail down, mandolin off	73	Violin pipes on, flute pipes off
4	Sustaining pedal on	74	Bass drum and triangle
5	Sustaining pedal off	75	Rewind
6	Snare drum		

A mechanism in the spoolbox switches the roll back into play after rewind.

4 + 5 = bells on	72 + 73 = xylophone on
2 + 3 = bells off	2 + 3 = xylophone off

WurliTzer Mandolin PianOrchestra Rolls
(See the Philipps PM scale on p. 201)

CHAPTER NINE
POSTLUDE—
TROUBLESHOOTING
AND MAINTENANCE

The previous chapters in this book are devoted to the complete, thorough restoration of player pianos, in which the entire action is disassembled and all perishable parts are routinely replaced. There are occasions, however, when it is desirable to diagnose what is wrong with a malfunctioning player piano without completely disassembling it; this chapter includes guidelines for troubleshooting a player action to find out why it doesn't play. While it is impossible to predict exactly what you will find inside an old player action, a few simple tests will help you to diagnose what is wrong, providing that the hoses and tubing are intact. This chapter also contains information on adding an electric suction unit, automatic rewind and shutoff to a foot-pumped player piano, and it concludes with information on the proper care of music rolls.

Diagnosing Problems

Prior to testing the player action, check the operation of the rewind/play lever. Make sure it engages the transmission as it should in both positions, and see that the action cutoff and wind motor accelerator are adjusted correctly. If any of these controls are out of adjustment it will be impossible to arrive at any valid conclusions.

Put a roll which is in good condition on the tracker bar, set the rewind/play lever in rewind, hold the top spool to keep it from turning, and pump. If the pump offers no resistance, the pump and wind motor are probably both leaky.

Set the rewind/play lever at play, set the tempo lever at 0, and pump. If the pump provides good resistance with the lever in rewind, but provides none with the lever in play, the stack valves are leaking. Either the lower valve facings or seats are bad, or the pouches are holding the valves up off the seats. If the piano has pouch input channels running through a gasketed junction, as in a Standard or Autopiano, try to tighten the screws holding this junction together. If the screws are all stripped, or if the gasket is rotten, chances are that atmosphere is leaking under the pouches, causing them all to lift the valves off their seats a little.

With the rewind lever in play, and the tempo lever at 0,

if the pump offers good resistance this indicates that the pump and stack valves are holding suction. Set the tempo lever at 70. If you must pump extremely fast in order for the piano to play, the stack pneumatics and/or top valve seats and faces are leaky.

If the piano offers resistance but the right notes won't play, check the alignment of the music roll with the tracker bar.

If the piano rewinds the roll at high speed with ordinary pumping, and you meet with firm resistance in play, but the piano doesn't play at all, the action cutoff is failing to turn the action on when the lever is turned to play.

If the pump offers no resistance and the piano won't play regardless of how fast you pump, rewind the roll all the way off the tracker bar, and pump hard to see if all 88 notes will play at once. If so, draw the V-shaped end of a good roll leader slowly over the tracker bar. If the valves seat and the piano plays once you start it this way, the pouches are holding the valves up off their lower seats.

If a player piano provides good resistance and plays fairly well only when played loudly with extremely hard pumping, but will not play softly, the old pouches are probably made of rubber cloth and are stiff, requiring high suction in order to work.

A note which "ciphers," or plays all the time, can be caused by the following conditions: a small piece of wood, hard shellac or other foreign matter lodged between the lower valve facing and lower seat, a tiny hole in the tracker bar tubing, a plugged bleed, a bad gasket or crack in the wood admitting air under the pouch, a tracker bar nipple leaking where it is soldered to the back of the bar, or any other condition which causes atmosphere to leak under the pouch or causes the valve to be held up.

A "dead" note which refuses to play can be caused by the following conditions: a small piece of foreign matter lodged between the upper valve facing and top seat, a plugged or kinked tracker bar tube, a hole in the pouch, an internal leak which admits suction into the tracker bar tube or channel or under the pouch, or any mechanical problem which prevents the valve from lifting.

If a note plays quickly but turns off slowly, the bleed is plugged or too small. If a note is slow to play but turns off quickly, the bleed is too large or the pouch has a tiny hole.

Pressing a piece of tracker bar tubing against a hole in the tracker bar and alternately blowing and sucking on it will provide clues as to the condition of a pouch. If you can hear the pouch crackling up and down, it is probably made of rubber cloth which has gone bad. If you can feel much more air flowing through the tube into one tracker bar hole than the rest, either the pouch has a hole, there is a leak between the tracker bar and pouch, or the bleed is too large. If you can't detect any bleed by mouth, either the bleed, tracker bar tube or an internal channel is plugged. If you can see the valve stems, and if you can cause one to move by sucking the pouch down, the pouch is holding the valve up off the lower seat.

If you can get at the top valve seats, cover one with your finger or tape, tape off the tracker bar, and pump. If the pneumatic slowly collapses with the valve on its lower seat and with the top seat closed off, the lower seat leaks. If you can tap the deck board and see the valves wiggle, the pouches are holding them up off the lower seats.

In an otherwise good player piano, if hard pumping causes the wind motor to speed up, the governor spring is too strong, the internal stop is turned in too far, the accelerator valve is not completely closed, or the tempo valve has a leak. If hard pumping causes the motor to slow down, the spring is too weak or the internal stop is not turned in far enough. Check the design of the regulator valve, adjusting screw or stop screw so you know what you are doing prior to making any adjustments.

If the wind motor lopes, or turns irregularly, either the slide valves are adjusted wrong, or one of the pneumatics leaks more than the others. Remove the suction supply hose from the motor, cover the nipple with one hand, and try to turn the motor backwards with the other. If it turns easily, the motor is not airtight. Listen for hissing noises, which will lead you to the leaks. If the motor refuses to turn with your hand covering the nipple, indicating that it is airtight, correct any binding or sticking slide valves, and adjust the slide valves to make it turn smoothly (p. 41).

If the electric pump in a reproducing piano or modern player piano won't turn on, check both ends of the power cord. If the cord isn't unplugged from the wall, it's probably unplugged from the piano. Once a year or so, every professional restorer gets a call from a customer who is convinced the motor "burned out" when actually the cord is unplugged at one end or the other.

Maintenance

A player piano is a complex mechanical device which requires a certain amount of maintenance. If you hope to restore a player piano (or buy a restored one) and use it year after year without taking care of it, it will perform less satisfactorily than if you spend just a little time taking care of it.

An important way to minimize the amount of maintenance, both for the piano and the player action, is to keep the humidity surrounding the piano at a constant level—ideally, 35%—all year. If this means running an air conditioner in the summer and a humidifier in the winter, do it! Professional rebuilders never cease to be amazed by some owners of valuable music machine collections who spend tens of thousands of dollars acquiring and restoring their collections, and who then permit the instruments to deteriorate instead of spending a little more money on humidity control! Get a good humidity gauge,

a room or furnace humidifier and an air conditioner, and pay attention to keeping the humidity and dryness under control. This not only keeps player actions working better, but it also keeps pianos from going sharp every spring and flat every fall, eliminating the pitch change that is usually necessary with every tuning. It also eliminates sticking keys, sluggish hammers, player actions which leak in the winter and other problems.

Keep the piano in tune. This means having it tuned no less than once a year; twice a year is better, and is the tuning schedule advocated by most piano manufacturers. Piano strings acquire little bends where they go around the bridge pins, and if you allow the pitch to drop lower and lower over a period of years, when you finally raise the pitch to where it belongs, the treble strings will have wild false beats curable only by replacing them.

A little lubrication goes a long way. Apply a drop of oil to the pumping pedal linkages if they squeak, and wipe all excess oil off to keep it from dripping onto your floor and into the piano pedal linkage inside the bottom. Apply a small drop of thin oil to the end of each shaft in the transmission once a year or so. Never oil the wind motor. If the slide valves bind or stick, burnish graphite mixed with alcohol into the wood as necessary. In a reproducing or coin piano, add a few drops of oil to the electric motor once a year; clean the dirty old grease off of the large transmission gears of a coin piano and apply a new thin coat once a year.

Keep the piano and player action regulated. The piano action and stack will get out of regulation the most during the first year of hard playing after new felts have been installed, so it is important to disassemble and reregulate it after the felt has packed down. If you leave significant lost motion between the jacks and hammer butts, the butt leather or buckskin will wear out much faster than if the action is regulated right.

Last but not least, pump the tracker bar regularly, particularly after playing a newly acquired batch of music rolls. New rolls contain a lot of paper dust and lint left over from the perforating process, even though roll manufacturers vacuum the paper as it exits the perforator. Old rolls which haven't been played in a years usually deposit generous quantities of dirt in the spoolbox, including some which gets sucked into the tracker bar tubes. Pumping the bar requires a certain amount of effort, and it is an easy thing to keep putting off, but it takes a lot more

Illus. 9-1. A tracker bar pump, available from supply companies. Use it regularly to keep the bleeds clean *before* they get plugged with dust and lint.

204

work to disassemble a player action after the bleeds have become plugged.

Adding an Electric Suction Box

Player pianos provide the most entertainment when they are pumped by foot, but some people enjoy being able to put a roll on the piano and let it do all the work itself. Piano and player piano supply companies all offer electric suction box kits, ranging from simple units with an on/off switch all the way to deluxe models with separate solid state speed controls for play and rewind. These kits include installation instructions and all of the miscellaneous hardware necessary to connect the suction box to the piano pump. Most of them contain an internal check valve which blocks the suction inlet automatically during foot pumping.

Decide where to place the suction box in the piano. In many players, the foot pump is small enough that the box may be located in the lower right hand corner with a lot of room to spare. In others, there is no room anywhere. Never remove the pumping pedals in order to make room for a suction box; sooner or later someone will wish they were still there. (Many player piano owners wonder if electrifying their player piano will lower its value. The only way this will reduce the value is if you remove the pedals to make room for the suction box). If it is possible to locate the suction box somewhere outside of the piano, cut a hole for the hose and power switch cord near the corner of the soundboard. This will have no effect on the tone of the piano. If locating the suction box away from the piano is out of the question, and if you are absolutely determined to electrify that particular piano, remove one of the reservoirs from the pump to make room for the suction box, and *save the reservoir!* This will alter the pumping characteristics of the player action, but in the event that the reservoir does get lost, it is easier to make a new one for a future owner than to make a new set of pedals.

Drill a hole into the trunk of the foot pump for the elbow for the new connecting hose. Locate this hole in an area *before* the suction from the bellows gets to the wind motor governor and action cutoff; usually, this is somewhere toward the center of the trunk. If there is no suitable location on the trunk, connect the elbow to one of the reservoirs.

Mount the power switch and volume control under the keybed, and neatly route the power cords, attaching them to the keybed with the clips provided with the kit. Run the power cord out through a small hole near the corner of the soundboard instead of draping it over the lower front panel of the piano.

A suction box with a two-speed power control has a microswitch which connects to the rewind/play linkage. If the player action is leaky, connect the switch as recommended in the instructions so the motor speeds up during play and slows down during rewind. In some well-restored player pianos, however, the stack and wind motor together require a lower suction level during play than the wind motor alone needs during rewind due to the gear ratio of the transmission, and it is necessary to omit the microswitch or even to connect it backwards, *increasing* the speed of the suction box a little during rewind.

Note that some less expensive suction boxes require air flow over the motor to keep it cool; this type will overheat if installed in a well-restored, airtight player action.

Adding Automatic Rewind and Shutoff

All player pianos which originally were equipped with an electric motor also had an automatic rewind and shutoff system. While it is easy enough to operate the rewind lever and shutoff switch by hand, it is also easy to walk away from an electrified player piano, letting it play merrily away in the background until it tears the roll off of the spool.

Obtain a medium size control pneumatic with self-contained valves from a player piano parts supplier or from an old technician's junk box—an old hammer rail pneumatic will usually do the trick. Rebuild it if necessary, install it on the side of the piano cabinet, and connect a pull wire from the pneumatic to the transmission linkage. Connect the pouch input tube to one of the extreme low or high holes in the tracker bar which is opened at the end of nearly all rolls, and tee the suction supply hose to the sustain pneumatic hose or connect it directly to the pump. Note that in player pianos which have one lever controlling both tempo and rewind (Apollo, Cable Euphona), these two functions must be separated in order to use automatic rewind.

A simple way to provide automatic shutoff is to cut a shallow slot in the takeup spool as in an Ampico upright, and to install a microswitch behind the takeup spool on the back of the spoolbox, wired in series with the main power switch. When the paper comes off of the takeup spool, the microswitch falls into the slot and turns off the power. Select a switch which requires very little pressure to move the blade over a full swing of one inch or more at the tip so it won't damage music rolls. To be safe, make sure the switch has a higher amperage rating than that of the suction box, and install an appropriate fuse in the line. Other more elaborate automatic shutoff systems are available from player piano parts suppliers.

Repairing and Preserving Music Rolls

In any given box of 100 old rolls, you will find an amazing variety of repairs—cellophane tape, electrical tape, masking tape, cigarette paper, glue, pouch leather, thread, string, etc., all of which are wrong.

To repair a small tear in a roll, use Scotch Magic Mending Tape (TM) or equivalent permanent "frosty" library tape. This is the *only* tape which provides a fairly permanent repair without turning gummy or falling off.

If a section of roll is damaged beyond repair, tape a piece of new roll paper down to a cutting board, and tape the old roll on top of it with the edges perfectly aligned. Trace through any remaining holes in the damaged area, and then cut through both layers with a new single edge razor blade. Remove the old damaged section, and attach the new section to the rest of the old roll with pieces of frosty tape no longer than 1½". Attempting to use long pieces of tape will introduce wrinkles, and the object is to make the splice perfectly flat. Cut out the holes where you traced through the old roll, untape the roll from the cutting board, and pick the remaining scrap of new roll paper loose. If you do this carefully, your roll will work like new.

If one edge of a roll is frayed from one end to the other, taping the entire length will cause the roll to wind up crooked and will make the paper buckle. If the roll is still currently manufactured, replace it with a new one. If it is an irreplacable, valuable collectors item or something you are willing to spend a lot of time repairing, lay it out on a long table with the damaged edge on a piece of waxed paper, fold the frayed pieces of paper flat, mix a 50/50 solution of white glue and water, and brush this along the edge with an artist brush. After the glue dries, cut the edge of glue off the paper with a new single edge razor blade, and peel the roll off the waxed paper. The paper will not be as strong as new, but it will be playable.

The right flange is always attached to the core, and in most rolls, the left flange is loose to allow for paper expansion. The core should be a little narrower than the paper so the flanges can be pressed snugly against the edges of the paper. After playing every roll, remove it from the piano and drop the right end into your right hand a few times to straighten the paper on the spool. Then tighten it *gently*, just until you barely hear the paper squeaking, and *STOP*. Do not tighten it beyond this point, or you might cause it to tear lengthwise. To keep the paper snug until next time you play it, use a rubber band just barely tight enough to hold itself in place. A rubber band which is too tight is worse than none at all, because it can tear the paper or cause it to warp.

An extremely fragile roll may need to have both flanges pulled away from the edges of the paper to keep from shredding it during rewind. If necessary, unroll the paper, reattach it to the core a little to the left of its original position, and insert a small rubber band around each flange as a spacer to hold it away from the roll. This will permit the paper to wander sideways during rewind without touching the flanges, but after each play the paper will have to be straightened by hand. Confine this treatment to irreplaceable brittle rolls.

Store your piano rolls in an environment with stable, moderately low humidity. If you keep them away from extreme dampness and dryness they will last for a long time.

Appendix
SAMPLE SERVICE ORDER
and
CHECKLIST OF REPAIRS

The following checklist may be used for three purposes: for appraising the condition of an instrument, for estimating a repair job, and for describing repairs which have been completed. Experienced restorers who are already good at estimating repair jobs will find the list unnecessary, but amateurs and less experienced professionals alike will benefit by careful analysis of each component of every player piano. If nothing else, read over the list prior to buying an old player piano or restoring one, to make sure you know what might be involved. For each item on the list, make note of labor and materials which might be necessary.

If you plan to make money at restoring player pianos, use this list to keep careful track of exactly how long it takes to restore your first dozen or so player pianos. This will help you to estimate future jobs accurately.

Obviously, if every conceivable repair were included in this list, it would form a major chapter, with entries for many repairs which the average restorer will never see in a lifetime. The author has tried to include everything normally encountered in an average major repair job.

PIANO BRAND & TYPE:
SERIAL NUMBER:
DATE MFD:
Repair estimate:( ) Appraisal:( )
Descript. of work performed:( )

THE PIANO

TUNE
RAISE/LOWER PITCH

REGULATE VERTICAL ACTION
   Remove action from piano
   Tighten all screws
   Reshape hammers
   Clean piano & action
   Align & tighten rails
   Straighten damper lift rod
   Travel hammers
   Space hammers to strings
   Space & square backchecks
   Space & square keys
   Set hammer stroke
   Regulate capstans
   Regulate key height
   Level white keys
   Level black keys
   Regulate letoff
   Regulate white key dip
   Regulate hammer checking
   Regulate sharp key dip

   Regulate dmprs.to lift rod,stgs.
   Regulate sustaining pedal
   Regulate damper spoons
   Regulate soft pedal
   Regulate bridle tapes
   Voice hammers

REGULATE GRAND ACTION
   Tighten plate & cabinet screws
   Remove action
   Tighten damper flange screws
   Clean piano
   Tighten all action screws
   Reshape hammers
   Clean action
   Remove actn,keys fr.key frame
   Bed key frame
   Regulate key frame glides
   Space & square keys
   Level keys
   Regulate key dip
   Travel hammers
   Space hammers to strings
   Regulate una corda pedal
   Space whippens to hammers
   Regulate jacks to knuckles
   Regulate rep. lever height
   Regulate hammer line
   Regulate hammer rail
   Regulate letoff
   Regulate drop
   Regulate hammer checking
   Regulate rep. spring tension
   Regulate key strip rail
   Regulate dampers to keys
   Regulate damper stop rail
   Regulate dampers to lift rail
   Regulate sust.ped.to lift rail
   Regulate sostenuto mechanism
   Regulate hammer lift rail
   Regulate striking point
   Voice hammers

REPAIRS

PIANO ACTION
   DAMPERS
      Polish lift rod
      Polish wires
      Replace blocks
      Replace felts
      Replace levers
      Replace lifter felts
      Replace spring cords
      Replace spring punchings
   FLANGES & BUSHINGS:(Type:Repin/Rebush/Replace)
      Action brackets
      Damper guide rail
      Damper lever fl
      Damper lift rod fl
      Damper wire fl
      Hammer butt fl
      Hammer rail fl
      Jack fl
      Pedal supports
      Rep.lev.fl

Sostenuto tabs
Stickers
Sticker fl
Sticker tongues
Whippen fl
Other
HAMMERS
Reglue
Replace
HAMMER BUTTS AND SHANKS
Lubricate knuckles
Replace bridle straps
Replace butts
Replace butt buckskin
Replace catcher buckskin
Replace knuckles
Replace shanks
Replace under cloth & felt
Reglue catcher shanks
Reglue knuckles
Reglue shanks
Repair knuckles
Repair shanks
HAMMER RAIL
Refinish
Replace cloth
MUFFLER: replace felt
PEDALS:
Overhaul lyre
Repair pedals
Repair trapwork
Replace lyre brace
Replace pedals
Replace pedal rod
REGULATING RAILS: (Letoff/Stop/Rest/Jack/Rep/Drop)
Repair ( ) holes
Replace buttons
Replace punchings
Replace rail
Replace screws
Replace supports
SPRINGS: (Polish/Replace)
Action shift
Damper rail
Damper
Jack
Pedal
Rep. lever
Sost. tab
Sost. rod
Spring rail felt
WHIPPENS
Polish spoons
Polish backcheck & bridle wires
Replace backcheck blocks
Replace backcheck felts
Replace backcheck wires
Replace bridle wires
Replace capstan cushions
Replace elbows
Replace jacks
Replace jack cushions
Replace rep. spring cords
Replace spoons
Replace whippens

KEYBOARD
KEYS
Clean sides
Clean entire keys
Ease
Paint sharps
Polish capstans
Polish white keytops
Polish white key fronts
Repair broken keys
Repair elongated balance rail holes
Repair ivories
Replace capstans
Replace bushings: front( ) center( )
Replace buttons
Replace sharps
Replace white keytops
Replace white key fronts
KEY FRAME & KEYBED
Clean, scrape, sand key frame & keybed
Polish pins:front rail( ) balance rail( )
Replace back rail cloth
Replace pins:front rail( ) balance rail( )
Replace punchings:front rail( ) balance rail( )
Shim & bed key frame

SOUNDBOARD, STRINGS & ASSOCIATED PARTS
BRIDGES
Repair/replace bass bridge
Repair/replace bass cap
Repair/replace bass shelf
Repair/replace bass treble bridge
Repair/replace bass cap
Replace bridge pins
PINBLOCK & TUNING PINS
Drive in tuning pins
Replace ( )broken tuning pins
Replace pinblock
Shim ( )loose tuning pins
Reglue pinblock/back frame
PLATE
Replace ( )broken agraffes
Replace ( )broken hitch pins
Replace ( )broken screws
Replace ( )screws with bolts
SOUNDBOARD
Reglue to ribs
Reglue perimeter to back/rim
Replace
Shim cracks
STRINGS
Liven, twist and tune bass strings
Replace ( )broken bass strings
Replace ( )broken treble strings
RESTRING PIANO: disassemble, repair & refinish soundbd, hone capo bar, rebronze & reletter plate, install plate, set downbearing, replace understring felt & braid, repl. tuning pins, bushings & strings, pull up to pitch

CABINET
Disassemble/reassemble for customer refinishing
Polish & lacquer hinges, locks, hardware
Refinish
Strip only

Reglue sides, toes, back
veneer, crossbanding
Repair/reinforce cracked bottom
Replace ( )casters, repair stripped screwholes
Replace ( )hinges ( )knobs
Replace nameboard felt
Shim key slip

MISCELLANEOUS
Replate action brackets
Replate duplex bars or plates
Replate hardware
Replate pedals
Replate plate screws
Replate pressure bar screws
Repair broken parts:
Replace missing parts:
Screws:
Polish
Plug & redrill holes
Remove broken screws & repair wood

THE PLAYER ACTION
Brand:
Single valve( ) Double valve( )

HEAD
Hardware: clean, polish & lacquer
Tracker bar: remove old tubing, polish
Tracking device: disassemble, replace pouches, gaskets, pneu.hinges & cloth, valve leather; reassemble, test & regulate
Transmission & roll spindles: clean, polish & lube
Replace broken pot metal transmission frame
Wind motor: disassemble, polish metal parts, repl. bushings, replace face board if necessary, seal channels, repair cracks, replace pneumatic hinges & cloth, replace slide valve cloth, lap & graphite slide valves & seats, regasket hose connector, reassemble & set timing

STACK
Disassemble
Pneumatics, fingers & decks: remove pneumatics from decks, remove fingers, clean off old glue, replace hinges & cloth, make new stationary boards as necessary, clean & repair deck boards, remove old glue from channels, seal channels, reglue pneumatics to decks. Reglue fingers.
Rebush fingers
Cover around built-in fingers
Cut off glued decks, resurface, add gaskets & screws
Gaskets: replace
Valves & seats
Replace inside facings
Replace outside facings
Replace valve discs
Replace stems
Replace stem guides
Replace Standard stem grommets
Polish stems
Polish & lacquer seats
Seal seats
Replace valve plate screws
Open unit valves & reseal
Regulate valve travel
Bleeds: remove, clean & seal( ) replace( )
Pouches
Replace & seal
Seal channels in pouch board

Clean/replace discs
Glue Baldwin pouches to stems
Seal pouch channels
Calibrate valve/pouch clearance
Open unit pouch blocks & reglue
Open glued pouch boards, resurface, add gaskets & screws
Remove, rehinge, recover & inst.pouch pneumatics
Regulate Schulz pouch hooks
Pushrods
Replace
Polish
Rethread
Replace leather nuts & cloth washers
Rebush guide rail
Rebush/replace flanges
Replace cloth hinges
Align top fingers to piano action
Lead tubing: replace with brass nipples/elbows
Replace ( )lead/fibre hose connectors/elbows
Remove white glue or contact cement from previous repair job
Repair ( )stripped screw holes
Other:
Reassemble, install new tracker bar tubing, bench test, install in piano & regulate to action

PRIMARY VALVE CHEST
Valves: disassemble, clean, replace leather, reassemble & set travel
Replace broken stems/valve buttons
Pouches: Replace & seal
Calibrate pouch/valve clearance
Gaskets: replace
Repair ( ) stripped screw holes
Other:

FOOT PUMP
Bellows: Disassemble, clean, replace hinges & covering, replace stiffeners, replace flap valves inside & outside
Replace face board of trunk
Replace flap valve springs/bellows springs
Reglue delaminated or cracked boards
Replace pedal mats
Clean & lubricate pedal linkages
Wind motor governor & accelerator: disassemble, replace pneumatic hinge & cloth, gaskets, valve facings, pouch, slide valve leather, reassemble
Action cutout: repl. valve facings, pouch, gaskets
Repair ( ) stripped screw holes
Other:
Reassemble pump, governor & cutout, install in piano with new hoses & control tubing, regulate governor, cutout & linkages

MOTOR-DRIVEN PUMP, ADDITIONAL
Replace ball bearings
Replace connecting straps
Rebush connecting rods
Clean, polish & lubricate crank assembly
Paint front & flywheel
Other:

ACCESSORIES
Restore sustaining pneumatic mechanism: replace hinge & cloth, releather valves, replace pouches & gaskets
Restore hammer rail control pneumatic assemblies
Restore mandolin pneumatic assembly
Releather finger buttons

Replace broken finger button springs, buttons
Replace mandolin curtain & clips
Add electric suction box
Add automatic rewind & shutoff
Other:
ADDITIONAL REPRODUCING & EXPRESSION PIANO
MECHANISMS
   Ampico A( ) B( ) Duo-Art( ) Welte( )
    Recordo( ) Other( )
Restore expression mechanisms
Restore automatic rewind/replay mechanism
Restore automatic shutoff mechanism
Disassemble/reassemble drawer
Install & regulate components in grand piano

Install & regulate components in vertical piano
ELECTRICAL COMPONENTS
   Replace wiring
   Disassemble, clean, reassemble & lubricate motor
   Repair motor starting switch
   Other:
COSMETIC WORK
   Refinish drawer panels( ) front( )
   Refinish internal parts
   Replate player action parts
   Polish levers/external drawer hardware
   Other:
MOVE PIANO/PLAYER ACTION TO AND FROM SHOP

GLOSSARY

accent. To increase the loudness of a note or chord in relation to the preceding and following notes.

accompaniment. The background part of a piece of music, as opposed to the theme. In a Duo-Art, the portion of the expression mechanism which controls the basic volume level of the entire keyboard.

accordion pneumatic. A pneumatic with two or more stages.

accumulator. Ratchet wheel or other mechanism which remembers how many coins have been deposited in a coin operated piano, causing the piano to play that many songs before shutting off.

air motor. See wind motor.

Ampico. Trademark of the *American Piano Company,* used on reproducing pianos.

amplifier. Pneumatic mechanism which increases the pump suction level.

automatic piano. Any self-playing piano, particularly a pneumatically operated coin piano with automatic rewind and shutoff.

band organ. Loudly-voiced self-contained automatic organ designed for skating rink, carousel, or outdoor amusement use. Models with brass trumpets and trombones are sometimes called military band organs. Synonyms: fairground organ, fair organ, carousel organ, merry-go-round organ

bass. The lower range of a musical scale.

beater. Device attached to a pneumatic which strikes a xylophone bar, drum, triangle or other percussion instrument.

bellows. Two boards covered with rubberized cloth or leather, usually hinged together at one end, which blow air out or draw it in when pushed together or pulled apart, or which move when air is forced in or out by an external source.

bells. See orchestra bells.

bilon. Brand name of extremely durable nylon pneumatic cloth coated with polyurethane on both sides, distributed by Player Piano Co.

bleed. Small orifice connecting pouch well to suction which allows pouch to return to "off" position.

bleed, adjustable. Bleed with small adjustable machine or wood screw for precisely controlling the size of its orifice.

bleed, ball. Bleed containing a small steel ball which floats up and down between two orifices; used only in Ampico B reproducing pianos.

box pump. See rotary pump.

brake, spool. A friction device in a player piano spoolbox which applies tension to the music roll or takeup spool, to cause the paper to wind up tightly.

calliope. Small, compressed air operated (usually) or steam operated (rarely) organ with large, extremely loudly voiced brass whistles. Many air calliopes play automatically from style A music rolls, as well as from a hand played keyboard.

cancel. See lock and cancel.

chain perforation. Extended perforation in music roll to hold a function on, (as opposed to lock and cancel).

choker. A pneumatic suction regulator.

chromatic. Having all twelve notes of the musical scale. Small band organs are not fully chromatic.

coin operated. Having a coin slot and coin mechanism. Insertion of a coin turns the instrument on, it plays one song, and automatically shuts off. Most coin operated instruments have an accumulator.

coin piano. Coin operated piano, usually with mandolin attachment and automatically controlled sustaining and soft pedals, and sometimes with pipes or xylophone, played by a large multitune music roll and powered by a motor driven pumping bellows.

coin switch. The mechanism in a coin piano which turns it on when a coin is inserted and which turns it off in response to the shutoff perforation at the end of each song.

coupled. Two notes or other functions which are played by the same hole in a music roll.

coupler. Mechanism for connecting notes or functions in a coin piano, orchestrion or organ. For example, some orchestrions have a bass octave coupler. Some couplers may be turned on and off; others are connected permanently.

crash valve. Valve which applies higher than normal suction or full pump suction to the stack.

crescendo. Gradual, smooth increase in loudness.

cutout pouch. Pouch which closes or opens channels on one side when atmosphere or suction is applied to other side.

damper. Device which mutes the tone. A piano damper presses against the strings after the key is lifted; a snare drum damper presses against the drum head to keep the drum from ringing when the beater is not playing.

deck. Board to which pneumatics are glued.

descrescendo. Gradual smooth decrease in loudness.

diminuendo. Decrescendo.

dish. The concave shape of a pouch.

drawing board roll. Music roll with the holes laid out on a drawing board, as opposed to one recorded on a roll recording piano.

Duo-Art. Trademark of the Aeolian company, used on reproducing pianos in the old days, and on ordinary player pianos in modern times.

electric piano. Usually, a coin piano or orchestrion powered by an electric motor; or, any piano with an electric motor including the reproducing piano.

end tab. Reinforcement attached to beginning of music roll with grommet or wire loop to hook onto takeup spool.

endless roll. Music roll connected to itself in a continuous loop stored in a bin, which does not require rewinding. Used in Link and some North Tonawanda and Peerless coin pianos.

equalizer. Spring-loaded pneumatic or bellows which evens out the suction level.

expression. Changes in loudness and tempo which impart a hand-played, human quality to music.

expression box. Mechanism which alters suction level to make piano play louder and softer.

expression piano. Player piano using special music rolls and containing expression mechanisms which automatically make it play louder and softer in imitation of hand playing. The expression is more limited than in a reproducing piano.

feeder. Pumping bellows.

fishing pole tracking device. An automatic tracking device which incorporates a long slender rod with a string connecting one end to a clutch mechanism. As the device responds to the movement of the music roll, the rod goes up and down like a fishing pole.

flange. The end of a music roll spool which guides the paper as it winds up.

flute pipe. Organ pipe which produces a simple tone imitative of a flute. Many coin pianos and orchestrions have a set of flute pipes.

forte. Loud.

fortissimo. Very loud.

forzando. See sforzando.

frein. Metal or wood tone regulating device mounted on the front of the mouth of a string (violin, cello, etc.) pipe, which helps to impart a raspy tone in imitation of the string instrument.

gasket. Leather or other material installed between two pieces of wood to form an airtight connection which may be disassembled.

general cancel. Device which cancels a group of functions or registers. See lock and cancel.

governor. A medium size bellows containing a regulator valve, which causes the wind motor to run at a constant speed regardless of the suction level in the pump.

hammer rail. Wooden rail in vertical piano action which supports hammers at rest.

hand played roll. Music roll made by pianist on a special piano equipped with recording mechanism. The master roll produced by most recording pianos has lines drawn by recording stylii, due to the difficulty of punching holes as fast as a pianist can play.

harmonic brake. See frein.

head. The shelf sitting on top of a player piano stack, which supports the spoolbox, tracking device and wind motor.

hinge. In a pneumatic or bellows, usually a folded piece of cloth.

hinge spring. A piece of piano wire bent in the shape of a square letter U, with the two legs inserted into the boards of a pneumatic to hold it open or closed.

hot glue. Ground animal connective tissue and bones available in granular form for use mixed with water and heated in a glue pot.

inner player. Early term for player piano with self contained mechanisms, as opposed to the push-up piano player.

inside valve. See valve, inside.

intensity. One specific level of loudness, or mechanism which causes a piano to play at a certain loudness. The Ampico A has three intensity pneumatics which in various combinations produce seven different volume levels.

key lock. Rail under keys in vertical player piano which, when lifted, prevents keys from moving as player action plays.

keyboardless. Having no keyboard. Many coin pianos and orchestrions, and a few reproducing pianos are keyboardless.

knife valve. See valve, knife.

ladder chain. Small chain used for wind motors and transmissions.

leather nut. Small nut made of hard leather with small diameter hole used for threaded connecting wires and pushrods. Leather nuts fit snugly on threaded wires and do not need lock washers to keep them from turning.

levers. Control levers usually located in the piano keyslip or spoolbox, used for manual control of tempo, rewind, expression and other functions.

lifter disc. Small cardboard or fibre punching glued to pouch, which prevents bottom of valve stem from indenting the pouch.

lock and cancel. Mechanism controlled by two different holes in the tracker bar; one hole turns it on, and the other turns it off, like a toggle switch. Used for turning intensities on and off in reproducing pianos, and for turning extra instruments on and off in orchestrions. Lock and cancel holes in the music roll eliminate the need for long extended chain perforations which weaken the paper.

mandolin attachment. Device which imparts a tinny sound to a piano.

manometer. Instrument used for measuring pressure and suction.

mechanical piano. Self playing piano which uses non-pneumatic mechanisms, such as a barrel-operated street piano.

mezzoforte. Medium loudness.

multiplex. To derive two or more functions from one tracker bar hole or mechanism, by using another hole to switch it. In the Ampico model A reproducing piano, tracker bar hole 1 causes a slow crescendo; hole 5 punched together with 1 causes a fast crescendo. In the Seeburg KT Special orchestrion, hole 1 switches hole 35 from bass drum and cymbal to tambourine.

music roll. Roll of paper with holes punched in it to play music on a self playing, pneumatically operated piano.

nickelodeon. Early day silent movie theater with five cent admission charge. Loosely, any coin operated device which produces music, including coin pianos, orchestrions and coin phonographs (juke boxes).

octave. Musical interval, the higher tone of which is twice the vibrational frequency of the lower one. One octave encompasses eight diatonic tones or thirteen chromatic tones.

orchestra bells. A set of tuned steel bars used in many orchestrions as an extra instrument.

orchestrion. Self playing piano containing 4 or more extra instruments; xylophone, bells, pipes, drums, etc.

outside valve. See valve, outside.

pallet valve. See valve, pallet.

pedal. Foot operated lever. Piano pedals control the dampers, hammer rail and other functions; pumping pedals are attached to the pumping bellows.

perflex. Thin polyurethane material which wears out very quickly when used for pouches and pneumatics.

perforation. A hole in a music roll.

pianissimo. Very soft.

piano player. See push-up piano player.

Pianola. Trademark of the Aeolian company, first used on early pushup piano players, and then used on player pianos from the early days all the way to the present.

play. Forward direction of the music roll, as opposed to rewind. Also known as "replay," "repeat."

player piano. Self contained, self playing piano which uses perforated paper music rolls and a pneumatic player mechanism.

pneumatic. (noun): Small bellows, typically less than 2" wide and 6" long. (adjective): suction or pressure operated.

pneumatic, unit. See unit pneumatic.

pneumatic action. Mechanism which operates by reduced or increased air pressure.

pneumatic cloth. Thin flexible cloth with airtight coating used for covering pneumatics. Traditional material was rubber-coated cotton cloth; a modern alternative is polyurethane-coated nylon.

pneumatic leather. See pouch leather.

pneumatic stack. Mechanism in automatic piano which plays the piano action or keys. The upper action of an old player piano housing the pneumatics, valves and pouches is known as the stack, with or without the head.

pneumatic system. A complete player action for a pressure or suction operated instrument.

polylon. Thin nylon coated with polyurethane on one side, used for pneumatic cloth.

pouch. Diaphragm or envelope of thin leather or other material which pushes or pulls on a valve or other part when one side is exposed to higher or lower air pressure than the other.

pouch leather. Thin tan or white leather used for pouches and for covering small pneumatics. Sold only by piano and organ supply companies.

pouch pneumatic. Tiny pneumatic used instead of a pouch for controlling a valve.

pouch sealer. Thin liquid rubber cement applied to a leather pouch to make it more airtight.

primary valve. See valve, primary.

puff. European and British term for pouch.

pump. Bellows or turbine which produces a supply of suction or pressure to operate a pneumatic action.

pump, tracker bar. Small cylinder (usually) or bellows (rarely) with aperture which fits over tracker bar, used for pumping accumulated lint and dirt out of a suction operated player action.

push rod. Wood or metal rod which connects a pneumatic to the device which it actuates.

push-up piano player. Automatic piano playing mechanism contained in a separate cabinet with "fingers" and "feet" which push the piano keys and pedals. Forerunner of the self contained "inner player" or player piano. A push-up with electric motor and reproducing expression mechanisms is known as a "vorsetzer."

quintadena pipe. Capped organ pipe which produces odd numbered harmonics, with the "quint" or third partial as loud as, or louder than, the fundamental.

rebuilt. A meaningless word in the player piano field, commonly used to denote anything from the replacement of one hose all the way to a complete restoration job.

regulator. Spring-loaded or weighted bellows, usually medium size, with a valve inside which regulates the flow of air or suc-

tion through it so the output is constant even though the input is irregular.

reiterating. Rapidly turning on and off, or moving back and forth. A reiterating snare drum beater strikes the drum repeatedly, producing a drum roll.

repeating. See reiterating.

replay. To switch to forward after rewinding.

reproducing piano. Player piano with sophisticated expression regulating mechanisms and usually with motor-driven pumping bellows, which reproduces or recreates the playing of human pianists by means of special music rolls.

reroll. See rewind.

reservoir. Bellows which stores suction or pressure, and which regulates or smooths pulsations to some degree, although not as effectively as a regulator.

restored. See rebuilt.

rewind. To reverse direction of the music roll, winding the paper onto the feed spool, usually at high speed.

roll. See music roll.

roll chuck. Removeable spindle and flanges which attach to a music roll and hold it in the spoolbox.

roll frame. Spoolbox.

rotary pump. Motor driven pump with four bellows surrounding the crankshaft.

rotary valve. See valve, rotary.

seat. Surface which valve closes and opens.

secondary valve. See valve, secondary.

shallot. In an organ pipe having a reed, a capped tube with a long slot down one side. In a beating reed pipe, the reed vibrates against the shallot; in a free reed pipe, the reed moves in and out of the slot as it vibrates.

shutoff. Mechanism which turns a motorized piano (coin piano, reproducing piano, etc.) off after the piece of music is done playing or after the roll is done rewinding.

sforzando. Heavy accent.

single stroke. Operating only once, as opposed to reiterating. Coinola O roll orchestrions have one single stroke snare drum beater and one reiterating beater.

slide valve. See valve, slide.

snake bites. Pairs of tiny holes in Duo-Art rolls used for controlling treble and bass theme.

spill valve. "Relief" valve which admits air into a motor-driven suction bellows system, or lets excess air out of a pressure bellows system. The spill valve is either attached to an adjustable spring or to a spring loaded reservoir, with an adjustment provided for setting the maximum suction or pressure level produced by the pump. Without a spill valve, an airtight pneumatic system would stall the motor.

spool. Cylinder, usually with flanges, around which a paper music roll is wound. The roll originates on the feed spool, and is pulled over the tracker bar by the takeup spool

spoolbox. Compartment in an automatic piano which houses the feed spool, takeup spool, tracker bar and transmission,

spool frame. Spoolbox.

stack. See pneumatic stack.

steamboat pump. Collectors' term for large motor-driven, slow moving six-bellows pump manufactured by Aeolian for use with early Duo-Art reproducing pianos. Installed in Steinway uprights and also made in a remote cabinet style.

suction. In player piano parlance, reduced air pressure.

swell shutters. Wooden shutters which control the loudness of sound in an organ or orchestrion.

takeup spool. The spool which pulls the music roll over the tracker bar while a player piano is playing.

theme. The more prominent musical part, as opposed to the background accompaniment. Also, a mechanism in an expression or reproducing piano which accents a note or group of notes.

tracker bar. Brass (usually) or wood (rarely) bar with holes which are connected to pneumatic mechanisms in a player action, over which the music roll passes to play the music.

tracker ear. Small metal tab or blade which feels the edge of a music roll, providing feedback to an automatic tracking device.

tracker scale. List of tracker bar holes and their functions.

tracking device, automatic. Mechanism which automatically keeps a music roll aligned with the tracker bar.

transmission. Assembly of gears, shafts, sprockets and chains which connect the wind motor to the music roll spindles, propelling the roll forward slowly or backward quickly as determined by a control lever.

transposing lever. Lever which shifts the tracker bar in a player piano one space to the left or right, causing the music to play in a higher or lower key.

treble. The upper part of the musical scale.

unit pneumatic. A pneumatic which contains its own valve and pouch, usually attached to the stack with screws for easy removal.

vacuum. Technically, a space absolutely devoid of air. In player piano usage, reduced air pressure.

valve, flap. A large thin flat valve usually made of leather or heavy rubber cloth which permits air to flow only in one direction.

valve, inside. A valve which is located inside of the top and bottom valve seats, with a stem connecting it to a pouch or other actuating device. When an inside valve is off, its output is atmosphere, and when it is on, its output is suction. Ordinary player piano stack valves are inside valves. (Also known as secondary valve in a double valve player piano action).

valve, knife. A valve which pivots over an elongated opening, gradually opening and closing it.

valve, outside. A valve which has two small discs connected by a stem, with the discs located outside of the top and bottom valve seats. When an outside valve is off, its output is suction, and when it is on, its output is atmosphere. (Also known as "primary valve" in a double valve player piano action).

valve, pallet. A simple valve which opens and closes one or more holes as it hinges open and shut.

valve, primary. A small valve which responds to a perforation in a music roll or some other source of atmosphere, which amplifies the small atmosphere signal to operate a larger sec-

ondary valve. In a simple double valve player piano action, the primaries are outside valves, but in a large orchestrion, they are sometimes inside valves.

valve, rotary. A simple valve which opens and closes one or more holes, or which connects and disconnects several channels from each other, as it turns.

valve, secondary. A valve which controls a pneumatic or other device, in response to a signal from a smaller primary valve. The stack valves in a double valve player piano are secondary valves.

valve, slide. A simple valve which opens and closes a hole, or connects and disconnects several holes, as it slides back and forth.

valve, tempo. Slide valve or other type of valve adjusted by the tempo lever to control the speed of the wind motor.

valve, unit. A block containing a valve and pouch, usually removeable for easy servicing.

valve block. A small wooden block containing a valve and pouch, attached to a pneumatic, deck or trunk board. Also see unit valve.

valve button. Small wooden disc used for a valve.

valve guide. Fibre, metal or wood strip with a hole in it for the valve stem, which holds the valve stem straight.

valve seat. See seat.

valve stem. Slender metal or wood rod running through the center of a valve perpendicular to its seats.

violin pipe. An organ pipe which imitates the sound of a violin with its rich harmonic series.

voicing. Adjusting or regulating the tone of an instrument.

vorsetzer. In German, "sitter-in-front-of," or push-up piano player. Collectors usually use it to denote an electric motor driven reproducing push-up piano player.

wind chest. Valve chest in pressure system which distributes air pressure to organ pipes.

wind motor. Suction powered device with medium size pneumatics and slide valves connected to a crankshaft, which turns the music roll.

word roll. 88-note player piano song roll with words printed along one side.

wind trunk. Thin box which conveys air pressure or suction from one place to another in a player action.

xylophone. A set of tuned wooden bars, used in some coin pianos. This term is sometimes used incorrectly to identify a set of metal orchestra bells.

zephyr skin. Thin animal intestine sometimes used for pouches.

BIBLIOGRAPHY

BOOKS

Barazani, Gail Coningsby. *Safe Practices in the Arts & Crafts/A Studio Guide.* College Art Association of America. 1978.

Bowers, Q. David. *The Encyclopedia of Automatic Musical Instruments.* The Vestal Press; Vestal, New York. 1972.

Bowers, Q. David. *Put Another Nickel In.* The Vestal Press; Vestal, New York. 1965.

Givens, Larry. *Rebuilding the Player Piano.* The Vestal Press; Vestal, New York. 1963.

Givens, Larry. *Re-enacting the Artist.* The Vestal Press; Vestal, New York. 1970.

Kitner, Michael L. and Reblitz, Arthur A. *The Mills Violano-Virtuoso.* The Vestal Press; Vestal, New York. 1984.

Ord-Hume, Arthur W. J. G. *Player Piano.* A. S. Barnes & Co.; New York, N. Y. 1970.

Ord-Hume, Arthur W. J. G. *Restoring Pianolas and other Self-Playing Pianos.* George Allen & Unwin; London, England. 1983.

Pierce, Bob. *Pierce Piano Atlas.* Bob Pierce; Long Beach, California. 1977.

Reblitz, Arthur A. *Piano Servicing, Tuning and Rebuilding.* The Vestal Press; Vestal, New York. 1976.

Reblitz, Arthur A. and Bowers, Q. David. *Treasures of Mechanical Music*. The Vestal Press; Vestal, New York. 1981.

Roehl, Harvey N. *Player Piano Treasury* (Second Edition). The Vestal Press; Vestal, New York. 1973.

Silver Anniversary Collection. An anthology of articles from the publications of the Musical Box Society International. Musical Box Society International; Summit, New Jersey. 1974.

PERIODICALS

"The AMICA." News bulletin of the Automatic Musical Instrument Collectors Association.

"Art Hazards News." Center for Occupational Hazards, 5 Beekman St., New York NY 10038.

"The Bulletin of the Musical Box Society International." Periodical of the Musical Box Society International.

"Fine Woodworking." The Taunton Press, Inc., Newtown, Connecticut.

Note: For a listing of current addresses of collectors' organizations worldwide, send a request to the Vestal Press, publisher of this book.

INDEX

215